State and Intellectual in Imperial Japan

Human intelligence—even in the case of the most intelligent—
falls miserably short of the great problems of public life.

Simone Weil

State and Intellectual in Imperial Japan

The Public Man in Crisis

Andrew E. Barshay

UNIVERSITY OF CALIFORNIA PRESS
Berkeley · Los Angeles · Oxford

University of California Press
Berkeley and Los Angeles, California
University of California Press, Ltd.
Oxford, England

Library of Congress Cataloging-in-Publication Data

Barshay, Andrew E.
State and intellectual in imperial Japan : the public man in
crisis / Andrew E. Barshay.

   p.   cm.
  Bibliography: p.
  Includes index.
  ISBN 0-520-07393-2 (alk. paper)
  1. Japan—Intellectual life—20th century. 2. Nanbara, Shigeru,
1889–1974—Political and social views. 3. Hasegawa, Nyozekan,
1875–1969—Political and social views. I. Title.
DS822.4B37 1989
952.03′3′0922—dc19   87-36767
                                                                    CIP

Printed in the United States of America
1 2 3 4 5 6 7 8 9

To KN:
non haec sine numine divum / eveniunt

Contents

Acknowledgments

In common speech, the word *litany* has unfortunately fallen on hard times. It has come to be associated with a formalistic recitation, rather than with multiple expressions of heartfelt gratitude. It is this latter sense I wish to recall here as I record my thanks to the many people who have given me so much help over the course of this project.

To the members of my dissertation committee at the University of California, Berkeley—Irwin Scheiner, Thomas C. Smith, and Robert N. Bellah: I hope they will not find this poor payment of the intellectual debts I have happily incurred over the past nine years. To my mentors and wise counsellors in Japan—Matsumoto Sannosuke, who guided my research at Tokyo University with grace and undue modesty; Maruyama Masao, who shared generously his time, reflections, convictions, and laughter; and Hashimoto Mitsuru, of Osaka University, for his exciting criticism and warm friendship. To Fukuda Kan'ichi and Tanaka Hiroshi, for sharing with me their extensive knowledge of Nanbara Shigeru and Hasegawa Nyozekan, respectively, and for their practical assistance. To my parents and to my family in Japan: for what they gave there is no substitute.

Colleagues at Wesleyan University contributed in many ways. I would like to express special thanks to two who read the manuscript in an earlier form—David Titus, whose enthusiasm and insights have been welcome and gratifying; and Thomas James, now of Brown University, who gave deep and close thought to what he read, and often gave lucid expression in his own words to my still tangled thoughts. His has been a nourishing friendship, which I hope I have requited. Additionally, in sharing with me her thoughts on the past and present situation of Chinese intellectuals, Vera Schwarcz has provided a valued comparative perspective.

I wish here to thank the readers for the University of California Press for their comments and criticisms. Thanks also to Peter Dreyer for his patience and sharp editorial eye.

In the course of writing I have had the opportunity to present aspects of my research to a number of audiences, whom I wish now to thank: the Minzoku Mondai Kenkyūkai at Kyoto University, especially Naka Hisao, Takahashi Saburō, and Hashimoto Mitsuru; the New England Japan Seminar; the History Faculty Seminar, Wesleyan University; the Japan Forum, Harvard University; and, finally, the Japan Seminar, Columbia University. Each has in its own way helped to shape my thoughts on the subjects discussed in the following pages.

Were it not for financial support, of course, little if any scholarly work would be possible. Thanks are owing to the Fulbright-Hays Commission and the Social Science Research Council for research and travel support at the dissertation stage, and to Wesleyan University, particularly the Mansfield Freeman Fund, for a project grant and travel funds that made possible an additional summer's research and time out to think.

The end of my litany of thanks brings me to the greatest of all my debts, and that debt whose intellectual, spiritual, and material elements are as indistinguishable as they are profound: I speak of what I owe to my wife, Kimiko Nishimura. Here, I despair of speech. In expressing my thanks, I borrow the words, and hope, of Newman: *cor ad cor loquitur.*

Note on Names and Transliteration

As is well known, the practice in Japan of taking pen names (gō), especially at the suggestion of friends—and sometimes of changing them—was once common among prose writers. It was also common practice to refer to those writers by this name. Thus Natsume Sōseki rather than Natsume Kinnosuke; Mori Ōgai rather than Mori Rintarō. Indeed, the family name too was often dropped, leaving only the pen name—all that was necessary—to identify the writer. Hasegawa Nyozekan is another case in point. "Nyozekan" is the gō he took early in the twentieth century at the suggestion of a fellow journalist and used for the rest of his life. The meaning, incidentally, is ironic. Taken at a time when Nyozekan was swamped with work, it means "as free and easy as you please." In this book I have followed common practice and refer to "Hasegawa Nyozekan," or, more frequently, to "Nyozekan" alone. In official records and some of his writings, one does find "Hasegawa Manjirō."

Japanese names appear in standard order (family name first), except where the individual has reversed it. This is frequently the case in English-language publications.

Japanese terms, including personal and place names, appear with standard diacritical marks. An exception has been made in the case of well-known place names such as Tokyo, Osaka, and Kobe; and of terms such as Shinto, which is now commonly seen in English.

Chinese names and terms are transliterated in *pinyin*, except when taken directly from published works where another system is followed.

Preface

This is a study of two modern Japanese intellectuals, one a professor of Western political thought, the other a journalist. Although the intrinsic interest of each of these lives emerges readily when they are set in context, I have deliberately chosen to study them together, and to focus on the imperial period (1868–1945), for reasons I wish briefly to delineate here. First, a word about the general approach I have taken: essentially, this book argues that the creation and development of the modern state in Japan simultaneously redefined both politics and society. In this process, a vast area of social thought and practice concerned with the national life, one that fed and transcended official and purely private activity, also emerged. This was the "public" sphere, whose emergence also produced the type of intellectuals I call "public men." Owing to the heavily bureaucratic character of Japan's political and institutional evolution, however, "publicness" soon ramified into positions distinctly "inside" and "outside." Public life pursued in large, especially official, organizations was accorded greater value and prestige; independent (and dissident) activity, while public, did not enjoy such approbation. Indeed, *public* tended to be identified with the state itself.

As a professor of Western political thought at Tokyo Imperial University, Nanbara Shigeru (1889–1974) was an insider. Hasegawa Nyozekan (1875–1969), as a critical journalist, was an outsider. With the crisis of early Shōwa (1925–45), involving the repression of the left, depression, the collapse of party government, mobilization for and defeat

in total war, Nanbara and Hasegawa as public men were called upon
to promote and adhere to an extreme cultural particularism. This was
a task both found onerous yet curiously irresistible. Nanbara, a neo-
Kantian in philosophy and a professing Christian, refused to yield entirely to the demands of orthodoxy, but his personal opposition remained just that, and depended for expression on his insider status.
Hasegawa, the outsider, sought to defend a humanely anarchic, almost
prepolitical, community against the demands of the state. But he was
actually mobilized to a greater degree than Nanbara, since the state had
both destroyed the left and effectively politicized the nation down to the
level of the local community, even of the family.

In short, I attempt in the pages that follow to show how, for public
men in imperial Japan, the intellectual content of public work and the
mutually defining status positions of insider and outsider were interrelated. I believe that this is something of a new approach—though one
by no means wholly original—to the intellectual history of modern
Japan. In the course of writing this study, I found myself confronting
certain methodological and philosophical issues concerning the relation
of social being to consciousness. These, frankly, I would rather not address at once, preferring to let the results speak through the text that
follows. "[Social] being determines consciousness" in any case seems to
me an unhappy, if compelling, formulation. It leaves out the interpreter
and his/her interests. The relation in question must emerge as a construction—though not an arbitrary one—of the interpreter. It is not
something objectively given and waiting to be seized, ready-to-wear,
from without. ("The Critique of Pure Reason," Ralf Dahrendorf notes,
"does not emerge by squeezing Prussian society.") At the same time, as
will be clear, I believe that a social perspective on intellectual work is as
necessary as close attention to text. My intent here has been to combine
these approaches as the situation seemed to require it.

More germane to this preface, perhaps, would be some attention to
my particular choice of protagonists. It would no doubt be possible to
pair a number of public insiders and outsiders in ways that would shed
light on the dilemmas and ambiguities of the public sphere in imperial
Japan. Some such pairings are suggested in the text. But as indicated
earlier, the choice of protagonists here was not accidental and needs
some explanation.

As with many Western students of Japanese history since the 1960s,
I got my first inkling of the importance of "problem consciousness"
(mondai ishiki) in Japanese scholarship through the work of Maruyama

Masao. It would be digressive to describe the impact on me of this
work, and I shall also forgo a discussion of Maruyama's achievement in
the context of contemporary Japan, since I intend to take up this question fully in a separate study. But Maruyama, as will become clear, figures prominently in my account, both in terms of substantive ideas and
personal testimony about the period under study. The persuasiveness of
the former is best determined in context, both here and, more important, in his own work. The historical testimony to which I refer is central because Maruyama happens to have had close personal ties to both
of the subjects of this work. Hasegawa Nyozekan was a longtime associate of Maruyama's father, the well-known journalist Maruyama Kanji.
Nyozekan was a frequent presence in the Maruyama household during
the 1920s and early 1930s and, along with his father, had a decisive
impact on the young Maruyama's views of Japanese society and politics,
particularly his understanding of "Japanese fascism." Nanbara Shigeru,
in a sense, took up where Hasegawa left off. As Maruyama's main academic tutor, and later senior associate at Tokyo Imperial, Nanbara was
also in a position to wield considerable intellectual and moral influence
over his pupil. All indications are that the personal tie was very strong,
though Nanbara's intellectual influence on Maruyama, as may be surmised, was of a more theoretical and philosophical quality than that of
Hasegawa. Nor did pupil follow teacher slavishly. Indeed, it seems that
the differences between them have much to do with the temperament
and social perspective inculcated in the young Maruyama by his earlier
mentors; and that the particular power of Maruyama's mature work
springs from his combining within himself the streams of insider and
outsider publicness represented by his two teachers. It is for this reason
that I follow the Nanbara/Hasegawa pairing only through 1945: their
intellectual significance for Maruyama, as a key representative of the
postwar generation, was greatest prior to 1945; and indeed, taken on
their own terms, each can be said to have made his chief contribution to
Japanese political and social thought under the imperial system. These
are not, therefore, complete intellectual biographies. In sum, while
Maruyama himself is not the central focus of study here, his presence,
both in broad matters of substance and close historical perspective, has
provided a kind of organic link between my accounts of the public lives
of Nanbara and Hasegawa. There are two points I wish to stress, however. My treatment of Maruyama is not uncritical; I am not simply
"taking his word for it" in shaping my interpretations here. Second, this
work is intended to stand by itself, to yield insights of its own as a study

of the dilemmas of public life in imperial Japan. I hope I have not failed
in either respect.[1]

Although this study concerns developments in the history of Japanese
social and political thought, and deals specifically with the lives and
work of a small number of public men, it is also meant to address a
broader problem: the price of national identity in the twentieth century.
In this sense, it is an illustration of the hard truth expressed in the statement of Simone Weil's quoted above as an epigraph. Indeed, Simone
Weil's brief life and her writings stand as proof that modern human intelligence cannot do otherwise than believe in its strivings and accept its
inevitable failures. This truth must be taken personally. Simone Weil is a
limit case in this regard, and it is with this limit case that I would like
to begin.
    Simone Weil believed that fascism is preceded, not followed, by the
state's denial to those subject to it of a personal and social need for the
free expression of thought. She did not, of course, mean simple license
for the tongue, but considered speech—words defined and intended to
refer to some reality, as opposed to the "myths and monsters" of collective slogans and the seeming absolutes of political rhetoric. Essentially,
then, fascism meant for Simone Weil the attempted reduction of rational life to absurdity. Leaving aside the question of whether *fascism* is
the word best suited to describe this aspect of the modern state's behavior, there can be little argument that our century has seen enough of regimes that have made just such attempts. None, it would seem, is wholly
exempt from the fear of public knowledge and discussion, or from the
temptation to set and define the terms of public discourse in ways conve-
nient to itself. That modern states do not, and cannot, succeed in the
attempt to monopolize social rationality is beside the point. They all try,
some on a national scale in the midst of crisis; others bit by bit, relying
on local reproductions of the process of denial. In this respect, perhaps
the most any people can achieve is to create and maintain a system that,
in Robert Bellah's phrase, is "*relatively* less problematic" rather than
wholly innocent of repression.[2]
    Simone Weil darkly regarded the modern bureaucratic state as mov-
ing ineluctably toward centralization of all its functions, this by necessity involving two linked processes. The first, already sketched in, might
be called the elimination of alternative rationalities from society in the

interest of managerial efficiency. The state, that is, is to become the end
of a good life rather than a means to its attainment. Having mobilized
the forces of instrumental rationality—the technological, capital, and
organized intellectual resources of society—on its own behalf, the state
marches, by fits and starts (as Max Weber also thought) on the "irrational," affective sphere, the realm of passion and compassion. This
process essentially consumes, or destroys, local attachments, love of
place, even of country; ultimately, it disallows all self-definition independent of the state. Simone Weil called this process "deracination":
uprooting. She considered that all modern states were inhabited by
more or less deracinated peoples, and urged (in a book written for de
Gaulle's Free French), that a movement toward "rootedness" be fostered in France as the country fought to win back its independence. The
central emotion of national rootedness was to be not a hunger for glory
but compassion for one's country and people. It is no surprise to find
that Simone Weil's program also called for post-liberation France to renounce all colonial possessions.[3]

The specter that haunted Simone Weil was the combined force of the
bureaucratic state and the national, collective "we": power and its enabling ideology. To counteract this deadly combination, she sought to
unite in her person the life of the intellect and of manual work. By this
means she sought to demonstrate that deracination could be resisted; a
life of conscious bonding to a community of work would be the model
for an alternative mode of social being. Indeed, Simone Weil accorded
to manual work a profound spiritual significance grounded in its painful, sacrificial nature.

Few have lived as Simone Weil did. Fewer still have died as she did: of
voluntary starvation and chagrin at her separation from her country in
its time of trial. The proposals she made to de Gaulle contain many contradictions and apparently undemocratic, elitist elements. The contradictions are as radical as her thought and way of life and death. Philosopher, mystic, and "revolutionary pessimist," she is, as noted, a limit case
rather than a modal personality. Yet it is the limit case rather than the
modal personality that inspires (and sometimes repels us). Many of Simone Weil's contemporaries throughout the developed world, both intellectuals and workers, have paid with their lives, or at least with their
livelihoods, for statements not half as radical as hers. Many more have
adjusted. By examining the relation of a number of Japanese thinkers
to "power and its enabling ideology," this study seeks to show how

inescapable, universal, and yet unique, are the contradictions of that relationship.

———————

No modern state could even attempt the total commitment of resources that has made possible the immensely destructive total wars of our time without the active support of those subject to it. To a degree this is an old story. "The king makes war," ran the medieval adage, "and the people die." In his own pathbreaking analyses of "Japanese fascism," Maruyama Masao cites David Hume: "Any government, however despotic, is based on people's opinions." And Maruyama comments further: "To be sure, the most despotic government cannot exist without a minimum of voluntary cooperation from the ruled."[4] We must leave aside discussion of Maruyama's questionable thesis that the academically unpedigreed "pseudo-intelligentsia" of Japan provided the backbone of support for fascism and war itself in that country. Our concern here lies rather with the broader question: How, and how well, does this mobilization work?

It is obvious, of course, that in everyday life, allegiance to the state is regarded as no paradox at all. It almost sinks beneath the surface of consciousness, just as our awareness of "nature" tends to become something of an abstraction, broken by intermittent sensation. Indeed, in a crisis, when it believes itself threatened by a foreign or domestic enemy, the state mobilizes the energy and resources of its people with an alacrity that seems, to most, only natural. Perhaps this is because people feel, not only that they are defending themselves, but that their own existence has been recognized by the state; that they can give not some alienated product of their work—their money—but their intelligent service and blood. In a democracy—and "we are all democrats today"[5]—mobilization becomes self-mobilization. In a larger sense, then, mobilization in crisis, while it entails an expansion of state power, also heightens the people's identification with the state; the people become the state.

Yet sometimes too great an accumulation of moral, political, and economic contradictions forces us to question the need for such mobilization. This is not necessarily the result of massive "failure" alone, as it was for the defeated regimes of 1945. It may also be the precipitant of long-standing social tensions within a still legitimate system, as in the confluence of the civil rights and antiwar struggles of the 1960s in the United States. At such junctures, an increasing and representative body of people begin to look beyond the immediate "crisis" to examine the whole nature of the state's relationship to smaller social entities and to individuals. While the exact form of the question varies according to time, place, and tradition, the thrust seems to be common: Why is it "natural" to submit to and promote the power of the state at a given moment? Can there be too much obedience? What is the ultimate end in view? Must the expansion of state power diminish a society's capacity to set humane ends for itself, and the mobilization of social rationality contribute inevitably to the further expansion of that power until some catastrophe brings a temporary halt to the process? Must the growing purview of the state tend to the deracination and demoralization of a people?

The journalist Hasegawa Nyozekan posed this question in 1921. How is it, he asked, that as servants of state men are permitted, even praised for committing, acts forbidden to the common conscience? What is it in the nature of the collectivity that sanctions such a differential morality? Why is it that one cannot even claim membership in a "nation" without "the sacrifice of part of one's humanity"?[6] Over the succeeding decade, Hasegawa came to believe that the resolution of the paradox of national identity lay in the development of a truly international proletariat, and set about a critique of the state that sought to lay bare the ideological roots of modern patriotism and its violent tendencies. Thus in 1931 he dared to claim that Japan's invasion of Manchuria signaled the advent of fascism in his own country and to predict that it would lead to a "second World War." He insisted that only the proletariat could prevent such a cataclysm. Yet this same Hasegawa Nyozekan, writing in the late 1930s, professed to see Japan's war in China as a liberating force, and upheld Japan's right and duty to compel China to accede to modernization by conquest. Hasegawa, finally, was at no loss for words to explain, in terms of a misunderstood national character, why Japan had gone to war with the Western world. His intelligence had been mobilized.

Nanbara Shigeru, on the other hand, believed that the state was indispensable to the achievement of true freedom and humanity. This was a view befitting his position as a public servant in an imperial university. Yet Nanbara remained unshakably opposed to the "pseudo-religion" of the *kokutai* (Japan's emperor-centered national polity), according to which the emperor was the font of all values—goodness, truth, beauty, justice—in the lives of his people. He clung to an ideal state. And in his private poetic journal, Nanbara confessed his hopes that England, whose utilitarian philosophy he scorned, would be victorious against Germany, his own country's ally.

In the end, Nanbara could only hope that a new Weltanschauung, grounded in individual Christian witness, would take shape and prevent a repetition of the events his country had set in motion. Japanese tradition alone, he felt, was philosophically and morally insufficient.

Both of these cases illustrate the daunting task of critical allegiance: to keep the comforting sanctuary that is one's nation from becoming a prison house, for oneself, for others. In this sense, this study may be read as a cautionary tale, whose focus on Japan is "accidental." Maruyama Masao himself, a brilliant and problematic disciple of both Nanbara and Hasegawa, looked beyond Japan for a formula to express the moral lesson of uncritical allegiance. In his essay "Politics and Man in the Contemporary World," Maruyama drew on the experience of Martin Niemöller, a German pastor and eventual prisoner of the Nazi regime. Niemöller crystalized his experience—the transformation of equanimity into opposition as Nazi attacks came closer and closer to the church—into two stark injunctions. First, *Principis obsta:* "Resist the beginning"; second, *Finem respice:* "Consider the end." [7] Niemöller's own awakening had come too late to prevent the evil that so seared his conscience. Ultimately, then, as Simone Weil thought, we may fail. Her example, however, and Niemöller's and Nanbara's, and Hasegawa's, shows us that we are bound, whatever the result, to continue our attempts to think *through* our condition. The alternative—to cease thinking altogether—permits no other choice.

Introduction: The Dual Senses of "Public" in Imperial Japan

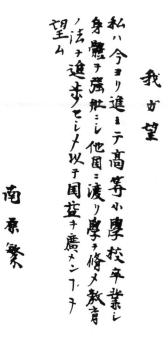

Text in Nanbara Shigeru's hand of "Waga nozomi" (My desire, ca. 1898; for a translation, see p. 52). Courtesy of Education Centre, Kagawa Prefecture.

Both Nanbara Shigeru and Hasegawa Nyozekan regarded the emergence of the modern state as a universal, defining condition of national historical development. And both recognized it to be a process specific to each national society: every history is unique. Hasegawa Nyozekan at moments embraced an explanation of Japan's history based on a conjuncture determined ultimately by the dominant mode of production in society as it articulated with external economic forces; at other times he relied for explanation on cultural formations handed down from the past. Nanbara Shigeru was more consistent. For him history was an unfolding of worldviews whose logical contradictions compelled further development via dialectical breaks with the past. Both were keenly aware of the "unique" aspects of their nation's history, especially its political development. But that very awareness of difference was born of a deeper belief in Japan's irrevocable and complete entry into the stream of world history, and bespoke, further, the conviction that all particular histories would ultimately converge.

In this basic outlook, the two men were very much products of the Japan that had been opened to the world in the mid-nineteenth century. For with the Meiji Restoration of 1868 and Japan's subsequent exposure to a bewildering variety of Western modes of thought, Japan's history and future development appeared in an arresting, even thrilling, new perspective. This was the view—one with indigenous roots to be sure—that all history, Japan's included, was inherently relative and manipulable; and that what Japan needed was to review its past and determine its future course in the light of the advanced state already reached by the powers that had made their appearance on the horizon at that crucial moment. This view, challenged though it has been by a powerful quasi-nativist reaction, has never been superseded.[1]

At the same time, Japan's spectacularly successful entry into the stream of universal development also produced recurring fears that someday the bubble would burst, that the nation would forever be forced to play catch-up with the West. This complex has given Japan's modern history an urgent, and sometimes violent and frenetic, quality. And it has, in most periods, fostered a preoccupation with national identity, with being "understood" by the outside world. In its efforts to "stand shoulder to shoulder with the West," Japan met great success at the turn of the twentieth century, only to find its "special relationship" to East Asia a source of friction, hostility and frustration vis-à-vis its fellow colonial powers (not to mention those actually subject to Japanese rule). Such experiences have in their turn produced spates of compensatory truculence and encouraged explanations for the actions of the state that look directly to cultural predisposition and the national character.

Whatever may become of this mind-set in the future, there can be no doubt that its proximate origins are to be found in the late Tokugawa and early Meiji periods, when the consensus was formed among the nation's leadership to make a forced march to national strength, lest Japan suffer the fate of China. In its urgency, this consensus on the need for a "rich country and a strong army" (*fukoku kyōhei*) also presupposed that the state itself would direct the nation's development toward its utilitarian end. But who made up the state? Who was to supply the resources and shape priorities and strategies? What was *fukoku kyōhei* to mean for the people?

In the years roughly between 1868 and 1898, an answer emerged from among the myriad factional conflicts, clashes of economic interest, and confrontations over matters of principle among the social forces struggling for a voice in the polity. This answer can, I think, be encapsulated in three contemporary formulas.

First, *kanson minpi*: "Exalt officialdom, slight the people/officialdom is exalted, and the people base." This is perhaps the key to the process by which the Meiji leadership sought to create a modern state. Influenced both by Tokugawa traditions of bureaucratism long divorced from actual feudal landholding and, after the 1880s, by imported Prussian models for administration, the "founders" built a state in which preponderant power lay with official bureaucracy and a transcendent cabinet rather than with an elected representative body. A description of this process is far beyond the scope of this introduction, of course. Here, let it suffice to say that the state, itself composed of power blocs frequently at odds with one another, managed to take effective, though not undisputed, charge of laying the infrastructure of national strength and identity: a conscript army, a new land tax system, standardized and compulsory education, a constitution, local and national assemblies, railroads, telegraph, post, and so forth. Stupendous popular energies were released, particularly among the upper segments of the peasantry, with the disestablishment of traditional statuses. But all at a price: vast numbers of legally equal imperial subjects were excluded from any political representation. The land tax did not ease the burden of the peasantry, but attempted to rationalize collection and concentrate revenues in the hands of the central authority. Warrior discontent over disestablishment split the leadership and had finally to be put down by force. Industrial development, spurred by military expenditure and transfer of ownership and management of plant to select private hands, took off in the mid to late 1880s, but did not proceed on a scale sufficient to absorb an increasing rural population. Instead, writes the economist Makoto Itoh, it created a "huge impoverished reserve army in the rural villages," which "served to hold back the improvement of industrial workers' wages." "In stark contrast to the rapid growth of capitalist production, peasants and wage earners continued to suffer poverty and insecurity. Labor unrest in the cities developed parallel with [indeed, independently of] socialist ideologies, including antiwar campaigns, and at the turn of the century began to attract the attention of a wider public."[2]

The second formula is *kazoku kokka,* "family state": it describes how the *kokutai* articulated with the nation as a whole. Thus "family state" will represent the complex legitimating ideology that took shape by the 1890s as the leadership rejected (and partly coopted) proposals, made from within the ruling group and by publicists close to the sovereignty question, for a "mixed" English-style constitutional monarchy and a more radical democratic system derived from natural-rights theory. The "family state" postulated a semidivine monarch whose family was the "great house" for all those of his subjects, at once chief priest of the Sun line and a modern ruler with enormous prerogatives who "presided over" (*suberu; tōchi suru*) but did not "involve himself" (*ataru*) in the actual administration of the state. Many of the implications of this pattern will be discussed in succeeding chapters. Here let us stress its valorization of organic harmony and patriarchal integration over any conflictual notions of the composition of the polity. This ties in, of course, with the "exaltation" of officialdom, which, along with the independent military, acted for the first three decades of the modern period as the structural expression, so to speak, of the imperial will.

In its fully elaborated form, the *kazoku kokka* also bound the *ethnos* (*minzoku*) to the state that ruled it in an ostensibly timeless relation. The system of rule was presented as wholly specific to the national culture; ideas that challenged the political system became threats to the national/ethnic identity of Japan. Under the auspices of modern education, from the imperial university to the elementary school; of the army and reserve organizations; and through untold private expressions, this consciousness permeated Japanese society. The identification of state and ethnic identity has had decisive consequences for the shape of critical thought on politics and society in Japan throughout the modern era.[3]

To these formulas, however, must be added an unstable and vital third—*banki kōron (ni kessubeshi),* a phrase from the new government's Charter Oath of 1868 that might be translated as "all measures [shall be decided by] public discussion."[4] What was meant by "public" (*kō/ōyake*)? Who was the "public" in the modern Japanese state? How represented in the polity? If the "people" were to be "slighted," where did "public" as the manifest subject of politics ("public discussion") reside? For the eventual victor in the contest over state sovereignty, and for those actually operating the state machinery, "public" equaled official.

Indeed, the term *public* had, from the time of Japan's first absorption of continental political thought from China (directly and via Korea) been connected with governing authority. Consideration of the meaning of the counterpart terms in classical Chinese political thinking is clearly beyond our purpose here. But it is noteworthy that the oldest layer of meaning attached to the Japanese term *ōyake* seems to be that of "sovereign," (imperial) "palace," "court," and "government." Associated with this term were (and are) ideas of impartiality; absence of bias, private intent or interest; joint possession; the realm of common human feeling; and (more recently) society. All told, although *ōyake* can now be understood to refer both to state and to society, history is on the side of those who would identify *public* with what pertains to governing authority.[5] Concretely, we find that in Japan *kō* (*ku*) referred to "public" lands and their inhabitants, the former having been declared the property of the imperial family at the time of the Tang-style Taika Reform of 645. It was also a term for the nobility, later for the shogunal authority and *daimyō*. Thus at the end of the Tokugawa period, "public discussion," strictly speaking, referred to the *daimyō*/court/*bakufu* councils designed to deal with the regime's deepening crisis. With the Restoration and abolition of the feudal system, of course, "publicness" reverted to the imperial institution and its bureaucratic guardians. In sum, then, we can say that *kō/ōyake* did not emanate from the *min*—the common people—but was from the first presumed to inhere in the entities that ruled over them, notwithstanding the more recent ambiguity in the meaning of the term.

We may also approach the "public" from the standpoint of ethics, in view of its association with Confucian conceptions of statecraft. *Kō/ōyake* was contrasted to *shi/watakushi*, denoting private interest or concerns. It was the cardinal sin of the official to mask selfishness with a public façade. It may be worthwhile to point out the constant presence of a countertradition in Chinese ethical thought that, rather than drawing a rigid distinction between the "public" (*kong*) and the "private" (*si*), or placing the latter in clear subordination to the former, stressed an ideal of government that was invisible, and, implicitly, did nothing to obstruct popular energy. Particularly relevant here is the fusion of this insight with the Spencerian notions we find in the writings of Yan Fu (1853–1921), Liang Qichao (1873–1929), and other late Qing reformist thinkers. In their work, the idea emerges that the energy of the *min* gives life to the larger, nonofficial "public" sphere, which might now be called "society." It was from this sphere, Yan Fu insisted, that the state derives its true strength. Yan Fu, of course, treated Spencer's Victorian "Old Liberalism" as a prescription for the state. It was as a formula for building a powerful state that he cherished the thesis of continuity between popular energy and national might.[6]

The irruption of Western ideas into Chinese political and ethical discourse, then, did not render the multiform deposit of tradition forever irrelevant. Neither did this hold in Japan. Indeed, the state builders and imperial myth makers of early Meiji, having prevented the colonial fragmentation of their country, were able to set about their task with far greater confidence of legitimacy than their counterparts in post-Taiping China. The official disestablishment of the four traditional statuses of Tokugawa society—warrior, peasant, artisan, merchant—and legal equalization of the populace as imperial subjects did more than lay the infrastructure of national identity. It created a "public world" not necessarily coterminous with imperial subjecthood *as officially defined.*[7] Indeed, Fukuzawa Yukichi (1835–1901), however much he went on to become a booster and apologist for the imperialist policies of the Meiji government, saw in this creation the true significance of the "revolutionary Restoration." Although his conclusion (at the time of the Freedom and Popular Rights Movement) that the people were too immature to assume a direct hand in their governance led him into the quasi-reactionary camp, Fukuzawa's valorization of a differentiated society of individuals—concretely, of middle-class property holders—remained a key alternative to the presumptive disparagement of "popular" (= individual) interest found in the *kanson minpi* formula. He had argued in *Gakumon no susume* (An encouragement of learning, 1872) that scholars should not seek government posts—official status—but should enhance their own personal independence, and promote that of the nation, from an "outside" (*zaiya*) position. Finally, Fukuzawa's own refusal to take any official position speaks to his conviction that real vitality lay *outside* the state. Fukuzawa's choice must also be understood in the context of the disbanding in 1875 of the Meirokusha, the high-level society for public discussion that was the very emblem of the Meiji Enlightenment. The Meirokusha, it will be recalled, faced a choice between publication of its journal under new, emasculating press laws or its dissolution as a body. After some debate, it chose the latter. For a brief period, then, "publicness" had remained undifferentiated. The publicists of the Meirokusha confidently proposed; the government, including some of their number, disposed. But this situation could not last once the state, pleading *raison d'état,* began to erect barriers between the two spheres.[8]

I discuss Fukuzawa only to suggest that in the early Meiji years a new discourse arose around the notion of a nonofficial public sphere of action based on the legitimate worldview of individuals and groups in, and as constituting, society. We may recognize in a number of Tokugawa thinkers the streams that fed this discourse: in the separation of public and private realms that, as Maruyama Masao argued, began with Ogyū Sorai; in Itō Jinsai, with his "vitalist" celebration of individual energy; in the widely shared discussion during the late Tokugawa period of "practical studies" (*jitsugaku*) as the concern of the man of "merit" or "talent" regardless of status (within the warrior class). (We must be content to suggest, rather than prove, any such genealogy.) The point is that the post-Restoration years, quite apart from the eclectic designs of the founders of the Meiji regime, saw the creation of the intellectual and social space for a new public discourse.[9]

Indeed, there were other alternatives besides Fukuzawa's middle-class public. Irwin Scheiner's study of Protestant converts among former samurai has shown that transcendent conscience, rather than property ownership, could define a basis for social action, criticism, and solidarity that was independent of—but did not reject—national identity.[10] We may point to a third alternative, one that has remained in undeserved obscurity. This is the "communitarian" public reconstructed by Irokawa Daikichi and other historians of the *minshūshi* (people's history) school. With origins in late Tokugawa peasant solidarism, this communitarian public saw expression, for example, in "underground" discussions of a proposed constitution for the new state drawn up by the local activist Chiba Takusaburō in the Tama district, west of modern Tokyo. This and other grass-roots proposals helped to shape the ideology of the Freedom and Popular Rights Movement, the struggle against which compelled the leadership to protect itself and the state via the illiberal "granted constitution" of 1889. Irokawa has shown how official hostility to these innovative and democratic "outsider" proposals for the political direction of the country issued in the multifaceted, but hegemonic, imperial orthodoxy of the years after 1890.[11]

As Fukuzawa himself feared, the "undue preponderance of authority" (*kenryoku no henchō*) in the government, especially after the Prussian option was taken in matters of sovereignty and state administration, worked like an albatross, stunting the growth of public consciousness, and forcing it into expression as a self-serving "nationalist" privatism: one cannot but be struck, for example, by the constant refrain of industrialists, through the 1940s—many from wealthy peasant families finally liberated from inhibiting status restrictions—that all their efforts were aimed at "serving the nation." [12] The success ethic of *risshin shusse* indeed equated self- and national aggrandizement. Even at their most acquisitive, however, Japanese would-be followers of Guizot's advice— *enrichissez-vous!*—could not conceive of enrichment at the expense of the nation. Call this hypocrisy—as it appeared to many critics then and now—the point is that the compulsion to identify private and national benefit was in part the legacy of Meiji's "revolution from above": the founders had amassed great prestige by creating, through autocratic means, an independent state at a time when (as it appeared) permanently debilitating subservience to the West was equally possible. An "undue preponderance of authority" thus persisted, producing a catalogue of apparently unapologetic factionalism and greed by those in and near power. The idea that some structural, systemic problem of political economy was at work in the seeming selfishness of bureaucracy lay unexamined until, with the advance of industrialization, a socialist critique developed in the 1890s. Once established, it remains to add, this critique represented a realm beyond the pale of official tolerance, and the government sought with extreme prejudice to bring its adherents to heel. [13]

The state, then, sought to bind the "public" to itself, along with the authority to define the identity and values of its subjects. The centripetal force of this identification was most evident among bureaucrats, where personal, official, and national identity were intertwined with a powerful sense of mission—to civilize the people, to acquire learning for the sake of the nation, to raise Japan's status in the world. [14] It is not difficult to imagine that social status and prerogative over "outsiders" went hand-in-hand with this attitude. Criticism of status abuses, by the same token, had to confront this interlocking set of identities. As we have seen, one method was to posit another valid realm—individual/social good or interest, conscience, preexisting solidarities—as a basis of criticism and counterideal. These "outsider" publics shared a common task: to disengage private and official from the circular logic of attacks on "selfishness" and create from them a sphere of values, and action, outside the state. The "public," therefore, was not something wholly separate from the state, or vice versa. Rather, "public" affairs entailed conflict and compromise with official and truly private interest. But the end public action served was different from these two. Publicness in practice partook of official and private bodies, but was coterminous with neither.

We must also give attention to a powerful variant of the "outside" critique. This we might call that of the "imperial" public. From this standpoint, an unfeeling and despotic bureaucracy had grown so privatized that the emperor's deep concern for his putative children was denied expression. The dominance of officialdom was a fact of life in Japanese politics. When the parties came into the ascendant at a later time, the same critique held. Only direct communication between sovereign and subject could ensure that the beneficent will of the monarch would be given voice.

Appeal to a charismatic emperor was a tactic available to a panoply of critics across the ideological spectrum and throughout the imperial period. Early in the Meiji period, disaffected loyalists such as Saigō Takamori and Etō Shinpei had raised armies against the new government in the emperor's name. Fukuzawa, while more accepting of the status quo, had seen in the sovereign a harmonizing cultural center and focus of loyalty outside the state. And he emphasized the emperor's potential "usefulness" in promoting moral and cultural progress, proposing in a number of editorials in *Jiji shinpō* that the imperial house ought to be provided with resources for supporting excellence among the people.[15] In formulating his ideologically eclectic *minponshugi,* the political theorist, journalist, and sometime activist Yoshino Sakuzō (1878–1933) treated the emperor's will as the ultimate justification for a vast broadening of the franchise. Finally, the radical antiparliamentarian agrarianist Gondō Seikyō (1868–1938) called for a virtually osmotic relation of emperor to subject in a number of influential essays and tracts, among them *Kōmin jichi no hongi* (Cardinal principles of autonomy under the emperor, 1919) and *Kunmin kyōji ron* (On joint rule by sovereign and people, 1932). The "Young Officers" of the 1930s who attacked "evil officials around the throne" (*kunsoku no kan*), therefore, represented only the most extreme form of appeal to the "imperial" public.

In contrast to other "outsider" critiques based on individual interest or conscience—here we exclude revolutionary, hence heretical, ideologies—the appeals to "imperial" publicness sought to make use of the

specificity of ethnic identity as a means to break the official monopoly
on proximity to the source of that identity, the emperor. But because of
their explicit particularism, such appeals were, compared to other "outsider" approaches, much more readily coopted by the state. Such would
seem to be the import, for example, of Kano Masanao's analysis of autonomous local youth, religious, and cultural organizations, which as
they came under state sponsorship were quickly disabused of their anti-
bureaucratic thrust.[16] The same may be said of post-Taishō political
movements with strongly anticapitalist elements in their radical agrarian and/or emperorist programs. Since such movements had ties to the
lower echelons of the army officer corps, their fates were often as violent
as the means they chose to eliminate obstructions between emperor and
people. In the long run, however, the radical critique was simply tamed:
how else explain Konoe Fumimaro's proclamation in 1940 of a "New
Order" whose program consisted of "putting into practice the Way of
the Subject"?[17]

It would be wrong, therefore, to imagine that the public types outlined above represented from the first clear-cut, status-bound ideological products. Their fluidity was their greatest virtue. The government
came only gradually and by twists and turns to assume its monopoly on
defining national identity. Still, there can be no question that the promulgation of the Constitution, Education Rescript, Rescript to Soldiers
and Sailors, and other hortatory edicts, represents the crystalization of
an enabling ideology that, combined with the proven power of official
bureaucracy, stamped Japanese political evolution with a heavily statist
character.

The ideological field, to put it differently, was valenced. Certainly
there was competition among official elites (oligarchs, ministries, the
armed services, Diet, peerage, and so on) for the right to use the imperial name, to "assist the throne" from a position of greatest proximity.
Nor can we ignore the voice of the public outsider as it implicitly claimed
legitimacy for itself through the act of speaking—in the press, journals,
local assemblies, political meetings, and in countless informal ways. In
the end, however, one must consider the lesson of the Meiji Constitution
itself: it may be true, as Joseph Pittau has argued, that the "hybrid constitutional monarchy" of Meiji was ambiguous enough to allow a "liberal" reading, once the political conditions for it had developed with the
passing of the genrō.[18] In theory, however, this liberalism was highly circumscribed, and in practice it had to live and grow in the interstices of
the imperial system rather than direct its operation. The parties, for ex-

ample, never overcame the taint of private factionalism attached to the word *party* (*tō*) itself; and their voluntary dissolution in 1940, following upon a decade of declining influence, speaks eloquently to this reality. And if this was the case with the established parties—as opposed to the democratic movement—how much more heavily must the sanctions against separateness have weighed upon principled dissenters from the status quo? A party qua party could not assist the throne. Its separate identity had to be denied first.

We have already seen that economic activity had to be justified in terms of its "service to the nation," lest it be condemned as "individualistic." (Here, to digress briefly, we must note that *individualism* itself refers to a kind of corporate self-seeking rather than to any preference for solitary activity.[19] It is for this reason that attacks on liberalism often took the heads of giant *zaibatsu* as their target, despite the fact that, objectively speaking, they were furthering capital accumulation to an unprecedented degree.)

But those who sought to make Japanese politics more representative had to face more than the immediate problem of wresting authority away from jealous bureaucratic factions and a hostile military; they had somehow to confront an intensely competitive society that tended to value qualification, status, and precedent over institutional innovation and experiment. And it is with that society and its values, as these bear on the problem of the public, that we must concern ourselves now.

Bureaucratic capitalism in Japan gave rise to a secular hierarchy in which unaffiliated, or "free," activity was in general held to be of less value than specialized work performed within a recognized organization, with service in the official bureaucracy assuming pride of place. This preference for affiliation and conformity, for "riding the rails of routine,"[20] bedeviled attempts to "liberalize" the empire, politically, socially, and intellectually.

That government service should occupy the top rungs of this hierarchy is not surprising when one considers the long supremacy of the samurai-bureaucrat under the Tokugawa system, and the resulting cult of public authority. ("Justice comes from the august authorities"—*Seigi wa okami yori*—was the watchword.) To this add the continued role of the state in overseeing the industrialization of the country and protecting it from external harm. Clearly this is a circumstance that bore on the social experience, perspective, and life choices of educated persons under the empire (though not, as I shall argue, in any rigid, deterministic way).

It is a matter of record that the staff of the empire and business world eventually proved unable to provide positions for all the bright young men who emerged, beginning in the late Meiji years, from the higher schools and private and imperial universities. As Maruyama Masao observes, "the rapidity of the establishment of higher education exceeded that of the industrialization of Japanese capitalism."[21] The competition for available posts was as intense as the school-inculcated ambition that drove it. An unhealthy commingling of "two contradictory principles of competition and status" soon transformed the search for talent into an exercise in formalism: no academic pedigree, no official appointment. Private bureaucracies in industry, business, and medicine followed this example. And as this formalism combined with an already utilitarian and compartmentalized approach to higher education, a prototype generation of "experts"—defined as such by their academic pedigrees—emerged from the classrooms of late Meiji academe. Very quickly, Japan moved—as the journalist and historical essayist Yamaji Aizan put it in 1910—from the "age of the [Restoration] hero . . . to the age of the student [*shosei*] . . . to the age of the specialist." Indeed, Maruyama asserts, "it is no exaggeration to say that the universally infamous tendency toward compartmentalization and sectionalism that everywhere accompanies specialization was in Japan very nearly the 'original sin' of modernization itself."[22]

Possession of academic pedigree, then, led for the fortunate to a position in the bureaucratic elite, official or private. The "experts" were organization men, the "insiders" of the empire. And it was would-be organization men who, among others, fed the "intelligentsia" created by the shortfall of positions in the bureaucratic apparatus of the late Meiji era. But the contemporary critique of the "success" ethic, it must be stressed, was more than sour grapes. It is not to be reduced to a by-product of unemployment. Rather, derailed or frustrated careers often served as the occasion for a radical and profound questioning of personal ambition, and of the unforgiving values of contemporary Japanese capitalism as well. Beyond this, we must remember that the social approbation and deference that were the nominal rewards of insideness[23] were matched, for some who chose outsideness, by freedom of movement and expression; a sense, perhaps, of unencumbered self-determination and spontaneity. This is certainly the impression one gains from the exuberant satire and flamboyant autobiographical writings of journalists such as Miyatake Gaikotsu and Yamazaki Kesaya. Indeed, Miyatake's autobiography bears the provocative title *I Am a Dangerous Individual* (*Yo wa kiken jinbutsu nari*)![24]

Described solely in occupational terms, the public man as insider was a would-be or actual organization man (including academics, researchers, and doctors at large institutions). What then was an outsider? Again, I refer to occupation; I shall try shortly to show how we may relate occupation—professional and social being—to consciousness. As Maruyama Masao has suggested in his typology of Japanese intellectuals, *outsider* would refer to members of "private sector professions" such as "independent scholars and critics, physicians in private practice, and attorneys."[25] We may also describe as outsiders journalists, artists, creative writers, and perhaps (paradoxically!) public school teachers and the operators of small private schools (*juku*). Broadly speaking, it is clear that insiders would by definition belong to large organizations and occupy (at least potentially) upper-level positions within them; outsiders would perforce work in smaller scale, or socially suspect, organizations such as labor unions. They would also enjoy less security or regularity of affiliation and more mobility, voluntary or otherwise.

Clearly, the public worlds of the insider and outsider impinged upon each other constantly. Students by definition remained still undifferentiated in their publicness. The journalist reported and editorialized on the activities of the bureaucrat and sometimes sought his patronage. The bureaucrat cultivated, tolerated, and manipulated or harassed the journalist as his authority and interests dictated. Circumstances of birth and background alone might neither provide safe passage to insideness nor bar the entrance to it. Nor did separation mean mutual unawareness and unconcern or prevent informal contact. But that did not change the fact that by the middle years of the Meiji era, walls had grown up between "inside" and "outside" that, once in place, did much to determine how, and among whom, Japanese from then on lived their public lives. The insider enjoyed prestige, status, and public trust inaccessible to the outsider. The outsider might win fame, but any deference paid would be conditional and specific to his personal achievement. Unlike the insider, he could not count on respect being paid by virtue of title or affiliation; quite the contrary. Exceptions such as Sōseki or Ōgai aside, the independent writer, the private scholar—in sum, the "free floater"—treated, and was treated by, the wider public world in a manner different to the insider; this solely on account, not of his intellectual ability or particular "calling," but of the circumstances in which he worked.

The two linked, yet distinct, public worlds outlined here provided fertile ground for self-conscious reflection, critique, and attempts at transformation by those whose lives were shaped by, and helped to shape, those worlds. In other words, the public world produced its own ideologues and ideologies. These intellectual specialists sought to interpret and guide the development of the public sphere, of public discourse, in imperial Japan. It is to such individuals that I have given the name *public men*. As intellectuals, they were "professionally committed to the independent and deliberate use of the word"[26] and to its transmission through largely impersonal means to audiences outside their own personal knowledge and immediate social milieu. This audience included a vastly expanding newspaper and book readership, especially among the urban middle classes, professionals, lower-level white-collar workers, business people, and students. It is obvious, however, that particularly after the second decade of the twentieth century, the audience for public questions was expanding beyond the urban middle class to include certain strata of the working class, and also, especially at the left end of the spectrum, crossing gender lines. (In this connection we may remark that public women and women's issues remained almost exclusively "outside," while labor and agrarian issues were taken up more broadly.)

The point is simply that the public world under discussion here was no longer one in which an undifferentiated and tiny number of enlighteners, such as the members of the Meirokusha, could gather to debate the issues. The growth of the state, of the industrial economy and working population, and powerful trends toward democracy all made this impossible. Public men occupied a valenced ideological field: a bureaucrat (including an academic bureaucrat) was better because he knew better. He had the academic pedigree and the proximity to power to prove it. This reflected the historical legacy of Tokugawa bureaucratism and status hierarchy, as well as the urgency of late capitalist development.

How are we to relate this bit of sociology to the actual intellectual content of public work? We may speak, I think, of public discourse in imperial Japan as being hegemonized by the state. The state controlled the boundaries of legality in public discourse by administrative, judicial, and legislative means. Moreover, it sought actively to define national values and identity; specifically to wed a patriarchal and corporate concept of family and society, an intensely competitive meritocracy, and an ethic of national service in the promotion of domestic capitalism and enhanced power and status abroad. As Japan entered the twentieth century, and the membership of the ruling strata of society shifted and expanded, the dissonances and conflicts of logic and interest inherent in the secular hierarchy began to tell on the system. The "rules of the game" also changed, in that "democracy" emerged as a tolerable point of contention among public men, if such contention would keep "socialism" at bay. Under these conditions, therefore, it became easier rather than otherwise to perceive where the real danger lay: in systems of thought and organizations that either questioned the sanctity of private property (that is, capitalism) or challenged the "imperial rule"—the constitutional system. An attack on either or both became heresy; the heretic ceased to be Japanese. Viewed in a negative sense (what they were not or tried not to be), public men sought not to be heretics. Sometimes they failed, often with devastating personal consequences. They also sought not to be sycophants. Here, too, they sometimes failed. The significance of the insider/outsider distinction in this context may be understood in this way: from the point of view of the state, an outsider was further from the locus of value—the emperor and the state that protected the *kokutai*—than an insider, and perhaps more susceptible to heretical claims. The ideological offenses of outsiders were thus less tolerable, because they were more dangerous: with less status to lose, politically dissident outsiders were far more prone to organize. On the other hand, outsiders could legitimately "withdraw" into (apparently innocuous) private, aesthetic concerns more easily than insiders, who were, ideologically speaking, "on call" all the time. And while being "on call" in fact permitted the insider greater access to "dangerous thought" (know your enemy), the insider also had status and organizational integrity to protect.

Short of a conscious decision for heresy, then, the insider might have experienced a greater sense of intellectual restriction in his public work. In return, to bring the discussion full circle, his ideological offenses were not always punished with the severity encountered by outsiders. Such were the rewards of insideness. In either case, insideness or outsideness, the state's own complex ideology, with its concomitant operating definition of heresy, became a reference point for public men as they made the personal, political, and intellectual choices that shaped their lives. Insideness and outsideness both created and reflected the choices they made.

Let us pass now to a consideration of the "positive" attributes of publicness—that is, those features public men sought to possess and enhance. Earlier it was noted that the public world of late Meiji Japan was far different than that of the immediate post-Restoration years. In another sense, however, we find an interesting continuity in what we may call the "informal," albeit crucial, criteria for public work.

Broadly speaking, all public men, whether insider or outsider, official or nonofficial, shared two features. The first is the nationalist mentality, perspective, and rhetoric of the entire period—from Meiji on—that we have been discussing. All felt that it was their duty to "bear the fate of the nation on their shoulders." This attitude, as Maruyama Masao pointed out long ago, was simply the "common sense" of Meiji Japan.[27] A public man felt it his duty to mold the consciousness of his audience in accordance with a public ideal. That ideal, of necessity, reflected the circumstances of its production. Insider public men tended to think of the state they served as (ideally) the proper means to the realization of "publicness"—the harmonious and organic unity of state and nation. They did not accept the view that the state was the mere instrument of a ruling class, but believed that it could transcend the conflicting interests of "civil society," and was indeed the only conceivable means to overcome the inherently corrosive tendencies of individualism, particularly in the economic sphere. Some went further, realizing that the officials of the state itself engaged in self-aggrandizement and private factionalism, and harbored a counterproductive turf mentality. The role and posture of the armed services were especially, but not solely, indicative of such evils. The point is that an insider—as the example of Nanbara Shigeru will show—need not be a supine agent of class or factional interest. This does not mean that the elitism of bureaucratic thinking, even among idealists, did not remain salient, or that certain assumptions about modes of expression and behavior did not tend to prevail among them. One could always spot the official.

Outsiders, as we saw apropos of Fukuzawa and other critics, held to a public ideal that took some other substrate as prior to the state. And they believed that it was necessary to defend this substrate from state encroachment for that ideal to be realized. There were of course outsiders who were more sympathetic to the state—notably moderate labor movement activists who preferred to deal with capital through the state rather than directly. And there were insiders, such as Minobe Tatsukichi and Yoshino Sakuzō, who did not automatically reject the idea that there ought to be popular checks on state authority. By and large, however, it is on the question of the proper role of the state vis-à-vis society, the nation, or the people, that substantive distinction between the two types of public men rests.

At no point did public men cease to be concerned that their work contribute to the national enlightenment. But as industrialization advanced, along with the power and complexity of the state, the meanings of both *national* and *enlightenment* shifted. In the late Meiji period, and increasingly as Marxism and other socialist thought made its influence felt among educated strata, we begin to find that the "nation" ceases to be simply an unexamined point of departure and becomes for some public men a problem in itself. Why, they asked, had Japan's development taken the course it had? Was it not perhaps "distorted" in some fashion—in favor of the official, the party man, the industrialist and financier, the absentee landlord? And was it not time for "enlightenment" to issue more directly in social reform, aimed not so much at uprooting the "absurd customs and evil practices" of Tokugawa feudalism as at breaking up the entrenched economic and bureaucratic interests that dominated *modern* society? In posing these questions, a minority of public men on the inside drew closer to those outside, and both flirted more openly with heresy. In a sense this became necessary as the moral and literary critique of "success" was joined by the conceptually more rigorous and radical critique of political economy embodied in Marxism. This was to prove an unstable combination, and the nationalist, humanist, and spiritual concerns of earlier critics soon were separated from the internationalism of class struggle. But in another sense, the nationalist mentality—the unwillingness to be separated from the nation—reemerged in the problem of *tenkō* (ideological apostasy from the left) in the 1930s. The "nation-as-problem" approach never entirely disappeared, however, even during the heyday of ultranationalism. Instead, it became the key component of the "modernist" social criticism that emerged from the interwar generation of public men represented, for example, by Maruyama Masao, the economic historian Ōtsuka Hisao (1907–), the sociologist Fukutake Tadashi (1914–), and others. Most of these men, whose work I shall discuss in the conclusion, were the products of "insider" education, and spent the bulk of their careers in national universities as luminaries of the postwar enlightenment.[28]

The second shared feature also relates to the role of enlightener. In modern Japan this profession has entailed familiarity with the ideals, symbols, and (less so) the actual conditions of the "West," past and contemporary. The more education and advanced training one had in higher school, university, and beyond, the more expert one became. (By this advanced stage, intellectual work in one's specialty would have become both habit and personal need, since it was in large part the single most important component in self-definition. For the insider, *where* work was undertaken was as important as its content.) Expertise, however, was for the public man more than a matter of keeping up with the literature in a limited area of specialization. Indeed, expertise brought with it the duty to interpret the intellectual, even spiritual, needs of Japan, and to contribute to the enlightenment of those not exposed directly to the influence of "Western" thought. This had been the case with the *yōgakusha*—the late Tokugawa "scholars of Western learning" who found their great champion in Fukuzawa. Who better than the independent *yōgakusha*, Fukuzawa's *Gakumon no susume* asked, to lead the way to civilization? Those who later posed this question revised it to emphasize official over private training, but the ethos of publicness was shared sufficiently to distinguish the public man, for example, from the scientific technician. In certain fields and individuals, this distinction, too, was lost. This overlap was most pronounced among the "technical intelligentsia" (*gijutsu interi*). Here we may take Yoshino Shinji (1888–1971)—younger brother of Sakuzō—and his protégé Kishi Nobusuke (1896–1987) to be representative. As pioneers of Japan's "industrial policy" in the late 1920s and as members of the heavily bureaucratic Kokuikai (National Prestige Maintenance Association), Yoshino and Kishi aspired to a "reform [*henkaku*] of the whole character of society" through the subordination of private interest to that of the "national economy." This effort was to follow a pattern of "leadership and assistance" in which technocrats were to occupy the former position. It is to be noted that as the policies of Yoshino and company were adopted, strong lateral ties were formed with sympathetic figures in the military, private industry, academia, and journalism, and that technocracy as a concept and a calling appealed to public men on both the left and the right. The bureaucratic presence, however, remained dominant. The aspiration to leadership—control—was nurtured by a philosophy of the technocrat as a "new man" who united "technology" (*gijutsu*) and "psychology" (*shinjutsu*) in his personality. The technocrat, in this vision, was a *shi* (that is, a samurai) who embodied the *Will zum Kulturleben*.[29] To coin a phrase, *expertise oblige*.

Let us summarize. The West never ceased to be the bearer of models of power and of culture to modern Japan. But, as we have seen, the development of national institutions for the training of experts and the dissemination of their knowledge brought with it a status distinction between insider and outsider among experts in public questions. The ramifications of this distinction will become clear in the studies that follow. But we need to bear in mind that, at least by the 1890s, the distinction among such experts, as among insider and outsider in society as a whole, was deeply and keenly felt.

At the same time, public men did share the two broad features of national outlook and expertise in "imported" knowledge. To this extent, both insider and outsider belonged to what C. Wright Mills called the "cultural apparatus" of their country,[30] an apparatus that was a product of the middle and late Meiji era. We may offer the following constellation of features as a definition of the public men under study here: (a) intellectuals concerned—though not exclusively—with (b) the public sphere, which as defined earlier, includes what Ralf Dahrendorf calls "representative" and "legitimative" activities, and contributes to the "reservoir of possible futures,"[31] who are (c) expert in the knowledge of "Western" ideas and concepts relating to their concern, and (d) perform the role of "enlightener" either from a high status position "inside" the state (that of professor in an imperial university) or "outside" it (as a journalist, for example, on a major newspaper or periodical).

Given these two public types, how did social position and the content of public work interact? How and when was the meaning of *public* defined, and how did it evolve? How did public men represent their activities? What purposes did they claim to serve? Did they identify more with the state? Nation? Society? How did these identities develop? To what action did they lead? How, in sum, did public men come to terms with the valenced ideological field within which public discourse was conducted in imperial Japan?

The preceding definition, rough though it is, will have to set the stage for a brief characterization of what the contemporary phrase called "the crisis of the state" of the early Shōwa period (1925–45).[32] It is with this crisis in mind that this study examines the lives and work of its subjects, and tries to answer the questions posed above. The significance of this period should need no explanation, as its broad features are only too well known: the collapse of parliamentary government coinciding with Japan's military expansion into Manchuria, China, and finally Indochina; the attempt in domestic politics to mobilize the population for war under the aegis of a failed quasi-totalitarian "new order"; world war, loss within two years of an immense empire, stupendous destruction by conventional and atomic weaponry used on major cities; abject defeat; occupation and the disestablishment of the imperial system. How did Japanese public men act and react under these conditions of unexampled and convulsive change? How did they adjust to the drastic eruption of their country onto the world stage and its destruction by the West? What did it mean to be Japanese in 1925? In 1935? In 1945? Who decided? Who set the terms of discourse? These are some of the questions posed by the Shōwa crisis.

Yet what was the internal crisis? How did it develop? The early Shōwa period brought a multifaceted crisis, involving both the resolution of long-standing tensions and the creation of new and explosive precedents.[33] Whatever the continuities with earlier periods, "something happened" between 1925 and (roughly) 1932 that sets the entire period apart, both from the years before it, and from those after 1945.

The first year of Shōwa began with the coordinated enactment of universal male suffrage on the one hand, and the Peace Preservation Law (*Chian iji hō*) on the other. The former ratified attempts since the beginning of the Taishō period to broaden the franchise, made in recognition of the vastly expanded number of industrial workers, and the spread of education and literacy. The latter defined the boundary between heresy and acceptability in political behavior: any expression of, or organization for the purpose of expressing, opposition to the *kokutai* as officially defined, or to the system of private property, fell outside the pale of orthodoxy. This measure also had its ancestors, from the late Meiji anti-socialist legislation of 1900 to more immediate precedents in the form of procedural changes in the Justice Ministry's approach to ideological offenders. Both, in short, grew out of developments during the Taishō years.

For our purposes, "Taishō" may be viewed as two linked periods, with the crucial fulcrum at 1917–18. Prior to this date, public discourse was largely institutional. Public men, notably Minobe Tatsukichi and Yoshino Sakuzō, tried to theorize a redefinition of the political community that centered on the political parties (Yoshino put greater emphasis on "democratizing" the system as a whole). The passing of the "founding generation" had made some broadening necessary. The Taishō political crisis, which coincided with the death of the emperor in 1912 and culminated in the emergence of a "two-party" establishment, along with a defiant rebuff of military high-handedness in ministerial appointments, bore this out. Hara Kei's "politics of compromise" ensured that the Seiyūkai would be allowed to form the cabinet in exchange for its promise to promote government legislation in the Diet. But even though the parties were brought into a more active governing role, the more deeply rooted discontent of the nationalized masses lay unanswered.[34] The emergence of formal party government after 1918 came only when the masses, inspired by the Russian revolution of 1917 and driven to the limits of physical endurance by the huge inflation of the war years, erupted in midsummer in the so-called "Rice Riots" that brought down the "transcendental" cabinet of Terauchi Masatake. Earlier popular unrest notwithstanding, it was the events of 1917–18 that introduced the concept of "society" into public discourse all across the political spectrum, and into the day-to-day workings of government. The late Taishō period saw the expansion of education at all levels, the decentralization of the imperial universities, government involvement in conciliation of labor disputes, the legalization of certain unions, and so forth. The combination, then, of institutional reform and the forceful impingement of society onto politics created the long-term conditions for reaction, and hence for the "crisis of the state" that was to come. In this context, enfranchisement was, as Katō Kōmei phrased it, an inevitable "leap into the dark," and the Peace Preservation Law the elite's insurance policy against an organized revolutionary threat. I shall have occasion further on to discuss the government's decimation of the left and its consequences.

Fear of the left, however, only reflected the economic conditions that had given dissent legitimacy. Economic crises, beginning with the postwar "bust" after 1918, a major financial collapse in 1927, and the devastating depression of 1929–32, alienated Japan's everyday people, not, to be sure, sufficiently to turn them en masse to revolution, but enough to swell the ranks of the many proletarian parties, however briefly. But the real significance of this growth lay in the impetus it gave to the right wing, both old-line bureaucratic and military forces unreconciled to the Taishō redefinition and their handmaidens on the newer anticommunist, pseudosocialist "mass" right.

For these groups, all the ills of the status quo—its openly pork-barrel approach to public policy, inability to come to grips with the maldistribution of national wealth (especially its tolerance of rural poverty and relative overpopulation), "weak-kneed" foreign policy, and general subservience to the capitalist Anglo-American powers—could be attributed to the "liberal-genrō-party bloc." This bloc had "usurped" traditional authority to the detriment of the masses and of Japan's national strength. Furthermore, it had allies in the bureaucracy and its "chief priests" in the imperial universities. Liberalism, in sum, was synonymous with economic ruin for the little man, overpopulation and rural poverty, weakness and humiliation abroad. And in due course, "liberalism" as voodoo doll, and as umbrella term for the institutional expansion of the ruling elite and broadening of the political community, was rejected, and decisively so.[35] However, this rejection, at least in its radical component, relied on the very broadening it decried. As against the "cosmopolitan" appeal of the proletarian parties of the left, the radical, "mass" right—the fringes of the "imperial" public—appealed to the masses *as* Japanese, and to the emperor on their behalf.

A drastic "renovation" was called for, a "Shōwa Restoration." This restoration, admittedly, had as many meanings as proponents. During the formative years of the crisis, the initiative lay with rebellious junior officers in the army at home, who embarked on a series of unsuccessful but bloody attempts at coup d'état, and above all with the Kwantung Army, which unlike its domestic counterparts, quite successfully set the future direction of Japan's foreign policy by overrunning Manchuria in 1931. Having demonstrated the weakness, and won the acquiescence, of the government, the military was in a position to compel Japan's reorientation from diplomatic cooperation to a regionalist power-bloc approach to foreign relations. And it should not be thought that the whole civilian establishment was unhappy with this rejection of internationalism, any more than it had been with the suppression of the democratic movement at home.

However, the "crisis of the state" was not resolved with the rise of the military (or by its reintegration after 1936). Rather, the state remained in crisis *because* of that ascendancy. For although party power per se had ebbed in the early 1930s, no new political actor had come to the fore with strength sufficient to control all the elements—in the military, industry and finance, the parties, peerage, and bureaucracy—that had ranged themselves to the "right" in the Taishō rearrangement. The end of party government was the fulcrum, not the conclusion, of the crisis. For other vestiges of liberalism remained subject to attack by "renovationist" forces in sometime alliance with segments of the bureaucracy and peerage. A series of coup attempts and assassinations of political and business leaders by the radical front of young officers and "outsider" civilian conspirators was only the raw and violent edge of anti-pluralist, antiparliamentary reaction. But it was this same general movement in Japanese politics that brought about the rejection of Minobe's "organ theory" of state—to be discussed below—and a purge in the late 1930s of noted liberal critics of fascism and Japan's China policy.

The key date, it would seem, in the development of reaction into a "positive" program was 1936–37. These years saw the defeat and absorption of the radical renovationist arm of the military, followed by the government's definitive commitment to an expanded war in China, and alliance with Germany. After this date the government, especially under Konoe Fumimaro, could focus its appeal to the nation on the need to "resolve" the situation in China. This was to mean the mobilization of all national resources, military, technological, capital, and ideological, in an effort to create a regional power bloc in East Asia with Japan at its core as an "advanced national defense state."

It is true, of course, that state authority remained fragmented. Elites, including party men, all competed for a role in the organization and control of the coming new order. Konoe's attempt to build a new, state-directed mass "assistance" organization to parallel the dirigist reintegration of the economy succeeded only in reducing constitutional government to a "mangled caricature."[36] Konoe's foreign policy meanwhile set in motion a chain of events that led Japan into world war. Nevertheless, national mobilization, "assistance" politics, and war itself put an end to the earlier "crisis of the state." After 1937 there was no more open internecine strife. The price of its solution was, of course, total war and total defeat.

Let us return now to the problem of how public men acted and reacted during the "crisis of the state" and the subsequent total war. Between 1931 and 1940 Japan's ideological orientation also shifted, in ways analogous to the overlapping of reaction and redirection that had marked the politics of the period. And with similar results: broad, surface conformity to the generally totalitarian tenor of the regime reproduced itself in public discussion of social and political thought.

Thus as *demokurashii* yielded to *yokusan* ("assistance" of imperial rule) in political practice, society—the "discovery" of late Taishō thinkers—yielded to the *minzoku,* or nation. The individual came to mean in political thought what the party meant in politics: a selfish center of interest and a hoarder of power. Materialistic Anglo-Saxon individualism was exposed—and not only on the radical right—as the great abettor of Bolshevism. Communitarian harmony became the desideratum, the ideal of all orthodox political thought, whether it wore Japanist or pseudo-Marxist dress. Thus the first decade of the Shōwa period brought not only a state crisis but a broad cultural struggle.[37]

Among the intellectual elite, public insiders and outsiders of status, the ingrained habits of thought and critical method that made them "experts" in imported knowledge also had to compete with the terrific pressure to conform to the antiliberal tendencies in national politics. Indeed, to an extent, conformity was a presumed concomitant of national/public status. But, just as in politics, an internal tension (between expertise and status) persisted, despite the totalitarian machinations of the regime. It must at the same time be borne in mind that however "pluralist" the system was in its institutional makeup, it was decidedly *not* so in its values. Under a *yokusan*-style regime, one did not have the right to say no to the system openly, for how could one "assist" that which one doubted or questioned? It was not the right of an individual to make such a judgment. One did have the freedom, given a suitable high-status environment such as a university, to make one's yes mean something as close to no as ingenuity and conviction would permit. Only a very few, whose resistance was grounded in an explicitly cosmopolitan or transcendent ideology, dared to utter a no that was no. Examples include non-apostate Communists; pacifist Christians, such as Yanaihara Tadao; Akashi Junzō and other members of the Jehovah's Witnesses; and certain Buddhists, such as Senō Girō. But in terms of insiders as an unorganized body, those who doubted relied on what E. M. Forster called "the slighter gestures of dissent"—individual, sanity-preserving declarations of opposition. And this only at the risk of accusations of hubris and defeatism by others more openly committed to the national purpose, however ill-defined.[38] Such "slighter gestures" shaded into, and were outnumbered by, vague, guarded, and unoriginal professions of loyalty, which, thanks to their very ambiguity, were the best protection of integrity and status. Together, these "slighter gestures" and hedged bets of loyalty make up what we may call the "intermediate strategies" for intellectual survival adopted by public men.

But beyond such essentially negative postures, we must also consider the gradations of voluntary—positive—service. What are we to make of those public men of both types who—in numbers greater than was imagined in the years immediately after the defeat—hewed to the state? Is their positive service reducible to sheer opportunism, or perhaps to coerced and self-protective enthusiasm? No doubt this is true in part. But we must admit that for many public men, "hewing to the state" represented the cutting edge of ultramodernity. For some academics and journalists, such as those studied recently (from disparate points of view) by Itō Takashi, Muroga Sadanobu, Sakai Saburō, James Crowley, and Miles Fletcher,[39] the "crisis of the state" and war meant a chance to acquire real policy influence; a chance to put into practice ideas that were the product not of a sudden "ideological apostasy" (*tenkō*), but of considerable reflection and personal conviction. There is no gainsaying the sometimes execrable political and intellectual judgment exercised by Japanese public men. But the relevant question is not why did they abandon (an undefined) "liberalism" and/or "individualism"? It is rather what did they hope to achieve through voluntary cooperation and mobilization? What did they think that "policy influence" might actually mean? What, furthermore, was the alternative to state service? And what in general was the circumference of possible postures vis-à-vis the system of ideological mobilization—set by status, personal background, experience, and day-to-day political developments within and involving Japan, as well as by the "objective" social and economic state of the country? Surely the range of action for public men was not unlimited; it is my purpose to show what those limits were, and how public men worked within them.

Mention has already been made of *tenkō*. For early interpreters of Shōwa intellectual history, this meant a sudden and coerced ideological apostasy, and was used to explain the trend, after the mid 1930s, toward state service (or in our terms, toward "crossover" into insideness by public outsiders). The work of Itō and others alluded to above has done much to demonstrate the limitations of the "coercion model" of involvement. There is simply too much that cannot be explained without so qualifying and stretching the category of "apostasy" that it borders on uselessness. Specifically, *tenkō* as interpretation rests on the assumption that roughly after 1930, no one should of his own free will have desired to serve the Japanese state or to give his talent to the officially designated national cause. But as I have argued, the nature of the public man's commitment was such as to disallow any total withdrawal from national life; and after the elimination or cooptation of alternative centers of organized public activity—opposition political parties, the labor movement—the public man was left all dressed up with no place to go except into the arms of the state, which was the sole repository of legitimate public service. For a public man, finding a way *not* to serve was the more difficult task.

Granted, then, that public men were predisposed to work within a national framework—"national" reflecting relatively stronger or weaker identification with state or with society depending on the individual and the period. In any case, *state* and *society* were defined in the light of theories imported from the West, naturalized and manipulated for the purpose of national enlightenment or reform.

The cruder discussions of *tenkō* sometimes give the impression that Japanese public men renounced the beliefs of their period of intellectual formation as easily as they changed clothes. To a degree, as Fletcher points out, some—the more superficial thinkers—might have felt it necessary to "digest" one after another "set of Western ideas."[40] Admittedly, some cases of *tenkō* to communitarian nationalism and, after 1945, to "democracy," have been quite spectacular. And perhaps, too, some public men shared a tendency to treat ideas not as they related to "actual" conditions of Japanese state and society, but only as they related to each other in the abstract. Such a tendency would certainly explain the apparent ease with which affiliations shifted.

Fletcher's work, however, proves a more important point: that if one looks not only at the content of particular concepts, but at the stated (or unstated) problematic and context, the intellectual reorientation loses its appearance of caprice. The "New Order" theorist Rōyama Masamichi (1895–1979), for example, urged that the Meiji constitution was better interpreted in the light of the "traditional and historical . . . internal principle" of the "national community" (*kokumin kyōdōtai; Volksgemeinschaft*) rather than of a plurality of institutional claims on the body politic. By arguing that "the fundamental principle in the political formation of the Japanese people inheres in the national polity," Rōyama sought to redefine constitutionalism so as to reflect more intimately "the actual life of the people."[41] It takes little imagination to see that his proposed (and tautological) reading both renders illicit *any* social conflict and justifies, implicitly, the suppression of such conflict in the name of some presumptive harmony. At the same time, the force of factionalism in contemporary Japanese politics was, under the system of collective irresponsibilities enscribed in the constitution, impervious to deterrence. (It was illegal, of course, to seek to amend the constitution.) Rōyama certainly erred in attempting to promote a fictive harmony to the status of a political principle. But in the context of the void in political thought left by the apparent internal collapse of European parliamentary systems, combined with the sorry performance of the domestic arrangement, his conceptual equipment—naturalized German state and administrative "science"—left him little alternative. In any case, one can see how easily Rōyama and others, like his young Tokyo University colleague Yabe Teiji, might have found in ideological mobilization a satisfying solution to the demands of status and expertise.

Or take the case of the *Asahi shinbun*'s Ryū Shintarō, whose mammoth bestseller *Nihon keizai no saihensei* (1939) proposed the corporatist "reorganization of the Japanese economy" along lines pursued in Nazi Germany. This controversial work set the terms for informed discussion of the measures necessary for Japan to "respond effectively to the economic problems caused by the China War." Ryū essentially argued that the government ought to create a network of cartels for strategic industries and regions; policy was to be determined by associations made up of industrial managers and representatives of appropriate political, especially bureaucratic, entities. Underlying this effort, Ryū urged, a "new economic ethic" based on the goals of the "national community" rather than individual (enterprise) profit had to be inculcated; to give this ethic bite, Ryū proposed the "separation of capital and management." This would ratify what had already begun to take place in large *zaibatsu* firms. Family-owned capital had become divorced from daily management of the enterprises with the rise of a new managerial class that did not own stock and hence felt "no responsibility toward capital." Ryū also supported the strengthening of dividend-limiting legislation, and called for government supervision of "surplus profit."

Some critics found Ryū's desire to suppress enterprise profits communistic; others objected to his assertions that "peace industries," rather than munitions, ought to be relied on to drive the economy. Clearly certain interests were threatened by Ryū's proposal, which formed the basis for discussion of economic matters in Konoe Fumimaro's think tank, the Shōwa Kenkyūkai. But it is noteworthy that Ryū's ideas were congruent in the main with the dirigism that marked the thinking of Yoshino Shinji and Kishi Nobusuke. The dual features of the "national community" and a technocratic thrust were fully evident in the thinking of all three men.[42]

A final example points to the convergence of activist thinking on the question of China. By the late 1930s only the myopic could have failed to see that Japan was moving toward a broad-front war on the continent. It comes as little surprise to find, then, that the ideological justification of that aggression engaged a number of prominent thinkers. Among them was the philosopher Miki Kiyoshi (1896–1945). Miki fused a heavily Lukácsian Marxism; a Heideggerian rhetoric of crisis and authenticity, being and national community; and Nishida Kitarō's category of "fundamental experience" into a philosophy of Japan's world-historical role. Vis-à-vis China, Miki advanced the thesis that Japan's mission was to supersede the West—temporally as the stage of capitalism was brought to a close through the force of "cooperativism" (*kyōdōshugi*) and spatially as Japan's dominance in East Asia was established in place of the ebbing Western tide. For Miki Japan's élan as a modernizing force was legitimate over and above any claim of Chinese nationalism for control of such processes. Why? Because "cooperativism" worked at home; it was authentic, and rooted, he claimed, in East Asian tradition. Japan was thus repaying a cultural debt to China with the point of a bayonet—very hard currency indeed. Miki sincerely hoped that this phase would soon end. He criticized an exclusively military approach to the resolution of the China problem, asserting that the country "clearly could not be occupied forever."[43] By 1942 Miki had had enough of Japan's world-historical role. Disillusioned, he fell silent and resumed contact with former colleagues on the left. Imprisoned for harboring a suspected Communist, Miki died in prison in September 1945, after the surrender but before the release of political prisoners was ordered. A better example of the public man *in extremis* can hardly be imagined.

Public men like Rōyama and Ryū embraced fascist or corporatist theories of political and economic organization because they seemed to suggest solutions to the nearly decade-long, and sometimes violent, crisis of state and polity; to the intractable problems of China policy; and to the question of Japan's position vis-à-vis a Europe reorganizing itself into power blocs. The ideas of the activist public men mentioned above were unexceptional in their antidemocratic, statist, and dirigist thrust—unexceptional both in the Japanese and European contexts. In the broadest sense, these activists felt themselves to belong to the "worldwide" reaction against the interest-oriented politics of the parliamentary status quo, and against the individualistic economic and philosophical assumptions underlying that status quo. These assumptions they subsumed under the category of "liberalism." But one must again understand that when such men attacked "individualism," they were referring, as a practical matter, to institutional individualism, to the force of faction, rather than to any deep-seated anticollectivist impulse in Japanese politics. In the light of their general reading of the situation, then, it was entirely consistent with their achieved status that ambitious public men should have reached out for antiparliamentary, communitarian models of social and political organization put forth by European fascist and totalitarian ideologues.

The fact that Japanese public men did not look to their own tradition also stems from their "public" background, the salient features of which we observed earlier. (Rōyama, I might add, buttressed his appeal to "tradition" with qualified citations from Nazi theorists of community, among them Rudolf Brinkmann, state secretary in the German Ministry

of Economics, whose writings supported Rōyama's belief that "the freedom of the [individual] personality consists in recognizing by oneself
the higher necessity of the cooperative body [*kyōdōtai*], entering into it,
and being placed under it.") [44] And it reflects the pervasive belief of such
men, across the ideological spectrum, that Japan had, to all intents and
purposes, moved into a historical stream alongside (even ahead of)
those societies that had provided models for Japan's own development.
Consider for example the prototypical position of the early "social policy" thinker Kanai Noburu, who founded the Shakai Seisaku Gakkai
(Social Policy Association) in 1896. For Kanai, Japan as one "follower"
country could not only learn "how to" from industrializing pioneers
such as Britain, it could also seek to avoid the pathologies of industrial
development—class conflict, revolutionary labor movements, and so
forth. Japan in Kanai's view could, along with other "followers" such as
Germany, apply the lesson of "don't let this happen to you." By practic-
ing meliorative social policy à la Bismarck, and attempting, specifically,
to preserve rural communities intact, Japan could spare itself the radicalization of rural migrants as they were caught up in the industrial process. The experience of Europe was regarded as wholly relevant to that
of Japan; it was seen as the duty of public men (such as Kanai) to arrive
at formulas for the manipulation by the state of social processes perceived as universal, so that these could benefit, protect, and strengthen
the nation. [45] Other examples of the belief of public men in the relevance
of Western thought to Japan come quickly to mind: the conviction of
the constitutional theorist Minobe Tatsukichi that the promulgation of
the Meiji constitution had transformed Japan into a modern state; and
of Yoshino Sakuzō that under this constitution, Japan could work out a
lasting democratic arrangement suitable to the spirit of the age, and in
keeping with a personalist Christian social ethic.

The "West," of course, was not one, but many. Antiliberal and revolutionary thinkers also turned there first. Indeed, for theoretical guidance no Japanese public man could or would turn first to the Japanese
past. Just as, for the most part, they did not write for the world, neither
did they seek to learn from their own society's past. Their concern with
it was instrumental; to illuminate and manipulate it in the interest of the
national future and their own role in it. The question was to which
"West," and when, would they turn?

It should be kept in mind, however, that Japanese political tradition
had, apart from its enshrinement in official propaganda since the late
Meiji era (when it was "invented"), [46] become largely the playground of

"national moralists" or obscurantist ideologues. It was only gingerly, and against much opposition, that critical method, beginning in the 1890s, had been applied to the national political past. Though not the first, the example of the cultural historian Tsuda Sōkichi (1873–1961) is instructive. Beginning in 1916, but particularly in the years from 1924 to 1930, Tsuda had published studies that argued a now-accepted fact: that Japan's mythic heritage, as recorded in the *Kojiki* and *Nihon shoki*, was the intentional product of a far later age, and of a ruling group in need of a legitimizing source for its hegemony. (Tsuda, as will be related below, eventually ran afoul of the publications and lèse-majesté laws on account of such views.) In general, the time was yet to come when learned and politically independent syntheses of "Western" and Japanese thought and culture, or, alternatively, attempts to argue for Japan's unique contributions to world culture, could be written without the taint of cultural imperialism. Notable attempts were made, of course. One thinks of the great philosopher Nishida Kitarō's *Nihon bunka no mondai* (The problem of Japanese culture, 1938), or Hasegawa Nyozekan's *Nihonteki seikaku* (The Japanese character, 1938). But whatever the value (which was considerable) that some such works might have had in themselves, many of them, even Watsuji Tetsurō's erudite study, *Sonnō shisō to sono dentō* (Imperial loyalist thought and its tradition, 1943) lent themselves, intentionally or not, to later cooptation. In some cases—for example, Tanabe Hajime's articles on the "logic" of social and national existence—the question was not one of cooptation so much as virtual, albeit unintended, prostitution. Witness, in recognition, the title of Tanabe's first postwar work, *Zangedō toshite no tetsugaku* (literally, Philosophy, path of confession, 1946), the manuscript of which, significantly, was already complete by the summer of 1944.[47]

A minority of public men, oriented to a "purer" West, or at least to a clearly defined political ideal of their own, were unwilling to lend their prestige to a too-obvious justification of current policy, feeling that it was rash to assign "world-historical significance" to a war that had yet to be concluded. Thus Nanbara Shigeru openly criticized Tanabe Hajime in print; the journalist Kiyosawa Kiyoshi (1890–1945) was more circumspect, choosing to record his misgivings and forebodings in his now famous diary, *Ankoku nikki* (Diary of dark times).

The presence of such a minority report, however, should not obscure the larger point. There was no organized "resistance" movement in Japan. No public man, however much opposed to militarism, fascism, and war, could have expressed or agreed with the political philosopher Harold Laski's dissent—in the midst of World War I—from the proposition that "in a crisis the thought and soul of the individual must be absorbed in the national life."[48] Some way had to be found to serve expertise and status, to be part of the "national life." Thus the fact that Japanese public men felt drawn to the state in crisis should occasion no surprise. This says nothing about their judgment, which was far from uniform. The same may be said of their European contemporaries in similar circumstances. Not all German intellectuals pandered to the Nazis; not all opponents of the regime were killed or driven into exile. Some stayed, unwilling to abandon their nation despite the hideously misguided undertaking it had launched. They tried to maintain conscience and sanity, believing that ultimately a decent order would be restored in Germany. Some, like the members of the Kreisau Circle—to be discussed later—tried to do so as a network; this cost them their lives. By the same token, we must consider the case of intellectuals in a regime like Vichy, which had, at least under Pétain, a plausible claim to legitimacy (so Robert Paxton argues) as a government of national salvation. One did not have to be fascist to serve; not at first. The philosopher Emmanuel Mounier (who might profitably be compared to Miki Kiyoshi) is a case in point. The time was to come when one did have to be a fascist, even a traitor, to serve the Vichy regime. This was never the case in Japan.[49]

Let us conclude. It is unhistorical to assume that there should have been wholesale resistance among public men to the trend of the times. (That we must argue so pitifully is of course testimony to the truth of Simone Weil's stern dictum.) We should rather begin with the presumption of basic, if initially passive, allegiance to the state in crisis. We have also observed a divergence of postures. In a few instances, there was explicit resistance to the war as such among Japanese public men. These are analogous to the recorded cases of domestic sabotage by Japanese workers of machines in wartime. Both public men and workers, that is, used the tools of their trade to act against the system.[50] The vast majority of Japanese, regardless of class, fell into the category of survivors.

How did people survive? How was it all—war, crisis, privation—to end? How were personal and national fates to be intertwined? We remain quite ignorant about how people actually felt as the situation grew increasingly desperate. And the time is not far off when those who do remember will be gone. We may imagine that there was no one, outside of the few genuine fanatics in the general population, who did not wish to survive the unnatural-become-natural condition of total war. One did what one had to do; nothing more or less. The public man's work, however, was verbal and ideological, and, in the case of insiders especially, was underlain by an ethic of organizational service. Thus every statement had to be weighed, its effects calculated. Responsibility cut both ways. For the unenthusiastic, as we remarked, some way of saying "no" while saying "yes" had to be worked out. On the other hand, there were among public men truly zealous servants of power who fought the "ideological war" to the end. There were opportunists who measured out their zeal in smaller and smaller portions as the situation worsened, so that they could claim to have "opposed" the war when defeat came. This attitude, however, dovetails with the nonopportunistic realm of survival psychology.[51] To sort out the ramifications—personal, political, and moral—of how individual Japanese regarded their wartime service in the light of defeat lies far beyond the scope of the present discussion.

Once the intangible but inescapable aura of defeat had formed over Japanese society, each individual had to cope with it in one way or another: by believing in the cause all the more; by resignation; by looking ahead; by simply falling silent, doing what one had been assigned to do, clinging to it, until the inevitable came. Some, such as Nanbara, actually sought to hasten its arrival.

When it did come in Japan, defeat was a foregone conclusion, but no less a shock. The instant of surrender on 15 August seems to have been experienced as an eternity of anguished uncertainty turning to eviscerating realization: the past fifteen years had been a waste. The élan of the imperial system, its entire legitimacy riding on the promise of victory, seems to have burst like a bubble. But soon there was a thrilling new feeling: that no one else, oneself included, would have to die. As the Catholic philosopher Yoshimitsu Yoshihiko remarked to a friend shortly after the end of the war, "It's like a Greek tragedy, Father; everyone is weeping, but everyone is happy."[52]

Whether or not they themselves felt the need for self-criticism after 1945, Japanese public men of this period have a lesson to teach about the nature of the modern state. The state demands the use of its subjects' intelligence in its service. In the absence, for obvious reasons, of conditions of civil war or actual invasion; and leaving aside contemporary polities of an internal colonial type (those that rest on the explicit exclusion of an exploited majority on racial grounds, for example), the state in crisis receives that service. Indeed, the capacity to mobilize it may be another way of saying that its rule is regarded as legitimate. This legitimacy cuts across ideological lines between and within states. It overrides (sometimes with violence) the moral objections of its own and outside critics. It exalts the nation and deracinates society: war is only the ultimate deracinator. (As the German legal philosopher Gustav Radbruch remarked, "War, which is the apex of the militaristic view of the state, is at the same time the nadir of national distinctiveness.")[53]

Yet mobilization must have a cause. Pressure must be applied; along with a national mission, a threat, real or imagined, foreign or domestic, must be invoked. For although—indeed because—national identity is the "very tissue of modern political sentiment,"[54] doubt and dissent breed in moments of slack and in corners only desultorily propagandized. Here resentment at long injustice or neglect combines with reason to produce withdrawal—and resistance. Such opposition may not aim to overthrow the state in toto but only to return it to its "proper" course. This in turn may mean only the least degree of interference in social life. Or it may entail an attempt to compel the state to live up to the values it itself propagates, even to infuse a new and healing vision of justice into a power-swollen system. In any case, such attempts must compete with the constant impulse to follow official dictates, to work for aims of the state. For it is never easy to deny the wishes of national authority, however vacuous, once it is admitted that some, even the slightest good, might be achieved through obedience. That in Japanese public men this conflict may be seen in heightened form is clear, I think, from the foregoing. And it is in this context that their "war responsibility" and unequal contest with the "great problems of public life" may and must be judged. Not to damn out of hand; still less to excuse; but to deny their "otherness" and assert the profound relevance of their experience and thought processes to the situation of thinking members of national societies in the present: this has been my underlying aim in writing.

This said, we are ready to begin our investigation: Nanbara Shigeru, political philosopher, and Hasegawa Nyozekan, journalist and critic, were public men, insider and outsider respectively. As "public" tended more and more to fuse with national community, and national community with state, both men, as I have noted, were called upon to adhere to and promote an extreme cultural particularism. This was a task both found onerous, yet curiously irresistible. How they attempted to resolve this paradox, at once personal and derived from status, is the central question of the studies that follow.

Nanbara Shigeru
(1889–1974)

Signature of Nanbara Shigeru. Courtesy of
Education Centre, Kagawa Prefecture.

MISE-EN-SCÈNE

Professor Nanbara Shigeru, holder of the chair in political science in the Law
Faculty of Tokyo Imperial, is not known to have published a single volume in
the over ten years he has occupied that position. True, he may periodically
publish an essay in the *Kokka Gakkai zasshi,* but the fact that his name is
unknown in intellectual circles generally is enough to show that he has
failed, even pro forma, to make the scholarly contribution one would expect
of a professor in the area of *Geisteswissenschaften* [*seishin kagaku*], especially politics, at an imperial university. One can only agree that he is the
epitome of a "scholar out of touch with the life of our people" that Minister
of Education Hashida [Kunihiko] has criticized.[1]

Nanbara was anonymous and he knew it. He may also have sensed
that his anonymity could not last. "Like a snail hunched in his shell,"
one of his *waka* reads, "a life hidden away I would lead."[2] But notoriety
came, albeit in a paradoxical way. In 1939 Minoda Muneki, at one time
professor of logic at Keiō University, and leader of the rightist Genri
Nihonsha, began another in his series of attacks on the Law and
Economics Faculties at Tokyo Imperial University (Tōdai), in which
Nanbara, among others, was singled out. The words quoted above are
Minoda's, and so perhaps are to be taken with a large grain of salt.
(Nanbara probably took them with aspirin.) What had Nanbara done
to warrant this attack? If he was anonymous, why not let sleeping dogs
lie? Or was anonymity dangerous? To answer, let us first look at what
Nanbara was, where and when. Having set the scene, we shall explore
his thought.

This was not Minoda's first attack on an imperial university. His
group, whose name translates loosely as "The True [or Fundamental]
Japan Society," was founded in 1925. As such it was one of a welter of
right-wing nationalist groups that sprang up in the wake of the Taishō
political crisis, the domestic movement for democracy, and socialist and
labor agitation—with the success of the Russian revolution looming
close in the background.[3] These developments, as is well known, brought
together a motley and unstable alliance of old nationalists, represented
both by bureaucratic statists such as Hiranuma Kiichirō, and China-
rōnin adventurists à la Tōyama Mitsuru; with newer groups propagat-
ing a national socialism marked by its virulent anticommunist (and later
antiliberal) emphasis. There was among both types a sharing of bureaucratic, political, business, and military patrons, as well as (at a lower
level of prestige) of academic epigones—not to mention duplication of

membership, especially among students, so as to give the illusion of strength in numbers. Power behind the scenes was not a problem.

The overlap and sharing of patronage just alluded to may be illustrated briefly with a look at the career of Minoda himself, and at the emergence of the Genri Nihonsha. As noted, Minoda was a former academic. His main ideological influence was Uesugi Shinkichi (1878–1929), a nationalist constitutional scholar and chief antagonist, from within Tokyo Imperial, of Minobe Tatsukichi's organ theory of the state. (The significance of Minobe's work, its ascendancy and ultimate renunciation, will be discussed presently.)

Ironically, Uesugi could claim "no disciples in any position of academic importance" at the time of his death, and it was left to Minoda, his "self-appointed successor," to carry on the struggle against Minobe's theory. The consequences for liberals and liberal thought were obnoxious, to say the least. With the depression, Manchurian incident, and collapse of party government, the field for effective right-wing agitation had opened far more dramatically than during the years after 1918. A nonentity, Minoda seemed suddenly to command attention. He had powerful friends, in the House of Peers especially, a powerful anti-Tōdai animus, and followers who were quite happy when push came to shove. The anti-Tōdai vitriol was obviously given fuller play than would have been possible under Uesugi's direct leadership, or had Minoda truly been "the heir to Uesugi's mantle as a scholar and teacher."[4] But Minoda knew himself to be an outsider.

In a sense, Uesugi was responsible for the whole mess. His efforts from the rostrum to provide a "theoretical basis for the merger of Japanistic and socialistic thought" had led him to take the further step of mobilizing rightist students at Tokyo Imperial in a campaign against "dangerous" (Marxist and anarchist) thought; this won for him the "extra-academic" favor of Hiranuma. Uesugi's vehicle was the Kōkoku Dōshikai (Association of Comrades of the Imperial Land), founded in 1920, with the patronage of Hiranuma, then public prosecutor general. The group, to which Minoda belonged, scored an early success in bringing about the expulsion of Morito Tatsuo from the Economics Faculty. But for our purposes, the spin-offs of the Kōkoku Dōshikai in the rightist movement are more significant than its own achievements. These spin-offs, as Frank O. Miller notes, followed two distinct lines. The first was the Kokuhonsha (National Foundation Society), which "stemmed directly" from the Kōkoku Dōshikai. Founded in 1924, it was to become the centerpiece of Hiranuma's "fascistic" activities. Not surprisingly, as Miller notes, "the role of academics generally, and the influence of Uesugi specifically, was submerged in the organization under the weight of the numbers, prestige, and influence of bureaucratic, business, and military members."[5] Such ties, in the relatively liberal atmosphere of the time, led to verbal attacks on Uesugi as the "running dog of the clan clique and bureaucracy" and an "academic sycophant"—criticisms duly noted in the Justice Ministry's 1940 report on the right-wing student movement.[6]

Passing over the "satellites" of the Kokuhonsha, in which Uesugi's direct influence was diminishing, let us turn to the "second line" of succession, those organizations where his legacy was perpetuated more directly. These were groups, based still largely in the universities and higher schools, which saw their role as one of direct combat against "leftist manifestations in the academic community," and who formed the overlapping contacts with the distinctly outsider movement for national socialism associated with Ōkawa Shūmei and Kita Ikki. Miller is unambiguous in his designation: Uesugi's direct legacy thrived in the form of fascism.

It was from among the members of this "second line" that the Genri Nihonsha was founded in 1925 by Minoda and Mitsukawa Kametarō, another academic follower of Ōkawa's and a battler against the *minponshugi* of Yoshino Sakuzō. Minoda by 1927 found himself at the head of an umbrella group of Uesugi-style academic watchdog organizations and set to work "grinding out a steady parade of extremely antiliberal, Japanistic diatribes under the banner of the Genri Nihonsha."[7]

Minoda's efforts first paid off in 1933. In this year the Genri Nihonsha, in concert with the Kenkokukai (originally sponsored by Uesugi to "provide a meeting ground between bureaucratic and national socialistic circles") began the campaign that resulted in the dismissal of Takigawa Yukitoki from the Law Faculty of Kyoto Imperial. Probably the first organized attack on a liberal, as opposed to a socialistic, heresy, Minoda's campaign prompted Education Minister Hatoyama Ichirō to demand Takigawa's dismissal on the grounds that the interpretations of the laws of rebellion and of adultery set forth in his *Keihō tokuhon* (Reader in criminal law) desecrated the national polity. Despite protest, the threat of mass resignation (one actually carried out by a small minority) of the entire faculty, and student demonstrations at Kyoto and elsewhere, Hatoyama succeeded.

Assured, then, of the support (direct or indirect) of high officials, Minoda continued. I shall defer for the moment discussion of the theoretical issues involved in the Minobe case—these are the subject of Miller's full and lucid analysis, and of a host of other works. Still, we must note Minoda's role at the forefront, not only of the revival of the old Uesugi-Minobe controversy, but of its function as a channel for the infusion of rightist energies into a deadly serious political attack on the so-called "liberal-*genrō* bloc."[8] As discussed earlier, this was the term used by conservative polemicists—supported by Hiranuma and various military claimants—to designate elites such as the surviving *genrō* Saionji Kinmochi, privy seal Makino Nobuaki, and Ichiki Kitokurō, professor of law at Tokyo Imperial, holder of various posts in the Home Ministry and House of Peers, and finally imperial household minister. My purpose here is not to privilege the political struggles with which the Minobe case was embroiled, but rather to point out the degree to which, by their nature, Tokyo and the other imperial universities were bound to become the focus of attention and attack whenever ideological questions concerning the state and its sovereignty arose. Long-term structural shifts in the power configuration within the imperial system necessarily involved the universities—especially Tokyo Imperial. Not only was it the chief training ground for officials and thus involved in terms of the career interests and prestige of its alumni (interests and prestige resented by outsiders such as Minoda); in a far broader sense, the university owed its life to the state. Article I of the University Ordinance of 1886 makes this connection explicitly: "It shall be the purpose of the Imperial University to teach the sciences and the arts and to probe their mysteries in accordance with the needs of the state." Thus the classic tension between state service and expertise in Western learning—and by extension its free pursuit—was inherent in the relationship.[9] For every one who stressed the need for scholars to follow their own light wherever it led, there were always others, such as the lawyer and Hiranuma crony Takeuchi Kakuji, who thought quite otherwise. Writing at the time of the Morito case, Takeuchi argued that "Tokyo Imperial University should become the quarantine office for imported [ideologies]. . . . If a thought is harmful, it should be treated as a harmful thought. For an ideology which is both harmful and harmless, the university should remove the harmful portion, and import the profitable part." There was no end to danger involved when a professor became infected by such ideologies (in Morito's case, the anarchism of Kropotkin), and then passed the radicalism on to his students.[10] But who was to decide the question of "harmfulness" versus "profitability"? How? The question was as political as any. Indeed, how could politics and learning help but be intertwined—not so much in the sense of any cheap sellout to power for reasons of individual ambition, as of a far more deeply rooted sense of belonging to, dependence on, and identification with a cultural apparatus that had been called into existence as (to borrow Thomas Huber's term) a "service intelligentsia"?

We are in a position now to explore a little more specifically the links between the basic tension of the university-state relation, the Minobe affair itself, and the issue—to be discussed at length—of "academic autonomy" under the imperial system.

Minobe's "organ theory," as we have already seen, was widely accepted in academia. The emperor himself had no objection to it, and regarded Minobe as an individual of the highest caliber.[11] The theory was elaborated in self-conscious response to—and in order to further—the "trend of the times" away from feudal subjection and toward individual liberty: "It can be said that the most important ethical imperative of modern constitutional government is that each individual be respected for himself, and that each be permitted as far as possible to give expression to his capacities. The history of modern cultural development is the history of the liberation of the individual." [12] In terms of the governing of the state, *liberty* meant not only autonomy and decentralization among state institutions, but also much fuller participation of hitherto effectively excluded social groups in the polity. As with the state itself, then, "liberty," too, had a corporate aspect. Minobe saw no constitutional obstacle to a vast broadening of the actual influence of the Diet; indeed, he regarded the establishment of the Diet as the key accomplishment of the constitutional system. Nor did he see any reason to refrain from broadening the franchise itself, with the impact that such broadening would certainly have on the Diet. There could be no question that a more representative system made for freer individuals. But how did Minobe justify such claims? It was only to be expected, he argued, that "time, place, and historical conditions" would be salient in determining the development of organs of the state *duly recognized in the text of the constitution.* Minobe vigorously rejected claims that the *kokutai,* interpreted to mean unlimited imperial prerogative, constituted a principle of historical immutability. Clearly, amendment of the text of the document had to follow prescribed procedure. But not everything in the "historical constitution" was written; and as was obvious, the historical constitution was hardly immune from change. Of far greater moment, in Minobe's view, was the promulgation itself. Not the "national polity," but the constitutional arrangement of state organs, determined the form of government.[13]

From this universalist institutional perspective—one animated by a belief in the "trend of the times" toward greater individual freedom—Minobe sought to establish the principle that "the state is a corporate body in which the emperor as monarch of the Japanese Empire . . . occupies the position of supreme organ." Governmental authority within this body, however, "exists for the common purpose of the entire nation and that is all that is implied when we say that the emperor is the supreme organ of the state."[14] Having to all appearances won this point, it was not difficult for Minobe to proceed to interpretations that sought to make licit criticism of the *exercise* of prerogative by state ministers; restrictive constructions of articles that, in his view, had served to aggrandize the power of certain organs over others in the name of inviolability; and so forth. The key to the whole lay in Minobe's application to the Meiji constitution of the "universal" category—revealed so far only in the West—of auto-limitation; a principle that by definition could not allow the unchecked autocracy that in Minobe's estimation was the hallmark of the former feudalism and of contemporary bureaucratic despotism. The emperor, not to speak of less exalted state organs, was bound by the constitution of the state.

In so arguing, Minobe was trying to free discussion of the state from the stranglehold of the orthodox identification of *kokutai* with unlimited imperial prerogative—and the de facto bureaucratic power of those who "assisted" the throne in its exercise. For Minobe, *kokutai* referred to "that unique and unbreakable faith of the Japanese people in the divinely sanctioned character of the Japanese monarchy *as the unifying principle of the nation from the founding of the state.*"[15] It was not a license for despotism.

It was and remains obvious that, as Miller shows, the differences in practical terms between Minobe and his opponents amounted to the former's embrace of government by a parliamentary, as opposed to bureaucratic, cabinet.[16] In this conflict, a host of ideological—even theological—issues, pursued for their own sake, became entangled with crucial questions of political power. Nor were these issues merely derivative; in some ways, they provided the conceptual language and symbols that made it possible to wage those struggles as they were actually waged. Herein, I think, lies the political significance of the Minobe case. Is it so surprising that the organ theory enjoyed the support of "antifeudal" segments of the political and official elite? Is it so surprising that those who objected to the ascendancy of these elites used and benefited from attacks on that theory to silence its academic proponents and displace the political configuration it stood for? Indeed not.

Nor is it surprising, in view of the relationship of Tokyo Imperial to the state, that the stormy political weather of the years after 1931 had serious, if ambiguous, effects on the institution, and on the intellectual work pursued within it. There can be no question that the official attack on and renunciation of organ theory (not merely the banning of Minobe's work) constituted a purge of liberal thought—understood as those intellectual currents that fostered the broadening of representation within the polity by nonrevolutionary means, and that placed the parliament at the *center,* if not the zenith, of the political system. In this connection, the Minobe case is to be understood as one in a long chain of events in the history of politics and learning in a strong, "late-developing" capitalist state.

This history has been represented as a struggle for "university autonomy"—which it in part was. (If this were all it was, one would have to pronounce the struggle a clear failure.) But this is to draw the issue too simply. Autonomy from what? For what? For whom? Who was the enemy? Who the ally? Such questions are not always easy to answer. This said, let us look briefly at the issue of "university autonomy" as it arose at Tōdai early in the twentieth century. As we shall see, it was in the context of a widening struggle over this issue, and of attacks from many quarters on "liberals" in the academy, that the names of Minoda Muneki and Nanbara Shigeru were eventually to be linked.

We have seen that old-line bureaucrats such as Hiranuma Kiichirō resented the assertion by subordinate bodies that ministries need not control every aspect of their operations. This was the case in education, where roughly since 1905, but particularly in the wake of the university reforms of 1918–19, Tōdai and its junior partners among the imperial universities had won a semblance of autonomy. This was a prized possession, analogous, one might say, to the expanded influence enjoyed by the Diet—also in the teeth of bureaucratic opposition. The years after 1918 coincide, at Tōdai, with the ascendancy of Onozuka Kiheiji (1870–1944), founder of Japanese political science, head of the Law Faculty, and after 1928, university president. (I shall have more to say of Onozuka later.) Accounts of these years, with some self-congratulation, speak of a "golden age" of liberalism and tolerance. Minobe's organ theory had indeed won acceptance as the standard interpretation. His texts were used not only at Tōdai but at other imperial universities and major private institutions. Thus a conservative, but resolutely parliamentary, order seemed well founded, and the Hōgakubu its collective theorist and supplier of administrators.

What did university autonomy signify? It referred largely to procedural matters. In the area of appointments, Byron Marshall notes, Tōdai presidents were chosen virtually in-house, since the university made a practice of submitting the name of a single faculty member for approval by the Ministry of Education. Full professors in each department voted for the chairman. Recruitment and promotion were similarly conducted, "on the understanding that the University Council [Hyōgikai] and President would merely rubber stamp departmental decisions." "In the first decade following the 1918 reforms," Marshall continues, "there were no frontal offensives by the government on the new provisions for appointments. . . . Only after the political climate turned hostile to intellectual dissent in the 1930's did officials of the Education Ministry directly challenge the status quo, and then only twice, with unsatisfactory results." [17] However, procedural autonomy did not guarantee freedom of scholarly inquiry, and it is important not to confuse the two. Or to miss the connection: usually a challenge to the former arose because the latter was being "abused." The question was whether the defense of autonomy alone, at the cost of freedom of inquiry, really meant anything.

Meiji-era ordinances designed to keep the faculty from making public statements on political issues or foreign policy remained on the books. There was, to be sure, some latitude in their application. But any expression of opinion even remotely endorsing socialism, Marxism, or anarchism, or objectionable for some other reason, would surely prompt ministry officials to pressure the administration into silencing the offender. Although it was permissible under civil service regulations to exert such pressure, the technique frequently galvanized a faculty to protest, either through its head, or via resignation en masse, until a settlement—usually a compromise—was reached.

For bureaucratic opponents of the "long leash" approach to supervision of the university, such a situation was unacceptable. They had long since recognized the need for more dependable methods of curbing the academy's independence and ridding it of dangerous intellectual elements. Hence the solution: "Elite factions within the government committed to silencing academic dissenters resorted to the . . . insidious tactic of employing criminal indictments for violation of the Peace Preservation and Press Laws." [18] Once hit upon, this method was used to great effect, and consistently, through 1939. The fact that its use required (and enjoyed) cooperation between the Justice and Education Ministries is of course the key point: a criminal charge was grounds for immediate and indefinite suspension. It was a simple and effective weapon for officials unreconciled to the idea of an independent academic body.

It is important to note the sequence in which this legal tactic was employed. Marxists and socialists (at least those so regarded) were the first target. The earliest case comes from 1920, in the so-called Morito incident. Involved was a study by Morito Tatsuo, a young Tōdai economist, of Kropotkin's social thought. The article, which did not *advocate* anarchism, was published in the department's journal, edited by Ōuchi Hyōe. Both Morito and Ōuchi were suspended (and eventually convicted) after ministry officials caught sight of the article and banned the journal's distribution. The precedent had been set. I shall have occasion below to discuss these years in detail. For now my interest lies in the period after 1933, especially 1935–40. For it was then, after the decimation of the organized left outside the universities, and the arrest of many leftist students and faculty (from 1928 to 1933) that the law was turned on liberals (along with the remaining academic Marxists, who were thought to constitute a vestigial "front").

Hardly anyone in the university system was prepared to make a full-scale defense of avowed Marxists as such. This is not to say that other defenses were not attempted. ("Ōuchi Hyōe is not a dogmatic Marxist but a scholar," Nanbara Shigeru told a court in 1944.) [19] But the presence alone of such people brought unfavorable official attention to the university, and that posed a threat to its procedural autonomy. By and large, Marxists, when they were not actually arrested and/or expelled— as in the second "Popular Front" incident of 1938—were silenced by suggestion. Their histories were known to the authorities in any case, so publication, without prior public recantation (*tenkō*), was impossible except when the subject could be considered innocuous. Admittedly, there were cases of academic Marxists publishing "daring" material. Some, like the economist Uno Kōzō, fell through the cracks. But they were the exception that proved the rule: Marxism was anathema.

So far, "so good." After 1933 there were hints that "liberals"—I use the term to indicate that they were regarded, or branded, as such— would be next to take center stage. The Takigawa incident was such a sign, of direct rightist influence in higher education, especially on those charged with its national supervision. But the full implications of this shift in focus by Japan's "academic vigilantes"[20] became clear, as we have seen, only with the Minobe affair of 1935. Again, let us note that with the campaign of public vilification of Minobe by Minoda Muneki's organization, the influence of "outsider" ultranationalist groups on educational policy grew more and more pronouned. Genri Nihonsha worked the street, university corridors, and the halls of power to create and sustain antiliberal feeling. The organ theory itself might now seem an arcane issue, but it served well, for reasons suggested above, to concentrate the energies of those unreconciled to the Taishō rearrangement. Bureaucratic opposition from Hiranuma Kiichirō has been noted. To this we must add military resentment of the theory on the grounds that it impugned the emperor's right of supreme command (tōsuiken)— which of course threatened the military's special prerogative and untouchability in the Diet. So, too, for certain segments of the peerage. It was in the House of Peers that the Genri Nihonsha associates Kikuchi Takeo, Etō Genkurō, and Mitsui Takayuki initiated the attacks early in 1934. The resulting government-sponsored "Movement to Clarify the National Polity" was no less than a bloodless purge. Ironically, in its wake a number of Minobe's former students became his prosecutors and judges, still others the censors of his works. It should be noted, however, that although Minobe himself had resigned from Tōdai in 1934, the Law Faculty continued to be known in rightist circles as the "Grand Temple of the Organ Theory." So the fight, for some, was not over.

Minoda and his stable of propagandists never really let up. After all, humbling Minobe did not mean that his disciples had been vanquished, or that other attempts, in the name of "scholarship," to desecrate the kokutai might not be forthcoming. Clearly, Minoda and the Genri Nihonsha, while they aroused the hostility and ridicule of many (but not all) at Tōdai, represented only one in a confluence of threats to the university. It did not do to be too openly contemptuous. Minoda had friends in high places. Some of them, as we have seen, made their homes in the House of Peers, others in officialdom. Yet another was General Hayashi Senjūrō, prime minister from February to June 1937, who concurrently held the education and foreign affairs portfolios. It will be recalled that the hallowed formula Saisei itchi ("Worship and governance are one") was the slogan of Hayashi's brief administration.[21] It suggests the tendency of the orthodoxy that emerged in the years after the "de-Minobiza-tion" of constitutional theory, and also the direction further attacks on Tōdai would take.

At this juncture two clarifications are in order. It would be mislead-ing to portray Tōdai—even just the Law Faculty—as quaking in fear. Though they had proven its obvious vulnerability, Minoda and his ilk remained resentful of the enormous prestige and exalted status of the institution. Tōdai insiders might still be confident that their home would outlast the fulminations of Genri Nihonsha or any other outside pres-sure group. It would be equally wrong, however, to imagine that the university was inhabited by complacent opportunists. Minoda himself might be a passing threat. But the real danger was the more worrisome as it came closer to home. Attacks by the right served to bring to the surface internal, and factional, conflicts within the departments of the university. This was manifestly the case at the time of the "Hiraga purge" of 1938–39—which brings us to the formative years of Konoe Fumi-maro's New Order, and particularly the role played in it by his educa-tion minister, General Baron Araki Sadao. In July 1938, Byron Mar-shall relates,

> Araki summoned the President and department chairmen of Todai to an un-precedented meeting with the upper echelon of the Ministry bureaucracy with the clear intent of browbeating them into abandoning university elec-tion procedures on the grounds that they had no legal basis and were con-trary to Imperial prerogative in appointment of government officials. Led by Law Professor Tanaka Kōtarō the professors offered a spirited rebuttal, re-peating most of the arguments familiar since the Tomizu incidents three de-cades earlier. Minister Araki, faced with the threat of unified resistance by all imperial university faculties, chose not to press the offensive any further.[22]

Araki's moves, however, were only part of a larger "housecleaning" (*shukugaku*), the chief precipitant of which lay in the badly divided De-partment of Economics. Factions there dated from the department's for-mation in 1919, and broke down to some degree, but not entirely, along traditional right-left lines.[23] There were "hard" and "soft" elements on both sides, as well as uncommitted faculty, not to mention nonvoting junior members and researchers who were affected by what happened. The atmosphere was so thoroughly saturated with factionalism, every issue so politicized, that for all intents and purposes the Economics Fac-ulty was paralyzed.

This situation was, of course, an invitation to the ministry to inter-vene. The Minobe affair and continuing rightist agitation had meanwhile convinced high university officials that only drastic measures would preserve the status quo. When it became necessary to replace President Nagayo Matao, who had been instrumental in the earlier rebuff to Araki, the university was open to pressure. Named to replace Nagayo was Hiraga Yuzuru, an eminent naval architect from the Department of Engineering. Hiraga, to put it charitably, was no diplomat. He insisted that the chief instigators of divisiveness in the department be punished, hoping that ultimately with the department quiescent, the university as a whole could make its proper contribution to the war effort. Hiraga singled out two men. One was Hijikata Seibi, a strong nationalist and leader of the anti-Marxist faction. Hijikata had (his later protests notwithstanding) been responsible for the expulsion from Tōdai of Yanaihara Tadao, a colonial economist and pacifist critic of the government's China policy. In an effort to break the leftist faction, which Yanaihara supported, Hijikata called for a vote of censure against the latter, in view of the banning of certain of his stinging articles on the China war. This had been only the latest in a series of such moves led by Hijikata. On the other side, Hiraga sought the suspension of Kawai Eijirō, a devotee of T. H. Green and an anti-Marxist, but vociferous, critic of Japanese fascism and its epigones. Kawai, ironically, had only just broken his modus vivendi with the Hijikata faction in anger over the treatment of Yanaihara. Kawai's works had recently been banned for violation of the press laws. In Hiraga's eyes, the grounds necessary for suspension existed, and he ordered the requisite inquiry by the University Council. A special commission led by Tanaka Kōtarō—a highly astute academic politician—found nothing ideologically "wrong," but objected to the stridency of Kawai's tone. Hiraga capitalized on this judgment to urge Kawai's resignation. Kawai refused, pending legal indictment and a faculty vote. In January 1939 Kawai was brought to the Justice Ministry for the first "of a long series of interrogations as a prelude to formal indictment."[24] Hiraga thereupon invoked his authority as president to suspend the offender, without waiting for a faculty vote. At the same time, he suspended Hijikata. In short order Hiraga also accepted the resignations in protest of a considerable number of faculty on both sides of the issue and appointed himself chairman. He then persuaded a rump faculty to stay on and instituted a program of outside recruitment. The purge was over. Kawai was indicted, convicted, and forbidden to publish. Losing an appeal to a higher court in 1943, he was broken. He died a year later.

Nanbara Shigeru had defended Kawai throughout. A number of his

colleagues felt that Nanbara had lost sight of the larger issue.[25] As Tanaka Kōtarō had defined it, it was imperative to throw a sop to the authorities in order to preserve the university from further depredations.
His strategy of appeasement carried the day. Realistically speaking,
given the power of the ministry, especially with Araki at the helm, Tanaka played his cards well. Hiraga was nothing if not obtuse. His methods aroused intense resentment. And the purge was all over the newspapers, even the radio. Nevertheless, the troublemakers were gone.
What Hijikata meant to the right is unclear. But it is obvious that Kawai, a "liberal" (in this case an unapologetic social democrat), was the
main offering. His sacrifice kept Araki and the forces he represented
out. Until the next time, when the pattern now established repeated itself: attack by the right / official persecution of an individual scholar /
political settlement in the interest of university autonomy.

Just as Kawai Eijirō's fate was being decided, Nanbara Shigeru's
number came up. His case deserves some examination in detail, since
it both introduces his thought and ties together a number of thematic
threads that the narrative has suggested. In mid 1939, as noted, Nanbara was singled out for attack by Minoda Muneki's Genri Nihonsha.
Nanbara's sins were twofold. First, he had placed himself beyond the
pale as a political theorist by declaring, in effect, that a scholar's first
duty is to truth: "Let the truth prevail though the world perish," he had
written in the *Teikoku Daigaku shinbun*.[26] Whatever the claims of the
political collectivity, be they legal, moral, historical, or emotional, they
could not be substituted for the critical use of intelligence. In pursuit of
a scholarly calling, it was the disinterested nature of criticism that rendered it true loyalty to the polity. The state need have no fear of truth.
Minoda branded Nanbara's article "a piece of vacuous political theoriz-
ing" typical of the ivory-tower ultraliberals at Tōdai.[27] In the new dispensation, Minoda claimed, truth inheres in the national community as
part of "life"; it cannot exist apart from it. Those who speak of disembodied "truth" or "justice" engage in rank subjectivism, which in a time
of national emergency is tantamount to disloyalty.[28]

There is more to the story. The Genri Nihonsha had in fact grasped
the full significance of Nanbara's piece. It was intended as a specific repudiation of the theories of Otto Koellreutter, a German legal scholar
then lecturing in Japan.[29] Koellreutter himself had recently replaced the
Catholic Carl Schmitt as the leading legal light of the Nazi regime.
Schmitt, he claimed, was really a neo-Hegelian who "viewed the state as
the sole authority to whom one owed a political obligation." Koellreut-

ter *dixit:* not so. It is the *Volksgemeinschaft* to which loyalty is due.
Politics is "the will of the community."[30] And although Koellreutter's
biologism did not necessarily sit well with his Japanese audiences, his
trumpeting of community possessed an undoubted appeal in the Japanese academic world. It could not but reflect the chauvinism characteristic of the period as a whole, in particular the influence of *völkisch* theory that accompanied the increasingly close diplomatic and political ties
between Japan and Germany. In this process the signing of the Anti-
Comintern Pact in 1936 only prefigured the full-blown commitment (on
paper) represented by the Tripartite Pact of 1940.

Nanbara had boycotted a luncheon given in Koellreutter's honor in
the Law Faculty on 1 June (1939), preferring to "eat by [him]self this
cold and rainy noon."[31] By 1939 there were few others who found the
mere presence of a Koellreutter more than they could stomach. This is
not to deny the deep antagonism and contempt many at Tōdai felt for
the openly fascist fringe in Japan. Yabe Teiji, a younger colleague of
Nanbara's, was also the chief theorist and scribe for Konoe Fumimaro's
New Order Movement. His diaries for the period do not lack for denun-
ciations of fascism and expressions of disgust and ridicule aimed at
Minoda and his student clones. Germany he took more seriously.[32]

Nanbara's second offense came closer to home, involving as it did the
teaching of East Asian political thought at Tōdai. Since 1931 the Law
Faculty had been lobbying the Ministry of Education for permission and
funds to establish a chair in that subject. Coincident with the "Movement to Clarify the National Polity" in 1935, the Faculty of Literature
at Tōdai as well as the Law Faculty at Kyoto Imperial had instituted lecture courses that were regarded as little more than vehicles for the propa-
gation of the "national morality" that went back to Inoue Tetsujirō
(1854–1944). Nanbara had from the first been involved in the effort to
establish the chair, but one, he was determined, that would present an
independent and critical viewpoint. Permission was finally given, likely
on the assumption that Law would follow the example of other departments and do its bit in the further heightening of national narcissism.[33]
Instead, the course proved an embarrassment. After long negotiations
Nanbara had persuaded Tsuda Sōkichi (1873–1961) of Waseda to give
the lectures. He was proud of his choice and regarded Tsuda's agreement as a great coup.[34] Tsuda was the author of *Bungaku ni araware-
taru waga kokumin shisō no kenkyū* (Studies in Japanese thought as revealed in literature, 1916–21), which sought to depict the "texture of
life as it was lived" (*jisseikatsu*) among the social classes that in each

period have "played [the] dominant role in the development of Japanese culture."[35] His work was for this reason viewed with sympathy by Marxists of the 1920s. The problem however lay in his rationalist de-mystification of ancient Japanese history and myth, and in his views of the relationship of Japanese to Chinese culture. In his *Shina shisō to Nihon* (Chinese thought and Japan, 1938), for example, Tsuda denied that the Buddhism and Confucianism propagated by "bookish" theorists actually represented a constitutive element in the daily life and mentality of the Japanese. What would first appear to be ideal fodder in the ideological struggle with the materialistic West (since it gave scholarly weight to the uniqueness of Japan) was actually inimical to it. For in denying any organic relation between Japanese and Chinese culture at the level of *jisseikatsu*, Tsuda had undermined the entire pan-Asian thrust of Japanese ideology.

In any event, Tsuda gave six lectures. At the conclusion of the final lecture he was forcibly detained by rightist students (and protected by the young Maruyama Masao, who intervened physically) and "questioned" for two hours. In its November 1939 issue, *Genri Nihon* attacked Tsuda, and Nanbara for complicity, in an article entitled "An Unprecedented Disgrace to Learning on the Eve of the 2,600th Anniversary of the Founding of the Empire." Two months later, Tsuda and his publisher, Iwanami Shigeo, were brought up on charges of "desecrating the national polity," a violation of Article 26 of the Publications Law.[36] The prosecution received a few lines' attention in the Tokyo *Asahi,* and none (so as not to grant the story any more attention?) in the 100,000 daily circulation *Teikoku Daigaku shinbun,* despite the petition drive among sympathetic faculty members in their defense.[37] Though convicted and sentenced to terms of three and two months' imprisonment, respectively, Tsuda and Iwanami were acquitted on appeal in 1944. Their successful appeal, however, should not obscure the larger point. Criminal indictment against individuals was an alternative used by the government, with the Justice and Education Ministries cooperating, to the less effective attempts to manipulate the in-house procedures of university departments or "brow-beat them" into submission. The earlier victories for university autonomy won by Onozuka Kiheiji and defended by his Law Faculty successor, Tanaka Kōtarō, against higher-ups in the ministry, were rendered hollow by this new tactic. What is more, the use of the legal system against "liberals"—the Marxists having been hounded out of the universities—seemed to follow attacks on them by "fanatical" right-wingers such as Minoda. Surely the sequence was not accidental.

Nanbara understandably felt responsible for the treatment Tsuda had received. At the same time it confirmed his belief that an unholy alliance of conservative bureaucrats with militarists masquerading as civil officials was systematically attempting to seize control of the university. These feelings he did not keep to himself.[38]

Such were Nanbara's perceptions of the situation. It is difficult to say how far the unholy alliance could have gotten in this attempt to eliminate dissent. The outbreak of the Pacific war brought a sense of crisis—and a national consensus for survival—so socially pervasive that much of the struggle over academic freedom was put on hold. The "liberals" in the Law Faculty remained in place, clinging to the rock of their official positions. Had the Pacific war begun later than it did, Maruyama Masao has suggested, a more total *Gleichschaltung* could have taken place, and Nanbara's work would also have been banned.[39]

The situation, of course, was highly anomalous. Unlike the Economics Department, which had been gutted and rebuilt from without, Law remained intact after the Minobe affair. In effect, it became an island of extremely circumscribed freedom, enjoyed, so to speak, by a small number of individuals sitting at the apex of the system's hierarchy. After 1945 this anomaly came to be regarded as the continuation of a "tradition" of tolerance. But it was just as obviously a matter of time before the Law Faculty as a whole would have fallen victim to the same pattern. In any case, this was the little island on which Nanbara Shigeru worked. For as long as he could, he lived inside his shell on this island. But as should be clear, once forced to confront those who had pried that shell open, Nanbara stood his ground. Let us now pick up the biographical thread from the beginning.

CHILDHOOD AND CONVERSION

Nanbara Shigeru was born on 5 September 1889 in Aioi, a village in Ōkawa-gun, Kagawa Prefecture, on the island of Shikoku. His rural origins remained a lifelong element in Nanbara's self-image. The poverty of his childhood, he said some years before his death, taught him shame and self-sufficiency. As a teacher Nanbara seems to have regarded students with urban roots as somehow less pure of heart; their relative sophistication seemed to him an impediment to the formation of good character. The eldest son of Nanbara Teikichi, a former samurai whose family had fallen on hard times, Nanbara was raised by his mother and grandparents after his parents were divorced in 1894.[40]

His mother, we are told, was a devout Buddhist, a member of the Shin sect, whose religious practice communicated to her son a sense that this life is enveloped by and leads to another, holier reality. To this source of inexhaustible blessing one expressed unending gratitude through prayer and acts of charity.[41] At the same time, Nanbara received, as did a countless number of his contemporaries, an education in the Confucian classics, Chinese literature, and dynastic histories. In this connection the *Analects* and *Great Learning* appear to have had the greatest impact on him. The dictum of the *Analects* (12:17) that "Government consists in rectification" (*Sei to wa sei nari*) remained the touchstone of Nanbara's political philosophy.[42] But with his later conversion to Christianity (to be discussed presently), the "this worldly and utilitarian" ethics of Confucian teaching was entirely swept away.[43] Obviously a later memoir, treating a period before religious conversion, must be viewed as filtered testimony. Nevertheless, it would be a serious error to regard Nanbara's lifelong philosophical engagement with Plato, Kant, and Fichte, vivified by the "pure gospel" faith of Uchimura Kanzō (1861–1930), as a mere elaboration of a "traditional" upbringing. Nanbara insisted so emphatically on the "transvaluation of values" wrought by Christian faith (both personal and in a world-historical sense) that there can be no misunderstanding on this point.

In another sense, however, Nanbara's life is a picture of childhood dreams fulfilled. In a composition written while he was a student in higher elementary school (perhaps around the age of ten) Nanbara had vowed to "move forward to graduation from higher elementary school, make my body strong, journey to other countries, be trained in scholarship, contribute to the progress of education, and therewith extend the interests of my country [*kokueki o hiromen*]."[44] Normally such a precocious fragment would have little meaning, if only because modern Japanese schoolchildren (particularly after the mid Meiji period, one imagines) were seldom encouraged to free composition. It serves, nevertheless, as a good example of what Maruyama Masao called the healthy and expansive personal nationalism that was "common sense" for Meiji thinkers, virtually regardless of political stance. Personalities as varied as Fukuzawa Yukichi, Uchimura Kanzō, Ueki Emori, and Kuga Katsunan saw themselves "bearing the fate of the nation on their shoulders." For these men, individual action that fed popular energy also built the nation. However, as Maruyama points out, this "healthy" nationalism fell prey to the peculiar conditions of its emergence. Born amidst the threat of possible colonization, Meiji nationalism all too quickly took on monstrous proportions, serving as the justification for imperialism and domestic political repression. The paradox of this growth lay in the fact that a good number of the adherents of freedom and popular rights had little problem rationalizing Japanese expansion into Korea and China as part of the "natural" process of national construction at a time when the Western powers continued to breathe down Japan's neck.[45] By the last decade of the Meiji period, this contradiction had come home to roost. Thinkers who sensed this found themselves trapped in a political system that allowed little freedom of expression. In consequence, some embraced an apolitical individualism that was a passive support of the system. A smaller number, equally heirs of the earlier nationalism, turned to antipolitics as, in the name of the original Restoration, they rejected the "national idea" that power was its own justification. For them, the Restoration had been betrayed.

Christians such as Uchimura and Christians-to-be such as Nanbara both shared and sought to transcend the logic of this nationalism. Nanbara, as we can see in the fragment quoted above, had outlined the form of his future, leaving its content open to radical transformation. If the nationalist imperative *kokueki o hiromen* ("extend the interests of my country") was continuous, its definition was not.

Nanbara left home in 1907, shortly after the Russo-Japanese war, to enter the First Higher School (Ichikō), then under the headship of Nitobe Inazō (1862–1933). He was seventeen, and thus belonged to the generation of late Meiji youth hardest hit by the "postwar malaise and generational conflict" endemic to urban Japan, much decried, little understood, and very intense.

The act most symbolic of this "age of anguish"—the suicide of Fujimura Misao at the Kegon Falls—came, fittingly, before the war with Russia. War, and victory in war, only punctuated the sense that Japan, having now won wealth and power, had, to paraphrase Sōseki, become an unbearably difficult place to live. The country had been victorious in war, but culturally was gnawing away at itself from within.[46] Late in life Nanbara described his own experience in these years. Introverted, alone in Tokyo, he was neither a sportsman nor a ferocious debater, nor yet an aesthete; not, in short, a man to be noticed. Yet like the majority of his confreres, Nanbara seemed destined to become a typical Ichikō product: strong in sense of self and service incumbent upon status, but practically faceless when seen from without. Although close to his class-mates, Nanbara, like so many, went through a season of disorientation, of a "groping search" for something he could neither identify nor ex-press.[47] He followed the fashion and read, in English, the novels of Dos-toevsky and Tolstoy. He was in the audience when Tokutomi Roka spoke in impassioned defense of Kōtoku Shūsui: "Muhonron" (On re-bellion) was delivered at Ichikō on 1 February 1911.[48] But these were to be the years, also, of Nanbara's "rebirth." Spiritually, the decks were clear. And after his encounter with Uchimura Kanzō, Nanbara suggests, reversion was inconceivable. With his entry into the gate at Uchimura's home church at Kashiwagi, he found his path marked out.[49]

Uchimura Kanzō was not the first Christian leader with whom Nan-bara had contact in these years. Nitobe Inazō was his master at Ichikō, and Nanbara's writings include the requisite tribute to Nitobe's pa-triotic cosmopolitanism. It was the polished force of Nitobe's person-ality and patrician mien that seem most to have struck the young Nan-bara. Nitobe broke the mold, forcing him to realize that the Education Rescript and "Japanese spirit" were not the alpha and omega of educa-tion. Nitobe combined an emphasis on latter-day noblesse oblige and full cultivation of personality with a more traditional reminder that the man so cultivated must not be a "vessel" (utsuwa)—a narrow spe-cialist—but an exemplar, and at home in the world. Others of Nan-bara's generation at Ichikō, the great writer Akutagawa Ryūnosuke, for example, found Nitobe uninspiring at best, altogether too self-regarding, even a poseur. Nanbara's reminiscences convey no such deflation. We must assume that he respected Nitobe, even if he found him spiritually unsatisfying.[50]

Nanbara also heard Ebina Danjō (1856–1937)—whose followers included Yoshino Sakuzō—speak at his Hongō church. For reasons that remain unclear, Ebina's message seems to have struck Nanbara as some-how artificial and "foreign," as unsatisfying as Nitobe's gentlemanly Christianity. It offered him no way out of his personal desert.[51]

Nanbara first ran across Uchimura's name shortly before he finished at Ichikō. A friend showed him an issue of Uchimura's *Seisho no kenkyū* (Bible studies), which carried an invitation to Uchimura's readers to at-tend his Bible lectures at the Imai-kan. Nanbara accepted. Attendance at these talks did not, of course, mean that one had been admitted to the Non-Church (Mukyōkai)—the small, anti-institutional body of believ-ers that formed under Uchimura's charismatic leadership. The gate was a narrow one. With time, Uchimura found Nanbara suitable; Nanbara was willing to entrust his soul to Uchimura. As Nanbara moved from Ichikō to Tōdai, we find his name in the membership list of the Hakuukai, a group of new disciples set up to initiate young believers into the ways of the Mukyōkai. Nanbara remained a core member of this small, tightly knit group throughout his university years. Even after the Hakuukai merged in 1918 with its senior groups, the Kyōyūkai and Kashiwakai, its members remained on intimate terms. Its religious style seems to have been distinctive enough to mark it off as a Mukyōkai subtype. Suzuki Toshirō, a contemporary scholar and disciple of Uchimura's, speaks, for example, of Nanbara's faith as "typical of the Hakuukai."[52]

The merger of believers' groups at Kashiwagi coincided with a major development in Uchimura's spirituality, his turn in 1918 to eschatology. In this year he launched his *Sairin undō* (Second Coming Movement), one aspect of which seems to provide a key not only to Nanbara's own religious style, but to his future work, both as an official and as a scholar. The Hakuukai minutes for 2 May 1918 note an essay written "by Brother Nanbara for the *Seisho no kenkyū* on the Lord's Second Coming, on which Dr. Uchimura has of late placed so much emphasis. All were moved." For Nanbara the import of Uchimura's teaching lay in the following: "It is vital above all, for those in public service . . . that until the Lord returns, they devote sufficient care to the position entrusted to them, keeping it in good order [*kirei ni shite*] with the intention of returning it to Him."[53] Life in the world is centered in a religious purpose. At the same time, Nanbara believed, one could not wait idly on God. Man was born to serve, service to nation being the highest form of service in this life. Thus were Uchimura's "pure gospel" and the commonsense nationalism of Meiji fused in personalities such as Nanbara's.

Yet there is more to this ethic. As is obvious from Uchimura's own life, how an individual interpreted the nationally oriented command of faith, and the nation-state's demands on that individual, could and did conflict. Yet in considering the Mukyōkai as a spiritual "elite," we cannot treat individual and state as mutually opposed. We are not dealing with alienated personalities. Particularly where Christians in the academic elite are concerned, religious commitment ipso facto meant state service. But not unconditional service. The point of contention was: who defines national welfare, national strength, the content of patriotism? In the eyes of Uchimura and his disciples, all fell within the purview of conscience.

Not that conscience spoke to all in the same way.[54] Nanbara, for example, never adopted Uchimura's pacifism. He never evangelized directly. In other respects, his interpretation of the "interim" ethic of Uchimura's *Sairin undō* seems not to cover all that Uchimura wanted to convey. The eschatology is much attenuated. There is a clear bias for earthly action in Nanbara's insistence that a Mukyōkai believer ought to remain in public service, there to fight any moral battles that might arise. For Nanbara, to use Albert Hirschman's phrase, religion did not form an "exit option" from earthly—read national and organizational—duties.[55] The nation was to be the object of religious action transmuted into expertise. Clearly this was an attitude that would be reflected in the development of Nanbara's political thinking. But we must defer such discussion and fill out more completely the picture of Nanbara as *homo religiosus*.

Certain of Nanbara's texts on Uchimura, both reminiscences and programmatic statements on the significance of non-church Christianity for the future of Japanese culture, will serve our purpose well. For in paying tribute to his spiritual father, Nanbara also revealed himself. The texts, which date from 1930 to 1935, seek first to distinguish Uchimura's anti-institutional Christianity from two modern errors: egoistic "individualism" on the one hand, and "syncretism" on the other. And they point to Mukyōkai Christianity as the prophetic resolution of this dialectic of errors.

For Uchimura the struggle for faith had begun amidst the rupture of feudal loyalties that conversion, and the Restoration, had engendered. Indeed, Uchimura sometimes spoke as if he sought merely to redirect upward an essentially positive value such as *chū* (loyalty), that is, to "graft Bushidō onto Christianity." But such values, while immensely important, had lost their "ultimacy" for Uchimura once he had recognized what Kierkegaard called the "infinite qualitative distinction" between anything on earth and the realm of God.[56] Once, in other words, Uchimura had shared Kierkegaard's experience of man's desperate need for faith, and his inability to manufacture it within himself, he rejected any necessary "upward" continuity between traditional ethics and Christian faith. It was no longer enough to profess traditional loyalties. They did not of themselves lead to Christianity: faith came from the other direction, through existential experience of grace, by nature untransmittable, which, as Nanbara wrote, "only silence could describe."[57]

Long religious struggle and personal tragedy, Nanbara wrote, led Uchimura to grasp the true relation of self and nation. But this understanding was not granted to all, and the walls of misperception were dauntingly thick. But Uchimura, Nanbara asserts, was driven to convey to Japan that the root of all error, and the cause of all discord and misery, lay in the "selfishness" of modern Japanese man, false faith in his own powers. As Nanbara paraphrased his teacher thus:

> By what sign do we identify this "modern man" who lurks among us? It is his "self" [*jiko*], a self sometimes hidden . . . from God Himself. Not "the Other," not "the Absolute," but the egoistic "individual" lies at the core of this self. In his self modern man seeks after God. And he proposes to do this by means of "knowledge" [*chishiki*]. (How long I myself, modern man that I am, clung to this egoistic self!)

It was in fact the modern condition—and Japan *was* modern—that Uchimura, in Nanbara's conception, sought to transform.[58]

At the same time, Nanbara emphasizes, Uchimura could hardly deny man's love of *place* on earth. Having been born in Japan in a time of turmoil, he owed that country the effort at spiritual revolution that faith compelled him to undertake. God had placed him where he was. Was he to deny God's will? In this sense, Uchimura loved Japan for the sake of God and for itself, a love that for that reason enveloped his entire personality, without turning into statolatry. The two loves were warp and woof for Uchimura, breath and sustenance. Who could give up breathing in order to eat, or eating in order to breathe? Both were indispensable to the spirit. Thus could Uchimura confess that "he knew not which, Jesus or Japan," he loved more.[59]

Yet this love, too, was misunderstood—at first, Nanbara implies, even by Uchimura himself. Indeed, we may recall that the Japan of 1894, flush with its newly acquired military strength, had appeared to a younger Uchimura to be the very instrument of God's providence. Japan would bring light and China would suffer for its obscurantist rejection of "civilization."[60] By 1900 Uchimura had begun to warn Japan that its own sins—the establishment of the empire and injustice at home— would soon expose the country to divine retribution. If Japan acted as the enemy of social justice and spiritual freedom, Nanbara paraphrased, it would face ultimate judgment—the judgment of logos—in the court of history.[61] A choice of destinies had to be made, triumphant or penitential.

As a young teacher, of course, Uchimura had refused, in a celebrated incident, to reverence the Education Rescript. He was called a traitor for following his conscience. And still thirty years later, Nanbara wrote, Uchimura was called an "individualist" in the worst sense of the word.

Yet he was neither traitor nor individualist! "Who dares call him an 'individualist'! Just as Dr. Uchimura's passion for our people and our country overflowed in his veins and in his personality, so too did it permeate his every teaching and act. This by no means bespeaks a trend of his later years only; it was so even at his very point of departure in his life of faith."[62] Nanbara reminded his readers of Uchimura's famous epitaph:

> I for Japan;
> Japan for the World;
> The World for Christ;
> And all for God.

Thus only had Uchimura acted, as his conscience dictated: for Japan, and "all for God."

It was perhaps unavoidable that Uchimura's claim of conscience above all, and his social criticism and pacifism, would be misunderstood by those outside his immediate circle. Indeed, there were many Christians (Nanbara was writing in the early 1930s, but the problem went back to the 1890s) who sought to lighten the burden of conscience through syncretism of Christian and "traditional" (that is, Shintoist) positions. Their patriotic zeal may have been admirable, but the adherents of such a stance fell into an error seemingly the opposite of "individualism." For fear of recognizing that God's judgment on Japan might bring it to a tragic destiny, and of ostracism for seeming to justify Japan's destruction, they gave themselves over to the collectivity. Confused and unsure of their spiritual identity, syncretists chose a false patriotism. For the "nation" to which they sold their consciences, Nanbara asserts, represented a vaster egoism, no more than the replacement for the smaller ego they sought to be rid of. Syncretism for Uchimura, and for Nanbara as (one) interpreter, was itself a form of egoism, in which the spiritual identity and prophetic calling of the Japanese Christian were absorbed into an exaggerated love of particularity. Itself an abortive response to modernity, syncretism was understandable only if the modern condition—rampant selfishness, personal and national, as Uchimura had said—was assumed.

As a disciple of Uchimura's, Nanbara considered himself and all Japanese who understood this message to be members of the Non-Church. Their consciences, not birth or institutional affiliation, bound them together. The day of the church as a temporal power had passed. It was now to be diffused throughout the social body of every nation, assimilating and transforming its traditions, giving them life and purpose. This "pure gospel" faith was to be the very breath, the invisible source of, all human good in society, of all meaning in human existence.

In sum, several strands of Uchimura's Weltanschauung made their way into Nanbara's early thinking. First, the characteristic spheres of concern (I, Japan, world) linked through the earthly work of the individual believer, as in the Christian nationalist formula of Uchimura's epitaph. There is the disdain for "individualism"—that is, the belief that the individual is self-sufficient by virtue of reason or "knowledge." Characteristic also is the conviction that the quest for objective individual freedom ("freedom from") had been superseded as the spiritual problem of the age.

Earthly destiny was bound up with that of one's nation, but all life was encompassed by and centered in the transcendent. Communication with God was possible only through the language of love and of faith, the action of God's grace in the individual soul. Here only could it find release from the bonds of sin. Religion, in this sense "beyond rationality," meant a relationship of the soul to God, of person to Person.

In terms of the political philosophy that eventually grew out of this position (here I must anticipate somewhat), we may put matters as follows: for Nanbara, the whole of reality was represented in the Augustinian formula of the two cities, the *civitas Dei,* and the *civitas terrena.* His religious identity was Protestant to the core: The Catholic church, its institutions and sacraments, was imprisoned in materiality and thoroughly politicized. As a result Nanbara faced the "Lutheran" dilemma of seeming, in the name of conscience, to yield to the state the institutional allegiance once reserved for the church. But the Reformation, despite its historical failure, represented a great spiritual leap and set the task for all subsequent endeavor. A "diffuse" church was to "complete the Reform" in a world of nation-states.

The two-cities metaphor dominated Nanbara's investigations into the history of Western political thought; that history, beginning with Plato, appeared to Nanbara as a series of attempts to approximate in human society the perfect freedom and perfect community found only in the heavenly city from which humankind, through sin, had become alienated. The central dilemma in all approximations was that the two cities spoke two different languages. As members of the church, people spoke the language of love and faith. In political society, they spoke the language of rationality. Although Nanbara is far from denying the role of tradition and ritual in society, he took rationality as the true legacy of Greece: the creative power that maintains and causes society to evolve. And, it is important to note, Nanbara identified political rationality as essentially democratic. Thus he began his lectures in political theory for 1936 with the following thesis:

> Politics is creation. It is an act of cultural creation. . . . It was by the [Greek] people that democracy was realized. Although it soon fell into corruption, it is most noteworthy that democracy was practiced in the most ancient state we know. Democracy was an act of conscious creation by the people. Taking pluralistic confrontation as a premise, and aware of this confrontation, the movement for self-creation that strives to overcome it is unique to politics.[63]

The human race can neither forget the origins of the earthly city nor cease to yearn for that of heaven. The problem of political thought could also be described as part of the larger task of coming to collective terms with the coexistence of faith and reason within the same creature. Both Rose and Cross, to borrow Hegel's figure, had to be granted their respective spheres in human—political—society. Neither Rose nor Cross, neither freedom nor community, could be denied except at the cost of tearing asunder the fabric of life in the earthly city. The conflation of Rose with Cross in the medieval church-state, the early modern state-church, and finally in the state itself had confused freedom with community and given birth to the modern crisis. The successive experiments at redressing this dialectic of broken promises made up the history of political thought in the West.[64]

NANBARA THE BUREAUCRAT

The statement above represents, albeit in simplified form, a position Nanbara developed after decades of thought. When he left Tōdai in 1914, the religious viewpoint he had formed in his early years with Uchimura had yet to acquire its political and philosophical complement. Nanbara thus far might be described as a Meiji nationalist who had got religion. What he lacked was a *gakuteki sekaikan*, literally, a "scholarly worldview." "Scholarly" here, I think, should be understood very broadly to mean an explicit, systematic, historically conscious, yet personal, interpretation of reality.[65] The rest of this chapter will be aimed at a reconstruction of the "scholarly" elements in Nanbara's outlook, and at seeing how his thought related, on the one hand, to the religious and nationalist elements of his personality, and how, on the other, he translated his worldview into practice.

For Nanbara this was first to mean experience in the day-to-day workings of bureaucracy. In November 1914 he passed the Higher Civil Service examination, and the following month he entered the Home Ministry. There he remained for seven years, until October 1921. In terms of the general career pattern among the elite, Nanbara was in no way exceptional. He was, to be sure, fortunate to have made it into the Home Ministry, which was, along with Finance, the most sought after appointment among Tōdai's young would-be officials.[66] The ministry was powerful, with control over vast areas of Japanese life. But what might Nanbara himself have hoped to achieve there?

The political scientist Ishida Takeshi provides a clue. Beginning with the late Meiji period, he remarks, a trend toward idealism had emerged in the ministry alongside the preexisting view that society was to be "administered" not by narrowly technical experts such as civil engineers so much as by (what sounds oxymoronic) "general experts." That is, officials whose task was to direct the use of knowledge, manpower, and resources toward a given social and administrative end were to be produced in the ministry out of the "semi-finished" material that came to it from the imperial university.[67] Although the neophytes who had requested entrance into the Home Ministry could be presumed to know something of its style of operation, the real work of inculcating in them a "consciousness of [their] authority" (*kenryoku ishiki*) could begin only after they had entered. Still, their exposure in the university to German constitutional, administrative, and social thought would have done much of the spadework in nurturing this consciousness.[68] The state they served was ostensibly neutral, not allied with factional or party interests. The object of state action was society; officials stood above it, ministering to its needs and creating a harmonious whole. Yet administrative thinking, as Ishida shows, cut two ways. Under the ideological cover of conciliation, Home Ministry officials, particularly the police apparatus that dominated the ministry, all too often used authoritarian methods, sought to expand their own "turf" at the local level, and treated the populace with contempt. The need to protect the nation from dangerous elements (like socialists, the intelligentsia, labor and peasant leaders, and the occasional outspoken Christian) frequently served as the excuse for repression. These tendencies Ishida terms the "negative facet" of the administrative mind-set.[69] Not that either group disregarded the ideal of social harmony. The idealists and humanitarians who surfaced during the late Meiji and Taishō years simply differed from their senior colleagues in matters of method. They feared that bludgeoning the people would conduce not to harmony but to a smol-dering awareness of injustice. Such awareness or consciousness, they claimed, would sooner or later express itself under Marxist aegis. Only social justice could bring harmony. Conflict had to be acknowledged and dealt with as such. In philosophical terms, society had to be ac-corded "subjectivity," the right to enunciate its own needs, not just have them dictated by the general experts in some government department.[70]

This is where Nanbara comes in; he rode this trend. At the age of twenty-seven, after three years' service in the Police Bureau, he was ap-pointed district commissioner (*gunchō*) for Imizu in Toyama Prefecture. His personal ideal as an official was to become a "shepherd of the people" (*bokuminkan*), and he applied himself to flood control, educa-tion, and in general to the attempt to "root democracy in the villages" that marked the years after World War I. It is interesting to note that at one point Nanbara sponsored and assisted the development of a live-in school designed to teach young members of the local elite something of the enlightened approach to rural government, so that these future local leaders would not be lost to the lure of the big city. Nanbara wanted to call the institution Nōgyō Kōmin Gakkō, an "Agricultural Public School." But the name met with determined opposition from the local and national Ministry of Education functionaries, who seem to have re-sented any infringement of the ministry's prerogative, and found the combination of "public" and "popular" in the designation Kōmin sus-piciously socialistic. Nanbara prevailed, however, and the name stuck.[71]

Early in 1919 (shortly after the school-name brouhaha had con-cluded), Nanbara was recalled to the Police Bureau to work on the min-istry's labor union bill. The draft, which Nanbara prepared, symbolized perfectly the idealism and acute social consciousness of the "left-wing" adherents of German social policy thought among Japanese insiders.[72] Like the articles he wrote at the time on the need for a labor union law, Nanbara's draft "oozed with Christian humanitarianism."[73]

As indeed it should have. This was the age of Yūaikai ascendancy under Suzuki Bunji. The evangelist Kagawa Toyohiko, although he had already left the Yūaikai, was also pursuing social reform along explic-itly Christian lines. (It is worth noting, also, that Kagawa had pioneered empirical sociology in his studies of the Kobe and Osaka slums.) But this was also a Japan still trying to take in the effects of the October revolution in Russia. Most Japanese were either dazzled or terrified; and the impetus the revolution gave to the socialist movement in Japan was more than matched by the extreme distaste with which the government regarded the Soviet regime and all it symbolized. Closer to home, the authorities, particularly the Home Ministry, had to contend with the Rice Riots of August 1918 and their aftereffects. (They had broken out in the district adjacent to Nanbara's in Toyama.)

Under these circumstances, Christian-inspired social reform à la Yūaikai and Kagawa took on a new significance. With its call for the recognition of the personality (*jinkaku*) of workers, and the amelioration of working and living conditions (in terms both of wages and dignity issues), it occupied a middle ground between Marxian socialism and the openly anti-union paternalism (*onjōshugi*) commonly attacked in the labor newspapers of the time.[74] As advocates of responsible unionism, Christian activists found themselves in a swing position. Regarded with suspicion both by conservative allies of capital and social revolutionaries, they tried to take advantage of the fact, seeing in their ambiguous position a chance to forge a third way toward social reform. Emotionally they were drawn to the side of labor. But what were the proper goals of social reform? They ruled out class struggle, believing as they did in the educability and redeemability of every individual and, be it noted, in private property.

For social reformers, and for their counterparts "inside" the system such as Nanbara, the postwar years represented a season of ideological play and uncertainty that they sought to use to advantage. So also in politics: the *minponshugi* ("democratism"/"people-as-the-base-ism") of Yoshino Sakuzō, alongside its view of the emperor as a harmonizing center, incorporated Christian personalism to justify its demand for universal (male) suffrage for the emperor's subjects.[75]

In a sense, however, this season of play and uncertainty came to an end in 1925, with the parallel passage of universal male suffrage and the Peace Preservation Law. This may seem to be jumping the gun; but the latter did explicitly define heresy in a way that decisively hamstrung the former. From then on it became simpler for the state to bring about the "migration" of those who had occupied the zone of uncertainty toward a center, or "inside," whose boundaries were now visible to all.[76]

What of Nanbara's labor union law? With the support of ministry councillors (*sanjikan*) such as Gotō Fumio and Maeda Tamon, the draft won the final approval of Home Minister Tokonami Takejirō, only to be crushed by Prime Minister Hara Kei.[77] Shortly after this defeat, Nanbara resigned from the ministry and reentered Tōdai, evidently at the behest of Onozuka Kiheiji, as a professor of politics. There is no clear evidence that Nanbara resigned in bitterness. He had never lost the contemplative disposition (which does not preclude an active life) that attracted him to Uchimura. At the same time, he had "gotten his hands dirty" in day-to-day government. The next generation of scholars at the imperial universities would not.[78] Nanbara, furthermore, drew no great distinction between government and scholarship. Both aimed at educating, the former in the life of the political community, the latter in the life of the mind, and to the benefit of the former. In any case, his return to the academy did not seem to be the result of personal crisis.

Nanbara's years in bureaucratic service coincided with major breakthroughs in Japanese society and politics. The general atmosphere of the times during which he served had set Nanbara's mind working in a definite direction. The explosive growth of the Japanese social movement was, as we have seen, tied in with Marxism, whose "efficacy" had now been proven in the victory of the Bolsheviks in Russia. For Nanbara, the force with which ideas bore on social reality through the agency of individual thinkers was thus driven home with great urgency. This insight spurred him to wonder about the philosophical sources of Marx's own conceptions, and he was led back first to Hegel, and further, via Fichte and the Romantics, to Kant. The history and the vast and contradictory legacy of German idealism were to hold sway in Nanbara's thought for decades to come.

Almost immediately after his appointment in 1921, Nanbara left Japan for three years of study abroad. The eighteen months he spent in Germany represent the crossroads of his intellectual life. The impact of German thinking on his mind was permanent. Before describing in detail how this was so, we must first have a clearer sense of what "Germany" meant as a whole for the life of the mind in the Japan of that period.

GERMANY ON MY MIND

By 1921 it had long been standard practice in Japanese academia for students in the *Geisteswissenschaften* (*seishin kagaku,* which included both philosophy and political economy) to spend a number of years in Germany for intensive textual research and to absorb methodology. The practice reflected first of all the overwhelming influence, since the mid Meiji period, of German scholarship in all fields related to the state: constitutional and civil law, administration, and political and social theory.[79] German philosophy complemented this hegemony of German statecraft. "The tendencies of German philosophy," writes the materialist Yamazaki Masakazu, "determined those of Japanese philosophy." [80] This was not simply a matter internal to philosophy. Not only did the problems taken up in German philosophical discourse dominate that of Japan. The problems—the weaknesses, the contradictions, the existential situation—of German philosophy were also transmitted to Japan. Furthermore, state service and the existential situation of philosophy were inseparably linked, but in a paradoxical way. A brief consideration of the Meiji constitution may suggest how, and shed light on the consequences of this paradox.

There was a basic gap between the views of Itō Hirobumi, the constitution's main author, and his Prussian consultant, Hermann Roesler, on the nature of imperial rule in Japan. Whereas Roesler envisioned an emperor who actually wielded power, Itō insisted on the insertion of the preamble and articles relating to the semidivine status of the monarch. Itō knew whereof he spoke. The emperor had not "ruled" in Roesler's sense for a millennium and a half. Itō acutely recognized the need for a state apparatus capable of realizing a strong constitutional order that simultaneously placed the source of its legitimacy out of mortal reach. Thus the emperor, under the constitution, became a mystical figure with vast prerogatives. The fact that the constitution was granted in accordance with the imperial will—in fact represented as "transmitting the immutable law according to which the land [had] been governed"—reinforced its inaccessibility and sacrosanct quality, and laid the basis for the manipulation of imperial prerogative by other organs in the state apparatus. [81] Not that Japan was an exception among the nation-states of the world. Monarchies predominated until 1914, and one would hardly expect Japan to have gone against the general trend in framing a constitution. Prussia under Bismarck in any case seemed to Itō to provide the clearest example of how a constitution should be drawn up in a situation analogous to that of Japan.

As Maruyama Masao has pointed out in a classic essay on Japanese political science, the enshrinement of the emperor made examination of the mechanics of state power a virtual taboo. The sovereign and the state over which he "ruled" (tōchi) stood enveloped in mist, untouchable, for example, by the mere scholars who populated the Kokka Gakkai (Association for State Science). State and politics were regarded as separate realms. The former was to be approached via the "general system" of laws deduced from the abstract idea of a state "in repose." Its operation in political reality—the application of its power, through law, to society—was not to be studied, except as a problem of administration. "Politics," to the extent that it existed, was conceived of in terms of the manipulation of law by neutral experts in the interest of maintaining the integrity of the state structure.[82] As industrialization progressed, bringing with it a labor movement and interclass hostility, the role of the state in preventing class conflict and possible revolution became a chief bureaucratic preoccupation. Members of the Shakai Seisaku Gakkai (modeled on the late Wilhelmine Verein für Sozialpolitik), which included both academics and bureaucrats, sought to involve the state in "prophylactic measures" that would head off social conflict.[83] As we have seen, this necessarily brought them into contact with socialists, and such contacts raised the suspicions of capitalist interests none too happy with the idea of any state involvement in society.

Until the rise of "Marxist" social science in the 1920s, the orthodox approach to the state effectively prevented any thorough dissection of the mechanisms of power. Those who threatened the state by manifesting any critical interest, who pointed to or advocated alternative modes of political and social life, were duly rewarded. Insiders such as academics could be censored, harassed, arrested. Real heretics—active organized socialists (Marxist or otherwise) and anarchists—were watched and followed. Arrest meant torture and in some cases outright murder. For such people, the fringes of the inner sanctum were guarded by vicious dogs, and it is small wonder that other Japanese concerned about the nature and quality of political life, compelled to steer clear of the sacred precincts, had difficulty both conceptualizing and expressing their heartfelt criticisms. Academics, for example, tended to cling to narrow "textual empiricism" or abstraction. Nanbara's mentor at Tōdai, Onozuka Kiheiji, was a good example. While he respected Onozuka tremendously as a person, and honored him for his long struggle for the procedural autonomy of the university, Nanbara could not deny the contradiction inherent in Onozuka's attempt as a scholar to make a "value-free" study of what was in effect a taboo—the nature of the emperor system, itself the font of value in the state.[84]

The point should be clear: the marking off of boundaries outside of which the investigation of reality was compelled to remain tended to turn officially propagated German thought as a whole into an ideological cover, admittedly imperfect, for a politically repressive system tied into the expansion of industrial capital. The state was protected by imported *Staatslehre* from critical inquiry within the academic elite, while social policy thinking provided formulas for its intervention (not always welcomed) in society.

At the same time, German philosophy attracted Japanese who wanted
(and had) to explore that sphere of life—the apolitical—not under
the direct eye of the state authority. That is, it appealed to the aesthetic
and metaphysical sense, to the cultivation of the affective, spiritual
life. A range of thinkers from the classical idealists and Romantics
through Schopenhauer and Nietzsche to the neo-Kantians all responded
to this need.

Yet it would be a gross error to see in the flowering of this philosophy
(as in the work of Nishida Kitarō) a mere substitute for, or conscious
abdication of, political responsibility. Apart from the dogmatism that
would reduce all of human experience to a single "real" sphere surrounded by epiphenomena, such a position (once advanced and now repudiated by Tatsuo Arima) fails to take account of the conditions of all
thought after the mid Meiji period. The state, as it were, stood in between politics and the *investigation* of political-social reality. Political
activity per se had only a calculus of interest to justify it. Japanese education and socialization in general were crowned by the imperative of
risshin shusse, in which service to self (including family) meant service
to nation and vice versa. In this "empiricist" reading of life, ambition
was to be commended so long as it could be channeled into legitimate
areas: public (civil and military) service above all, industry and large-
scale commerce, and "practical scholarship" such as administration, engineering, and natural science. The humanities occupied a more equivocal position. Art and journalism did not belong on the road to "success."

The affective sphere, with its own undeniable reality, was also left
to absorb the "excess" of intellectual endeavor that might have gone
into public involvement—whether in journalism, research, activism, or
teaching. The walls of this total "structure" were very thick. The state
made an effort to prevent crossover, to maintain each sphere in the illusion of self-sufficiency.

However, the national letdown and disquiet that came toward the
end of the Meiji era brought a challenge to the separate and unequal
valuation of the departments of life. *Risshin shusse,* "entrepreneurial
hustle," the boosterism and jingoism of empire went into partial eclipse.[85]

German thought itself reflected this change, particularly in the universities. Hitherto it had represented intellectual division. It provided
models for state administration, and for the cultivation of self (as well
as, in neo-Romanticism, ways of escape from the "vulgar world" [zok-
kai]). But it seemed to offer little for what came in between—for ways of
thinking about explicitly *social* life. In the closing years of the Meiji era,

we begin to see examples of Japanese thinkers not satisfied with this
situation, both within the academic elite and on its borders.

Minobe Tatsukichi, whose organ theory of the constitution relied "on
theoretical language from the German legal scholar Georg Jellinek" [86]
sought to show that a liberal political order could legitimately be derived from the Meiji constitution. He viewed Japan, a modern nation by
virtue of its having adopted a constitution, as a "corporate entity," of
which the emperor, Diet, people, and so forth, were "organs," the emperor supreme among them. The interests of each were legitimate, to be
articulated and responded to within reason.[87] Minobe's view, as we
noted, gained official acceptance, after 1913 becoming the preferred
(though not the only) interpretation taught in universities, public and
private. But this was not a permanent state of affairs. A reaction against
the liberal, decentralizing, and "democratic" tendencies of the Taishō
years was inevitable.[88] Not everyone was pleased with the new assertiveness of the parties and subordinate government agencies. And since
Minobe's ideas were regarded as the theoretical grounds for the new arrangement, political reaction just as inevitably meant a rejection of the
ideas and their propagator. In other words, Minobe's final downfall in
1935 came because his theory, by demystifying the emperor and rendering the state susceptible to critical examination, had enabled "organs"
hitherto held in check by old-line bureaucratic and military manipulation of imperial prerogative, to exercise something like genuine constitutional rights. Minobe was thus an especially inconvenient creature
in the eyes of renovationist factions in the military and their civilian
allies. Along with Yoshino Sakuzō, whose influences included both
Johann Bluntschli and Hegel, Minobe represented the possibilities for
self-generating reform under the old dispensation. (It remains to add, of
course, that the liberalization attempted in these years was not totally
displaced in the ensuing reaction. It is true, nevertheless, that the influence of "liberals" was felt more despite, rather than because of, the institutional environment.)

A further example of the changing role of "Germany" recalls the
major intellectual development of the late Taishō period: the rise of
Marxism. Kawakami Hajime (1879–1946) is one of many examples of
budding insiders impatient with the either/or choice—state and self versus society—that university education and official career entailed. Kawakami had early on begun to question the state's monopoly on political definition. He had begun his public life as a lecturer on agricultural
economics at Tōdai, gradually metamorphosing from a virtual phys-

iocrat to a kind of humanitarian socialist. During his long stint teaching economics at Kyōdai (preceded by a firsthand look at what industrialization really meant to Europe), Kawakami came under Marxist influence and turned his back on the orthodox terms of service. He could no longer treat society as something to be molded to the needs of the state. Neither could he stomach the bourgeois view of self as an object of cultivation for its own sake—let alone economic individualism. Rather, Kawakami had sought (from his early youth) to give himself totally to others, eventually finding his intellectual orientation in Marx and personal salvation in Communist Party membership. He went as far outside as it was possible to go without taking up arms himself.

A great number of insiders ranged themselves in between Minobe and Kawakami. Contemporaries such as Takano Iwasaburō, doyen of "left-wing" social policy thinkers, found themselves uncomfortable within the academy, but unwilling to call for the whole system's overthrow. Takano, for example, left Tōdai in 1920 to head the private Ōhara Shakai Mondai Kenkyūjo (Ōhara Institute for Social Research). Some younger scholars, such as Ōuchi Hyōe and Kushida Tamizō, embraced Marxism; others went as far as fleeting activism.

The point: that under the pressure of political and social change concomitant with industrialization and colonial expansion, the walls that separated intellectual endeavor into "autonomous" departments began, ever so slowly, to crack. With the introduction of Marxism, German thought as ideological instrument was compromised, and in part transformed, into a weapon of criticism. Not every insider followed Kawakami, of course. Nanbara, to whom we now return, began his encounter with Kant in 1921 and was never remotely close to renouncing the critical philosophy in favor of dialectic in either its Hegelian or Marxist incarnations. What held him back? Perhaps the continuing impact of Christian faith? He shared in any case a common philosophical starting point in German thought, wherever that journey might end.

NANBARA AND THE PHILOSOPHY OF VALUE

Nanbara's three years abroad brought him into the orbit of a veritable who's who of European scholars. In London, where he spent half a year (at the London School of Economics), Nanbara met the socialist Graham Wallas and the radical political philosophers Harold Laski and L. T. Hobhouse. (Hobhouse played an important role in the thinking of

Hasegawa Nyozekan—to be discussed below.) In Grenoble, where he passed his last six months before returning to Japan (via the United States), Nanbara attended the lectures of Jacques Chevalier on Pascal. But it was in Berlin that Nanbara enjoyed sustained personal contact with, and discovered the work of, a disparate group of German intellectuals, both "mandarins" and "outsiders." [89] Among the mandarins were the chief representatives of both the Baden and Marburg schools of neo-Kantian philosophy, and it was through neo-Kantianism, especially that of the "value" philosophers of Baden, that Nanbara approached not only the work of Kant, but politics itself. He also fell heir to the problems and fallacies of that philosophy.

Among representatives of Baden, Nanbara's mentor, the legal theorist Rudolf Stammler, the philosophers Heinrich Rickert and Emil Lask, and the jurist Gustav Radbruch were the most influential—although he cannot be called the disciple of any one of them. From the "logical" school of Marburg, Nanbara was most familiar with the work of Hermann Cohen and Ernst Cassirer. In addition, he knew economists such as Eduard Meyer and Werner Sombart. Among Marxists, he made the acquaintance of the "Austro-Marxists" Max Adler and Karl Vorländer, and "revisionists" such as Karl Kautsky and Eduard Bernstein. (Bernstein, of course, was heavily influenced by Kantianism.) Nanbara also met a young theologian, Paul Tillich. Finally, he became conversant with, and deeply opposed to, the thinking of the literary coterie that gathered itself around the poet Stefan George, known as the George-Kreis. Aside from George himself, Nietzsche was the great inspiration of the circle's work, both poetic and historical. Nietzsche's "Dionysian" view of the Greek polis, as mediated by George-Kreis intimates Edgar Salin, Wilhelm Andreae, Kurt Hildebrandt, and Kurt Singer, provided the critical springboard for Nanbara's own study of Plato. This study, to which I shall turn later, rested on the neo-Kantian view that political and philosophical inquiry into the polis of Plato's *Republic* and the *Laws* had to be conducted in terms of a rigorous dualism, ideal and phenomenal. Nanbara followed his neo-Kantian mentors in believing that the scholars of the George-Kreis had dissolved this tension in the poetic and mythic interpretation of Plato, with ominous consequences for political philosophy.

Nanbara's mentor in Kantian philosophy, as mentioned, was Rudolf Stammler (1856–1938). One of the most faithful followers of Wilhelm Windelband's antipositivist call for a movement *"zurück zu Kant,"* Stammler had gone on to become the preeminent neo-Kantian legal mind of his time. Nanbara's studies with Stammler came toward the end of his mentor's career, but they were by no means years of obscurity. To attempt here even a summary of Stammler's theory of the *richtiges Recht* (just law) is impossible, given our purpose and Stammler's voluminous legacy. Strictly speaking, it may also be beside the point: nowhere in Nanbara's writings do we find any reference, any allusion to Stammler as a substantive or methodological influence. However, Stammler did direct Nanbara's line-by-line reading of Kant's three *Critiques,* and (probably) of *Zum ewigen Frieden* (Eternal peace, 1795). It was this latter, and Kant's philosophy of history and world order in general, that Nanbara embraced with the greatest fervor—areas with which Stammler seems to have been but little concerned.[90] In fact, Nanbara shared the widespread contemporary sentiment that Stammler's systematic theory of the "just law," while "infinitely rich," subtle, and original, suffered from extreme formalism and abstraction.[91] This much was admitted even by Stammler's admirers. Stammler spoke, for example, of "just law," but provided no criteria for such laws' determination; for him the "constitutive concept" (*Grundbegriff*) of social science held that "the form of human society is nothing else than the idea of external regulation as the logical condition under which alone it is possible to form the concept of the social co-operation of human efforts."[92] He postulated a "natural law with variable content" (*ein Naturrecht mit wechselndem Inhalte*), by definition unspecifiable in theory.[93] True, one can certainly see in Stammler's idea of a community of "free-willing" individuals one similar to Nanbara's; what Nanbara did was to apply certain national criteria to the community. But the congruence may be owing not so much to Stammler's influence as to their common reading of Kant. After all, such a concept of community is hardly original with Stammler; it belongs to the common stock of neo-Kantian thinking on the constitution of society.

In Stammler's concern for theoretical purity in legal philosophy, one can see (as Ogata Norio points out) continuities with Hans Kelsen's "pure theory of law" (*reine Rechtslehre*). Both were enormously influential in Japan, especially in Nanbara's alma mater. But just as Nanbara had reservations about the formalism of Stammler, so too did he about Kelsen.[94] In sum, we may say that Stammler's significance for Nanbara was, first, instrumental, in that it was Stammler who taught him to read Kant; second, it was tangential, in that the state, and the moral and spiritual constitution of the national community, which lay at the forefront of Nanbara's concerns, mattered to Stammler insofar as they involved the law; third, it was critical, in that Nanbara saw lacunae in Kant's concept of state *because* they were so faithfully reflected in Stammler himself, and vice versa.

One wonders, however, what sort of psychological impression his years in Germany made on Nanbara. Here was the great Reich, exhausted and bled white by a war largely of its own making, humiliated in defeat, and resentful of the exactions on it under the Versailles Treaty. The politics of the early republic promised nothing but nervous exhaustion. The Weimar coalition, formed after two attempts at revolution and beholden to the bloody methods of the Freikorps, which defended it against "Bolshevism," managed to promulgate a constitution. The right, a tangle of militarists, Prussian monarchists, and "vaguely socialist" anti-Semites went on the attack against the revolutionary left; assassinations of socialists and centrists caught in between marked these years. Feeding this instability was the fantastic inflation, which began at a creep in 1921, but by April 1923 defied belief. This was the time of trillion-mark loaves of bread and wagon-load wages. Though brought to an end by Hjalmar Schacht through "ruthless" cuts and the creation of the Rentenmark, one can only guess how much bitterer popular feeling grew, not only toward those nominally in control, but toward the Powers who, as many believed, held the fate of Germany in their hands. By the end of 1923, a semblance of stability had been achieved, even a "mask-like" prosperity sufficient to raise expectations and fuel confidence that, strength regained, Germany would rise again.[95]

At the same time, the massacre of 1914–18, despite its "unhealthy aftereffects," produced the desire to put an end to imperialism—at least as it had been practiced hitherto. "Kaisers, Emperors, academies, dogmas, everything associated with the 'old men' should be swept away," the British critic Richard Rees writes.

> Oppressed workers and sweated coolies should come into their own. On the ruins of authoritarianism and paternalism a universal Liberty Hall should be built, whose foundation had been laid in Russia in 1917. Freedom was in the ascendant—educational, artistic, sexual, moral, every kind of freedom; not the four beggarly freedoms of a later and sadder generation, but a thousand.[96]

In this climate of hope, whose only grounds lay in Europe's need to bury a horrific past, Nanbara began his studies. It is unfortunate that, unlike his close friend Ōuchi Hyōe and Tōdai colleague Morito Tatsuo, Nanbara left no memoirs discussing German politics and society. We do know that his personal hopes for world reconstruction through the concrete means of the League of Nations were rather cool. It is important, however, to note the reasons. Another of Nanbara's contemporaries, Konoe Fumimaro, was also in Europe, roughly at the same time, and came to the same conclusion. But for Konoe, the League, and the idealism that it seemed to embody, actually did little more than ratify an Anglo-American world order. This, he felt, was unjust, as it worked against Japan's interest in China both as an "ally" and as a "follower" country. Nanbara, already deeply influenced by Kant's *Eternal Peace*, had a far different perspective. He held political reality to a higher standard, and found it wanting. Similarly, he refers (in an essay written in 1929) to the "pacifism advocated after the Great War by sentimental humanists and religious dogmatists"; this too, compared with the rigorously deduced proposals of *Eternal Peace*, Nanbara found wanting. But instead of despairing of any possibility of genuine world order, he defended the League:

> Yes, its organization was imperfect in the extreme; yes, the motives for its creation included many impure elements; and yes, it was formed on the essentially mistaken basis of utilitarian ideas. Yet it was also a manifestation of an idealistic effort to establish a new world order, a great historical fact whose like is bound to be repeated in future. We must not commit the injustice of undervaluing it.[97]

Fukuda Kan'ichi, Nanbara's direct successor at Tōdai, and himself a Mukyōkai adherent, has remarked that Nanbara's views reflect the quietism and eschatological bent that emerged in Uchimura Kanzō's thinking after 1918 (the Second Coming Movement referred to earlier). Given his background, Fukuda is certainly in a position to know. And it is true, as he says, that Uchimura was bitterly disappointed in what he regarded as the moral failure of the United States.[98] However, aside from the reference above, one finds little in Nanbara's writing to link his doubts with Uchimura. On the other hand, his study of Kant in the context of Weimar's economic and political travail jibes completely with such coolness, and helps to explain Nanbara's refusal to put his faith in institutions per se. These could too easily become fetishes masking a spiritually vacuous politics. Nanbara is said to have regarded "institutionalism" as the most serious flaw in the democratic movement of the Taishō period, along with a penchant for pure theory represented by Marburgers such as Hans Kelsen—who, as noted, enjoyed considerable influence in Nanbara's own Law Faculty after the mid 1920s.[99] It is not difficult to see why in Nanbara's view these two flaws could complement each other. For they bespoke precisely the absence of a "spirit" of democracy and a nuts-and-bolts commitment to seeing it through, which Nanbara considered the key legacy of his seven years' service in the Home Ministry.

Nanbara's hands-on experience in local government in his rural "second home," and his involvement in drafting the labor union bill of 1920, might indeed have brought home to him the tenuousness of the democratic prospect in Japan. But in terms of his explicitly philosophical commitments, value judgments, and the basic disposition underlying them, Nanbara was most deeply marked by Weimar neo-Kantianism. Not surprisingly, this influence is most evident in Nanbara's political thought, especially in his concept of the state.

Nanbara's mentors (the term is taken broadly here) included a number of Weimar's high academic elite. Whether "mandarin" or not, however, all were products of Wilhelmine education.[100] And whether adherents of the Marburg school, with its concern for the critique of the logical conditions of all knowledge, or of Baden, with its efforts to articulate and systematize absolute, universally valid values in the midst of a contingent, historical particularity, all faced a number of common tasks. They had, first, to come to terms with the massive and catastrophic repudiation of rationality that they all perceived in the slaughter of 1914–18, with its aftermath of defeat, and its repercussions in the realm of culture and philosophy. Though one is hesitant to minimize the differences between the two schools, it may be said that the epistemological premises and ethical imperatives of Kantian philosophy did enjoin on Nanbara's mentors, their predecessors and confreres, a kind of "liberalism."[101] This was not, as it was not with Nanbara, a laissez-faire liberalism based on the privileging of individual economic activity. Rather, it was one that for philosophical reasons attached highest value to practical reason and to the inviolability of personality. Politically, this meant a rejection of any system of dictatorship or collective compulsion; and thus a general acceptance of the Weimar Republic. The more cosmopolitan logicians of Marburg especially tended toward a universalist, ethical socialism. Their politics, after the crushing of the 1918 revolution and the hammering out of the constitution, ran to the left of center. The Baden philosophers, by contrast, with their concerns for *cultural* wholeness guaranteed by the embrace of common values, were perhaps more elitist and conservative. Yet though it is true, with some exceptions, that the value philosophers tended to be more susceptible to the claims of culturally based nationalism, at the same time their ethical focus led them to be more immediately suspicious of collective actionist thinking, and of any kind of "irrational decisionism." [102]

Given the fate of Germany under the National Socialists after 1933, later observers of the Weimar scene have been quick to note that the neo-Kantians (when not exiled or killed) stayed away in droves from those tendencies of thought that seemed to feed the Nazi ideology of *Blut und Boden.* The neo-Hegelians, neo-Romanticists, and certain phenomenologists, on the other hand, will stand eternally condemned for the alacrity with which they adapted themselves to the new dispensation. Much modern intellectual history has been written in answer to the question, "Which side were you on?" This is but natural; the issue of intellectual allegiance to brutal regimes has hardly been settled. And one can only assent to Jürgen Habermas's lifelong feeling of abhorrence for that aspect of Heidegger's thinking that permitted him to prevaricate on and mystify his involvement with Nazism.[103]

At the same time, we must recognize that the neo-Kantians, from the very beginning of the Weimar period, inherited a profoundly disoriented philosophical milieu in Germany, and that their philosophy alone did little to prepare them for any confrontation with the forces in society and politics that seemed to reflect and to weaken further the tenuous hold that rationality had over Germany. (I do not speak of personal commitments as if philosophy alone determined them. Nor am I forgetting that some neo-Kantians became deeply involved in politics: one has only to think of Max Weber, Ernst Troeltsch, Eduard Bernstein, Kurt Eisner, Gustav Radbruch, even Rudolf Stammler. But a glance at *when* they were active is revealing; when it came to the period of decline and final repudiation of the republic, neo-Kantians found themselves ill-equipped to counteract it.)

Many intellectuals, not necessarily of malevolent intent, had come to distrust the purely logical and methodological approaches of Marburg to questions of truth and law. After 1914—though of course the trends had begun much earlier, in the nineteenth century—reasoning by category and deduction seemed unbearably arid, so unconnected to any tangible reality as to be meaningless. And, indeed, legal philosophers like Stammler and Kelsen explicitly disavowed any concern with the content of law in favor of the systematization of "pure principles for ordering consciousness." [104]

Not so different were the implications of the value approach. A value represented something wholly apart from being, a transcendent and universally valid object of consciousness, "an unconditioned standard of what 'ought to be.'" [105] It is true that value philosophers in Weimar sought, for and within a historical particularity, to articulate a system of values. And they did so in the service of peace and order, national belonging, and wholeness. Yet this "synthesis" (as Ernst Troeltsch termed it) of elite and mass in society, and of real and ideal in philosophy, while it bespoke an awareness of need, offered nothing to guide practice. It was almost as if enunciation itself were sufficient. The point here is not to assign blame. It is simply that the emphasis on the "noumenal freedom" of personality to choose to act according to universal norms and values left the solution of social and political problems to the rational will of the individual; this may have been a compelling philosophical postulate, but it hardly pointed the way to social solidarity.

The field was left almost entirely open to adherents of philosophies that placed phenomena, especially collective phenomena, first. The primacy of intuition and action, of being and life—indeed of circumstance and blind necessity—represented an assault on the deepest of Kantian convictions that these "must, and therefore can" be overcome. Recent history, moreover, stood as a reproach to the faith of neo-Kantians in the "power of mind." [106]

Neo-Kantians, Nanbara included, philosophized about politics and society in terms that avoided the problem of power. They did this because they addressed their primary concern with "noumenal freedom" in terms of the individual will struggling against unintelligible necessity. This struggle, in their view, was to be waged through law, an inner moral law and an outer legislative compulsion that resided in the state. Law and freedom, as distinguished from law and power, was the relationship they saw at the core of the "civil constitution." Thus when, as in the case of neo-Hegelians such as Carl Schmitt, this distinction was transformed into an identity and a justification for the expansion of state coercion, neo-Kantians had no answer. Kant had advanced the view that the state was indispensable in its "external" function as a "guarantor" of "inner" freedom. This was the liberalism that had fired Germany's revolution of 1848 and been attenuated so severely under the empire. It was for this reason that, as Dahrendorf observes, "Kant did not really survive Hegel" in Germany. [107]

It had seemed to many that under Weimar precisely such a conception of state and law had finally come into its own. Despite the bloody pact made by Ebert and Noske with the Freikorps, it was true that at least in terms of the moral and philosophical integrity of those who framed its enabling document, the republic could scarcely have asked for more. Even so, it was all too clear that Weimar's mandate was a tenuous one. Sympathizers and critics alike perceived this; to the internal threat of political disintegration and economic collapse, the philosophical corrosion of Weimar's "principle of hope" was now to be added, along with (for conservatives) the menace of "Russo-Asiatic" imperialism.

From the start, then, the atmosphere was one of crisis and anxiety: would the rational center hold? And what if it did not? In the event, as we know, those neo-Kantians who remained alive in Germany held themselves aloof from national socialism, abhorring it without confronting it. Many of them, like Rickert, were advanced in years and survived only briefly after 1933. Somewhat younger scholars like Ernst Cassirer, whose Jewish origins immediately placed him in grave jeopardy, fled. None was prepared to abandon the belief in the intimate relation of freedom to law. A situation in which this belief was repudiated by state fiat and ideology was by definition unintelligible nonsense. Precisely for this reason, they were defenseless against it.

It was as these developments were beginning to unfold—first with the striving for cultural synthesis and social integration under a state committed to the universal law of freedom, and then with its repudiation—that Nanbara undertook his own studies of Kant. Although he considered himself something of a Kantian fundamentalist, in fact many of his texts are pregnant with the terminology and concerns of value philosophy; this despite his long studies with Stammler. This may help to explain why, as Nanbara sought to be true to Wilhelm Windelband's dictum that "to understand Kant is to go beyond him" (*Kant verstehen heisst über ihn hinausgehen*), he did so by moving toward the nationalist metaphysics of the later Fichte. For it was in this direction—the realization of national wholeness—that he considered the most pressing tasks of philosophy to lie. Indeed, Heinrich Rickert, who had built upon Windelband's work to synthesize value philosophy, had followed the very same path.[108]

In the pages that follow, I wish, in the light of Nanbara's orientation to value philosophy, to explore his particular mode of "going beyond" Kant. What, first, did he find of enduring value in Kant? What was insufficient, what questions left unanswered in Kant's work? Why did Nanbara undertake his long and arduous studies of Fichte? The final and central question will be, How did these studies reflect, and relate to, the intellectual milieu, specifically that of insider public discourse, of Japan during this period? In what way was it different from that of Germany?

Nanbara's first publications after his return to Japan in 1923 might be described collectively as a critical testament to his years with Stammler. Two in particular, published within one year of each other, deserve brief notice. One was a longish schematic essay on the end of utilitarian liberalism, published in 1928. The other, although chronologically prior, in a sense answers the question—what next?—implied in the former. This essay, "The Ideal of International Politics in Kant" (Kant ni okeru kokusai seiji no rinen, 1927), was incorporated into Nanbara's first major work, Kokka to shūkyō (The state and religion, 1942). Here it was preceded by studies of the Platonic and Christian views of the state, and followed by a searching contemporary critique of the Nazi Weltanschauung, which Nanbara treats as a perversion of the conceptions of the state explored in the earlier studies. These texts will be considered in due course.

To turn then to Nanbara's critique of liberalism: perhaps its most noticeable feature is that it is largely derivative; there is little original in it in either a European or a Japanese context. The liberalism it attacks is best understood, I think, as the philosophy of economic individualism, with "liberty" referring to unrestricted pursuit of individual economic benefit. As such, this was a critique associated with the work of Friedrich List and other founders of the historical school of economics, which dates from the 1840s.[109] Its philosophical origins, however, lie deeper, in Kant's refusal to justify goodness through an appeal to utility. The sort of liberalism Nanbara affirmed (without using the term) was, by the same token, that of which the neo-Kantians also approved: namely, the absence of despotic compulsion—compulsion not permitted by a law recognized by all members of a polity—that encouraged the free development of the moral faculty within the personality. This did not, in Nanbara's view, require that unrestricted pursuit of individual happiness or pleasure be placed above all other concerns. Indeed, it was to be subordinate to the needs of the whole community (whose national character at this point remains formal), and to the moral needs of the noumenally free individual.

Nanbara nevertheless gave credit where it was due. He recognized lasting achievements in the liberal tradition that ran from Locke and Rousseau through Adam Smith to J. S. Mill and beyond. It had brought scientific method to bear on the study of society; it championed the individual conscience and the responsibility of each for his own acts. At the same time, liberalism had grave limitations. It rested on a belief in individual happiness as the highest good, turning the state into a mere mechanism for that purpose. It propagated a corrosive, atomistic view of society and rationalized exploitation in the name of economic individualism. It placed dogmatic faith in a spurious cosmopolitanism of trade, in which the pursuit of self-interest by individual rational calculators somehow added up to a self-regulating world order. All he had absorbed from Uchimura, all he had seen, perhaps, of postwar Europe gave the lie to these sanguine and self-serving beliefs. The idealism he learned from Kant was no shallow optimism but a rigorous, unyielding command. *Du kannst*, Kant had said, *denn du sollst*. Here, instead of a philosophy of happiness, was a philosophy of freedom.[110]

At this point, we enter into the subject matter of the other essay mentioned above. Here, however, I wish to avoid a tiring recapitulation. Much of the ground Nanbara covers is no more than an able, though perhaps unexceptional, account of the Kantian antinomies and of Kant's linking of freedom to moral action: the idea, in other words, of the categorical imperative as a law inscribed in the tissue of reason. This is not to deny the importance of this groundwork for Nanbara's later critique of Kant, but simply to say that, given its nature, it is duplicated in many places and languages.[111]

Instead, let us pursue more directly the aspects of Kant's philosophy that Nanbara found problematic. These are found at the intersection of Kant's treatments of religion, on the one hand, and the historical and political implications of his moral theory, on the other. We may call to mind here Leonard Krieger's observation that Kant, in the systematic development of his critical philosophy, moved ever closer to the border area between freedom and necessity. Thus, writing in his *Idea for a Universal History*—a work Nanbara discusses at length—Kant had stated: "The greatest practical problem for the human race . . . is the establishment of a civil society, universally administering right according to law." It was in this context, as Nanbara notes, that Kant had introduced the idea of "nature's secret plan" for human concord as a reflection of the dualism of the human makeup. For though a "radical evil" lies at the heart of the species, nature (understood as providence) has conspired in its salvation: Nature exploits men's "unsocial sociability," bringing them into conflict with others, forcing them together out of their benighted condition into changing the conditions of their lives. In this way men discover reason. Thus have they "progressed" and seemingly blundered into enlightenment. As Nanbara put it, Kant saw nature "assisting man in doing what he cannot do for himself," but only on condition that he make use of the capacity for reason that he finds within himself. No regress, no stasis is tolerable for Kant. The *end* of nature is man (literally—Kant explicitly excludes women from his considerations); the end of man is the reunification of nature with reason, the realization of the human—rational—essence. Nature thus conspires in the salvation of the human species. This is the great teleology that is history.[112]

Kant's moral theory, then, is teleological. And since by implication it involves the mutual relations of men, it has a political moment. As such it also involves the state. Kant has told us, Nanbara says, why man is free. But how and where is he free? First, it must be grasped that freedom has two aspects, inner (*innere*, the freedom to follow the moral law) and outer (*äussere*, the legal guarantee that permits man to follow the dictates of the former).[113] The state exists to make possible the application of the categorical imperative to social life. It is the "guarantor of freedom." As such it deals in *Legalität*, with deeds springing from motives other than obedience to the inner moral law. Given the moral end of the state, the means it employs can justifiably include coercion (which is why even "a people of devils" can be made to live under a good constitution). Thus the *Reich der Sitten*, the "moral community" of rational persons, exists within a national-legal framework, the *Reich des Rechts*. The guarantee provided by this dual subjecthood frees the individual to strive for perfection. The important point for Kant, Nanbara stresses, is that human freedom forms the core. And that the state, as the individual, is endowed with a moral personality. Rather than serving in Kant's system as a means for the attainment of individual happiness (which would tie it to the state of nature), the state is the legal expression of human freedom, obedience to which becomes a moral duty, an end in itself. The important point for us is the emphasis Nanbara places on Kant's deduction that men cannot be free except by being bound to the state.[114]

Nanbara's concern did not stop here, however. Instead, with obvious and passionate approval, he went on to give an account of the internationalist proposals contained in Kant's late writings. These, Nanbara saw correctly, were no fortuitous product of Kant's dotage, but evidence of a compelling logic in the development of his whole teleological philosophy.[115]

The state, Kant had seen, was not an orphan. It existed among other

states. Just as the individual, however rational and subject to the prescriptive (not automatic) moral law, must strive to overcome evil, passion, desire, and cruelty, and so become "worthy of happiness," so too
the state. It may not take its own "happiness" as an imperative and justify the use of other states as a means to that end. (Coercion is licit
within, but not between, states.) Kant recognized no "national interest"
in the sense of a self-justifying pursuit of power or repression of popular
aspiration. What he sought was to provide philosophical grounds for
international order in a way analogous to moral-legal order among men
in a state. Individual, state, and world order thus stand in concentric
circles, with a common core.[116]

In *Eternal Peace,* Kant tried to define the highest political good of
human society and outline the means for its attainment. Kant had taken
a revolutionary step in recognizing that "the problem of establishing a
perfect civil constitution [was] dependent upon the problem of a law
governed relationship between states."[117] Perpetual peace was *the* political task of humanity, to be pursued by states on a universal scale, assisted, as we saw earlier, by nature itself.

If men within states had to struggle against egoism, states themselves
faced the analogous, yet far more horrific, "egoism" that was war. Kant
in his *Conflict of Faculties* had called war the source of all evils and
moral corruption.[118] He saw clearly that as nation-states became the
norm in the organization of political society (under American and
French-style constitutions, he passionately hoped), their mutual competition and antagonism could not but doom society to ever more dangerous and bloody warfare. Kant feared the disintegration of all order as
long as states regarded the condition of chronic war or preparation for it
as natural. He was sure that only nature—experience—would teach
them by appalling example that no justice could be established through
war. He rejected the belief of contemporary theorists such as Grotius in
the "right to war" based on national interest. There could be no right to
use or destroy others in one's own "interest," even in a limited way, followed by peace through haggling. Such a right guaranteed no more than
eventual, mutually assured destruction.

Kant turned, as always, to law in search of a solution. In *Eternal
Peace* he proposed that a small group of pioneer states "inaugurate
peace-intended-to-be-perpetual" through treaties of nonaggression that
pledged the signatories to certain rules of intercourse.[119] Their example
that "nonaggression pays" marked only the merest beginning. But it
was the only conceivable beginning, for it relied on the moral commu-

nity's internal compulsion to duty, on the belief that states "must, and therefore can" act positively, through embrace of law, to live at peace.

There could of course be no cure-all, and as Nanbara points out, Kant recognized each state's right to self-defense. This presupposed the individual citizen's duty to fight also, provided that the life of the state had been made precarious by the aggression of another power. Even here, war was at best an irrational, desperate last resort. Kant's rejection of pacifism became Nanbara's also, which placed him in an ambiguous position vis-à-vis not only Uchimura, but the postwar Japanese constitution as well.[120]

But let us return for a moment to Nanbara's philosophical education. Nanbara, we must admit, failed to appreciate that Kant's view of war was a very narrow one. To be sure, Kant condemned war as "the most extreme form of the general evil—the natural egoism" in human nature, and he abhorred the "misery and atrocities" that accompanied the revolution in France. But in Kant's terms, "war" meant declared wars between sovereign states. Thus it is difficult to say how he would have theorized civil war, or (as is now everywhere common) undeclared wars as in Vietnam or Afghanistan. For Nanbara, Kant's formalism might have presented problems in trying to think about the war in China, for example. Still, it is not difficult to understand Nanbara's enthusiasm for Kant's vision. What a leap of philosophical and moral imagination it must have taken to make a premise of the possibility of peace, without surrendering any awareness of the brutality of men and states as they are.

For Nanbara, however, it was Kant's concept of the state that was of greatest consequence. As we have seen, Kant had viewed the state as a "moral community" with a distinct personality, the freedom of which is to be guaranteed externally by its common acceptance of law under a sovereign power. As always, the sanction of law remained the key. The state was a deduced necessity, a "particular totality" in the logical chain that stretched from individual to cosmos. "Nationality" per se was no more than a category, in this case abstracted from commonsense observation (for once, Nanbara says, Kant descended into the realm of experience). There was such a thing as a nation, but its characteristics were of no import except in a purely formal sense. Kant had indeed refused to follow those who made of the state an "absolutized egoism" whose only relations with other states were based on the balance of physical force. (Not the *only possible* relations, that is.) There could be no return, nevertheless, to Hellenism or a universal church: this would constitute no more than a suppression of rivalries through coercion, of uncertain duration. Similarly he rejected the idea of a free federation capable of enforcing peace on those outside. It would either become a world state, or, if insufficiently strong, would disintegrate into hostile factions. No, the state was to be a permanent reality, and any solution to the problem of conflict in human society would have to take it into account. As W. B. Gallie remarks, Kant was simultaneously the first systematic internationalist and "one of the most steadfast of 'statists' in the history of political thought." [121] In his very cosmopolitanism, Nanbara asserted, Kant elevated the nation-state to the level of a philosophical ideal. The *civitas terrena,* alongside the *civitas Dei,* had now arrived.[122]

If Nanbara accepted Kant's assumptions about the permanence of the nation-state, he also discovered Kant's concept of nationality to be empty of substance. What makes a nation a nation? What is a "people"? The term Nanbara used is *minzoku:* it will dominate our discussion for some time. A question pestered Nanbara relative to nationality. What sort of lasting international order could arise out of the merely formal recognition implied in Kant's demand that "legally protected status" be accorded to would-be peacemakers? Was that enough? Was not some understanding of particular qua particular necessary in international politics? What, for that matter, distinguished Kant's politics from mere legalism? Was there not some critical defining element lacking? Yes, politics aimed at the establishment among nations of a just order. But one has first to understand what *nation* signifies before any synthesis of particular and universal—national and cosmopolitan—is conceivable. In this respect, on the question of *where* men are free, Nanbara found Kant's political philosophy "woefully insufficient." [123] As inheritor in part of the cosmopolitanism of the Enlightenment, Kant had only been able to make a start at anchoring the autonomous moral agent in a social substrate, the national community.

In the early 1930s, therefore, Nanbara set himself two tasks. As was consonant with Kantian method, he would first try to work out a statement of his own philosophy in which the position and value of politics would be given firm theoretical grounding. This would take him not only beyond Kant, but beyond Rickert, Emil Lask, and Gustav Radbruch also. The statement that emerged, in 1931, was Nanbara's "philosophy of coordinate values." And it was from this position that Nanbara sought secondly to formulate, where Kant could not, a more substantive idea of national community that could speak to the spiritual crisis that faced the modern, specifically the capitalist, world.

The work that combined these two tasks took the form of a critique of the philosophy of Kant's pupil, Johann Gottlieb Fichte (1762–1814). It was above all Fichte's "popular" work, and the sense of mission he injected into his philosophy, that became central to Nanbara's own self-definition from the time of his first exposure to Fichte, remaining so until his death. This Fichte was the "later" nationalist of *Der geschlossene Handelsstaat* (The closed commercial state, 1800), *Grundzüge des gegenwärtigen Zeitalters* (Characteristics of the present age, 1804–5), *Reden an die deutsche Nation* (Addresses to the German nation, 1807), and finally of the *Staatslehre* (Theory of the state, 1813). Between 1931 and 1942, Nanbara devoted a number of studies to the combination of nationalism and socialism in these works. The first of these, to be considered presently, was entitled "Gendai tetsugaku no mondai toshite Fichte no imi hihan" (The critique of Fichte's significance as a problem in contemporary philosophy).[124]

As may be imagined, neither the subject nor the timing of Nanbara's work on Fichte was innocuous. This was true in the context of both Germany and Japan. Let me explain briefly.

By 1931 many of the forebodings of rationalist thinkers in Germany had been borne out: in the vital fields of jurisprudence and politics, Jellinek (d. 1911), Stammler, Radbruch, and Kelsen (who also bore the influence of Viennese logical positivism) were soon to yield to Carl Schmitt—and soon thereafter to others of far less brilliance, such as Otto Koellreutter.

Just as "Kant did not survive Hegel" in the nineteenth century, neither did the neo-Kantians survive the "neos" of the twentieth: the neo-Hegelians and neo-Romanticists who came after Schopenhauer and Nietzsche. The apostles variously of community, irrationalism, and decisionism had been received with alacrity in late Weimar. Philosophers of being such as Heidegger, brilliant and spellbinding (and later, like Carl Schmitt, a member of the Nazi Party), tried to fill a "hunger for wholeness" that Peter Gay sees as a central motif in the cultural life of Weimar Germany. Nanbara, in a similar vein, spoke of Germany's search for a collective identity as a response to shattering defeat and loss of philosophical certainty.[125] Thinkers of far lesser stature than Heidegger, such as Othmar Spann and Julius Binder, won audiences who lapped up their talk of rediscovered primal communion in the *Volk*. It was a hunger that could not be filled with Kantian criticism, logic, or the mutual relation of values within a cultural system. It was one thing to assert the inherent capacity of reason to formulate values—aesthetic, scholarly, political even—but another to empower them to reweave a society disintegrating outward from a nominally republican core. Values did not *exist*.[126] By what authority could they claim the right to regulate human action? Blood, on the other hand, existed. It was basic and real. Pain and fear, love and anguish could be felt. These were the categories of philosophy that mattered.

It is clear from his writings on neo-Hegelianism and phenomenology that Nanbara recognized and feared the growing absorptive power of *Sein* as opposed to *Sollen*. (Also, because Nanbara concentrated on politics, he seems to have read much that was simply second-rate. Unaccountably, one finds no reference to Schmitt's work, though it was probably the sole exception, its implications notwithstanding, to the numbing mediocrity of contemporary political thought.) Nanbara presaged the outcome in politics of an excess of *Sein*.[127] Blood, race, tradition, sentiment, all would come to be defined as constituent of true national community. Rationality had lost its mandate: no longer could it be identified with the utilitarian interest of a liberal citizenry for which the state served as a means to private ends. This, as we have seen, Nanbara did not lament. No longer could rationality crown the eternal present of the Kantian imperative, where free-willing individuals formed a state possessed of a moral personality. This Nanbara did lament. What was worse, the critical separation of empirical from rational, and rational from nonrational that Kant had undertaken to salvage human knowledge would soon lie in ruins.

As we have seen, an analogous process was soon under way in Japan: Minoda Muneki's scorn of "disembodied" truth was of a piece with what had come to pass in Germany. But with this difference: neither the traditional symbols of national unity—the imperial house and its associated cultural furniture—nor the modern Meiji constitution had been destroyed in the process. There had been no devastating defeat, no failed revolution in Japan. The basic framework of the national order remained. It was this fundamental difference that permitted Nanbara to sustain his ethic of service; of "remaining in place." He had to hope that the spiritual and philosophical disaster that had befallen Germany would not ultimately swallow Japan.

Such were the fears, then, that both spurred Nanbara to write and to do so within the status order and world of public discourse of which he was a part. Thoroughly immersed in this order and this world, he sought, in a sense, to protect it from itself. And that required him to sound

philosophical alarms against the tendencies of thought that had arisen
in Germany: he knew very well that, if the past were any guide, they
would reproduce themselves in Japan.

We can recognize in Nanbara's Fichte studies an attempt to steer a
course between philosophies that explicitly rejected Kantian premises,
by now triumphant in Germany, and a die-hard rationalism that had
nothing meaningful to say to the public world. The prospects for this
project were mixed at best. During this same period, a number of Kyoto
school philosophers had published new works on Fichte (whose early
criticism of Kant's epistemology had appealed to them). Fichte's *Addresses* were also being used by the Ministry of Education for its own
purposes.[128] A cursory reading of this work suggests that the intent was
to raise the prestige of the "new" communitarian West (represented by
Germany) to the detriment of the "old" individualistic version. Whatever
their virtues, then, Nanbara's own efforts must be seen as parallel to, if
not part of, a wider trend: the attempted elimination of the individual as
a meaningful entity in all public discourse. It is, of course, questionable
whether in this attempt Fichte was a truly apposite weapon. All would
depend on how one treated the relationship of the early to the later
work: the stronger the emphasis on the transcendent ego that was so
prominent in the early Fichte, the less propaganda value would accrue
to his name. Nanbara, typically, steered a middle course between the
exaltation of the *Ich* and its repudiation. True to his (and Fichte's) Kantian training, he focused on the theme of freedom-in-community.

I noted earlier that Nanbara's initial work on Fichte emerged simultaneously with his basic statement on the idea of "coordinate values,"
and that the Fichte studies are in a sense an elaboration of one area of
value, namely the political. Before examining Nanbara's treatment of
Fichte, therefore, let us give some attention to Nanbara's overall scheme.

In Nanbara's systematization, each value—the true, good, beautiful,
and just—was accorded to its own sphere, from which, in the life of the
intellect, it reinforced the others without competing for primacy. The
first three, of course, Nanbara derived from the Platonic Ideas. But now,
projected forward as it were through Kantian lenses, the true was identified as the end of reason alone. No longer, as in Plato's *Politeia,* could it
represent an end of political life—that is, it was not for the state to define what was true. Such an identification, for Nanbara, also constituted
the cardinal sin committed by Hegel. In his panlogism Hegel had absorbed all of cultural (that is, rational) life into the logic of the dialectic,
of which the state was the manifestation.[129] The good in similar fashion

became the end of the moral life of the person, neither embodied in the community nor legislated by its anointed leader. The beautiful likewise represented the end of aesthetic endeavor. Creation represented an attempt to attain perfection in and through the work of art, which in turn tied it to the capacity of the mind to grasp the idea of perfection: perfection and beauty were one. But the point Nanbara wished to establish was that the community, however much its traditions bore canons of beauty, could on no account be identified with beauty itself. The soulcraft Plato regarded as the domain of the philosopher-king, and by extension of the state, could not take beauty as its end, any more than it could seek to enforce truth on its own authority. That end, rather, was the just.

The just—right order among men—was in Nanbara's system raised to a level coordinate with the Platonic Ideas, with this difference: the true, good, and beautiful each defined a value realizable in the relation of person to the Absolute (values taken as rational "emanations" of the Absolute). The just, while derived from the Absolute, was in its expression inherently social or "relational." It was *political* in essence, realizable only among the members of a community. The political entity existed, in fact, for that purpose and could only on that account justify its power.[130] On this issue Nanbara parted ways with Rickert, who did not recognize distinct political values and tended to view values hierarchically; and with the admired Radbruch, who, while recognizing the "value of the supra-individual social community," treated it as derivative, existing in order to serve the "absolute" values of the true and beautiful.[131]

Now the ultimate philosophical question for Nanbara was, what can philosophy know about what is *beyond* philosophy? Its greatest service would be to point to that *beyond* and say, "without this, there is nothing." Nanbara followed Windelband in the assertion, made in his *Einleitung in die Philosophie,* that all values required a priori metaphysical certainty springing from a superexistential essence,[132] and identified this essence with the Absolute, with God. Communication with the Absolute—"religion"—did not, could not, constitute one among a plurality of values. Values, after all, were rational constructs, whereas religion bespoke a relation with what was beyond, and productive of, value. In the Absolute, all contradictions and antinomies were resolved, something impossible in the sphere of value itself: "Indeed, those who hold values, those who do not, nay even those who oppose any value, are all alike called to a new relation of love."[133]

FICHTE AND THE PRICE OF EXCESS

Both the high-mindedness and potential difficulties of Nanbara's system are striking, but to comment on all their aspects would take us far afield. Clearly, Nanbara's insistence on an autonomous value of justice as the end of politics contains liberal implications. He had separated critically the values of the good, true, beautiful, and just, defining the state as that which safeguards and "sponsors" the moral autonomy of individuals in a community. How was this sponsorship to work? How tenable a distinction was Nanbara making when he insisted that the state was not a definer of value, or its source, but rather the locus of its realization? How, in short, was Nanbara's neo-Kantian liberalism supposed to pan out?

Nanbara's conception of the state did not really stop with "sponsorship." Here lay the problem. For he could not, just as Plato, Kant, and Fichte could not, conceive of genuine freedom outside a state. He followed closely the tradition that saw the state as an educator in freedom—and not necessarily in a participatory sense. Not only did the state guard the material life of the national community, it also raised its spiritual level—defined in terms of the moral freedom of its members. It is not hard to see that this protective, sponsoring state could easily become identified both with freedom, and with the national community. (Freedom, equaling membership, became formal and tautological.) Yet as we shall see, Nanbara resisted such an identification. How? And how convincingly?

Aristotle had said that those outside the polis must be either beasts or gods. The problem of twentieth-century politics, Nanbara had come to realize, was that those who dwelt within increasingly assumed the character of both beast and god. What was more, they had philosophies to justify their transformation.

It was this spiritual condition that Nanbara sought to combat. His vehicle, as noted, was the work of the later Fichte. In political terms, Nanbara found in Fichte's notions of nationalism (*kokuminshugi* or *minzokushugi*) and socialism the seeds of a viable philosophy of freedom-in-community. Not that he accepted Fichte's thought in toto. Some aspects of it troubled him deeply. But he found in it weapons to use against those worldviews whose inherent brutality had, to his mind, brought humanity to its present state. Nazism and Marxism each represented for Nanbara a reductionist "positivism," one of race, the other of class. Each had absorbed and twisted part of Fichte's message. How had that been possible? Fichte had to be defended. More important, he had to be understood anew.

Nanbara devoted immense labor to explicating Fichte's "science of knowledge" as it was set forth in successive editions of the *Wissenschaftslehre* (1794–1804). But it was in the "popular" works, the lectures and tracts published after Fichte's embrace of nationalism in 1800, that Nanbara saw the ideas and moral force that could lighten the spiritual burden of his own age.[134]

The central thesis of Nanbara's Fichte studies holds that the unsystematic political writings of the later Fichte must be viewed in the light of his epistemology, even as that epistemology shifts from an ethico-practical (heavily Kantian) to metaphysical (proto-Hegelian) basis. Fichte's notion of the state and its relation to the *Volk* grew progressively more "totalistic," in that he came to abandon the Kantian distinction between legal and moral (objective and subjective) order. He moved from a conception of the political state as the legal mechanism for the enforcement of Virtue (the *Notstaat*) to one in which, as the embodiment of reason, it "not merely leads to the land [*kokudo*] of heaven; the very idea of state must represent the kingdom of God on earth."[135] In the *Theokratie des Verstandes,* the highest form of state, we have the ultimate in what might be called Lutheran metaphysics. Nanbara himself, as we have seen, believed in a kind of national providence for Japan, but this was based on faith in a God whose will is not accessible to unaided reason. The closer Fichte approached Hegel in his identification of reason with the divine, and of the state with its embodiment, the more wary Nanbara grew. Such an identification removed purposeful human action from history, stripping the idea of subjectivity of any meaning. The panlogism of Hegel was inhuman, Nanbara thought, and it pained him to see Fichte anticipating Hegel in any sense.[136]

Now it is vital to keep in mind, as Nanbara constantly reminded his readers, that Fichte, although he had rejected Kant's *Ding-an-sich* as a "relic of dogmatism," had done so in order the more to exalt the self-conscious freedom of the "transcendental" ego (*Ich*).[137] Nothing material outside the subject was to bind it. But the members of the nation had to be educated in this self-conscious freedom; it was a normative construct, not an automatic capacity of the empirical self. Hence Fichte's "pedagogical mania"[138] and his view that the state was not only to provide but was itself the means of education in freedom. The state, as national community, was to educate itself, at first (and only at first) by relying on an elite that would eventually educate itself out of business.

There is no *Führerprinzip* in Fichte. Education was to be oriented toward the unity of state (polity) and culture (nation). For Fichte political sovereignty and cultural nationality were not coterminous. But such unity was the end of all cultural endeavor. A nation (*minzoku*) without sovereignty would not stand for much in the end. It would inevitably come under the conqueror's heel, its culture—beginning with language—to be extirpated.[139] Such was only to be expected. This is not the place to discuss the historical and political background of Fichte's work. It should suffice to point out that he had lived through the Napoleonic invasion and seen Prussia occupied by the very army whose revolutionary legacy had fired his own Jacobinism. The turn in his thought from Enlightenment cosmopolitanism to an increasingly metaphysical nationalism reflected this history of dispossession.[140] There is no question that his nation's humiliation was for Fichte a personal abyss, and that the vision of a united, sovereign Germany powered his philosophical impulse toward the identification of history and metaphysics in the state. Fichte learned from his times the power of negation. The "present age" was one of corruption, humiliation, and "sin run rampant." Yet it was in the depths of national despair that the seeds of regeneration waited. The divine logic of history would effect a new synthesis of culture and politics. Germany would rise again.[141]

But who were the Germans? What made them? What was the particular genius that assured their rise from the ashes? Why, indeed, should history look to Germany to inaugurate the "reign of virtue"? What sort of state would Germany establish? These were the questions that Kant could not ask—he had not needed to. Fichte did. And so did Nanbara.

For Fichte the Germans were an *Urvolk*, an "original people" (*genminzoku*), a spiritual essence produced by history in order to accomplish its work. The past had seen such peoples in Greece. The once great vitality of the Latinate civilization that followed was now "played out," and it had lost its original genius. The Germans were the *Urvolk* to come. Fichte's criteria for originality seem to have been twofold. The first lay in language—more accurately, the "spirit" of the language, its genius for expressing transcendental ideas. Second, the *Urvolk* had achieved consciousness (*jikaku*) of its historical mission of translating reason into action in historical time, of serving as the vessel of reason.

Fichte did not conceive of Germany's regeneration as an imperialistic crusade.[142] Germany was not to turn around and attempt to subjugate those who had humiliated it. Rather, the reborn state was to lead spiritually, by example. What Germany achieved within, other nations could regard as a moral law to be made their own. Nations were to be preserved as such. This is a theme we have encountered in the earlier discussion of Kant, but one that for Nanbara extends back to his education and non-church religiosity.

What qualified Germany—we can see the circle of reason closing—was its self-consciousness of mission. Fichte's Germany, despite a long historical past, was to enter fresh "into a stream of time which had already corrupted other peoples." [143] This through the realization of what *ought* to be, of the progress of *Humanität,* by Germany. The urgent need of the present thus impinged on the past, and the more urgent need of the future on the present. Thus Fichte's Germany, as Windelband described it, was a "Germany lying in utopia." [144]

Fichte saw with great specificity what features of social organization would characterize his German utopia and the steps toward their attainment. These he described in the work that announced his "later" period, *Der geschlossene Handelsstaat* of 1800. Since Nanbara professed to find in it suggestions for the organizing principles of a just, postliberal order, his account of it may serve as a bridge to our discussion of Nanbara's Japan.

Nowhere in Fichte's oeuvre, Nanbara points out, are the notions of nationalism and socialism systematically linked. [145] *Der geschlossene Handelsstaat,* while it recognizes problems in the economic order insoluble by the individual moral agent, retains traces of the distinction of legal from moral that would disappear from its author's later work. The state at this point is limited to a regulative function over the national community. Its historical particularity was barely established. It was thus the task of later interpreters, Nanbara said, to attempt such systematization, and of critics to distinguish potentially valid syntheses of Fichte's ideas from violent imposters.

We saw earlier that Nanbara found in Fichte the concept of the nation as a "spiritual essence," one united linguistically (although in an abstract sense) but most of all by a shared consciousness of personal freedom and national mission. Such a community was the ideal underlying Fichte's economic thought. What sort of system would best reflect man's nature as a self-creating "active being" among like beings? Each individual was to be guaranteed basic rights—life, property, labor—mutual recognition of such implying that individual freedom is self-limiting. The common good of the community necessarily requires (as in Plato's Republic) a division of labor. But in Fichte's conception occupation is "freely" chosen, given what nature has provided and the prior development of the requisite civic consciousness. Society is further divided into corporations, whose activities are directed by a class of "civil officials" who serve the common good, not the state apparatus. Their regulation of work is also educative. Given the rights each individual possesses, and the materials provided by the state for the pursuit of his chosen activity, all should be free to "act on their freedom." This is what the state seeks to make possible. But a problem arises that Nanbara does not address. Utopian schemes that place a class of supervisors to assist in the attainment of freedom are plagued by the nagging question, "Quis custodiet ipsos custodes?" Where do the self-conscious, nonegoistic civil officials come from? Who appoints them? What guarantee is there against abuse? There is an infinite regress in idealist thinking on society. Sooner or later one runs up against the unyielding core of faith that *Sollen* will become *Sein*. It is from this core that the system is spun out. It seems to be part and parcel of such thinking that an elite is required to regulate activity until it becomes self-maintaining. Nanbara certainly never outgrew this sense of his own indispensability, with its concomitant administrative bent. But this did not make him authoritarian, and there is a difference.

To return to Fichte: as the title of the work implies, the state is closed to foreign trade by individuals, Fichte believing that control of trade by the state was the only guarantee of economic self-sufficiency. Self-sufficiency in turn was the only guarantee that the state could pursue its *moral* end, which was "to promote . . . conditions which facilitate the moral development without which there is no true freedom." [146] Freedom, that is, not to possess or accumulate, but to act. At this point in his philosophical development, Fichte believed that as planner and controller of economic activity, the state was fated to "wither away." When the moral level of the community had risen so that individuals spontaneously "manifested reason," the *Vernunftreich* would have arrived, and the state would give way to the nation.

Nanbara recognized the potential for excessive centralization and power hoarding by the elite in Fichte's outline. He was, of course, aware that the economically backward Prussia on which Fichte based his thinking at the dawn of the nineteenth century scarcely provided a standpoint from which to prescribe remedies for the inequities of industrial capitalism. [147] But he believed that Fichte's precocious insights into the nature of laissez-faire economy remained valid. Fichte had warned that such a system would produce ever greater disparity of wealth and be consumed by class conflict. No system premised on egoism could provide a foundation for moral progress, period. All these were ideas Nanbara found apposite. In terms of his philosophy of coordinate values, it is evident that economic activity, while an indispensable means in cultural life, could never be an end in itself. It had to be directed to serve the end of justice, that is, political value. Left unregulated, it would subject the community to "unease and contingency" that would corrode the material foundation of cultural life. At the same time, Nanbara admitted the existence of independent laws of economic life (never spelled out), the attempt to gain total control over which would produce injustice far worse than existed already.[148] Presumably these laws have to do with the "basic rights" Fichte had defined: life, labor, property.

With its regulation of production, distribution, and foreign trade, Fichte's closed commercial state did indeed add up to "national socialism." But Nanbara makes an immediate qualification. First, the "nation" in Fichte's sense is above all a cultural—rational, normative—concept premised on a community of free individuals. The state to which the regulation of the economy is entrusted serves this community, not itself, by ensuring the just distribution of goods as the foundation of moral progress. Fichte's socialism, Nanbara ventures, could best be termed "cultural." All of which, he admits, sounds very utopian. But do we not all of us desire "a social order in which all individuals participate in social labor, and to the degree that they do so, also participate in the enjoyment of the fruits of that labor; [a social order] in which, in this sense, the rights and duties of the multitude are held equally, so that one segment of the whole membership may not be exploited by any other?"[149] Such an order is socialist. "However much one may despise the name or try to force it into oblivion," Nanbara concludes, "socialism remains the task [kadai] of our age."[150]

Nor was there any question that "contemporary socialism"—national and Marxian—had failed to bring about such an order.

In Marxism Nanbara saw a doctrine that remained imprisoned in a nineteenth-century positivist framework. If Nazism erred in identifying the national community with race, at least it had recognized the deep yearning of the postwar generation for some sort of identity. Marxism, on the other hand, continued to buy into a utilitarian concept of society in which individuals were atoms in aggregate, with "needs" to be satisfied through the application of social mechanics. This was happiness: the satisfaction of want.[151] The hard kernel of truth in Marxism lay in its recognition of the exploitative nature of class structure in capitalist so-

ciety, its reduction of individuals to means of acquisition. Philosophically, the concept of alienation derived from the "activist idealism" of
Fichte and Hegel (in fact there are hints of "proto-alienation" in Kant).
Nanbara duly recognized this lineage. He fully acknowledged the nobility and moral passion of Marx's desire to "humanize" the proletariat
through the restoration to this basic class of the means of production,
deprived of which it had fallen into an intolerable state of alienation
from its "active" essence. But Marx and Engels, Nanbara believed, had
committed an error as grave as their insight was profound. Despite the
claims of their socialism to be scientific, they in fact based their hopes of
utopia on a value judgment far more irrational than any Fichte had
dreamt of. This lay in their postulate of a self-propelled dialectical motion of economic "laws." At some future date, "history" would begin
with the restoration to the working class of its productive essence. With
this collective control of matter established, happiness (the satisfaction
of wants) and liberation would follow. Nanbara thus understood Engels's famous "in the last analysis" to mean that the laws of motion in
the economic base were "irrational" and lay beyond human power to
direct with any constant certainty.[152] They had first to be believed in,
then elucidated in objective reality: this was their "scientific" aspect.
Even a cursory look at Nanbara's references (he wrote in 1940) shows
that he relied almost exclusively on Engels, always tending to absorb
Marx into Engels, attributing to Marx a materialism so total as to be
untenable.

Nanbara's main objection, however, was not to the scientism of
Marxian thought. To his mind, Marxism reduced humanity to an empirical and psychological amalgam. At one level, it denied any primary
noneconomic bonds between human beings. The notion of a national
community that had inspired Fichte was rejected as at best historically
necessary, the ideological expression of a bourgeoisie in quest of a national market; like the state, concern with "nationality" was fated to
wither away. Marxists, of course, had gone deeper, denying humanity's
spiritual nature. In so doing, Nanbara recognized, Marx was reacting to
the tenacious hold of institutional religion over society and trying to
show how deeply embedded relations of dominance, expressed in religious terms, maintained humanity in alienation. But had Marx not done
away with humanity in the process? Nanbara wondered whether there
was any human essence left to liberate once its spirituality was denied.
Marxism as a worldview had, in fact, condemned itself to permanent
poverty.[153]

If Marxism "could not feed the hungry heart," Nanbara's opposition to it, philosophically, and politically, paled in comparison to his visceral horror of Nazism. To his mind Nazism posed a far greater threat, and he poured his heart into his wartime essays on the Nazi Weltanschauung.[154] Nevertheless, it had first to be understood that Nazism was itself a "counterattack," a racial naturalism opposed to the "social" (economic) naturalism of Marx, which had arisen initially as part of the nineteenth-century critique of bourgeois individualism. It was the answer of the postwar middle classes to socialism, and had, in fact, incorporated socialist elements into its ideology.[155]

Nazism was a dangerous failure because it had mistaken blood for community, vitalism for spirit. Its concept of freedom consisted in the collective right of Germans to treat other peoples as things (*Sache*). As such it was a direct repudiation of the entire idealist tradition, essentially a doctrine of race and power-worship, divisive and hostile. It vaunted the community but reduced its members to living as a herd.[156]

Nanbara found particularly odious the myth making of Alfred Rosenberg, to whose *Mythus der 20. Jahrhunderts* he devoted, in 1942, a searing critical essay. His hostility stemmed partly from the fact that Rosenberg had concocted a wretched "Germanic Christianity," which he intended as a heroic religion fit for the *Herrenvolk*. That Rosenberg had misappropriated Nietzsche's *Übermensch* for gross ideological purposes was obvious. Nanbara refused to indulge in a hunt for the "roots of Nazism," however, distinguishing Nietzsche's essentially individualist will-to-power from Nazism, which he regarded as a phenomenon of the mass.[157]

Not that Nanbara was so terribly concerned to defend Nietzsche. What Rosenberg had perpetrated symbolized something far worse. His "Germanic Christianity" parodied an idea that Nanbara, as we know, took very seriously. In the modern world, he believed, "national" forms of Christianity would be called upon to "complete the Reformation." Rosenberg, ironically, used precisely the same terms to describe the mission of his brainchild. We have seen how much Nanbara owed to Uchimura, and his debt to Kant and Fichte. It should not be difficult to imagine how intolerable it was for him to see his deepest hopes mocked under the aegis of a regime of nihilists. It goes without saying, also, that Nanbara's attack on Germany in 1942 (before the tide had turned against the Axis) was no cheap shot. The Hitler regime was his country's ally in war.

Nazism was diabolical, an inverted form of what Nanbara took to be the most profound of human values. Freedom was not to be enjoyed in isolation; historically as well as morally, it is within the life of the political community—its paradigm being the Greek polis—that freedom takes on meaning. This idea of freedom-in-community was then immeasurably deepened by the intrusion of Christianity into the classical world. Nazism twisted this truth into its monstrous opposite.

Nanbara admitted the apparent similarities between Fichte's nationalism and Nazi ideology. His response—that simply blaming past thinkers for the uses to which their systems are put ignores more immediate problems—has a certain validity. But it also skirts an important issue. Is the "use" of the system merely a willful abuse? Is it only an accident—would not the national socialists try anything, claim anything, twist anything, in order to broaden their appeal? Perhaps. On the other hand, was there no underlying pattern, a persistent logic, of the idealist philosophical discourse that was also problematic? Why the virtually presumptive philosophical capitulation to the state, particularly after Kant? Why the privileging of the *national* community? Was this inevitable once the tense dualism of Kant was resolved, as Fichte and Hegel resolved it? And was this ultimate identification of freedom with obedience for the ruled, and with power for the state or party, simply a question of ambiguity and misunderstanding?

Perhaps all this is to say that Nanbara was in the end caught in his own idealist web. He was intensely self-conscious in his interpretation of Fichte; he had made a value choice, a commitment to read Fichte along lines that seem hopelessly strained. It was an audacious attempt to use Fichte to overcome what Nanbara regarded as a desperate cultural and philosophical crisis. We may, indeed must, question his choice of weapons. At the same time we are bound to recognize the logic underlying that choice. Deeply repelled by the "false totalities" of race or class, Nanbara urged a redeparture along idealist lines. Only idealism—the only philosophy not soiled by idolatry—recognized and cherished the autonomy of the prime values. Only idealism could save modern societies from the common fate of total systems, the total politicization of life, which was at the same time its depoliticization.[158]

In Fichte Nanbara found his own voice. This said that nationality lay in essence in a spiritual ideal. True, Fichte had given far too much weight to the metaphysical claims of the state. He had nearly mistaken the glimmerings of his own intellect for the "separate light" of the heavenly city. "Man must conceptualize," Fichte had said.[159] But he tried to do too much. Still, he had come as close as anyone to the "synthesis" Nanbara held to be the unending project of Western—and now Japanese—culture.

MEUM AND VERUM

We now face the question of Nanbara's intellectual and political position in Japan. We had a glimpse at the outset of this chapter of the somewhat anomalous institutional setting in which Nanbara worked. But where and how did he fit into the larger discourse of the early Shōwa period? By what means did he make his views known?

Nanbara sought to spiritualize and universalize the national consciousness of the Japanese people through his philosophy, as Fichte had sought to do with Germans. Classical German thinkers, including Fichte, sought to "restore the expressive unity of the polis," which they considered Greece's legacy to Germany. Similarly, Nanbara sought to combine the "universal history" of the West with his own past. Fichte and Nanbara alike pursued nations, as Windelband had said, "lying in utopia."

There are two major flaws in the analogy of Nanbara to Fichte that may be illuminating. First, the religious context. Japan had no Christian tradition. Fichte's religion, however much it may have struck contemporary critics as "Fichtianity,"[160] was inconceivable without the entire history of an actual and avowedly universal church, and of the impact made on it by the Lutheran Reformation in Germany. In its religious foundation, Nanbara's vision seems a greatly attenuated version of Fichte's, and its realization was even more indefinitely postponed than Fichte's German utopia. Moreover, Nanbara's thinking was symptomatic of the intellectual culture of Japanese public men, in its assumption of a basic congruence in the historical development of Japan and the West. Fichte could pronounce upon a long history of which his nation was entirely a part. For Nanbara, however, history had begun, in a sense, only at the point of convergence.

Such, indeed, was the key assumption of the liberalism Nanbara, along with Minobe Tatsukichi, embodied. The "trend of the times," Minobe had insisted, was toward individual liberty, and it was up to public men to make sure that Japan was no exception. But something had gone dreadfully wrong. The cause was not far to seek: internally, individualistic liberalism had atomized the societies to which it had promised so much. Its political and economic systems seemed to have collapsed, leaving the way open for systems of subjection, one based on the "false totality" of race, the other on that of class. As these systems grew in power, their effects could not but be felt everywhere. Japan was in no respect an exception. The clamor grew louder for unanimity and control, for the elimination of all threats to the state, including threats in the realm of thought. Aggression was applauded; a spurious communalism and appeal to myth treated reasoned opposition as selfish disloyalty or as a mask for revolutionary intent.

Particularly after the Manchurian incident, Nanbara seems to have felt that Japan simply lost its bearings. In a sense the analogy to Fichte may not be so far-fetched. For although Japan was a sovereign state, in Nanbara's eyes political rationality was fast declining. At once ideologically "on call" and deeply troubled, Nanbara sought to respond. Two means, sometimes combined, were available to him for the expression of such a conviction—"pure scholarship" read as prophecy, and professions of "qualified loyalty." As an example of the first, consider Nanbara's account of the "third period" of the historical scheme Fichte set forth in his *Grundzüge des gegenwärtigen Zeitalters*, 1804–5. This was the age of complete national abasement, of "sin run rampant," where reason is despised, freedom equated with egotism, the sense of wholeness and belonging entirely subordinate to selfish impulse. It is an age, as Nanbara put it, in which "people believe that they can perfect themselves simply by getting what they want." Nanbara's conclusion is of particular interest:

> In the extreme development of egoism, the motive for all political action in the national life is decided thus: the politicians and military who make up the governing class are all corrupt, lacking both "insight into the lofty dictates of political wisdom" and "an understanding of true interest." Driven by the schemes that they latch on to for immediate benefit—benefit from the standpoint of their own class, that is to say, nothing more than selfish impulse—*they recklessly expand armaments and plot the extension of their own territory at the expense of their neighbors. That such action may earn them the distrust and animosity of other nations, they show not the least concern. Forgetting that, vis-à-vis the outside the state is a member of an international body, and seized by egoistic self-deception, they faithlessly walk away from the unity of the whole, and find themselves, in the end, isolated from the world.*
>
> At home the people in general who make up the class of the governed, driven by selfish impulse, turn their back on the whole of the national order, and act only in accordance with what they happen to desire. But because this egoism recognizes no end whatsoever outside itself, it may result in the unforeseen imposition on the people of the ends set by another—leaving them willy-nilly under the control of a small number of powerful individuals. The dictatorship of these strongmen is in itself carried out for its own benefit; to

protect the interests of the whole is merely a claim they make to further their selfish ends. As a result the ties of unity that bind the whole are cut, the people summoned finally to their own destruction. This is precisely the political fate that befell Germany, a national tragedy that the radical changes of the age brought about.[161]

Nanbara had seen the handwriting on the wall, and it spelled Kwantung Army. Yet it was not, Maruyama Masao reminds us, Nanbara's sole purpose to use "pure" scholarship as a mere cover for *Zeitkritik*. Rather, the "purity" of his scholarship (i.e., the fact that it does not mention Japan!) was a vehicle for Nanbara's highly normative worldview to express itself. It was a code, but more than a code. For even in coded form, the content, an account of a genuine philosophical problem, was meaningful. Nanbara wrote trusting that his small circle of educated, largely academic readers would grasp both the pure and prescriptive message of his text.[162]

Even in terms of the latter, however, Nanbara's concern was not with militarism or corruption per se. It was with the Japanese state itself, that which was, especially after the Minobe case, beyond scrutiny. For one who believed as deeply as Nanbara in rationality *and* nationality, the dilemma was acute. The object of criticism, first of all, was also the object of love. (What was patriotism if not love of community illuminated by the "separate light" of faith?)[163] But it was also an object whose unworthy guardians forbade any searching inquiry that might have public consequences and weaken their power. Writing about the state presented difficulties for a third reason. Japan's evolution since Meiji toward the sharing of worldviews with the West, Nanbara declared early in 1941, was beyond anyone's power to stop. Thus, given the emergence of Japan as a modern state and the thorough involvement of Japan in "Western" culture, an ideological war *against* the West, we may infer, was for Nanbara a war by Japan against itself.[164]

Nanbara's central concern, therefore, was to repudiate as false the view that, having absorbed the technology of political, economic, and military power sufficiently to build an anti-Western empire with itself as the motor, there was nothing to prevent Japan from now "purifying" its culture—the "materialism" and "individualism" of the West jettisoned and the spirit of the *minzoku* freed from the Western forms that suffocated it. To Nanbara (however anti-individualistic his own views) the idea of any "return" was intolerable—shoddy, reactionary, and ahistorical. The more refined argument of "overcoming the modern" theorists, that Japan was actually on the cutting edge of *ultramodernity*, he

regarded as little more than a variation on the theme of "return," and
gave it little credence. Far from "returning" to or "purifying" the *Nihon
seishin*, the real task of the present was to grasp the soul of the West.
"There can be nothing more laughable or dangerous than to speak of
'Western' or 'European' culture without penetrating to its root, and to
act instead only on the extreme forms to which it has been driven in
modern times; on the changes it has undergone within this single generation."[165] To a significant degree, understanding the West meant understanding Japan, in terms not of contrast but of likeness, not of cultural
debt but of a common predicament. Underlying this defense of "convergence" lay the fear that the nightmare that had come upon the West
(Nanbara must have had Germany in mind) would soon be Japan's
own.[166] Because this was so, Nanbara could, as we saw above, use accounts of remote historical and philosophical problems to make criticisms of Japanese reality that, if expressed openly, would have made him
a criminal.

Hence the double meaning of Nanbara's study of Plato, which was
written in 1938. It deals with the ambiguities of Plato's Republic and
specifically with the controversy over its interpretation between neo-
Kantians on the one hand, and followers of Nietzsche, especially the
George-Kreis, on the other. Nanbara's animus, as we remarked earlier,
was directed against the "poetic" or "Dionysian" interpretation of the
polis as a "community of life" (*sei no kyōdōtai*) bound, through the
charismatic action of the philosopher-king, to a particular myth and its
own gods. For Nanbara and his mentors the danger of such a notion of
polity was twofold. First, it rendered the concept of justice (*dikē*) a "national emotion" and the relation of ruler to ruled one of charismatic
authority dispensed from above, matched by devotion from below.[167]
Second, with obedience to a "mystical aristocracy"—spiritual dictatorship—the only conceivable mode of political communication, the freedom of the citizen dissolves before the authority of the community, and
only the elite are free. The entire dialectic of ideal and phenomenal,
which Nanbara took as the key to understanding the *Politeia*, is lost.
Whether intentionally or not, the proponents of the "mythic" view of
the polis in effect handed political philosophy over to the ideologues of
"nationalist" reaction:

> To become human becomes possible only under the aegis of the state. Not
> only must individuals approach the world of truth and beauty through the
> state, the national community represents [all] moral ideals, and men only as-

sume their personalities in the state. In addition, even the realm of religion is
understood in an exclusively mundane [*chiteki*] sense; no *Civitas Dei* exists
to transcend the state. No, the state itself means the realization of the heavenly kingdom. What is established here is the ideal of a "religion of the state"
or a "religion of the *Volk*" [*minzoku shūkyō*] along the ancient pattern. The
eternal salvation of the soul does not—indeed, must not—take place outside
the terrestrial state. That the emphasis on the this-worldly, here-and-now
sense of religion ends in the mystification of the political state simply follows
of necessity.[168]

True, Nanbara himself virtually reverenced the state as the necessary
locus of the realization of justice in human society. But, he insisted,
there is a great difference between saying that the state *is* the font of all
value, and that the state ought to protect, and provide the material
foundation for, values that it does not itself embody. It was in such a
distinction that Nanbara saw the salvation of any future politics. One
wonders, however, whether in practice this crucial distinction would remain in sight. In the absence of strong restraint by Tocqueville's "intermediate powers" and a lively social self-consciousness, could the state
simply "protect" and "provide"? Could the state, as many neo-Kantians
envisioned it, really unite "cultural individualism" and "state socialism" without inevitably vitiating the former?

Nanbara probably sympathized more with the Nietzschean critique
of the "bourgeois liberal" view of the state than he lets on at times. The
turn to myth, he recognized, bespoke a deep need to bring life to political society. Liberalism had so totally identified politics and individual/
group interest that the political community was reduced to a venal club.
But the danger, for Nanbara, of confusing myth with a concrete social
program, and attempting to put it into practice, was all too obvious.
Return to myth was not part of the solution, but of the problem: "The
'crisis' of the state currently bruited about lies less in the modern state
itself than in the very advocacy" of reactionary programs of "return."[169]
It was the attempt to substitute a "mythic" or "poetic" understanding
of the state for a solid epistemology and critical sense that was responsible for turning the twentieth century into a wasteland of dictator-
ships.[170] For with the advent of such "theocracies" (*shinsei seiji*)

the development of scholarly thought in general is eliminated, and together
with it all theoretical consideration of society is blocked also. There is no
longer any freedom [*yochi,* lit. "space"] for inquiry into the meaning and
value of the life and behavior of the state. The reason is that matters pertain-
ing to the political sphere become identified with religious mystery. And if

the latter is placed beyond our reach, basic reflection on the former becomes impossible.[171]

"The most urgent duty of the present," Nanbara wrote on another occasion, "is first the establishment of political and social values."[172] Nanbara directed this fundamental indictment at a state he never names. He had communicated in "pure" code what his student Maruyama Masao was to make explicit in his essays on "ultranationalism," written scarcely a decade later. For Maruyama had identified as "ultra" nationalism the ideology according to which the state reserved all right to define its subjects' values and shape their consciences. Thus we can see that, whatever Maruyama's other influences, and allowing ample room for his undoubted genius, Nanbara's writings of the late 1930s and early 1940s were broaching themes that assumed prime importance in the work of his "unworthy disciple." Without the intervention of catastrophic defeat, all would have remained in code.[173]

Nanbara held it an article of faith that the spread of the "rational spirit" of Greece, whatever obstacles history might place in its path, could never be stopped. His greatest hope was to make this spirit the "common sense" of his homeland. Along with a noninstitutional Christianity, it was to shape a new Japanese culture. I shall leave aside for now the question of how much Nanbara's hopes reflected the desperation of his time and place. Did he seriously expect Japan to convert? I shall defer for the last chapter the opportunity to sort out the myopia from what, I believe, is of enduring value in Nanbara's position.

Meanwhile, another issue emerges. What would be "Japanese" about the culture Nanbara envisioned? Was there to be a final contest between *meum* and *verum* after all? Nanbara could see no need to choose. It was not as if it were demanded that one swear allegiance to another *country*. Thus his occasional writings on Japan from 1934 to 1945 never waver in their appeal to the critical spirit. At the same time, in seeking to answer this question, they reveal the strain of constant calculated dissociation from the immediate policies of the state he served.

In "Man and Politics," Nanbara had called "for truth to prevail, though the world perish," the utterance that caught the eye of Minoda Muneki and the Genri Nihonsha, earning Nanbara a diatribe in Minoda's *Kokka to daigaku*. "Man and Politics" does a good job of pulling together many of the threads that run through Nanbara's studies of Plato, Kant, and Fichte (the work on Nazism came later). We need not detain ourselves with the arguments of this essay again here. But the conclusion is of interest as a profession of "qualified loyalty."

Having pushed our inquiry to this point, we reach the final problem to which we must give our attention. Namely, what can we in Japan learn from the problems outlined above? From ancient times, the Japanese spirit, with the imperial house at its center, cohered in and developed out of the "land born of the Eight Great Islands"; that is, out of the life of the political state. Justly deemed the formation [*kessei*] of the pure sentiment and will of the Japanese people, with its profound spiritual tradition in the realm of politics above all, this spirit knows its like nowhere in the world. Recent years have prompted many to reflect on this. In the future development of Japanese culture (and in contrast to the situation of totalitarianism), we must strive, without losing any of our passion for our Japanese people and historical culture, to establish firmly the spirit of human freedom and critical rationalism. Just as in the past through Confucian culture and Indian Buddhism, so over the next centuries Japan will, through confrontation [*taiketsu*] with world culture, ceaselessly create herself [*taezu mizukara o sōzō shi*], bringing to development the Japanese culture that is to be. The problem: the "worldedness" [*sekaisei*] and universal historical significance of that culture. [In the creation of such a culture,] I believe, lies our mission as scholars, and the mission of this university.[174]

It becomes clear that this continuous political tradition, the *bansei ikkei no tōchi* of the Meiji constitution, most characterized Japan. This was the genius of the nation. Fichte could only dream and manipulate history to place German genius in a typically intangible "spirit" of the language. This somehow linked the *Volk* to a communitarian ideal that, in turn, united it with Hellas. Nanbara in his Fichtean persona could point to the "actual" past, one that had been all but created, of course, in the restorationist intellectual endeavor that began with Mito. There was no need, now, to strain after universality. The Restoration and subsequent creation of the constitutional order had brought Japan into the stream of world history.[175] In placing the imperial house at the center of a Japan both traditional and modern, Nanbara joined the cultural historian Watsuji Tetsurō and a great company of other Japanese of the modern period. Although Nanbara speaks of the emperor as effecting the "organic unity" of the people, he downplays the vaunted "inherent" Japanese reverence for, or the inclination to worship, the imperial house. And while acknowledging the traditional identification of the emperor as *arahitogami* ("living" god), he stresses the "realism" of the relation as one based on fear and affection directed toward the sovereign as the nucleus of a familial national community with natural, historical origins.[176] For Nanbara the *kokutai* is a historical and "spiritual" datum (an element in *mentalité?*) without consideration of which the nation can neither be understood nor attain the "worldedness" he desired for it.

Nanbara's concern that the Japanese attain "worldedness" (i.e., in-

clusion *as particular* in a temporal totality) as a nation, rather than as
individual persons, seems significant. The contrast with another contemporary philosopher also heavily indebted to Plato, Simone Weil, is
rather striking, the more so because on some points her thought and
Nanbara's resemble each other. In "Forms of the Implicit Love of God,"
an essay written in 1941–42, Richard Rees notes, Weil "instances one's
mother tongue and one's city or native countryside as examples of the
metaxu, things which, without being of absolute value in themselves, can
serve as intermediaries between man and the absolute beauty which is
the real object of his love." [177]

Clearly, for Nanbara nationality was more than an intermediary in
the salvation of an individual. [178] As we saw in his assertion that Uchimura's greatness lay in his standing "as a *Japanese* before God," nationality signified an eternal and collective identity, providentially fixed. All
of Nanbara's deep concern for freedom of personality, which is unques-
tionable, must nevertheless be understood in the light of this belief. Even
vis-à-vis eternity, Nanbara could not assert an absolute universality that
pertained to personality. How could he possibly do so for contingent
man? Rather, he venerated an ineradicable personal and community
identity, and fought, on this ground, the claims of the contemporary political state to absorb them both.

Nanbara remained consistently uncomfortable with the empirical individual—or, better, with the individual acting out of self-interest, or
joining together with others to do so. This is abundantly clear in his
most specific statement of principle in defense of the constitutional
order, which came in a talk given in 1938 on "Contemporary Political
Ideals and the Japanese Spirit." In it Nanbara dramatizes the ever-
present dilemma of the public man "on call": the tendency to wrap potent criticism in an affirmation that defuses it. To wit:

> The parliamentary system, especially, represents throughout the world the
> political method for the self-determined popular will of human individuals
> who have come to consciousness with the advent of modern times [*kinsei*].
> In contrast, recent years have seen that system denied and ignored, not only
> from the communist standpoint, but from the fascist and "national essen-
> tialist" [*kokusuishugi*] as well. But can we not . . . on the foundation of the
> national community [*kokumin kyōdōtai*] as distinguished from the individu-
> alism of liberal democracy, breathe life into the parliamentary system and
> build it anew? In this way we can rescue it from the conflicts of interest be-
> tween parties, factions, and individuals. . . . The problem for the future be-
> comes rather how on this basis to make politics reflect the will of the Japa-
> nese people [*kokumin taishū*]. What we have in mind, then, as opposed to an

individualistic "liberal democratic government" [*jiyū minshusei*] is a new "communitarian democracy" [*kyōdōtai shūminsei*]. . . .

In the actual conduct of politics, provided that the various organs [of state] identified in the constitution adhere strictly to their allotted functions [*bun*], no conflict or tension ought to arise either among them or between higher and lower officials within them. For one organ to abuse its authority, especially by the use of force, is entirely incompatible with the fundamental character of our state. As long as the spirit of our constitution is rigorously upheld, there should be no room for the establishment of a dictatorship [*dokusai seiji*].[179]

Thus Nanbara tried to satisfy the demand of critical reason with an attack on abuses of constitutional authority—although not stated, the targets were the military and Education Ministry bureaucracy. The criticism rests, as it did with Minobe, on pristine constitutional principle. But the offense of those particular organs lay precisely in their "individualism," in their attempt to "privatize power."[180] The terms have shifted from Minobe's emphasis on individual (and, by extension, corporate) *liberty,* to the protection of the true, constitutionally defined "national community" from those who would represent it falsely. Only now, included among the "parties and factions" who obstruct the formation of this community, Nanbara numbers the military itself, along with segments of the civil bureaucracy. He is unable (constitutionally, as it were) to defend individual rights as such. Modes for gaining consent within a "communitarian" democracy remain totally obscure. To this extent, Nanbara's criticism of abuses, while to the point and deserved, blended all too easily into the communitarian rhetoric of those who were far more willing to destroy, rather than rectify, the parliamentary system as a whole.

At a deeper level, however, Nanbara was true to Minobe. For his argument rested on the traditional division of *kokutai*—as a historical principle of unity rather than license for unlimited prerogative—from *seitai,* on which Minobe had placed his own defense. It was an argument, moreover, that held both entities to be susceptible of rational examination. If Nanbara's critique of contemporary politics—an area admittedly not his strong suit—was uncertain in its implications, the same may not be said of his perceptions of the ideological use of the term *kokutai*.

As we have seen, Nanbara, like Minobe, viewed *kokutai* as "the cohesion of the Japanese spirit." (Frank Miller's observation is apt here: "While [Minobe] could not quite escape from, he would not escape into the world of 'national polity.'")[181] Yet that spirit was incomplete. For all its peerless, open simplicity and realism, it was entirely specific and un-transmissible to the world as a whole. It needed a universal (rational, critical) and transcultural foundation. The "Japanese spirit" was not a Weltanschauung.[182]

It was from this position that Nanbara made his strongest attack on the philosophical manipulation of *Nihon seishin*. As we have seen, the greatest danger he recognized lay in the potential for statolatry if a criti-cal separation of values was neglected. A case in point was Tanabe Ha-jime (1885–1962), whose work Nanbara castigated in a section of *Kokka to shūkyō*. The successor to Nishida Kitarō as doyen of the "Kyoto school" of philosophy, Tanabe had given generously of his philo-sophical talent in an attempt to identify "ideological war" (*shisōsen*) as the manifestation of an "absolute dialectic"—the violence of history it-self. This held that the state was the only logical mediator between "kind" (*shu* = *minzoku*, the "self-alienation of the absolute") and "in-dividual" (*ko,* its negation). The state is subject (*shutai*), "absolute so-ciety" and the "archetype of existence." As such, Tanabe claimed, the state in the East Asian universe, one informed by Mahāyāna and par-ticularly Zen Buddhist thought, represented the functional analogue of Christ in the West. The state was a structure that "completed the dia-lectical truth of Christianity and liberated it from its mythic limita-tions." People as "kind" thus participated in the state as revealed (logi-cally disclosed) being, and were thus "saved." Tanabe's religion of the dialectic, Nanbara claimed, was a "religion of the state." Despite its pre-tensions to universality, he pressed, Tanabe's system lacked any political principle that could guarantee world order—"which is what we really need"—since it had merely divinized the state. "People might think" that Tanabe's ideas represented the great cultural synthesis of East Asia and the West, which could only have come from Japan; only here had sufficient intermingling taken place for this world-historical mission to be set under way. As a Christian, of course, Nanbara refused to allow that the state could logically absorb personality, since the core of per-sonality lay in the created soul of the individual. Having drunk too deeply at the Hegelian spring, Tanabe had produced a "synthesis" that eliminated the difference between religion, philosophy, and state. It was a pantheism of a subtle theoretical kind, with a long philosophical pedi-gree, and more insidious than Nazism for that reason.[183]

We are now in a position to look at Nanbara's thought as a whole.

There should be no need to list its constituent elements or the religious motives that inspired it. The main issue, it seems to me, remains that of freedom and community. As we have seen many times, Nanbara believed humanity to be called to a freedom greater than that of the liberal "freedom from." Its attainment involved a paradox in that this freedom was inherently political. In order to be free, individuals had to live in a modern polis; that is, a community of persons recognized as such. Could such a polis be realized in the modern world? It had the interest politics of individualistic liberalism, and its negation, the all-*and*-nothing politics of collectivism and statolatry, to overcome. This was the dilemma of the modern. Fichte had pointed—truth subsisting in error—to the divine in resolving the dialectic that history had revealed. Freedom seen as "freedom for" or "freedom to," oriented toward an ideal, would involve individuals in a cultural collectivity (a *Volk*) with a shared spiritual purpose. That ideal was the realization on earth by each nation, as providence ordained, of the perfect freedom and perfect community of the kingdom of God. By participating in such a realization, the person would find freedom.

Each nation was unique; the stamp of nationality on every individual was eternal. The person inherited the cultural uniqueness that was his nation's own genius. Fichte saw the German genius in its language and sense of mission. Nanbara saw the Japanese genius in an idealized continuous tradition of imperial "rule" over the Japanese people. Fichte had also pointed out with great cogency that a culture without a state would not last, that the end of culture is to achieve perfect "statehood." Nanbara inherited this position. His eyes meanwhile were directed toward a Japan lying, as surely as Fichte's Germany, "in utopia."

This basic position enabled Nanbara to make some extremely daring criticisms of contemporary political reality. It gave him a standard that was reinforced by status. As a member of the "cultural apparatus" of his country, Nanbara defended a philosophical liberalism that he considered to be consistent with both the *kokutai* and universal reason.

Nanbara was not comfortable with the empirical individual. His defense of uniqueness was restricted to the cultural sphere, which implied, to be sure, the affective life of the individual. But, as the example of his spiritual hero Uchimura makes plain, nationality was privileged in defining individuality, even with respect to eternal destiny. At the mundane level, Nanbara largely eschews mention of conflict within the cultural community, having made the implicit value judgment that any economic conflict ought to be harmonized through the development of the proper consciousness. Such consciousness would be created through community life, inculcated for some indefinite period by an elite.

The account so far, however, omits the salient fact of the whole development of Nanbara's thinking. It came in the midst of unprecedented political crisis, and ultimately of total war. His elite consciousness brought with it a sense of responsibility for, and of the need to suffer with, those who sacrificed themselves for the nation. Along with his criticism and opposition to Japan's war policies, therefore, Nanbara felt bound to his nation by a sense of responsibility that was both liberating and paralyzing. He was a responsible witness. This attitude hearkens back to Nanbara's understanding of Uchimura's interim ethic: Remain in place. It also reflected the organizational imperative of the academy as a segment of the bureaucracy. Public, organizational, and personal identity were closely aligned. The more desperate Nanbara's need to serve critically, the more he clung to his role. This was an operation that required highly developed rhetorical "feelers" as to what speech, under what circumstances, would threaten that role, and what would not. There is no questioning the depth of motive and sense of a higher calling that powered the evident calculation that went into his work.

It is this balance of calculation and urgency that both constricts Nanbara's writing and gives it its great pathos. Its subject was the state, the summit of political achievement, and now the cause of folly, misery, and death on a worldwide scale. Whole civilizations faced destruction, including Nanbara's own. The political message of his work, clearly discernible despite its protective covering of Germanic rhetoric and abstraction, sought to address the causes of the crisis. Writing of Japan, Nanbara warned and pleaded with the nation to abandon its suicidal ideological struggle, all the while seeing that catastrophe was inevitable.

How to prevent the reduction of Japan to a gutted relic? How to preserve the *kokutai*? Nanbara's only weapon was logos: the "independent and deliberate use of the word." I shall trace below Nanbara's growing sense that the center had not held, as it is recorded in his poetic diary. And I shall briefly examine his attempt to persuade the ruling elite to bring the war to a close. Together, these explorations should demonstrate the fusion, in crisis, of Nanbara's private and public being.

WAR AND LOGOS

By late 1944 informed opinion and common sense had long confirmed that Japan's war effort was doomed.[184] Earlier in the year,
Nanbara had recorded in his poetic journal an all too familiar event:

> Greeted by cherries in blossom
> [Another] twenty-thousand and five departed heroes
> Come home to the shrine of Yasukuni

Occasions that prompted poems of mourning were repeated time and
again. Long before the war, Nanbara had lost his first wife, and had
remarried. His mother did not survive the war. Nor did his mentor
Onozuka Kiheiji, his intimate friend Mitani Takamasa, and a host of
others. But it was the death of students that seemed to hit hardest. Students killed, students dead of illness—both equally victims. Learning of
the death of one, Nanbara wrote of his parents

> Grieving by Ōtsu's shore in the province of Ōmi
> Grown old, so old.[185]

Anyone could have written such poems, since death was no respecter of
political stance.

Similarly, Nanbara's *waka* record the experience of survival in war as
a "natural" phenomenon: the endless lines, the lack of food, and, after
the air raids had begun, the stupefying destruction. There are many
poems of anger, meant for this inverted "nature" but taken out on family. Then again, one finds poems of family solidarity, as by force of will,
a moment of happiness is seized and savored. Such poems, of course,
appear less often. And there are the descriptions of "real" nature, the
cycle of seasons, birth and death untouchable by war.

Much of what Nanbara wrote in poetic form expressed sentiments
that were criminal or close to it. At the least, his poems reveal sympathy
where political savvy would put bristling defiance or contempt, doubt
where orthodoxy would insert a slogan. Taken as a true record of his
innermost thoughts on the times in which he lived—such was his intention in publishing them[186]—the *waka* reveal Nanbara's sense of the progressive decay of political rationality in the leadership, and his forebod-
ing of the consequences.

> Now summer, and martial law
> Still not lifted
> **What the hell is happening**
>   (25 June 1936)

When the people cease
To put thought into word
What are we to make of that nation's politics?
                                        (late 1936)

General Ugaki forced to decline
The imperial mandate
Why must not be forgotten
                            (early 1937)

"Beyond Good and Evil" there is politics:
Damned if that doesn't fit
These times
                                    (1939)

I read the paper
Trying to ignore the dispatches from Berlin
As if this were enough to console me
                                    (1940) [187]

On the occasion of the Tripartite Pact, and the Battle of Britain, September 1940:

England, I know, will fight to victory
Against Germany and Italy
My admiration, so great, must remain private [188]

Closer to home, Nanbara addressed a series of poems "To the Konoe Cabinet" in autumn 1941:

Decisions made in these few years
Without any basis in objective reality
Are what I fear

Leaving aside the question of right and wrong
Think, honored sirs,
Are you talking about things that are even possible?

All this talk about
"Renewal of People and Government"!
Every damn one talks around it, nobody gets at the core

Minister Konoe who vowed
To give his all for the nation
Has departed after three months
                                    (17 October 1941) [189]

On the formation of the Tōjō cabinet, October 1941:

With the power of premier, army, and home minister
All vested in one man
How is the nation to feel at ease?

To leap of one's own accord
Into the vortex of world war
This I do not call "dauntless courage" [190]

You who hold power
Even Hitler failed
When he dared fight on four fronts

With Pearl Harbor, the country literally went over the edge:

What has happened
No human common sense
No theory can explain
Japan is at war with the world

"A people is a community of fate":
How painfully the theory sinks in
Accede to it? I suppose we must [191]

The resigned tone perhaps requires some comment here: "My admiration, so great, must remain private . . ."; "Accede to it? I suppose we must" (*ubenawamu ka*). Clearly such statements raise an implicit question: Why no more than this? Why no public protest, perhaps some sort of organized resistance? One possible answer is fear, not only of physical punishment or death, but of intolerable ostracism from the nation, which would enjoin such caution. In Nanbara's case this is plausible, given his long-engrained bureaucratic commitment to "remain in place" and perform his service. His Christian faith, as noted, was private and unevangelical, and strengthened this commitment. We know, of course, that others with similarly profound doubts about what Japan had done tended to express them in the same way. Nor was this mode of expression restricted to public men. An example comes to mind of *haiku* circles among leftist workers, which provided them with a vehicle for "putting thought into word" without making that thought available to police scrutiny. Not that there were no exceptions—those of unreconstructed Communists, certain Christians, and so on. But these prove the rule. What solitary individual would dare to speak out unambiguously in opposition, at the risk of devastating legal retribution and social ostracism? Organization was necessary, for inspiration, for support, for

the overcoming of fear, for the willingness to take that step into the void
that was open resistance. And what had the Japanese state succeeded at
best over the decades after 1925, if not the destruction of those possible
bases for dissident organization and all that such organization implied?

Between 1941 and 1944 few of Nanbara's *waka* mention Japan's
war. He records no victories, only the mordant lament:

> The news so one-sided
> I begin to doubt
> This people's intelligence [192]

The fall of Italy brought him close to unmixed joy. But where the collapse of Germany was concerned, Nanbara's relief and happiness were
tempered by the belief that Germany's violent repudiation of all that
was humane would have to be paid for in kind. A nation could not assume the role of *humani generis hostis* without suffering for its sins. It
was not that Nanbara felt that the worldview of the "old" West—of England, America, France—had proved its inherent claim on higher truth.
It had only pleased God to use them in bringing Hitler down. In fact,
Germany's transgression was the greater because what it had tried to
destroy in its own past was, in Nanbara's eyes, of far higher philosophical value than what the victors could offer. To understand Nanbara is to
understand the depth of his immersion in "the land of Kant and Goethe."

> With the war in Europe at an end
> I fold and put away
> The world map that hung on the wall

For what followed, Nanbara would need no map.

> If beginning today I recite
> One psalm for a hundred fifty days
> Perhaps peace may come [193]

The religious tone at such a moment is to be expected. It echoes the prophetic tone of an earlier poem:

> One day the prideful heart
> Will be struck for all to see
> History shows it:
> That nation will be no more [194]

Nanbara's poetry is testimony to exhausting internal struggle. Clearly
he did not wish for his country's victory. Neither did he pray for its de-

feat. He worked in expectation of its awakening. The work he did—the essays on Nazism and the publication of *Kokka to shūkyō*—he pursued in the hope that it would hasten that awakening and lessen the suffering to come. All depended on consciousness; this was his conviction, that if the consequences of a worldview were truly made plain, a spiritual revolution would occur. He was sure, for this reason, that he had been born to write *Kokka to shūkyō*.[195] It is in *Keisō* that Nanbara revealed the swings of emotion, inexpressible in public, that grew from his simultaneous opposition to, and sense of responsibility for, the actions of his nation.

> In the office, alone I take my meal
> But mine is not the heart of one
> Who turns his back on the world!
> (1937)

> In a fit of anger this morning
> I crush underfoot the insects lying
> In the primrose
> (1937)

> Y[anaihara]'s resignation decided this morning
> All gathered together
> As at a burial
> (1 December 1937)

> The year's lectures come to an end
> I sit facing the desk
> Hot tears unceasing
> (1938)

> Trusted friends one by one
> Driven out, this winter
> I will huddle alone in the cold
> (1939)

> Such purity of heart
> As when one has given the last full measure
> I have known two days only, or three
> (1940)

> Having chosen, in these days
> To do this work
> No anxious thoughts
> Just believe
> (1940)

Every line, as my mind prompted,
That I wrote today
I tear to shreds and throw away
                    (1943)

My first book, with time, has now
Appeared and my teacher
Takes it in his hands
Glad for me
                              (1942)

On the death of Mitani Takamasa:

Learning of your death
I hear my voice
Cry out in grief
                    (1944)

Not only at the front
Do we offer our lives
In struggle
        (1 January 1945)

This flower I see
Lord, what beauty
And the clouds
Precious beyond power of speech
I am alive!
                              (1945)[196]

Nanbara stopped writing poetry in April 1945. Does this mean that he simply fell silent in anticipation of the end? It does not. He could not face the idea of watching with equanimity as Japan entered its season of abasement. Logos had more than poetic use.

Toward the end of 1944, Nanbara had begun, in deep secrecy, to plan a "peace operation" (*shūsen kōsaku*), which he set in motion in May 1945.[197] Assembled and directed at every step by Nanbara, a group of professors in the Law Faculty was to approach and cultivate members of the ruling elite and military who were thought to favor a quick settlement. Nanbara's action stemmed from the *yūkoku*, "heartfelt concern for the nation," proper to a man of his status and position. He also felt that the Tōdai Law Faculty had to assume special responsibility in view of its "close relationship to the state."[198]

On 9 March 1945, Nanbara was elected chairman of the Law Faculty by a vote of twenty to two. The choice of Nanbara at this time raises an interesting question. It is conceivable that in both the Law Faculty and Ministry of Education, plans were being made in the expectation that Japan would before long come under foreign occupation. If so the choice of a consistent "liberal" like Nanbara would be very politic. There was the organizational integrity and prestige of the faculty to consider, after all. It would be an effective symbol of the capacity of the elite (and the nation as a whole) to reform from within to have an antiwar patriot in the position.[199] (There is no written evidence in this matter that I know of.) Nanbara's new position might have lent somewhat more credibility to his peace proposals, although we know that planning had begun long before his election. How he planned and made his contacts, chose his collaborators, and what his sources of information were, we do not know in great detail.

To work with him Nanbara recruited six colleagues. Some are familiar to all Japanese as architects, in one way or another, of the postwar order. One, Tanaka Kōtarō, a professor of commercial law, had contacts in the navy. He was among the first postwar ministers of education, and later served as chief justice of the Supreme Court, and as a judge at the International Court of Justice in the Hague. Tanaka was also a "renegade" disciple of Uchimura's who had converted to Catholicism during the 1920s. There may have been antagonism between the two men, but this was certainly a family affair. Another member of the group was Takagi Yasaka, dean of American studies in Japan and particularly close to Privy Seal Kido Kōichi. Like Tanaka, Takagi was a Christian who had at one time been an Uchimura intimate. Takagi was furthermore a member along with Tanaka and Yabe Teiji of the navy "brain trust."[200] Wagatsuma Sakae, a professor of civil law, had directed the compilation of the Civil Code in Manchukuo, and later served as head of the Law Faculty. During the Occupation he was active in land reform and revision of family law, serving also on the Constitutional Problems Study Commission. (Sometime after 1960 Wagatsuma was discussed by elements in the Liberal Democratic Party as a possible candidate for chief justice, until it was recalled that he had suggested that Prime Minister Kishi Nobusuke "go fishing"—in other words, resign[201]—at the time of the demonstrations against the U.S.–Japan Security Treaty.) Other members included Suenobu Sanji, a specialist in comparative law; the eminent political historian Oka Yoshitake; and Suzuki Takeo, who had training in economics and was an expert on finance and lending law.

The group had four types of contact in the elite. Among the *jūshin*, Konoe Fumimaro and Wakatsuki Reijirō were thought sympathetic and willing to keep the group's activities secret. Kido Kōichi, the Privy Seal, was, as noted, close to Takagi. Active cabinet members included Foreign Minister Tōgō Shigenori and Agriculture and Commerce Minister Ishiguro Tadaatsu. Finally among the service ministries, contact was made with Yonai Mitsumasa of the navy and Ugaki Kazushige (Issei) of the army.[202]

The diary of Nanbara's erstwhile colleague Yabe Teiji sheds some interesting light on the group's proposals and activities from May to July 1945. Obviously Yabe had been far too involved in the creation of the New Order and with the navy for Nanbara to put great trust in him. In terms of political theory, Nanbara felt that Yabe had crossed the indelible line, however much he might protest, into quasi-fascism. Of course, Nanbara's own writings resemble Yabe's at times. Both rejected "individualistic" liberalism in no uncertain terms, Nanbara as early as 1927. Both saw their ideal government as *shūminsei*. Nanbara had, in *Kokka to shūkyō*, called for a "cooperativist" world political order (*kyōdō-shugi*) reminiscent of Miki Kiyoshi. (Miki, however, spoke only of an East Asian cooperative body.)[203] Given the similarity in education and position, it is only to be expected that they would share some assumptions. And as we have seen, Nanbara waged a continuous struggle to dissociate himself from any but the strictest constitutionalism. But apart from problems of censorship, when it came to discussing specific state structures, Nanbara was not in his element. The rhetorical overlap with Yabe thus becomes more pronounced here. Still, the differences are crucial. Nanbara explicitly defended the idea of parliamentary government. Yabe rejected it. In any case, they shared not essential agreement but the limitations of insider consciousness.

Yabe has received attention elsewhere.[204] Suffice it to say that Yabe saw himself as directly involved in making history. He was a small man who wanted to be big. He talked tough to students and flaunted his military contacts, but could not overcome his feeling of isolation in the Law Faculty. If we judge by his diary entries on Nanbara's peace offensive, with which, thanks to his navy contacts, Yabe was tangentially involved, he did not know a great deal about the plan as a whole. Yabe's diary for 4 May notes:

> Hearing that Prof. Nanbara wished to speak with me, went to his office. "Germany is finished; the situation in Okinawa is generally desperate. We need to give our deepest consideration to the prospects for the nation. If I could [it would?] be of use, I would tell those in charge to take steps before what happens to Germany happens to us." We talked for a while about the

crucial question of what the navy's view is. I promised to give the matter serious thought and to let him know my feelings.[205]

On 19 May Nanbara approached Yabe to continue their discussions about ending the war. "He seems to be terribly anxious to do something. But it's still too soon." [206] By the time of their next conversation—a long and evidently detailed one on 4 June, we sense a change in Yabe's attitude. He resigned as a consultant to the navy. On 17 May he had, as requested, reported to the Navy Ministry on "research into a U.S./Britain versus USSR confrontation." His closest contact, Yabe then learned, had been maneuvered into resigning his post in the Navy's Office of Investigations (Chōsaka), with which Yabe had been associated. This development seems to have set Yabe's mind working. After an evening spent listening, over drinks, to his navy associates' reports on "the battle for Okinawa, the diversion of troops from Europe, and [the projected] battle for the mainland," Yabe wrote out his resignation, feeling "as if a great weight had been lifted from my shoulders." The underlying reason, historian Itō Takashi speculates, was the surrender of Germany. All bets, Yabe seems to have realized, were now off.[207] But this does not mean that Yabe had joined the peace party: the point should be kept in mind.

The substance of his conversation with Nanbara on 4 June, Yabe notes, was that "no one but Ugaki [Kazushige] can handle the job of bringing the war to an end. If Ugaki moves, then Mitsuchi Chūzō [home minister] and Yoshida [Shigeru] can become operators [operētā]." [208] Three days later Yabe (at Nanbara's request?) was making arrangements for Nanbara to meet Rear Admiral Takagi Sōkichi. Takagi was chief of the Office of Investigations in the Navy Ministry, and on the staff of the College. He thus held positions with ties to policy making, and had furthermore been on close terms with Yabe for some time.[209] On 29 August 1944, Navy Minister Yonai Mitsumasa and Vice-Minister Inoue Shigeyoshi had also given Takagi secret orders to explore channels for bringing the war to an end.[210] Takagi was thus someone Nanbara would want to see. A meeting was arranged for 8 June. Takagi's notes (contained in *Takagi Kaigun Shōshō Oboegaki*) record a "serious setting forth of opinions" between the two men. Nanbara reportedly asserted that if, on the basis of the situation prior to the outbreak of hostilities, "Japan was not ready and determined to go to war against the great powers, it should not have started the war. Despite the navy's hard fighting and victories won in particular battles . . . the war has taken the course it was bound to take." The task for the leadership now was to end it.[211] In this exchange Nanbara condemned the "conventional argument" (*zo-kuron*) for an all-out fight to the death: *ichioku gyokusai*. The logic here was that "if we fail to fight to the end, we leave our descendants no legacy as a source for their regeneration." This legacy, of course, was the intangible, bittersweet comfort of having destroyed oneself for a common, hopeless cause with which all that is good has come to be identified. Propaganda of the time tended to associate such an attitude with quintessential Japaneseness.

Presumably Takagi sympathized with Nanbara's argument that the policy of *ichioku gyokusai* would ultimately destroy what it set out to save, namely, the imperial house, the *kokutai*. "America will want to exploit the imperial house for all its worth. A policy of *ichioku gyokusai* will seriously diminish its usefulness [in maintaining public order and guarding against attempts at revolution], and its preservation will lose all meaning in their eyes." Besides, the Japanese people, if forced to fight to the end, would turn their wrath on the imperial house. "It is not His Majesty's will that with our allies destroyed, the homeland should be left to fight alone. It is our bounden duty [*taigi meibun*] now for the sake of mankind, to turn our eyes homeward, and rescue our people from their abjection and misery by bringing an end to the fighting."

After the battle for Okinawa, Nanbara told Takagi, the navy, from the standpoint of strategy, ought to convey to the emperor its opinion on what had to be done next. Nanbara thought the *jūshin* likely to agree. "But the Suzuki cabinet cannot end the war. We need one that can. The war is being dragged on by a small group of young army officers: and there can be no settlement without a purge of the army."

The final meeting with Takagi (also arranged by Yabe) covered the same ground. "The American proposals for the treatment of Japan 'do not touch' [*furenu*/harm?] the *kokutai*." If it was true that Japan must not seek to save itself through a bloodbath, neither could it simply wait passively for the end. Although the attempt to "engage the USSR as a mediator" was an important element, "the road we should take . . . toward peace" was to deal with the United States and Great Britain. "There is all the difference in the world between moving of our own accord toward peace and fighting until we drop. If we can prove through our own reform of government that we have abandoned aggressive policies, we will not suffer the fate of Germany." Nanbara's final words to Takagi (as the *Oboegaki* records them) adopt the rhetoric of the right: "We need to prepare for an administration that can carry through with the Shōwa Restoration."[212]

Yabe's diary for the day following this meeting records Nanbara's disappointment with Takagi. Their meetings had proved "a step backward." Nanbara now believed that "one would wait in vain for decisive measures" from the navy. But, Yabe notes, "Prof. Nanbara tells me he has been seeing Prince Konoe."[213] And we learn from a later entry that Nanbara had also met with Ugaki, Wakatsuki, and again Konoe. Other sources note visits by Nanbara, Tanaka, and Takagi Yasaka to, and sympathetic hearings from, Kido Kōichi and Tōgō Shigenori.

These visits were not only secret. They were physically dangerous. Yabe's diary records raid after raid by U.S. bombers, noting the names of colleagues whose houses had been destroyed. Just going about a daily routine was an enormous risk. To travel in and out of Tokyo as Nanbara and the others did simply added to the chances of death. The meetings, nevertheless, continued until the end of July. Nanbara believed, with good reason, he thought, that the principal objects of persuasion had agreed to the proposals. But it would have taken independent action by Kido, Tōgō, and the rest to translate them into actual policy. None showed quite that much enthusiasm. However, a historian of civilian peace efforts, Mukōyama Hiroo, has concluded that if "compared to the steps actually taken later in concluding the war, there are not a few points at which, albeit partially, the ideas of the [Nanbara] group were translated into reality. Much of such agreement is owing to the scholarly standpoint that was the basis of the . . . group's activity, and to the accurate analysis they made, as one would expect, of the information they obtained."[214]

There were many such attempts by civilians to bring peace. That they failed is sad but not surprising. We have seen that contacts among the high civilian elite promised much but delivered little, at least directly, before the atomic bombings of 6 and 9 August. Judging from Yabe's diary, Nanbara was left feeling that Takagi and the navy were unwilling or unable to do what many saw to be necessary. We know that by July 1945, Nanbara's views—on the importance of preserving the emperor, on the moods of the army and navy, and on the insanity of *ichioku gyokusai*—were far from unique. It is Yabe, unwittingly, who demonstrates the mind-set that likely prevented ideas like Nanbara's from becoming reality:

> Now that Okinawa has fallen I want to record my state of mind. . . . The only way to victory lies in disregarding victory or defeat and establishing a true, ideal total-war system. Even if we are defeated militarily we shall still have lain the cornerstone for the emergence of the Japan of the future. If we

allow the divisions in the nation—of army from navy, political from military strategy, faction from faction within each ministry; and the alienation of our people from politics—to continue as they have, defeat would indeed be miserable, and [I] would have to say that hope for the future of Japan is scant. I believe that laying the cornerstone of a true national community [*kokumin kyōdōtai*] is ultimately *the* road to victory. To take domestic disunity as a premise, and by using that disunity seek to save the imperial house, would only divorce it from the people, and would be fatal for the achievement of future unanimity. The United States and Great Britain have preserved governments in exile that they will use in conducting [government] postwar. The USSR, on the other hand, tries to win [*toraeru*, lit. "catch"] the masses of people in setting up a government. We ought to draw a lesson from this way of operating.

Viewing the problem of ending the war purely in military terms, as stages, viz., Okinawa, mainland shore, inland [defense shows that] total-war guidance has yet to become the paramount concern. The question of ending the war cannot even be considered apart from the establishment of a national order [*kokumin taisei*] or from the moral power [*dōgiryoku*] of the nation [*minzoku*]. The hour is late, but this is the goal for which we should strive.[215]

One suspects that for Nanbara, talk of "total war" in the face of annihilation was simply obscene.

And so it ended. Within months of the surrender, Nanbara came into his own. After the purge, he was appointed to the House of Peers and twice named president of Tōdai. His speeches published in the daily press were a combination of austere, eloquent idealism and a passion for national reconstruction. One should not overlook the religious, even liturgical, tone in Nanbara's addresses, which mattered as much, if not more, than the content. Nothing he had said during the war had to be recanted.[216]

The rest of Nanbara's public career lies beyond the scope of this chapter. Suffice it to say that he became a pillar of the moderate left establishment. Conservatives such as Yoshida Shigeru found him annoyingly utopian, if not "pink," in his call for a peace treaty that included the USSR among the signatories; on one occasion Yoshida even castigated Nanbara as an "academic sycophant"—the same term, it will be remembered, that had been applied to Uesugi Shinkichi four decades earlier. For those who shared Nanbara's non-Marxist, nonrevolutionary views, he appeared as the embodiment of critical intelligence in the national service.

In his moving eulogy for his teacher, Maruyama Masao distinguished Nanbara's wartime stance from that of other "thoroughgoing liberals and Marxists" who had also managed to preserve some objectivity.

Nanbara was never a "defeatist" or an "outsider" looking in on the collapse of a system he had no part of. Nor did he ever claim to be in sole possession of truth and justice, "censuring and indicting" "the Japanese" from on high. The war had indeed made of Japan a "community of fate," but not in a sense that would make criticism an act of family betrayal. For Nanbara, it meant accepting as his own and enduring the "sins of his country." [217]

We must not indulge in cheap criticism of such contrition. It is true that an attitude like Nanbara's might have appeared politically expedient under the new dispensation. But we find expressions of such a view in Nanbara's thinking from its earliest articulation. Nanbara was never anyone's patsy.

Maruyama considers Nanbara closest in attitude to "those few intellectuals in Germany who, while rejecting Nazism, refused to flee, and remained instead to share their countrymen's fate." [218] Let us pursue the suggestion briefly. There is a resemblance between Nanbara's ideas and those, for example, of Count Helmut von Moltke, who headed the Kreisau Circle, a small group of religious, socialist, and military figures who after 1940 sought to lay the groundwork for a new, Christian order in Germany. The group was tangentially related to the von Stauffenberg plot of 1944, but was first and foremost an intellectual endeavor. Many of its members, including von Moltke and the Jesuit sociologist Alfred Delp, were executed early in 1945. Delp, a trained philosopher also, left a diary and meditations that he wrote while literally in chains. [219] As a philosopher Delp was certainly more profound than Nanbara. In his study of Heidegger, *Tragische Existenz* (1935), Delp developed the idea of a "missing center," which resembles and deepens Nanbara's view of philosophy—and politics—as reflecting the dialectic of worldviews, swinging from excess to excess. Here we must leave aside the vast differences in their interpretations of this dialectic. Delp, not surprisingly, held Nanbara's heroes Luther and Kant "responsible for the total disintegration of human personality and existence." [220] And his view of human life as a totality of "orders" (*Ordnungen*) is somewhat troubling in its implications. Despite these reservations, one finds oneself wishing at times that Nanbara, like Delp, had looked more seriously at contemporary German thought, not only of "existentialist" philosophers such as Heidegger, but of the Marxist Georg Lukács and of sociologists such as Karl Mannheim and Max Weber.

Quite apart from the question of Nanbara's originality, Maruyama's comparison of Nanbara to figures in Germany raises problems of some complexity, as we saw in the earlier discussion of the Fichte-Nanbara analogy. I believe, however, that at the level of attitudes and motivation, the point Maruyama makes is just. Without entering into a discussion of "comparative tyranny," let me point out that von Moltke and Delp belonged to a long-standing, active organization and were executed. Nanbara to all intents and purposes worked alone, and he rose to the highest rank in the Japanese academic hierarchy after the war. He was no heretic, yet he moved against the current. He rejected "orthodoxy," yet performed his public duties without interruption. Nationalism, Christianity, elitism, and rhetorical instinct all combined in tense balance to ensure that Nanbara would do more than survive. He served. And that had always been the point.

Hasegawa Nyozekan
(1875–1969)

Signature of Hasegawa Nyozekan.
Courtesy of Chūō University.

AN INTERESTING MISPRINT

Sometime early in 1937 Hasegawa Nyozekan took in a film, *Atara-shiki tsuchi* (New land), made in Japan by the German director Arnold Fanck.[1] What he saw did not please him, and he took the opportunity to explain why via a short piece in the March 1937 issue of *Kaizō*.[2] Indeed, "did not please" is an understatement. The film, in its composition and argument angered and disturbed Nyozekan so much that he found himself trying to rationalize in print an unexpected burst of national chauvinism. The crux of the matter was this: a key scene depicted a young German woman, a journalist, lecturing the young Japanese hero on the meaning and proper expression of "Japanese morality." Thanks to this act of enlightenment-from-without, the man "recovers his Japanese-ness" (*Nihonjin o torimodosu*).

Leaving aside the merits or otherwise of this "too obviously pro-pagandistic" film, let us follow Nyozekan through his somewhat unpleasant "self-discovery." Plainly, he felt, Germans had no business attempting to teach the Japanese anything about being Japanese. Even if they had, the film failed to capture any sense of Japan. The scenario was so implausible that the "Japanese technicians who accepted [it] without the least resistance" ought to have been ashamed of themselves as artists and as Japanese. It could not show that what the young woman inexplicably understood and what the young man, even more inexplicably, had lost sight of in himself was in fact "Japanese" at all.

But all this, Nyozekan admits, is a rationalization of his visceral anger. The film awoke a "fierce nationalism" (*jikokushugi*) in him. "I do not call it 'Japanism'. This is not out of modesty, but only because my 'nationalism' is, purely and simply, 'my-country-ism' [*oragakuni-shugi*], and nothing more." That is, it was a relative matter, a cultural identification anyone might feel. Still, this pure and simple feeling did not seem consonant with the gut-level anger it produced. It challenged Nyozekan's conviction that the Japanese were, above all, tolerant people.

> We have never, like barbarians or the ancient Chinese, been so stupid as to regard outsiders, ipso facto, as barbarians. Whoever is excellent in any way, foreign or not, such people are to be respected. As the saying has it, "Where three so act, there I find my mentor" [*San nin okonaeba waga shi ari*]. From my youth, I have been proud, as a Japanese, of our modesty in being willing to learn from other peoples.

A revealing statement: can one, without falling into self-contradiction, be "proud of [one's] modesty"? We shall see that in some ways this self-contradiction is a recurring motif in Nyozekan's thought. There is certainly some truth in what Nyozekan says; Japan is a composite culture, formed largely in the absence of violent impositions from without. Nevertheless, to represent such tolerance as the only posture ever assumed by Japan toward the outside world is, of course, quite absurd. This is something Nyozekan seems to realize: Hence his professed bewilderment and shock at his own outburst. But there it was.

Nor was Nyozekan willing to yield on the basic point. This particular expression of pride in the Japanese national character (*Nihonteki seikaku*—a phrase, incidentally, of Nyozekan's invention)[3] has a history. "Nyozekan has become a nationalist in his old age," the novelist Masamune Hakuchō had asserted, it seems. Not so, Nyozekan countered. "My preference for things Japanese is not new."

But now this "Japanese character," so open, so tolerant, so locally rooted and unmetaphysical, was belied by Nyozekan's own feelings. What was more (to return to the film), Nyozekan suspected that a German audience, steeped in the highfalutin idealistic nationalism of their homeland, would view the film as a validation of their own self-satisfaction and sense of superiority. This suspicion made Nyozekan feel even worse. It was "un-Japanese" to react with such angry emotion; something "new to me in my life as a critic." Compelled to acknowledge these feelings, Nyozekan at the end of his reflections ventures to attribute his reaction to "the work of my liberal sentiments."

Liberal? The word would seem to make little sense in this context. But in Japan, as in Prussia, the dominant pattern of political autocracy and state-directed industrialization had tended to produce an identification by default of liberalism with "internationalism." It is true that Japan's industrial revolution of the 1880s owed much of its impetus to the transfer of state-run industries to select private hands—and to drastic deflationary measures; and that compared to the 1930s, Japan's economy operated with less state intervention and planning of priorities. At the same time, a basic collusive pattern remained, and in any case, the ultimate *legitimation* of profit seeking lay in "service to the nation." This claim became problematic with the rise of forces in the military and the civil bureaucracy opposed to the assertiveness of political parties and apparent domination of the political system by a Diet with close ties to private business and industry. These latter were put on the defensive; their "liberalism" had come to be associated with bourgeois internationalism, and was attacked from all sides as a prop of the parliamentary status quo, a futile, corrupt, and antinational enterprise that ignored the masses and catered to the interest of the elite. For some, liberalism spelled intellectual anarchy and fed directly into the Red threat. Such views, of course, placed liberal values in the worst possible light. Free trade, a rational interest politics, and cultural tolerance were more common and positive formulations.

Indeed, even when liberalism as a mode of political and economic organization "wore thin," its cultural values—freedom of speech and association, of conscience, of scholarly inquiry; in short, liberalism as a "moral category"—commanded the allegiance of many. Thus Hasegawa Nyozekan in 1935: since genuine laissez-faire (as opposed to state protection) had never really taken root in Japan, the country should have little trouble moving to the next historical stage of economic organization, that of dirigism (*tōseishugi*). But in order to grasp this situation, scholars and journalists had to be free to analyze and criticize what they saw happening.[4]

This, admittedly, is not a very convincing argument for the inviolability of conscience, and it is typical of Nyozekan, as we shall see, in its utilitarian premises. (But remember that it was in part a rhetorical tactic to argue in such terms.) A modification of this argument, that "cultural" liberalism remained valid as a guardian of "objectivity" in a reactionary political situation, was advanced by a number of Marxists, among them Tosaka Jun and Nagata Hiroshi. It is ironic, as Maruyama Masao has remarked, that these theorists, who had so recently attacked claims to a "value free" approach, were now compelled to retreat into the bourgeois citadel of "objectivity" in order to continue *thinking* as Marxists. But one must also admit that their reading of the situation has a certain plausibility. Theory and practice would have to be mediated by such categories for the time being; to think otherwise was to court disaster.[5] (It is to be noted, however, that when "practice" was extended to include state service, the argument ran into real problems.)

Why then would Nyozekan have ascribed his "unworthy" chauvinism and intolerance to his liberalism? In fact, he did not. A small note at the bottom of the last page of the next issue of *Kaizō* explains that the characters for liberalism (*jiyūshugi*) had inadvertently been printed in place of those for nationalism (*jikokushugi*)!

Given the history of the journal as the very emblem of mainstream Taishō democratic thinking,[6] perhaps the error was merely a typographer's reflex. But the editor's explanation, in its sheer matter-of-factness, unwittingly reveals, as no manifesto could, the displacement in self-image and public personae of Japan's public men during the first two

decades of the Shōwa era. Conceiving a new justification for their activity, the adoption of new paradigms and rhetoric had become the key
to intellectual survival and to the performance of their preferred social
roles. "Liberalism"—economic and political liberalism particularly—
had been superseded. To be sure, there was disagreement among public
men as to the nature and fate of the beast. Had liberalism been an error,
a historical misprint? Or had it simply been overcome by the development of its own logic—that with the capitalist system in crisis, the state
now had to step in and maintain that system; that social equity, as determined by the state, took precedence over the free pursuit of economic
benefit? Had liberalism, furthermore, lost its ideological usefulness? Its
critics, as we have seen, adduced many reasons for saying that it had,
reasons that reflected the range of ideologies from Marxism to "god-
possessed" Japanism. The feeling predominated that liberalism was best
the subject of a postmortem, or at least of worried consultation among
its sympathizers.

Our concern for the moment lies not with liberalism per se, but with
the question of how and when the intellectual orientation of certain
public men shifted. From what, to what? What was affirmed, what denied? We saw that for Nanbara Shigeru, whose private Christianity
acted on a strong "Meiji" nationalism, the passing of continental liberalism meant, in essence, the end of *individualism* as a social and ethical
philosophy valid for Japan as well as Europe; or, alternatively, of individualism to the extent that it was merely synonymous with selfishness
and calculating privatism in economic and social life. Nanbara, indeed,
had used the nationalism and professedly anti-individualist Christianity
of Uchimura Kanzō as a kind of shield against overcompromise with
communitarian Japanism. The intellectual and spiritual cost of Nanbara's insider calling should by now be clear, as should the degree to
which "insideness" provided him with a self-definition that he refused
on any account to renounce. Hence the question of *tenkō* never arises
for Nanbara. For Nyozekan it does. Why?

In Nyozekan we treat a figure generally considered one of the "great
liberals" of the prewar period. What then was the substance of his liberalism? Does the label accurately describe Nyozekan's development as a
thinker? Does it do justice to his public life?

We must approach Hasegawa Nyozekan differently than we did
Nanbara Shigeru. A preliminary list of contrasts will suggest the reason.
Nanbara was, as we have seen, virtually anonymous outside the mini-
cosmos of the Tōdai Law Faculty until 1945, and only grudgingly gave

up his snaillike existence. Nyozekan, born in 1875, was universally known for his journalism and political progressiveness by the middle years of the Taishō period. His semiautobiographical efforts of a decade earlier had attracted the interest and criticism of no less a figure than Natsume Sōseki.[7] While still in his forties, Nyozekan had begun to publish a serial autobiography, and much of his social commentary is personal in tone. He was, in short, a public personality, and fully aware of the fact.

Nanbara was a proud country boy, Nyozekan an "Edo urbanite," the son of a Fukagawa lumber wholesaler. Nanbara in his youth followed the stereotypical path to "success" from Ichikō, through Tōdai Law into bureaucratic service. Nyozekan (here the difference in their ages becomes a factor) was privately educated in various Tokyo *juku* and at the predecessor of today's Chūō University. Nanbara, though he returned permanently to the academy, considered himself all his life a public servant (which technically he was), "a shepherd of the people." He devoted himself to studies in German political philosophy, which, he passionately hoped, would in small part elevate the political consciousness of his country and aid in the creation of a humane nationalism enlightened by personal—not institutional—Christian witness. (The contradiction with Nanbara's anti-individualism is only apparent: "institutions" could easily become self-justifying and privatized, resulting in what we may call "ecclesiastical individualism." Thus a church supported by diffuse, individual witness was in fact to be preferred.) Nyozekan the public man refused any direct participation in politics, especially in the activities of the state, which—until 1933—he felt called upon to dissect rather than to assist. Over the years, however, he was associated with a number of groups that questioned the status quo from a leftist, though not communist, position. But it is important to keep in mind Nyozekan's watchword, which seems to have been a product of the years between 1895 and 1905. This was *danjite okonawazu*, literally, "[Be] resolute in not taking action." As with so much in Nyozekan's thinking, it involves an ironic twist—in this case on a more conventional phrase from the ancient *Book of History:* "Act resolutely [*Danjite okonau*], and neither the spirits nor the gods will hinder you."[8] This position, no mere tactic, clearly bears on matters of intellectual substance, where the differences from Nanbara are no less telling. Nanbara's overwhelmingly idealist mind-set, with its concomitant ahistoricity, has been discussed earlier. His neo-Kantian political philosophy was virtually innocent of any concern for power. Nor did Nanbara convey in his writing a sense of the subject of politics: the life and movement of society as it interacts with the state. Nyozekan by contrast took "life," especially the complex and dissonant life of society as an organism made up of real individuals, as the chief category of his thought. He knew about power from the receiving end. The milieu of his childhood and journalistic career taught him this lesson. To all questions he took what he called an antimetaphysical, Anglo-Saxon empirical approach; this in contrast to Nanbara's Germanic value philosophy.

Too mechanical a parade of contrasts, however, does injustice to the subtleties and ambiguities found in both thinkers. Let us focus therefore on Nyozekan. Some general comments on his "style" are called for to get us rolling.⁹ All of Nyozekan's writing radiates warmth, openness to ideas, and ingenuousness and good-heartedness that make reading him a pleasure. This is obvious in his autobiography, and in his fiction and drama—the former to be discussed presently, the latter lying beyond the scope of this book. Nyozekan could be acerbic, even stinging, in his combination of wit and social commentary. The best example of this may be *Shinjitsu wa kaku itsuwaru* (Thus the truth deceives, 1924), the first of many collections of short lead essays and sketches from his journal *Warera*. Nor, finally, did Nyozekan shrink from passionate polemic. His best work in this vein—for instance on the problems of the Japanese labor movement in the years after World War I—is quite moving.

The range of Nyozekan's concerns is evident in the sheer mass of *words* he produced: the (so far) definitive bibliography runs to a hundred pages; it is estimated that his complete works would fill fifty volumes. Not a rigorously analytical thinker, Nyozekan chose rather to adopt provocative attitudes and make intelligent (and sometimes idiosyncratic) criticism. He was not a man of system—though, as in his posthumously published *Kokka kōdō ron* (On the behavior of states, 1970), he could certainly sustain and elaborate an argument. Overall, Nyozekan preferred free association and sometimes grandiose generalization to close analysis and demonstration.

Still, a number of constant themes run like a ground bass through Nyozekan's work. Earlier we saw that "life" in society was the greatest of these. Its key complement was perhaps the idea of progress, or better, of evolution toward meaningful complexity through cycles of social/ institutional destruction and creation. At the same time, and related to this "dynamic materialism," there is a sense of the need for, and appreciation of, restraint, whether personal or social. Indeed, to some degree Nyozekan's social and ethical philosophy seems to boil down to making

a virtue of necessity. All this brings us back to the remark on "style."
Style, discipline, and tradition all mattered. "Being there"—at home,
attuned to one's surroundings, mattered. It conveyed an awareness of
limitations, of what was necessary and possible in a situation and what
was not. Nyozekan liked to refer to himself by the names of various ani-
mals, some of which are very revealing.[10] In his autobiography, he is a
"mosquito larva"—an insignificant member of the mass. In the farewell
piece he wrote for his beloved journal *Warera* (1919–30) he is a "can-
tankerous donkey" who, despite the pressure of changing political and
intellectual fashion, will not be moved. Finally he is a *musasabi*—a
giant flying squirrel. The image comes from Xunzi:

> He is good jumper, but can't reach the roof; a skillful climber, but can't make
> it to the top of the tree; an easy swimmer, but can't cross the stream; a deep
> digger, but can't cover himself up; a fast runner, but can't outrun a man.

In sum,

> Five skills you possess
> Yet not in one are you accomplished.
> Flying squirrel, how can you brag?[11]

It was with the flying squirrels among his countrymen that Nyozekan
sympathized and identified, their attitudes he professed to share and
sought to represent, their collective action he aimed to stimulate, and,
when necessary, criticize. This basic position had its political, social,
and moral moments, which it is the purpose of the following pages to
examine. How did Nyozekan come to form his attitudes? What sort of
public career took shape around them? What made him both "public"
and an "outsider"?

UPTOWN AND DOWN: NYOZEKAN'S YOUTH

Nyozekan begins his autobiography, *Aru kokoro no jijoden* (1950),
with a description of his "life in the womb"—a description, that is, of
the world that formed him, the world into which he was eventually
born. This was a complex of communities—the family and its business,
schools (especially teachers), in general the separate realms of "life" and
"thought" in the first two decades of the Meiji era. Formally, *Aru
kokoro* treats only the years up to Nyozekan's first journalistic venture
in 1903, when he signed on at Kuga Katsunan's *Nihon*. Not surpris-

ingly, however, in view of his preference for pithiness and disdain for single-mindedness, Nyozekan digresses frequently, ranging from remarks on Heian art to Meiji crowds to postwar advertising. From his early youth, Nyozekan had aspired to be a historian. Though this desire was frustrated, history remained a lifelong avocation, and many of his digressions turn into mini-essays on the "stage" of world history through which Japan was passing during the period under discussion. The frequency of such digressions tends to derail whatever narrative Nyozekan may have had in mind. In fact, despite the straightforwardness of the chapter titles, one feels that Nyozekan's sense of history, as a personal matter, was associative rather than linear. This quality constitutes *Aru kokoro*'s chief interest but lies beyond the scope of my immediate concern, which is to use *Aru kokoro* to provide a general setting for Nyozekan himself.

At the same time, it must be borne in mind that *Aru kokoro* is a self-interpretation, a work of "art," a reconstructed life. It is not a recitation of facts about Nyozekan, but a retrospective on his own development, and, as seen through his eyes, that of modern Japan. At times, indeed, Nyozekan seems to project onto his own youthful self attitudes he held in maturity, so that their emergence is attributed *to* a certain period because they affected Nyozekan's later view *of* that period. This is very much the case with the reconstruction of his early childhood and schooling. Perhaps this is in the nature of autobiography. In any case, we may say of Nyozekan that he had seen much. And despite his "wretched" memory and scant concern for the trappings of conventional narrative such as names and dates, the autobiography is a pointed and richly textured memoir. It is at the same time premised on Nyozekan's (professed) insignificance as a life *in* history rather than one who *made* history.

Aru kokoro may also be read as an attempt by Nyozekan to explain, in retrospect, his decision to stay out of any struggle for personal power and influence. Many intellectuals of the prewar years felt compelled, after 1945, to make such explanations in the face of charges, direct or implied, of "war responsibility." This in turn is a problematic represented by the term *tenkō*, now a metaphor (of diminishing explanatory power) for the intellectual experience of the generations in question.[12] Nyozekan relies for explanation in part on the cultural milieu into which he was born: witness the first two chapters of *Aru kokoro*, "Taiji jidai" (In the womb) and "Watakushi no umareta koro no jidai" (The age I was born in).

What then was Nyozekan's generation? What was the "womb," the *seimeitai* (life-world) that formed him? Viewed broadly, the most salient feature of Nyozekan's account is a sense of "not fitting in" (*zure*) either temporally or spatially, with the world that surrounded him. Or rather, the world that *formed* him was no longer the world he lived in, except in his mental habits and "style." This *zure* was not merely an individual, personal concern, but, he implies, one imposed by generation and geography on entire sections of the nation. For this reason, because he was decidedly *not* alone, Nyozekan felt no impulse to retreat into or champion his own sensuality as the only "real" or "valid" thing in life. The point is important in view of the apparent ubiquity of precisely this attitude among many creative writers of the late Meiji period. The pioneer in enunciating this sensual or aesthetic individualism was a near contemporary of Nyozekan's, Takayama Chogyū (1871–1902). Chogyū had created a sensation with this proclamation in "Biteki seikatsu o ronzu" (On the aesthetic life, 1901), which signaled his abrupt turn, under the influence of Nietzsche, from the idealist Japanism he had hitherto espoused.[13]

Unlike Chogyū, Nyozekan felt himself to belong to the "open" generation of early Meiji, genuinely individualist, spontaneously patriotic, unrestricted in the expression of curiosity about the world and its deep concern for the fate of the national community. For this generation, "Restoration" remained a valid ideal and charge, an attitude Maruyama Masao, with indirect reference to Nyozekan's intellectual genealogy, terms "nationalism from below."[14] This generation, Nyozekan asserted, did not suffer, as succeeding generations did, from the effects of sclerotic bureaucratism, institutionalized nationalism, and rigid specialization. Echoing the lament of the journalist Yamaji Aizan, Nyozekan mourns the advent of the "age of the specialist," dominated by conformist functionaries for whom the only knowledge of any value pertained to bureaucratic obligation and would further their "success."[15]

Nyozekan goes further, pointing to the sheer waste of talent involved in this abnormal attachment to official pedigree. The careers of two of his middle-school teachers provided him with poignant examples. Hirase Sakugorō and Makino Tomitarō were two self-taught botanists whose work, while winning both of them international recognition, was nearly ignored in Japan because it had been pursued outside the academic establishment. Both Hirase and Makino remained for long years in low-level teaching jobs. Finally, Makino, at least, won the patronage of a wealthy Kobe industrialist, who built a research center for him. In his inaugural speech Makino was unable to hide his bitterness toward academia—thirty years of neglect!—and as a result of his outburst the prefectural governor, who was to have given a congratulatory speech, flew into a rage and left. To Nyozekan the governor typified the bureaucratic mind in all its narrow defensiveness. And at the same time his behavior confirmed Nyozekan's unpleasant suspicion that the universities, too, had become the breeding ground of a buzzing "column of mosquitoes"—petty men whose positions allowed them to mask their selfishness and insularity with their "public" titles. It comes as no surprise to find that Nyozekan closes this vignette by concurring with the novelist Tsubouchi Shōyō's opinion that the bureaucrat is indeed the lowest form of life.[16]

Nyozekan never ceased, then, to be uncomfortable with, and critical and at times disdainful of, the "successful" Meiji state. At the same time, he never fell into despair over the oppressiveness of his society. He did not see himself, as did the poet Ishikawa Takuboku (1886–1912), as a suffocating victim of *jidai heisoku:* a sense of claustrophobic desperation that overwhelmed the poet as one by one avenues of outreach, to both local and global experience, were blocked or arbitrarily channeled by the heavy hand of the state.[17] Instead, since his mentality (Nyozekan claimed) had been formed independently of the ethic of *risshin shusse,* of "making it big," Nyozekan could choose to adopt the attitude of a witness, of a bystander *already present,* rather than that of the victim of a system whose existence preceded his own. This, indeed, was the privilege of *zure*—one that, combined with the individualistic nationalism imparted by his middle-school teachers, yielded its own brand of elitism.

Nyozekan's *zure* was a matter not only of "when" but of "where." Here lies the key to Nyozekan's ambivalent self-image. The "where" of Nyozekan's youth was formed by the magnetic poles of "downtown" (*shitamachi*) and "uptown" (Yamanote). On the one hand there were Fukagawa, his birthplace, from Tokugawa times the home of Edo's lumber dealers and carpenters, a world of craftsmen and merchants; and Asakusa, *shitamachi*'s raucous entertainment district, where all classes of society mixed. On the other lay Hongō, Koishikawa, and Kanda, where he went to school. For Nyozekan these districts represented "Yamanote" culture. To be sure, Hongō, Koishikawa, and Kanda were none of them geographically part of uptown Yamanote—the site of former *daimyo* residences, and still the preferred home of Tokyo's *crème de la crème*. But they pointed to Yamanote in the sense that the "Western" education offered in their schools led to a style of life found uptown rather than down. Between these two magnetic poles, and in response to events in his public career, Nyozekan's intellect and emotions oscillated, and, oscillating, evolved. Let us look a little more closely at these two orientations.

Hasegawa Nyozekan Manjirō was born on 30 November 1875, in Fukagawa, Tokyo. His ancestors had "for generations" worked as carpenters-by-appointment at Edo Castle (and presumably to various *daimyo*). His father, Yamamoto Tokujirō, a lumber wholesaler (*zaimoku don'ya*) and builder, seems by the time of Nyozekan's birth to have amassed a sizable fortune.[18] (Nyozekan claims that his father's greatest pleasure was building houses.) He was in business with an ex-samurai, a former retainer of the Hitotsubashi house—Hitotsubashi, of course, being one of the collateral houses of the Tokugawa. By Nyozekan's account, the man, "an ignoramus," lived on the considerable prestige of the name of his former masters. The partnership brought great mutual benefit, and several years after his birth Nyozekan moved with his family (parents, elder brother, grandparents, and great-grandmother—"always a guest in our house") to Asakusa. There his father, having sold his business, turned to the management and expansion of the Hanayashiki, a public garden first laid out in 1853. At the hands of Yamamoto Tokujirō, it grew into a hugely popular amusement park, with a zoo and open theater in addition to the original peony and chrysanthemum garden.[19] The partner, along with these business successes, also seems to have been exposed to a dose of English liberal thinking (how this squares with Nyozekan's description of him as unlettered I am unsure) and encouraged Hasegawa *père* to educate his children along these lines. In doing so, the partner apparently played on some strong feelings of dissatisfaction in his way of life with which Nyozekan's father was then contending. He felt it necessary somehow to put distance between himself and the deeply conservative world of the Edo builders and wholesalers. Here, by Nyozekan's account, was "a world unto itself," for which events in the political realm "were as a sheet of oil" floating on a vast sea. This sense of separation—but not irrelevance—extended even to the Restoration and to the popular rights agitation of the late 1870s and 1880s—to many minds the continuation of the Restoration struggle itself. Nyozekan claims that it was not until he went to middle school that the political significance of these events first impinged on his consciousness.[20]

In *Aru kokoro* Nyozekan describes in quick strokes the workplaces
and living spaces, the craft of the carpenters and labor of the lumbermen
on the river Sumida. He shows clearly that custom and taboo, relating
to the visible and invisible in everyday life, remained strong. Nyozekan's
father thus hesitated to share his dissatisfaction with his fellow *zaimo-
kuya*, expressing it instead by sending his two sons to school in Hongō,
and refusing to allow his employees to read the "vulgar press," such as
the early *Asahi*. He preferred to read aloud to them from the highbrow
papers, those without *furigana* to assist their readers with the many
Chinese characters.

Eventually, of course, Nyozekan's family did move out of Fukagawa. But the imprint of that densely cohesive society, though it may
have faded, was never to leave Nyozekan. Its mark on him only sank
beneath the surface, in fact, in his family's new surroundings in Asakusa. In addition, Nyozekan had an extraordinarily close tie to his
great-grandmother. He recalls listening to her as she recounted (with
the help of much *sake*) her many acts of Buddhist piety, and was struck
by her refusal to discuss the family's "shame": they had not always been
townsmen (*chōnin*), but had fallen to that estate from warrior status.[21]

In filling in the image of his early life, Nyozekan attempts to link it
with the collective past of generations of Edo *chōnin*. He shared their
world, one of "escapist" thinking, of a detached, wry skepticism, even
scornfulness, about the other world "out there." The *chōnin* sought entertainment and "escape" in Kabuki, and especially in *gesaku*—the
popular urban fiction that had developed during the mid Edo years,
with its characteristic mixture of tales of love, passion, and morals,
broad comedy, and general Edo with-it-ness. In many ways the entire
ethos was one of comic defense, of laughing at what one was powerless
to change. But this powerlessness was only political. It did not entail a
lack of economic influence. Still, that influence was of a behind-the-
scenes variety, just as for the big merchants, "real" business went on in
the back, or in restaurants and pleasure-houses, outside the formal,
stage-set public structure of the shopfront. As play, Nyozekan insists,
the *chōnin* satire he knew as a child was most important as a valve for
letting off steam, though to be sure playwrights and satirists were also
the "unconscious" prophets of the end of warrior rule.[22] In any case,
this "urbanity"—the objective, satirical, skeptical, and escapist traditionalism—formed one of the intellectual/emotional magnets that drew
Nyozekan's allegiance. It filled his earliest years, and reasserted itself decades later, after his bruising political confrontations as a journalist

with the police, the courts, and the government. Nyozekan freely admitted that in the 1930s, he "returned to the womb" of *shitamachi* "urbanity." The degree to which he represented a major intellectual current in doing so forms part of the larger question of *tenkō*, and will occupy us further below.

At the intersection of the "downtown" of Nyozekan's infancy and early childhood and the "uptown" of his education and public career stands a key figure, the writer Tsubouchi Shōyō (1859–1935), whose publisher (the Banseidō) Nyozekan's father supported, and to whose *juku* in Koishikawa he sent his sons. Overall, Nyozekan counted among his teachers some of the best-known educators and publicists of the generation that had witnessed, or found lifelong inspiration in, the Restoration of 1868. Nakamura Keiu (1832–91), a member of the Meirokusha and translator of Samuel Smiles' *Self-Help,* ran a school in Hongō (the Dōjinsha), which Nyozekan attended; Sugiura Jūgo (1855–1924) and Shiga Shigetaka (1863–1927), members of the Seikyōsha, gave Nyozekan his first taste of nationalist sentiment. But first there was Shōyō, who stamped Nyozekan with the ambiguities and conflicts of his own life and career. Shōyō was the failed paragon of *zure.* Or such, at least, was the "text" an older Nyozekan read back onto Shōyō's life. Nyozekan attended Shōyō's *juku* in Koishikawa from 1885 to 1887. The lesson Nyozekan learned was taken from life. Shōyō and (later) he himself stood with their feet in two worlds at once. Shōyō with his *gesakusha* training had taken the "modern" novel as a model for the representation of reality. The problem was that his dislike of "modern" Japan—the trendy Westernizing craze of which the ballroom dancing at the Rokumeikan was the epitome—impelled him toward an "older" reality quite unsuited to the dictates of the novelistic ideology he espoused. The success of Shōyō's *Tōsei shosei katagi* (The character of present-day students), Nyozekan points out, was owing not to the self-prescribed method of its author's *Shōsetsu shinzui* (The essence of the novel), but to its congruence with the genre—*gesaku*—it sought to displace.[23] Unable to bear this tension, Nyozekan feels, Shōyō took refuge in the consuming task of translating Shakespeare into Japanese, work that could be done entirely within himself. Here Shōyō could pursue activity that did not exacerbate the contradiction, of which he was all too aware, between his "modern" artistic credo and *gesaku* aesthetic preference.[24]

In his maturity Nyozekan came to share the conviction of Shōyō that the breakneck, indiscriminate Westernization of the time was turning

Japan into a nation of crude, superficial power seekers. Was it really necessary to emulate the worst features of the West in order to win approval? For Nyozekan, however, the intellectual and emotional conflict was not contained within the sphere of artistic engagement, but arose between the urgings of "urbanity"—the independent observation of the world, especially that of affairs, of power, of politics—and activism, the actual quest for power and influence. Nyozekan's recognition of the *existence* of the activist realm, leaving aside the question of how he was to deal with it, he tells us, was the legacy of "uptown," his middle school years at the Kyōritsu (later Kaisei) Gakkō and Tokyo Eigo Gakkō in Kanda.

Nyozekan was not a diligent student. As often as not he failed his exams, read what he wanted, and chose to follow his own lights. This independence was partly the result of long battles with tuberculosis and associated illnesses, which forced extended periods of solitary convalescence, and no doubt overworked his imagination. They also compelled him to think of himself as a perpetual observer, certainly an attitude that remained strong in him. In any case, Nyozekan became a habitué of the Ueno Library by the age of fourteen. At this time he added to the Chinese classics he had studied as a child virtually the entire canon of Japanese classical literature, as well as "whatever came to hand" in English about history and science. It was at this time that Nyozekan first read Herbert Spencer.[25] Nyozekan's father was unhappy with his son's precocity, and for a combination of reasons (not least some embarrassment over his egregious failure) withdrew Nyozekan from Keiu's Dōjinsha and enrolled him in the Kyōritsu Gakkō, a day school. The move was doubly significant. First it meant that Nyozekan was again living in Asakusa among the artists and tradesmen—animal sellers, noodle makers, geisha, and the like. The change from the "Yamanote" atmosphere of his boarding schools came at first as an unpleasant shock. Nyozekan recalls thinking that he had been cast onto a "human rubbish heap" (*ningen no hakidame*).[26] But as the years went by, Nyozekan spent more time selling tickets to the Hanayashiki, literally observing face-to-face the afternoon crowds coming for a few hours to walk in the sun and drink a little. He came to feel emotionally at home with the mixed humanity on the other side of the ticket booth. In the end, Nyozekan remained divided, committed to life in the wider world (*mi no okidokoro wa Yamanote*), but never to cut his ties to the little universe of his childhood (*kokoro wa shitamachi*).[27]

Nyozekan's change of schools also meant the beginning of sustained contact with teachers who, as much by the style as by the content of what they taught, were to form Nyozekan's first articulated political attitudes and commitments. Almost to a man, Nyozekan's teachers at his schools in Kanda subscribed to the "healthy," "open," "wholesome" Japanism of the "new generation" of the 1880s. Usually designated "national essentialism" (*kokusui hozonshugi*), or simply "nationalism" (*kokumin*, as opposed to *kokkashugi*), it is associated with Miyake Setsurei (1860–1945) and Kuga Katsunan (1857–1907), founder and close associate, respectively, of the Seikyōsha. Nyozekan entered the Kanda middle school operated by another Seikyōsha figure, Sugiura Jūgō, just when Japanist opposition was beginning to crystalize over the issue of revision (as opposed to abrogation) of the Unequal Treaties proposed in 1889 by Ōkuma Shigenobu and others in the government.[28] Nyozekan's teachers joined the agitation against indiscriminate Westernization at the expense of the "national essence"—the term used to signify what the newer word *dentō* ("tradition") does today.[29] Among these men were some of the founders of Katsunan's paper *Nihon*, including Sugiura, the principal, Kon Tosaburō, and Shiga Shigetaka, a prominent geographer. Shiga in particular had done much to convey to the "national essentialist" audience the message that "the West" was no monolith, but was itself made up of nations and peoples with diverse, conflicting, even violent, histories; people who were themselves struggling to maintain their own modes of life and language, their "essence." Japan was no different, and indeed might in some respects—especially in the continuity of its central political institutions[30] and organic social development—be said to be at an advantage. This was particularly so in comparison with China, a nation Japan was within six years to challenge and defeat, to virtually universal acclaim, in war. Nyozekan had begun to read *Nihon* at the Ueno Library, "at first uncomprehending, just as I had read the *Analects* as a child." Along with *Nihon* he had begun to read the journal of the recently founded Historical Society, *Shigaku zasshi*.

In *Aru kokoro* Nyozekan describes the national essentialist position as reformist, opposed alike to the "unthinking" Westernization of Ōkuma, to radicalism à la Itagaki Taisuke, and to the reactionary Shintoism of the "Takamagahara" faction, which urged a return to isolation. It may be germane here to point out that, despite the justifiable contrast often drawn between the Seikyōsha and the more thoroughgoing Westernizers of Tokutomi Sohō's Min'yūsha, Katsunan himself took great pains to place himself close to the Min'yūsha, lest he and the Seikyōsha be painted as obscurantist reactionaries whose program seemed (superficially) similar to their own. Nyozekan himself was drawn to Katsunan's writing and conception of nationalism precisely because of its *liberal* content. A nation, Katsunan insisted, *was* its people, and relied on the people's spontaneous, but constant, efforts to live from the past, not in it. This effort and energy could not be produced by fiat. The state could only benefit from encouraging it, but could not produce it at will. The state was responsible rather for the protection of livelihood from external threat. It was in this context that the treaty issue arose. Japan, for Katsunan, was fully capable of protecting itself and maintaining its institutions. Further tutelage was sure to be debilitating. Abrogation now was a tough step, but it would spare all parties later strife. Above all, Japan deserved autonomy.[31]

Nyozekan, then, admired the commitment of his teachers both for the principles that inspired it and for the individualism and high-mindedness that characterized their conduct. From them he learned contempt for conformism, for intellectual laziness, and for ambition devoid of serious national purpose. In the national essentialist intellectuals of the years before the Sino-Japanese war, he saw representatives of enlightened *opposition*, men of varied talents and professions who "could not sit still" while their nation's character was on trial. Not the hacks of today, Nyozekan sighs. Indeed, he asserts that Japan (in 1950) would benefit from greater caution, less extremism, in its reforms, an approach the Japanists of the 1880s—not the "national moralists" of the 1890s, and decidedly not the pawns of the military of his own time—appeared to him to represent. Of course, as Maruyama Masao pointed out in an essay on Katsunan's life and thought, in the atmosphere of the late 1940s when Nyozekan was looking back on his life, Japanism and national essence were scarcely distinguishable, in many minds, from ultranationalism and its catastrophic legacy.[32]

Nyozekan's suggestion thus stands as a good example of the out-of-jointedness he regarded as the chief characteristic of his own outlook. It goes back, as we have seen, to the particular timing and geography of his youth. Nyozekan felt fortunate to have been educated during the first two decades of the Meiji period, when institutions in society had yet to be centralized and made to adhere to fixed and detailed regulations, such as those for moral education in the public schools, beyond the broad imperative of *fukoku kyōhei*. His education in a succession of *juku* meant education as an individual by individuals. This outlook, which he never sought to overcome, left Nyozekan out-of-joint in the company of people educated after the schools had been standardized and, he implies, politically compromised, in their curricula. One senses a mixture of disdain and pity in Nyozekan's description of a younger generation of Japanese emerging like parts on an educational assembly line, or pressed, molded, and pushed one after the other through uniform tubes, like jelly.[33]

What was the problem? What had led Japan to transform itself thus? With what consequences? Clearly, the state had claimed a monopoly on patriotism, and had set about molding the young as it saw fit. Yet how could one resist this monopoly without placing oneself outside the pale as a Japanese? This was the problem Nyozekan's education led him to address. It is, in fact, the essence of the "public" problem as I have defined it. But did that same childhood and education, with their particular "where" and "when," hint at a method?

THE MAKING OF A PUBLIC OUTSIDER

There was a way "out" of Shōyō's failure and "in" to the public world. This was journalism, on which Nyozekan had set his sights sometime before his fourteenth birthday.[34] In this ambition he patterned himself after the multifaceted careers of his politically aware teachers. More directly, Nyozekan had the example of his elder brother, Yamamoto Shogetsu, to look to. Trained as a *gesakusha*, Shogetsu had gone on to become a journalist, first with the nationalist *Yamato Shinbun* and later with the Tokyo *Asahi*. Shogetsu also had contacts on a number of influential papers. But above all, Nyozekan admired Katsunan, the central figure at *Nihon*, eloquent spokesman for the humane and liberal nationalism of the new generation. Katsunan was, in contemporary opinion, one of the three "greats" among journalists of the day— the others being Tokutomi Sohō and Asahina Chisen.[35] A reminder, again, of *zure*: Nyozekan's *kokuminron*, like Katsunan's, is "prelapsarian," a product, that is, of the years before the Sino-Japanese War and Japan's definitive turn toward imperialism. Though there were few indeed who were disillusioned and radicalized by the events of 1894–95, it was among young and independently minded nationalists such as Nyozekan that the seeds of doubt found nurturing soil. Conversely, Japan's stunning victory brought even a Westernizing extremist like Tokutomi Sohō into the nationalist fold. Japan had *proven* its right to conquest by exercising it. This was an attitude that Katsunan never adopted. He opposed expansionism and military influence in day-today politics, and his follower Nyozekan kept the faith. For Nyozekan, Katsunan was everything a journalist should be: realistic in assessing politics, independent in viewpoint, unceasing in the effort to enlighten.[36]

The decade from 1893 to 1903 (from age eighteen to twenty-eight) hardly seemed to promise Nyozekan the career he sought. Apart from the belligerent turn of political events, personal and family travail took their toll in these years. The Hanayashiki and other ventures went broke and had to be sold. The family sank into poverty. Nyozekan fell ill so frequently and so seriously that a doctor informed his mother that her son, even if he were to recover from his current illness, would never make it past his thirtieth birthday. (This news was kept from Nyozekan's father.) Meanwhile, Nyozekan attended a succession of schools of law, where between illnesses he read English and Japanese jurisprudence. He graduated from the Tokyo Hōgakuin on 15 July 1898, fourteenth in a class of two hundred in the faculty of Japanese law (*Hōgo gakka*).[37] Penal law and the empiricist Italian school of criminology (best represented by Cesare Lombroso and Enrico Ferri) were of consuming interest, and Nyozekan continued research in criminology on his own at Ueno. He had also begun to study Italian. One can see here further hints of the concern for "society" as the collective (but competitive and conflictual) relations of real individuals, to which Nyozekan gave primacy in the *Critiques* of state and society he wrote in 1921–22.

As with his earlier schooling, Nyozekan's higher education was necessarily eclectic—and for the same reasons. The schools he attended could not count on state support. The student body ranged in age and background from the young and green (Nyozekan) to scarred veterans of the internecine struggles of the early political parties and the popular rights movement. Most notable, he adds, was the strong personal motivation of his confreres to complete their studies, not in the interest of advancement along a preordained career path, but out of the desire to have an impact, whether via law, journalism, or politics, on their times. Unlike their counterparts at Tokyo Imperial University, none of them believed that choosing a career had to be synonymous with filling a bureaucratic cubbyhole. (Nyozekan's disdain for the academy was tempered somewhat by his close association after 1920 with radical young economists from Tōdai who had gathered under the protective wing of Takano Iwasaburō, a former economics professor and victim of department factionalism who headed the Ōhara Institute. Nyozekan had in fact studied public finance under Takano at Tokyo Hōgakuin.)

It was also in the late 1890s that Nyozekan first studied Marxism, this under the auspices of the economist Tajima Kinji, a *Kathedersozialist* whose course he audited. Nyozekan's initial impulse was to set Marx and Engels aside in favor of the Chinese classics (the *Analects, Book of Songs,* and *Dao de jing* remained closest to his heart). But in due course he overcame this disinclination and read (in English) *Capital,* Engels's *Socialism: Utopian and Scientific,* as well as whatever anarchist, non-Marxist socialist, and nihilist writings came to hand at Ueno. In retrospect, Nyozekan found these latter of interest not so much for their applicability to the Japanese situation as because they illustrated the gap between the "real world" of Japan, and the vastly different environment that had produced the works he read. Japan was a poor, late-developing bureaucratic capitalist state, with semifeudal, territorial imperialist pretensions. On the other hand were wealthy, advanced capitalist powers now struggling with the consequences of their earlier territorialist approach to imperialism. In their own societies, these states faced strong labor movements, budding and multiform revolutionary organizations, and a sense of decadence and apocalypse among their intelligentsias. Japan on the contrary faced the shock of the *new.* Its capitalism was precocious, as was its labor movement. Its intelligentsia, though sincere in striving to approximate what it deemed the proper course, took its cues from the imported printed word rather than from the situation of its own society. The Japanese intelligentsia in consequence turned in on itself. It was self-consuming, suffering not only political repression but a self-imposed closure. The emergence, Nyozekan asserts, of a genuine revolutionary movement from the Japanese intelligentsia was historically "unnecessary." (We must bear in mind that this was a retrospective judgment, and that, indeed, the *Russian* revolution of 1905—not to speak of 1917—was hardly a gleam in the eye of history.) Thus Japanese nihilists, "more realistic" than their East European counterparts, could turn to literary nihilism, for which there was an audience, or to gangsterism, for which, in capitalist circles, there was a demand.[38]

To return to Nyozekan's own career: during this same decade, 1893–1903, he began to contribute essays and short stories to a variety of publications. His early short story "Futasujimichi" (The crossroad) tells of a young pickpocket who commits a daring robbery to prove his love for a woman. It was published by *Shinchō gekkan* in 1898, and its author applauded in Sohō's *Kokumin no tomo.* The story, Nyozekan says, was the product of "sheer boredom," written during a periodic convalescence.[39] He had not expected this success. Spurred on to further efforts, Nyozekan on Shogetsu's advice began to send work to the

Tokyo *Asahi,* and soon after this to the apple of his eye, *Nihon,* which began to publish his work in 1900. Again through Shogetsu, he arranged an introduction to the acting editor of *Nihon* in 1901, and was encouraged to continue his contributions. These included a partial translation of Kropotkin's autobiography and a critique (significantly) of the views of Shōyō and the Tōdai moralist Inoue Tetsujirō on suicide, discussion of which was rife after Fujimura Misao's celebrated plunge over the Kegon Falls in June 1903. All of this activity culminated in Nyozekan's signing on at *Nihon* late in 1903 as a "roving reporter." But instead of chasing down leads, Nyozekan was soon assigned to write feature stories, which better suited his talent. His duties in addition included translation of foreign press reports and preparation of Sunday supplements. In any case, at a monthly salary of thirty yen, Nyozekan realized what had been his greatest ambition. (For purposes of comparison, the starting salary for an official after passing the civil service examination was fifty yen per month; a college-educated bank employee made thirty-five; an elementary school teacher, ten to thirteen; a policeman, twelve.[40]

For all that joining *Nihon* had been his single desire, Nyozekan's career there was short, lasting only until late 1906. At that time, Kuga Katsunan, seriously ill (he died at fifty the following year), withdrew as owner and editor, leaving the paper open to factional disputes that ranged Miyake Setsurei and Kojima Kazuo (who in particular had treated Nyozekan as a protégé), against the new owner, Itō Kinryō. Himself once a reporter, later a corporate executive, Itō fired Kojima, prompting a majority of the editorial staff to resign en bloc with the aim of shutting the paper down. But with two or three hands remaining, *Nihon* managed to publish, moving its headquarters to the old *Hōchi shinbun* office. Meanwhile some of Katsunan's loyalists joined the Seikyōsha monthly, which soon changed its name to *Nihon oyobi Nihonjin.* In this journal, Setsurei published a "declaration" denouncing Itō's purge. Katsunan finally called his employees to his sickbed and gave each three or four months' salary in compensation for their loss. Nyozekan, in any case, was out of a job.

This is not to say that Nyozekan's four years at *Nihon* were a disappointment. He worked in a number of departments and wrote a daily column, while continuing his study of penology and Italian until the press of newspaper work forced him to give these up.

Finally, at thirty-three, Nyozekan joined the Osaka *Asahi,* a post he obtained through the offices of a friend and colleague at *Nihon,* Andō

Masazumi. Nyozekan's association with the *Asahi* lasted until 1918. This decade, during which Nyozekan served under the prominent editor Torii Sosen (Teruo), saw the real rise of Nyozekan's journalistic star, along with that, for example, of his colleague Maruyama Kanji. Nyozekan's forced departure from the *Asahi* was a crucial moment in his public life and will be discussed presently. In many ways it was the precipitant of his own changing perceptions of Japanese society and coincided with that confluence of intellectual currents generally treated as "Taishō" thought.

Nyozekan's years at the *Asahi* do coincide roughly with the first half of the "Taishō" period—not the Taishō of imperial reign titles, but those years beginning around 1905 (some would say 1900) and continuing until 1918, the year of the Rice Riots. To many observers then and now, "Taishō" ushered in a season of national redefinition. The self-possessed Meiji civilization had "broken up," the victim of its own success. Earlier I discussed some of the consequences of this breakup for the professional and affective lives of young, educated Japanese: a pervasive malaise and sense of uselessness, widely discussed at the time. This, of course, was a condition only a minority could afford, but as we shall see, Nyozekan came later in life to assign great intellectual importance to this discontent. Of no less moment were the broader social consequences of the breakup, suggested by the sometimes violent restlessness of workers and "petty bourgeois" in the cities and towns. Small property owners and business people in older urban centers (like Nyozekan's own Fukagawa and Asakusa) may indeed have felt themselves betrayed, and their aspirations smothered, by the obvious preferment given to later arrivals on the scene: those who had come to prosper in newer, more strategic industries and enterprises after first gaining an education in the higher rungs of the system. It is among those shunted aside and passed by, then, that the social roots of "Taishō democracy" may also be sought.[41]

Heavy industry was riding high atop an economy dependent on agriculture and labor-intensive light industry. New wealth flourished. The army and navy were strong. Japan had an empire. The emperor's children (*tennō no sekishi*) worked more and more in white collar. Their children went to elementary school, for a while at least. More and more went to middle school, fewer to high school or some technical institution. A talented, but not always wealthy, few went to university. Japan was growing its own middle class.

Yet the Meiji emperor had died. General Nogi had followed him of his own accord: it seemed so right, yet so incongruous. Not every boy became a minister; not every boy had a job. And it seemed that the newly wealthy, like Daisuke's father in Sōseki's *Sore kara,* made money while "serving the nation." Dangerous radicals like Kōtoku Shūsui were saying that the success of the empire was in fact a betrayal of the Restoration promise of a just society, rid of grasping factionalism and built upon univerally shared ideals. Instead, "civilization" had turned Japan into a nest of capitalist hypocrites. But increasingly, radical analyses of Japanese society focused not so much on the moral failure of power holders as the economic and social mechanisms that perpetuated the misery of workers and peasants and led Japan to build an empire on foreign toil. Such analyses often went hand in hand with the conviction that organized revolutionary change was necessary and desirable. Those who espoused such views met with harassment, censorship, sometimes torture, even murder. Sympathetic bourgeois intellectuals, academic and literary, faced surveillance and suspicion as they strove to link their energy with that of an emerging industrial proletariat. Police were always present in force at meetings, waiting for a speaker to utter any dangerous word associated with "socialism," whereupon the gathering would be broken up.

But what of workers themselves? What did the despised *shokkō* want? How did they express themselves? In letters by workers to contemporary union newspapers, one theme seems to stand out. What workers resented was moral humiliation, the fact that low status seemed to equal low moral worth. This was proven to them every day, not only in marginal wages, but at any point where their dignity could be denied: compulsory uniforms *outside* the factory; body searches to which white collar workers were not subject; denial of opportunity despite manifest ability, solely on the grounds of a scant education. In sum, for workers, the "right to benevolence"[42] was denied. Even the lowliest clerk or streetcar conductor could ride roughshod over a worker, apparently with impunity.

Underlying this consciousness of the "right to benevolence" was the strength of the village community sense newly urbanized workers brought with them. Even if, as in most cases, workers did not return to their villages to farm, their traditions of solidarity in struggle against authority remained with them. Thus it is not surprising that when, as early as the 1890s, but in great numbers after 1917, workers organized and struck for change, they voiced their demands in an amalgam of moral, economic, and trade unionist rhetoric. The "right to benevolence" is only apparently a contradiction in terms; it represented real expectations and a firm demand for basic human dignity in the workplace and outside it.

Similarly, we find that the chain of urban violence that runs from the first years of the century to 1918—to the extent that its ideological character can be reconstructed—reflects a mix of "inconsistent" political positions: nationalist and belligerent in 1905, democratic and antioligarchic in 1912–13, anticapitalist and to some degree antimilitarist in 1918. Nor, finally, is it surprising that the spontaneous, ad hoc character of some "incidents," while never lost, gives way as the years pass to larger-scale, even nationwide, semicoordinated outpourings of popular anger. Perhaps none of the urban violence, from the Hibiya to the Rice Riots, including the highly political disturbances of 1912–13, could be construed as revolutionary. That did not mean that the government saw no danger of it becoming such. It had long since taken legal and administrative steps to cut off such a threat, relying on police and prisons to keep the peace.

The end of the war had indeed brought alarming news from Russia. Anomalous as it might seem to the theorists of revolution, socialism had come first to Russia. Could there really be any guarantee that Japan would not follow? But that is not really the point. Japan had its own grave internal problems that had to be resolved, regardless of what happened elsewhere. Russia's revolution, as I remarked earlier, was either terrifying or dazzling, but it was no more than a reminder that Japan's own "civilization" had brought heavy discontent in train.

Such, in sum, was the problem of Taishō that Hasegawa Nyozekan meant to make his own. The essence of journalism as he conceived it was to treat civilization in its daily ramifications. The form was Katsunan's; the problem his own. The historical "gap" that marked Nyozekan's life compelled him to take up the critic's pen; he would never seek power for himself. He resolved to remain public in his commitments and an outsider in his mode of approach—even, to anticipate somewhat, at a time when, as in the late Taishō and early Shōwa periods, the realm of "insideness" seemed to expand with the passage of universal male suffrage and formation of proletarian parties.

Nyozekan's choice was, of course, only one among a number open to his contemporaries. In fact the typology of Japanese intellectuals in this period, beginning with the account drawn by Tokutomi Sohō in his famous *Taishō no seinen to teikoku no zento* (The youth of Taishō and the prospects for the empire, 1916), is not so much sociological as psychological. It is a typology of intellectual choices forced upon young educated Japanese by the "breakup of Meiji nationalism."[43] In his autobiography Nyozekan presents his version. At the time his ambition to become a critic of civilization took definite shape, he recalls, there were three ways to go intellectually:

> First there were those who sought to "live" the history of the "Japanese" age—to put it another way, to "live" the history of a modern state from which all things feudal had been swept away. This group made up the "nationalist type." Next there were young minds aflame with the demand for the "social liberation" that followed upon "political liberation" and corresponded historically to the end-stage of capitalism then in worldwide advance. These, in contrast to the nationalists, were the "internationalists." Then, third, was a group . . . that hovered, enveloped in a vague skepticism. They were a dismal crowd, so few as to seem nonexistent at the time. They were too much individuals, too innerly, to be jerked about [lit. "made to dance"] by the history of that period. In them, potentially, lay a dominant element that in the near future was to exert a decisive force on the history of the intellect and sensibility of all Japanese. The modern character, with its virtues and foibles, its strengths and weaknesses, of the Japanese intelligentsia from late Meiji to late Taishō, was the responsibility of this generation of young people, who underwent their "age of anguish" in these years.

Nyozekan, as may be surmised, placed himself in the first group, only to find himself, as his decade with the *Asahi* progressed, increasingly preoccupied with the "internationalist" concerns of the second.[44] While never renouncing Katsunan's nationalism, he shifted his perspective from politics per se to society, which, it seemed to him, enveloped the state as one dynamic element within itself.

The *Asahi*, with Nyozekan holding a steadily more powerful editorial position, came to reflect this shift. Its reporters tried to enter the toilers' world,[45] now finding its voice amidst the tinny blare of national self-advertisement. Indeed, for Nyozekan and Maruyama Kanji reminiscing some forty years after the fact, the *Asahi* had taken it upon itself to be "the conscience of the nation." Herein lay both the continuity with the nationalist layer of both men's thought and a new awareness of the function of criticism. The newspaper—with circulation now reaching the million mark—was in a position to "mediate" between state and society, to act as the advocate of society to the state.[46] This might seem an unexceptionable statement of the role of any mass-circulation daily in a capitalist society, where a newspaper can not only expose state policies but also express (and coopt) popular disaffection by offering it an accessible organ. But for a journalist like Nyozekan, the paper's role was all

the more crucial in the virtual absence of political representation for society in the Diet. Suffrage was as yet in the process of gingerly expansion. Parties had no social program whatever. All material improvement
in society had either to come from an enlightened bureaucracy or to be
sought independently of the state, as for example in the "human construction" undertaken by Kagawa Toyohiko in the Kobe and Osaka
slums. Attempting to promote legislation by organized social pressure
such as labor unions, let alone taking violent direct action, could call
upon any organization the fate that awaited "socialists" hostile to the
national polity.

In this context we can readily understand why Nyozekan took the
social role of the *Asahi* so seriously. At the same time, he had to be cautious. While certainly never the "organ" of the party, the *Asahi* did tend
to maintain close ties to the Kenseikai and its allies, and took the corresponding anti-Seiyūkai editorial stance. This was especially true of
Nyozekan's colleagues Maruyama Kanji and Torii Sosen.[47] The position
the *Asahi* took on political questions, independently of their social concomitant, could and did affect its standing with the government. How
far the paper was permitted to go in reporting on a given issue depended
not only on the government's vaguely formulated idea of "dangerous"
facts, but on how the paper assigned political responsibility in issues
where the social good was ignored or flouted. A concrete example is
called for here. This we have, one involving a confrontation with the
state of decisive importance for the *Asahi* and for Nyozekan as a public
man, and one, indeed, that demonstrates the dramatic emergence of
"society" during the Taishō period. It came in August 1918.[48]

The Rice Riots, as is well known, began at Namerikawa, a remote
fishing village in Toyama Prefecture. Some fifty women stevedores,
having protested in vain against the impossibly high price demanded by
local rice merchants, finally seized the rice stores themselves on the early
morning of 3 August. Women in neighboring villages followed suit. Reports of the demonstrations in the newspapers sparked protests, sei-
zures, and demonstrations nationwide. Doubtless the root cause was a
common one, but the specific issues differed from locality to locality,
depending on the mode of livelihood, as did modes of protest. In order
to suppress all the protests, raids on shops catering to the *narikin,* and
later attacks on police and government officials and buildings, the government of Terauchi Masatake had had to call out some 92,000 troops
and dispatch them to 120 locations in all but four of Japan's forty-six
prefectures. After its outbreak in largely rural *ura Nihon,* the unrest had

spread within ten days to the major cities of Kansai—Kyoto, Osaka, Kobe, Nagoya—and thence to Tokyo. But the cities were merely more noticeable by virtue of the concentrated effects of the disturbances. In fact, shows of force and actual violence by local people were reported in 38 cities (*shi*), 153 towns (*chō*), and 177 villages (*son*). Of all the cities, Kobe suffered the greatest damage, with the burning of Suzuki Shōten, a huge rice wholesaling and import firm with many subsidiary factories and other agencies. These, the *Kōbe shinbun,* and a number of large moneylenders, all symbolic of the "plutocratic despotism" attacked in contemporary leaflets, were the object of intense hostility.[49]

The root cause of the disturbances was, as noted, a common one. The massive outpouring of popular hostility took rice merchants, speculators, and profiteers as its primary targets. The basic demand was for a fair price: three years earlier a typical rice dealer would have charged less than twenty *sen* per *shō.* By 1918 the price had more than tripled. The wartime boom years, especially since 1916, had brought a huge inflation; "the real income of low-paid workers and farmers fell, and merchants', landlords', and industrialists' income rose sharply." [50] The rice price had gone through the ceiling at the beginning of August, affecting that of all other commodities. The situation was only made worse by a heat wave. Merchants who complied with the demand for a price reduction, about half the total number, did not face the destruction of shops and stock that resulted from obstinacy.[51]

The initial efforts of local police to stop the raids failed almost totally against crowds armed with bamboo pikes and stones. This failure may have been owing in part to the secret sympathy many police felt for the "rioters"; the quality of life on both sides was close to identical. And the Rice Riots were nothing if not an attempt to restore immediate, if not lasting, justice to lives pushed to their material limit. It is significant in this connection that a wave of strikes began at the same time as the Rice Riots themselves. Most notable for their militancy were miners in Kyushu. For the most part, their demands for a 30–50 percent increase in wages and a reduction in prices (paid in company stores) were met to some satisfaction. When refused, strikers, in some instances using dynamite, attacked and burned mine offices and the houses of company officials. It was not until well into September that these strikes, some including "pitched battles" with troops, ended. In general, government troops, presumably insulated from any sympathy for local people, were able in a matter of weeks to take the situation in hand, without, it is reported, any loss of martial discipline.

Once "peace" had been restored, with hundreds dead on both sides and thousands injured, the government began the legal mop-up.[52] The number of prosecutions exceeded seven thousand, and sentences were severe, "running into years" for what was far and away the most common offense: "buying rice . . . at forcibly reduced prices." Life sentences were not uncommon.

With the situation "normalized," the government froze the rice price. Along with a nationwide official call for social relief—to which wealthy individuals contributed "for the first time in their lives"—this action brought some respite from the conditions that had been the immediate cause of the "riots."[53] But, ironically, it was not until Japanese agriculture fell into a prolonged depression after 1920 that produce prices as a whole ceased their "vertiginous" four-year-long rise.[54]

The quelling of the Rice Riots did not mean a return to the bad old days entirely. First of all came the fall, on 17 September, of the "transcendental" Terauchi cabinet and its replacement ten days later by the Seiyūkai cabinet of the "commoner" Hara Kei. This may have been the signal event in the political history of the period. However, the government had also proven, "though no intelligent person had doubted it," that it was "strong enough promptly to crush any popular revolt, and that the soldiers could be depended upon to be loyal."[55] This must have been a comfort to the government and to the Seiyūkai, which had consistently "acted on behalf of the merchants," convincing the people that "the government was in league with the profiteers." This feeling "was in no way bettered" by the fact that funds gathered in zaibatsu-sponsored relief efforts "largely found their way into the pockets of corrupt local officials and dishonest merchants, or were used for bettering the conditions of policemen."[56]

At the same time, the Rice Riots were the vox populi. As Matsuo Takayoshi observes, however, the people were unable "to extend the uprising into a movement demanding reform of the political system."[57] And it is true that the demand had to be taken up by minponshugi publicists in newspapers and journals, and transformed into a program that called for the "drastic reform of the despotic political structure," including universal suffrage, freedom of labor unions, an end to the practice of appointing service ministers from the active list, abolition of the genrō, and establishment of genuine party government. Political language indeed, but words that owed their force to workers and peasants now conscious of their latent power. "In the voice of the new intelligentsia," Wakukawa Seiyei wrote in 1946, the masses "heard the expression of their own discontent and rancor. Some of the more intelligent peasants began to talk of class struggle. The hope of self-liberation was beginning to dawn among them."[58] Indeed, following the Rice Riots there was a florescence of attempts to bring about this hoped-for self-liberation. The Yūaikai came into its own. The largest-ever strikes by Japanese workers up to that time came in 1921 and 1922. In rural districts peasant unions and a movement for reform of the *buraku* began their contentious and harried existence. Thus the events of August 1918 "swept away for good the self-contempt of the proletariat. . . . [They] gave confidence to the working class, . . . conveying the gospel of 'power' to the masses." Thus Suzuki Bunji, whose Yūaikai was the main—and nonrevolutionary—beneficiary of the end of the toilers' winter years.[59]

A final point about the Rice Riots will lead us back to Nyozekan and the Osaka *Asahi*. A connection is frequently made between the Rice Riots and the Siberian Expedition—the dispatch of troops to Siberia by Japan and the Western powers in hopes of putting an end to the Bolshevik regime and stabilizing the Powers' colonial holdings in the East. Another aim, for the Japanese government at least, according to the contemporary account of the journalist Tsurumi Yūsuke, was to fire up patriotic sentiment. This had slackened noticeably amidst what Matsuo terms the "sundry contradictions born of wartime prosperity."[60] By projecting domestic dissatisfaction into support for "the boys in Siberia" the government hoped to save itself from the fate that had befallen the tsarist regime. Its success was partial at best. Rather than being caught up in a mood of "national unity" (*kyokoku itchi*), the masses displayed a decided antipathy to the expedition and distrust of the government's intentions. Though never taking up antiwar slogans, neither did they cheer the departing troops—a stark contrast to the raucous welcome home accorded the victorious army returning in 1905 at the height of popular demonstrations against the Treaty of Portsmouth. For Matsuo the "resistance" to the expedition reflected the awakening of the popular mind to the fact that (as Inoue Narazō put it at the time) "the police and the army protect the upper classes. The lower classes, they do not protect."[61] A further point that might help to account for the unpopularity of the expedition is the effect it had on rice prices. It was rumored that the government had been buying up the rice market in order to provide for the anticipated needs of the expeditionary force, so that when in August agreement in ruling circles to dispatch troops was made public, the news came as confirmation. This was the proverbial last straw.

These and other long-term factors in the breathtaking rise in the rice price had been the subject of articles in the Osaka *Asahi* for months.[62] It was against this background that the government in fact banned reporting on both the Siberian expedition and the Rice Riots: on 30 July it prohibited six Tokyo and fifty local papers from reporting on the proposed dispatch of troops; on 14 August reports and comments on the Rice Riots were banned from the press. The newspapers mounted a concerted protest, and the government, via the Home Ministry, relaxed the ban, agreeing to provide these media with "regular official reports for publication."[63] But this decision hardly satisfied the newspapers, and on 17 August the Osaka *Asahi* and *Mainichi* jointly sponsored a mass rally at the Osaka Municipal Auditorium to protest the Terauchi government's suppression of free speech. The meeting drew 173 representatives from fifty-three newspaper organizations. A "Reporters Accuse" (*Dangai kisha*) meeting on 25 August brought together 166 representatives of eighty-six Kansai news organizations, which passed a resolution of censure against the cabinet. The Osaka *Asahi* report on page two of the evening edition was pulled, and became the trigger for what was subsequently known as the "Osaka *Asahi*," or "White Rainbow" incident.

The government charged the principals in the story with violation of the Press Law. In itself, the "incident" apparently revolved around reporter Ōnishi Toshio's use in his account of the phrase *hakkō hi o tsuranuku* from the "Exemplary Biography of Zou Yang" in the classic *Book of History*:

> Those gathered at the meeting sat down to eat, but were unable to relax, enjoying neither the flavor of the meat nor the fragrance of the wine. For as they silently set their forks to the meal, down upon their heads, as lightning, flashed an inauspicious portent: as the ancients had it, "The white rainbow pierced the sun" [*hakkō hi o tsuranuku*] the burden of which was that our peerless empire would soon face a fearful day of final judgment.

Normally *hakkō hi o tsuranuku*—"certainly no slight to the imperial house," according to Sugimura Takeshi, then of the *Asahi*—was understood to refer to a celestial portent of military disorder. A "common sense" association of the time, however, linked the "sun" with the Son of Heaven—that is, with the emperor. Being pierced clearly signified a threat of assassination.[64]

Evidently Ōnishi's use of this phrase gave the signal to the right wing, which seized the opportunity the trial afforded to vent a good deal of spleen over the *Asahi*'s long-standing attacks on Terauchi. It is true that the paper had been hostile to Terauchi ever since he had served—the first military man to do so—as governor-general of Korea, in which capacity he had presided over its annexation to Japan. The hostility was particularly marked in Editor-in-chief Torii Sosen's writing, which tended (as Nyozekan remarked) "to blame the Terauchi cabinet for everything." [65] Torii's special animus was directed at Terauchi's China policy—his support, presumably, for Duan Qirui (Yuan Shikai's successor as president of the Chinese Republic) as against followers of Sun Yat-sen, for whom there was much sympathy among Japanese intellectuals. In any case, a number of journals and organizations joined in the campaign against the *Asahi,* which continued for a month after the "White Rainbow" case went to court. One publication, Suginaka Shukichi's *Shinjidai,* had the backing of Terauchi's home minister, Gotō Shinpei. [66]

For the trial, the government had prepared (but did not use) a list of articles that had appeared between February 1917 and September 1918, some of which Nyozekan had written. In the event, the prosecutor focused on the "White Rainbow" story, and in due course, Tai Shin'ichi, an *Asahi* editor, and Ōnishi Toshio were indicted on a charge of subverting public order. [67] The "incident" continued, however.

At the time, Nyozekan was the *Asahi*'s city editor and ultimately responsible for the affair. Tai, "who actually handled the story" was deputy editor and had put Ōnishi on the story. It soon became apparent that with the anti-*Asahi* campaign continuing, a number of government figures, along with a pro-Seiyūkai faction at the paper, had more in mind than putting away these two small fry. At one point Murayama Ryōhei, founder and president of the *Asahi,* was seized, in Sugimura Takeshi's words, by "right-wing punks [*uyoku no gorotsukidomo*] from the Kōkoku Seinenkai at Nakanoshima in Osaka." They tied him to a stone lantern with a leaflet pinned to his kimono that said, "On Heaven's Behalf We [Will] Execute This Traitor to Our Country" (*Ten ni kawarite kokuzoku o chūsu*). [68] Whether because of this incident, or owing to the cumulative effect of the campaign, Murayama felt compelled to resign as president of the *Asahi.* In their turn, Torii Sosen and Nyozekan also resigned, thus assuming responsibility for the entire affair. This was not the end of the resignations, however. The pressure from outside—including the government, where some wished to see the *Asahi* shut down completely—had brought to the surface a long-standing split on the editorial board between Torii Sosen's anti-Seiyūkai faction and another headed by the noted stylist Nishimura Tenshū. Among the dominant figures in the latter was Honda Sei'ichi (Setsudō), an "absolute backer" of the Seiyūkai. Murayama Ryōhei attempted to appoint Torii managing editor as a way of denying Nishimura's faction control of editorial policy. The attempt failed when Murayama was presented with the government's "deal": if Torii and Hasegawa Nyozekan would leave, "things would go lightly" for the *Asahi*. They agreed. But Maruyama Kanji, the news editor, knowing that his own anti-Seiyūkai stance was sure to cause more trouble, urged the two men to stay. (So that they could hang together?) Torii and Hasegawa demurred. Maruyama himself was given little choice. An executive of the paper visited him shortly, and after some discussion proceeded to take from his pocket a letter of resignation for Maruyama to sign. Realistically, he could not expect to get much done at the *Asahi,* and so acquiesced. Leaving along with him were the Investigation Bureau chief, Hanada Daigorō, and Ōyama Ikuo, who had been active as an editorial writer. Eventually Inahara Katsuji, who headed the Overseas News Bureau, and Kushida Tamizō, a guest editorialist, followed suit.

Nishimura's faction, represented by Nishimura himself as a consulting editor, along with Honda Sei'ichi, was now in charge. With some bitterness, Maruyama Kanji remarks that the change in editorial staff "brought the tinge of the Seiyūkai, of political parties, into the *Asahi.*" Deep down, he did not hope for great things from Japan's old-line party men and looked to the intelligentsia (*interi*) for a "rational" parliamentary politics, "a politics that does not push" (*isoganu seiji*). Like Yoshino and Minobe, Maruyama assumed a fundamental congruence between the Japanese and English, French, and American constitutional systems. That is, politics in these systems was a matter of "compromise." In the 1930s Maruyama asked publicly, "to whom should the system entrust the responsibility of 'dialogue' with the military?" His answer: again the *interi,* and he challenged the army in print to explain itself and to compromise. As Kobayashi Hajime remarks, the "logic" of this compromise, once overturned, "proceeded to wring Maruyama Kanji's neck."[69] Nyozekan, too, regarded Nishimura's dispensation—in the event an interregnum, with Murayama back a year later—as a blot on the *Asahi's* history. Murayama's quick return seemed to restore the paper to its "traditional" status as a critical force, attracting such *minponshugi* luminaries as Yoshino Sakuzō (who was also badly in need of money) as editorial consultants. But as Sugimura Takeshi observes, beginning with the "White Rainbow" incident, "the relative importance of the critical function in organs of opinion gradually diminished." The vast expansion of readership in the years after 1918 brought about the rapid com-mercialization of all communications media. With it, the price of "fail-ure"—being shut down, pressured, or otherwise threatened by the government—grew that much higher. A newspaper had to publish, pe-riod.[70] And although Nyozekan himself retained close personal ties with his *Asahi* colleagues, he never returned to the paper in any official ca-pacity. On 4 December, the Osaka District Court found Ōnishi and Tai [Yamaguchi] guilty, and they were sentenced to a month's imprison-ment.[71] The following day, Nyozekan moved to Tokyo, renting a house on the outskirts of the city. That night, his mother, Yamamoto Take, died of a brain hemorrhage.

THE FOUNDING OF *WARERA:*
"WE OURSELVES"

The account, just completed, of the breakup of what has been called the *"Nihon-*style left" at the Osaka *Asahi,* was based on nearly forty years of hindsight. But at the time, Nyozekan wrote early in 1919, "we were all in the dark," not only about what was afoot in the *Asahi* board-room, but about the ultimate outcome of (what seemed) a permanent and depressing compromise of the paper's "strict neutrality." But this was to prove a fertile darkness. Not knowing when or if the *Asahi* would return to itself, Nyozekan opted to reconstitute the *Asahi* "tradi-tion" in a new, smaller-scale, and more personal mode. None of those who left the *Asahi,* in fact, had expected their "base" at the paper to be permanent. A crack, as it were, had opened in time and space, and it was imperative to leap into it. Difficult as it was to cut loose, this was the only condition for advance. Only struggle could bring strength. The "base" or surroundings did not matter at that point. "Otherwise we would have held on . . . but it was *we ourselves* who had to grow strong."[72] This was the name of the journal Nyozekan established to carry on the direction of the Osaka *Asahi. Warera* was published monthly in Tokyo between 1919 and 1930. In setting up this new jour-nal of opinion, Nyozekan gathered around him not only colleagues from the *Asahi* but also friends like Furushō Tsuyoshi (Ki?) from Katsu-nan's *Nihon.* In addition, and appropriately, for *Warera* was anything but an exercise in nostalgia, Nyozekan's venture also attracted two new groups. First, there were young, mostly Marxist social scientists from Tokyo and Kyoto Imperial, as well as other universities, disciples of Takano Iwasaburō who had gotten together in 1920 to defend Morito

Tatsuo. Morito, it will be recalled, had along with the budding economist Ōuchi Hyōe published a study in Tōdai's *Keizaigaku kenkyū* (which
Ōuchi edited) on Kropotkin's social thought. In an "unprecedented use
of the press laws against a scholarly publication," [73] censors in the Home
Ministry hit upon the article (which did not *advocate* Kropotkin's anarchism) and ordered distribution of the journal halted. Morito and
Ōuchi were suspended and eventually convicted on criminal charges.
Morito resigned, while Ōuchi, after a year's probation, returned to
teaching. Takano meanwhile had left Tōdai for other reasons and assumed directorship of the Ōhara Institute, which became a magnet for
Marxists, socialists, and "left-wing" social policy thinkers. (Nyozekan
joined Ōhara as a consultant in 1922, and in the following year became
one of its directors.) *Warera*'s connection with the Takano group was
owing not only to intellectual affinity: the journal was one of Morito's
most vigorous defenders. The significance of this "incident" for all who
wrote from a dissident position was largely overlooked at the time—
except by *Warera,* which made a habit of defending those who ran afoul
of the government's machinery for rooting out "dangerous thought." [74]

A second new group active at *Warera* were students, again largely of
Tōdai and Waseda provenance, who had in 1918 formed an equally famous organization, the Shinjinkai. Both of these new groups shared a
kind of radicalism, more or less informed by a working knowledge of
Marxism and social science. The emphasis in both cases was on society
and away from state and nation, indicating the direction in which all,
including Nyozekan himself, considered that "real life"—the only source
of meaningful thought—was to be found. But there were definite gradations in this attitude among the members of the *Warera* circle. There
was no "line," no consensus on the implications for social practice
springing from their "discovery of society." *Warera* reflected this grada-
tion, with Nyozekan and Maruyama Kanji ranged alongside writers,
both young and established, who were more explicitly socialist, such as
Ōyama Ikuo, Kawakami Hajime, and his student (and critic) Kushida
Tamizō. Nyozekan's ideas, too, were changing. But this was not, he
would have insisted, the result of exposure to a "new wave" at *Warera*
that was somehow destined to reach the "shore"—society itself—ahead
of those who had preceded them. Such a view would bespeak only intellectual arrogance. For no notion in the world of thought was valid if not
responding to, or generated by, the slower and more powerful undulation that was social change itself. Indeed, Nyozekan saw in *Warera* a
record of that undulation. The journal was to be both product and cre-

ator of social consciousness. It could only hope to capture the dynamism of the reality that moved all around it.

In more traditional political terms, *Warera* projected both the older nationalism of the old *Nihon* left and the new ideal of "social reconstruction" that had also inspired the journal *Kaizō*. It would be misleading to consider this nationalism a narrow party or factional orientation. It embodied an entire outlook on public life. As with "social reconstruction," it was an ideal as much as a position taken on concrete issues.

Nyozekan captured this *Warera* "moment" in an eloquent maiden essay, "Osaka *Asahi* kara *Warera* e," published in February 1919. Much of the essay is concerned with the atmosphere at the *Asahi* and relates some of the details of the breakup of its editorial staff. We have already covered much of this ground. As a statement of *Warera*'s program and ideals, and as a suggestion of the ideas then gestating in Nyozekan's mind, the essay could hardly be more lucid. It is a declaration of "publicness."

All life is struggle, Nyozekan avers—to be born, to eat, to stand and walk, to run, to express oneself and "be" in the world. The characteristic of human life is consciousness. It is the awareness of what one is *about,* and what is *about* one. Life is inevitably a painful awaking, "from happy unconsciousness to unhappy consciousness."[75]

An individual? From a biological point of view, close to nonentity. The "volume" of a single human being is microscopic in terms of the universe as a whole. Nothing could have less significance. But its *essence* is another matter. The fact that it is aware constitutes its "substantiality" and significance. And in asserting this, no human being must yield.[76] From this statement of premises, Nyozekan draws parallels between the life of individuals and that of organizations—that is, of individuals functioning in an "organic" collectivity. The discussion of consciousness shifts to one of freedom. Indeed, the exercise of the latter is inconceivable without the former, and if not taken together, neither term has any meaning.

The assumptions underlying Nyozekan's disquisition bear some attention here. They belong, clearly, to the "humanist psychology" of the bourgeois nineteenth century. It is the way of thinking associated with the great European theorists of progress, evolutionary and revolutionary: Comte, Marx, and above all Spencer. Animating this humanism was the belief that "progress" or evolution, both individual and social, is inevitable (though not unilinear), and also that evolution must and *can* be made to entail an ethical or moral advance through the applica-

tion of reason.[77] In some of his later writing on the "Japanese character," the *seimeitai,* and Laozi, and in scattered remarks, Nyozekan
seems to embrace a kind of Tolstoyan intuitionism—à la Platon Ka-
ratayev in *War and Peace*—and to disparage the "Greek" tendency
toward abstraction. But this never displaces, and in fact is meant to
"complete," his firm belief in a process of world evolution susceptible of
discernment and analysis by rational individuals.[78]

The moral and material advance with which Nyozekan is concerned
is preeminently social. He was not an "individualist," if the term is
understood to take the development, happiness, or liberation of an abstract individual as a paramount concern. Rather, individuals are real
and important because society is, and vice versa. They are "dual aspects
of the same life."[79] The view is integrative in the sense of William
James's remark that "the community stagnates without the impulse of
the individual; the impulse dies away without the sympathy of the community." Thus freedom is a matter not so much of inherent individual
capacities as of individual and social need. Consciousness demands it,
as it were, instinctually. No society will survive without the evolution of
organs to allow freedom to express itself. This is as true in politics as in
society. In politics, possession of power sometimes creates the illusion
among rulers that power alone suffices and is self-justifying. In society,
law, tradition, and convention as embodied in institutions tend to fossilize. In both cases the freedom of human beings (which, because individual capacities and goals vary, often appears as conflict) breaks through
entrenched "system" and leads to advance.

In the progress of society in general, and now in particular when "society" has become the active concern of politics, the realm of freedom of
debate and of association becomes vitally important. Apart from the development in economic organization that ultimately mandates change in
social institutions and ways of thought, the free "competition" of ideas
in society spells the difference between revolution and "rational" advance. Nyozekan, we must remember, was writing in the aftermath of
the Russian revolution and the Rice Riots. Neither then nor at any later
time did he advocate the violent overthrow of the state.

Nyozekan's strictures concerning freedom in Japanese society are
double-edged. On the one hand, he was optimistic about the "discovery
of society" that had taken place among the Japanese masses and intelligentsia (and to a lesser degree among bureaucrats and "scholar functionaries"). It seemed to promise genuine reconstruction. The combination of
actual social development with the *recognition* of such development

would dictate action that was both realistic and progressive. On the other hand, a politically retrograde ruling class, even a well-meaning "enlightened" bureaucracy, could easily frustrate this development, with catastrophic consequences. The Rice Riots were but a foretaste of what could be expected when a politically undereducated people is forced to give vent to an irrepressible demand for social equity: "People who cannot use their mouths will use their fists." [80]

The "political impoverishment" of the Japanese people was in part a historical product of Japan's forced march from a feudal to a bourgeois state. The weakness of the "bourgeoisie" compelled the state, in its place, to oversee (to its own benefit) what should have been a social transformation fueled by popular energy and intelligence. But with the hard-won self-discovery of Japanese society, "elite charity" would no longer suffice. [81] A politically impoverished people is impoverished in all areas of life. Aware of this condition, it will seize control of processes of wealth-creation dependent on its own labor. It will take back what is its own.

The only rational policy under the circumstances was the intense political education for which the people were fully ready. But this was not something the "shepherds of the people" could provide. Even with the best of intentions, bureaucracy would only retard social progress. By its nature, it tried to force the members of society into the same mold. The point was to "let go," to allow each Japanese to develop the political sense by *doing* politics. [82] This meant, of course, the *minponshugi* program discussed earlier. The whole point of the program was that the social and political worlds now impinged on each other as never before. In fact, each political demand had a social concomitant and vice versa. To claim to have achieved freedom and equality in politics without freedom and equality in society was to ratify inequality and unfreedom in both spheres. (Concretely, for example, this would mean the passage of universal suffrage without any legislation guaranteeing the right of labor to organize.) Thus the opening up of the political process to society was the only way, short of revolution, for the state to resolve a contradiction that was dangerous to itself. [83]

The present age of social reconstruction had afforded the state a great opportunity to tune in to the popular will (*min'i*). This had been the secret of success of the advanced nations of Europe. By listening (at least just enough) to the voice of the people, states such as Britain, France, and the United States had retained their social orders, and proved that "the greater the volume of freedom granted to a people, the more natural it is that they secure for themselves positions of excellence in the

world. It is not the act of one solicitous for the progress of the state
[*kokka*] to accommodate a single group of individuals by suppressing
that freedom *when society does not in the least demand it.*" [84]

Nyozekan's gesture to the nation here is not purely formal. It is the
essence of what he called the "safe nationalism" of the Osaka *Asahi.*
This was the "tradition" it had "to its shame" repudiated in 1918 and
that he intended *Warera* to continue. It was the democratic and liberal
nationalism, he claimed, of the Charter Oath itself. And not only the
Asahi, but all independent newspapers and media of opinion, because of
the *moral* sanction only they could apply, had a unique role to fulfill in
the "national progress." This fusion of moral sanction, democratic impulse, and national outlook amounted for Nyozekan to the "publicness" (*kōteki seishitsu*) of journalism. In this sense, the period of transition from Osaka *Asahi* to *Warera* may have represented the deepest
flush of the Taishō redefinition. This was all the more so when a further
principle—probably the first victim of reaction—was added: national
morality was to be matched by international morality. What a nation
professed at home had to characterize its relations with other nations;
there could be no democracy at home that fed itself on the fruit of colonial exploitation.[85] In this Nyozekan shared with Nanbara Shigeru an
idealist tenet applied most often to the "real world" in the process of
displacing an old colonialism with a new one. This, at least, was the
lesson Japan learned at Versailles. The insistence on this continuity of
moralities soon disappeared from Nyozekan's writings as he came to see
a world united by its common implication in a process of production
rather than by shared values.

Domestic threats to this optimism, and to "publicness," were also
close to hand. The danger posed to the Osaka *Asahi* by bureaucratic,
party, and business interests was to Nyozekan's mind all too obvious.
But in society itself lay another danger, a by-product of the long-standing
exclusion of the people from political life:

> Many young businessmen, since coming into contact with advanced eco-
> nomic conditions, have grown dissatisfied with the status quo. But in many
> cases, owing to the meagerness of their moral, especially intellectual, life,
> that dissatisfaction expresses itself in a superficial hankering after formal
> "culture," a deliberate unconcern for the life of our people; in following the
> trend to live as an individual wholly cut off from society; in claiming to need
> [things] of generally scant value.[86]

In sum, Nyozekan was demonstrating the dual nature of "publicness"
by pointing out the dual nature of what threatened it. On the one hand

lay self-justifying institutions and programs, with the state as *primus inter pares:* let us call this the danger of the organizational imperative. On the other, there was an exclusivist privatism and self-centeredness. If publicness is created through the openness of both state (official) and individual (private), so too its negation came through this closure. That was the danger Nyozekan seemed to see. And it was up to the media to "work out" the public sense. If Nanbara attempted this from within the official world, from "inside," Nyozekan's place was "outside." As we have seen, he did not put great hope in "shepherds of the people." He doubted whether they could let go enough, and trust the people to act for themselves. But that was the very direction in which the real world was tending. The time had come for its submerged voice to be heard.[87]

Warera, Nyozekan proclaimed, was an organ of "safe nationalism" that represented the socialized public of late Taishō. But within months, the journal and Nyozekan himself began to show signs of a deepening radicalism—an awareness of the essentially conflictual nature of class relations in a capitalist society, and a concomitant belief that a harmonious, state-maintained consensus for stability and social peace was at best a bureaucratic illusion, and at worst a prettified form of militaristic coercion.[88]

Intellectually, the concern of Nyozekan, Ōyama Ikuo, and others was to uncover the root causes of what appeared to be an increasingly reactionary political situation. The signs were all around, in the reaction of the powers to the Russian revolution, in the events in Germany; in the entrenchment of capital for a long struggle with an awakened working class at home. Nor were occasional shudders of fear of the populace entirely absent from the pages of *Warera.* But the logic of the situation was too compelling, and politically Nyozekan came to associate with people and causes that led to suspicions in some circles that he was a "dangerous" individual.

Even those sympathetic to what Nyozekan and *Warera* stood for grew overly cautious. Yoshino Sakuzō and his associates in the Reimeikai—an organization that formed around Yoshino, Fukuda Tokuzō, and the jurist and universal suffragist Imai Yoshiyuki in 1919—provide a suggestive example. The occasion of its founding was Yoshino's famous public debate with the nationalist Uchida Ryōhei and members of his Rōninkai, whose stalwarts had been responsible for the long campaign against the Osaka *Asahi* and for the violent attacks on its publisher. The Reimeikai, buoyed by the dramatic show of support given to Yoshino, defined its chief purpose as the "stamping out of bigoted thinking" (*ganmei shisō no bokumetsu*); its political platform was *minponshugi* par excellence. But here experience had shown caution to be necessary. The membership, particularly Yoshino, was extremely anxious to avoid suppression by the authorities. Thus although he was interested in forming a united front on the suffrage issue within academic and critical circles (*rondan*), Yoshino explicitly refused membership to Marxists and socialists such as Sakai Toshihiko. The latter, to be sure, had their own strategic interest in making common cause: to overcome the police repression that had already rocked them. They wanted back in. Yoshino was convinced that any link to Sakai and the others would imperil his own wing of the movement.

It was amidst this atmosphere that Hasegawa Nyozekan was also denied membership. The official reason given—plausible in a formal sense—was that Nyozekan was not an academic, as were the other members, including Ōyama Ikuo. But behind this decision, Matsuo Takayoshi argues, was the fear not only of divisiveness within the group over its uncertain political complexion, but of the threat to its survival if it took in figures perceived as dangerously radical. (From this point on, Nyozekan sarcastically referred to the "professors' democracy" of the Reimeikai. But it is to be noted that it was Yoshino himself who apprised Nyozekan of the internal dissension that had led to his exclusion from the organization.)[89]

Matsuo goes on to upbraid Yoshino—though mildly and with respect. He accuses Yoshino of timidity for failing to take a chance on a united front, not only with people like Nyozekan, but with committed socialists like Sakai. More fundamentally, he faults Yoshino's condescension in not recognizing that a worker-led movement was quite capable of enunciating its own goals and ideology. This, of course, brings the discussion into the realm of "if only." My suspicion, however, is that a united front would have required more than personal courage and conviction on Yoshino's part; the entire intellectual and political culture was in question. However these matters may be, it remains true that by the early 1920s, Nyozekan had come to embody a radical, suspect outsideness that would remain with him into the 1930s.

A final vignette will bring the narrative here to a close. Following *Warera*'s vigorous defense of Morito Tatsuo, Nyozekan joined with the novelist Arishima Takeo and the dramatist Akita Ujaku to plead the cause of Vassili Yeroshenko, a Russian associated with the younger *Warera* crowd. A blind poet and revolutionary, Yeroshenko had come to

Japan for training at the Tokyo Blind School, and for a time he was associated with Ōsugi Sakae. Home Ministry documents from 1919 include warnings from the British Embassy in Tokyo that while in India
Yeroshenko had made contact with known revolutionaries and had to
be watched. He had attended a series of lectures given in the spring of
1920 by Nyozekan and others at the YMCA in Shiba, and later accompanied Nyozekan on speech-making tours to the poverty-stricken north-
east of Japan.

On 28 May 1923, the Home Ministry ordered Yeroshenko's deporta-
tion. He went into hiding, but was finally seized and taken to the Yodobashi Police Station. The following day, Nyozekan went with Arishima
and Akita to Yodobashi, but they were refused permission to see Yeroshenko. They decided to take the issue to the Home Ministry, where
they demanded, in a meeting with officials, to be allowed to see the prisoner. They were refused.[90]

THE TWO *CRITIQUES*

It was just at this point that Nyozekan published two major works,
to which we now turn our attention. These were the *Gendai kokka
hihan* (Critique of the modern state) and *Gendai shakai hihan* (Critique
of modern society), both published by the Kyoto firm Kōbundō, the former in June 1921, and the latter the following January. Taken together,
these books run to over a thousand pages and are as ambitious as their
titles imply. They represent Nyozekan in his "critical" period—universalist in his approach, Spencerian in method, yet never losing sight of
Japan as the object of ultimate concern. The *Critiques* are not academic
treatises but a knotted string of hundreds of mini-essays given unity
through a shared method and the clearly interrelated problems of state
and society they address. Most of the essays appeared first in *Warera*,
but other and larger-scale publications such as *Kaizō* and *Chūō kōron*
are well represented.

In writing his *Critiques* Nyozekan synthesized a huge amount of
reading in British and continental sociology, political thought, and
pragmatic philosophy.[91] And while it might be possible to trace the influence of individual authors (besides Spencer and Hobhouse, whose
impact Nyozekan recognizes explicitly), it seems to me that the more
relevant question to ask is twofold. What, first, is Nyozekan's general
orientation, the critical base from which he judges both the social forms

he observes and the content of the ideas that purport to represent and analyze those forms? A second question also arises: What did Nyozekan *not* see? What remains ambiguous or puzzling in the *Critiques?*

We noted earlier that Nyozekan had absorbed the "humanist psychology" and evolutionary viewpoint of the nineteenth century. In the *Critiques* this remains evident. But here, the focus is more specifically placed on the nature of *institutions* themselves, how they arise, function, and decline. One helpful formulation of the evolutionary view of institutions that Nyozekan absorbed (and modified) may be found in a recent work, Gianfranco Poggi's *The Development of the Modern State.* In one passage Poggi describes what he terms the "theory of institutional differentiation" as the signal contribution made by the classical sociology of Spencer and Durkheim to the modern understanding of the state/society relation:

> Since it is in the very nature of the modern state that there should be many states, and since modern states have historically exhibited an enormous variety of institutional arrangements, clearly one speaks of *the* modern state as *one* system of rule only at a high level of abstraction. At such a level it seems appropriate to some sociologists to regard the formation of the modern state as an instance of "institutional differentiation," the process whereby the major functional problems of a society give rise in the course of time to various increasingly elaborated and distinctive sets of structural arrangements. In this view, the formation of the modern state parallels and complements various similar processes of institutional differentiation affecting, say, the economy, the family, and religion.
>
> This approach has illustrious proponents both among the great sociologists of the past, who used it to get a conceptual hold on the nature of modern society, and among their contemporary epigones. It has attractive links to other disciplines dealing with evolutionary change. And it can be applied at various levels. Thus one might say that the key phenomenon in the development of the modern state was the institutionalization, within "modernizing" Western societies, of the distinction between the private/social realm and the public political realm, and that the same process was later carried further within each realm. In the public realm, for instance, the "division of powers" assigned different functions of rule to different constitutional organs; in the private realm, the occupational system became further differentiated from, say, the sphere of the family. And so on.
>
> Thus a proponent of this approach has the considerable advantage of applying a single more or less elaborate model of the differentiation process, with appropriate specifications and adjustments, to a great range of events, showing how in each case the same "logic" applies.[92]

One could hardly ask for a better outline of Nyozekan's general approach. His *Critiques* rest on deeply held Spencerian convictions. In

fact he states that his purpose in the *Critique of the Modern State* is to
write a "natural history of the state."[93] The phrase is a transfer from
Spencer's critique of the narrow politicism of contemporary historians.
Spencer wrote:

> That which constitutes History, properly so called, is in great part omitted
> from works on the subject. Only of late years have historians commenced
> giving us, in any considerable quantity, the truly valuable information. As in
> past ages the king was everything and the people nothing; so, in past histo-
> ries the doings of the king fill the entire picture, to which the national life
> forms but an obscure background. . . . That which it really concerns us to
> know, is the natural history of society.[94]

For Nyozekan, the state is part of society. It is a partial society
(*bubun shakai*), one of a number of institutions (*seido*) into which modern society has become differentiated. For this reason, although his critique of the state was published first, it should be considered together
with the *Critique of Modern Society* and viewed much as a blowup of a
crucial piece of some larger canvas: only through this enlargement can
the peculiar aspects of the state's evolution be grasped as they should. It
would be wrong to assign to the state any logical or philosophical pri-
ority in Nyozekan's thinking. That goes to society as the vessel of human lives (*seikatsu*). It is undeniable, however, that his development as
a thinker came by way of Katsunan's liberal *nationalism*—after an early
youth spent in a realm where political events "were as a sheet of oil"
that covered the *seimeitai*. In this tension we can see a kind of experien-
tial dialectic, of which the *Critiques* form a momentary resolution.

But there is more to these works than a personal dialectic. They are a
critical exercise prompted by an external problem. Indeed, just as Spencer took as his target the scribes of "great men" and their minions, so
Nyozekan wrote (especially in part 1 of *Critique of the Modern State*)
with the conscious purpose of laying bare the premises of the "metaphysical" state theory produced by the functionaries of Tokyo Imperial
University. These scholars, wholly indebted to German state science and
jurisprudence, had in Nyozekan's view served only to modernize the
mythology of the state. Regardless of intent, they mystified what they
ought to have clarified, idealized what they ought to have criticized. In
dealing with the problem of ideology as "cover," Nyozekan revealed a
partial debt to Marxism as true "science," although his conclusions
regarding social practice did not point to revolution. More directly,
Nyozekan followed the example of the British social theorist and political activist L. T. Hobhouse, whose *Metaphysical Theory of the State*

(1918) had subjected to critique the work of the British neo-Hegelian Bernard Bosanquet.[95]

In outlining the main themes of the *Critiques,* we may most usefully begin literally at the beginning. We need to understand Nyozekan's point of departure. *Gendai*—"modern times" or "the present"—is above all a problem, personally identified and experienced. It arises from a contradiction between social reality as perceived and an imposed normative and conceptual model. That model is ideological, the expression of power. It distorts and hides reality, and retards evolution, with which Nyozekan identifies himself. This situation that demands critique is *gendai,* itself a normative position. The "present" from which Nyozekan works is that of a Japanese state compelling society, despite its continuing poverty, to support an imperialism it is unable, materially, to sustain. The price is exploitation of the producing classes, human suffering, and thus ideological crisis. The latter is important because it is the occasion both of repression by the state and of hope for social reconstruction.

It is important to remember that despite the titles of their respective works, neither Hobhouse nor Nyozekan take an antistate position. Both concede the need for the state (bureaucracy plus political parties in a representative body) to assume a positive role in the realization of liberty and equality. In *Liberalism* (1911) Hobhouse emphatically denied—*pace* Spencer—the Old Liberal thesis that the pursuit of equality, a "positive" goal, entailed the curtailment by state power of individual liberty, and hence that liberty and equality were contradictory as ends. Hobhouse rejected the argument on two counts. First, "liberty" did not equal unrestricted indulgence, but included as a corollary *self*-restraint by the individual in the common good. That the restraining force had of necessity to originate in the *state* was a false assumption. Second, Hobhouse considered that industrial capitalism (as least in Britain) had developed to the point where equality of opportunity could be attained. The economic and political system *could* support an effort by the state to remedy the appalling inequalities that had resulted from the perpetuation of Old Liberal economic and social policies in a world of unionized labor and concentrated capital. The state, though it could not legislate "morality," had the duty to create the conditions for it, which meant structural changes in the system by which public resources were distributed.[96] The state was to be an instrument for the achievement of social ends, rather than the guardian of an anachronistic and unjust social arrangement.

Nyozekan, it is true, regarded the Japanese political system, especially the parties, as suffering the consequences of decades of bureaucratic tutelage. They seemed interested only in carving out spheres of power for themselves, and unable to take the initiative in promoting the social good. Organized around personalities and regional factions, they were given to the adoption of reformist positions simply as a wedge *against* a current power holder. And whatever criticisms could be made of parties on this score, the same was true for their elders, officialdom itself. All in all, the state ruled in its own interest, and to a great extent remained a "feudal"—private—institution.

Still, Nyozekan felt that in the long run the future belonged to the parties as at least potentially representative of society. Thus he calls for the parties, rather than the bureaucracy, to take the initiative in encouraging the growth of labor unions. The ultimate goal, he states explicitly, is the emergence of a British-style Labour Party. Nyozekan was not sanguine about any rapid achievement of this goal. But one can see his reasoning. By allying themselves with the working masses, the parties could "surround" the state with society and considerably strengthen their hand against bureaucracy by turning the Diet into a truly representative institution with broad popular support.[97]

The particular political actors notwithstanding, Nyozekan, like Hobhouse, considered that the state as a whole was moving away from minimal and "negative" control over society to its "positive" administration or management (*kanri*). But this did not have to mean simply the greater *intrusion* of the state into society, so long as "society" (which Nyozekan identified with the producing classes) possessed institutions strong and independent enough to compel bureaucracy to share the duties of *kanri*. To ensure that *kanri* indeed meant a scaling-down of state power, a representative political body elected by a universally enfranchised populace was obviously of great importance. Why, then, do the *Critiques* seem at times to waffle on the suffrage issue? In fact, they do not. But one has to take into account Nyozekan's perspective and priorities. First, he was alarmed at the tendency among *minponshugi* publicists to treat suffrage as a cure-all for Japan's political ills. Nyozekan believed that an unorganized society would too quickly be coopted and split by preexisting forces. Second, Nyozekan considered that the regional and bureaucratic factionalism that bedeviled Japanese politics was far stronger than that found in the social and economic spheres. Thus to expect the political system to take the lead in "socializing" itself was simply myopic. The most that could be expected at present was that the state would do its best not to obstruct movements for reconstruction already at work in society.[98] At some future date, its role might be different. And the key to the reconstructive process was, of course, the legal growth of unions among the working class. Without this basic guarantee (an assumption Nyozekan never examined) of *quality* and *equality* in social life, no political reform could have genuinely progressive consequences. But that society was headed toward an age of *kanri* and away from Japan's version of the antisocial selfishness of laissez-faire (in the sense that bureaucracy did nothing to protect workers—the true producers—against the built-in abuses and dangers of capitalist economy) Nyozekan did not doubt.

What we have above is no more than a sketch of Nyozekan's position on the immediate question of what ought to be done to make *minponshugi* viable. The position amounts, indeed, to the institutionalization of the will of the people, both socially and politically. It is a position quite specific to Japan as a late-developing industrial capitalist state, but one having much in common with other such states: a constitutional political form that needed socializing; a working class emerging into self-consciousness; a petty bourgeoisie frightened of the working class, yet itself excluded from political power; a bourgeoisie itself newly hatched from a feudal shell.

The fact that the *Critiques* were concerned with the present, then, does not imply that the past has ceased to matter. Indeed not. For in adopting a Spencerian view Nyozekan accepted the idea of an unbroken chain of social cause and effect, and that social forms arise from functions determined, not by conscious intervention at any given "present," but by conditions inherited all along the line. For Nyozekan, as for Spencer, "society is a growth and not a manufacture."[99] The present does not exist versus the past, but because of it. The conservative implications of Nyozekan's assertion that we live "from" the past emerge more fully in his postcritical period after 1933. But as we have already seen, Nyozekan's inaugural essay in *Warera* warned of the need to foster evolution, lest revolution become inevitable. Let us only remind ourselves here that even this position, in the context of Nyozekan's political associations, must already have seemed dangerous enough.

Two corollaries of this past-consciousness soon become clear: impulses to fix origins and to identify universal principles of development. Nyozekan does not, however, succumb to any genetic fallacy. By asking the question of origins, he did not seek to mark out ineluctable fate, but rather to identify mechanisms and functions that could "explain" the subject. His real interest was in the evolutionary process itself.[100] Still,

Nyozekan does rely on a single universal and cyclical principle to explain the organization, development, and destruction of all institutions. Institution (*seido*) may here be defined as an action system (*kōdō taikei*) for the realization of the collective ends of the individuals who compose it. For Nyozekan, individuals are bound to institutions from birth, so that it is a delusion to posit a "total" individual freedom, or to lament its undue usurpation. Human beings cannot but act socially. Similarly, the only freedom that means anything is the "socialized freedom" that issues in action. Freedom is something one *does* (as is *speech*). This is not to deny that as institutions fossilize, they encroach on the "socialized freedom" of their members, hence wounding the entire social body. In this sense, "every institution . . . is a tyrant."[101]

Every institution—state, economy, family, church—may be said to participate in the struggle for existence. Each seeks to continue in existence and maintain its power structure in the face of changes of modes of production (Nyozekan used the Marxist formulation), and the social relations determined by them. In this competition, institutions are forced to evolve. It is precisely the force of consciousness expressed in action that powers this challenge to institutional hardening.

With particular regard to the state, Nyozekan subscribes to a developmental scheme according to which the state has a dual functional origin. On the one hand, he posits an "instinct to subjugate" (*seifuku honnō*) that arose from the need of tribal groups to eliminate threats from without. Such threats felt among ancient civilizations (synonymous with the state) led to the evolution of means of organized self-defense; the alternative was to perish. But what was there to be defended? A way of life, a "society" following its own instinct toward "mutual aid." It is this instinct that Nyozekan, following Kropotkin, identifies as the primary feature of human society. (Spencer, indeed, had made the same argument: the chances of species survival were, and remain, better through interaction and cooperation.) "Society," however, needs the state, and the state is social to the degree that it "looks after" society's growth. Accompanying decisive shifts in (not elimination of) dominant modes of economic life and the increasing complexity of processes of production, distribution, and consumption came the "institutional differentiation" necessary to sustain social life. Not least among these institutions was the state, increasing in power as the life over which it watched grew in prosperity and complexity. Depending on geography, environment, and culture, furthermore, the state developed in multiform and competing modes. Nyozekan is not interested in describing these except in large abstractions generally associated with a dominant productive mode: feudal/military, absolutist/early capitalist, bourgeois/liberal, and so on. The key point he wishes to make is that the state, in the course of its evolution, cannot cease to express the two instincts from which its function derives. And when, as in the present, a shift in the social relations of production becomes imminent, the state like any other institution seeks to preserve itself and its power. It does so through resort, on the one hand, to its ostensibly legitimate monopoly on the use of force. But when it turns the instinct to subjugate inward on its own social body, with naked force, the benefit to itself is only temporary. The state must rely in this sphere on the social "consciousness" its presence has inculcated. It is, however, precisely this consciousness that has come into question. What happens when the state's (or any other institution's) ideology fails? Nyozekan seeks to answer historically, sociologically, scientifically. That is, the failure of ideology is not attributed to any teleology, to the unfolding of spirit in history in a dialectic. Instead, Nyozekan treats the production (and overcoming) of ideology as an institutional dynamic. Hardly unique to the state, it is a feature of all institutions, since, as "the basic form of organized human activity" all involve relations of power that are mutable. There is no question, in this connection, that for Nyozekan the growth of state power and of its intolerance of social "deviance" is the mark of the modern world. For this reason, his attention is given to state ideology in particular.[102]

Ideology then is no mere imposition, analogous to physical force. It is not a restraining ("negative") but a propelling ("positive") element in the state's institutional makeup. It is reproduced not only by the state itself but within other organs of the social body. Hence the "consciousness" of the state inculcated by its particular pattern of domination in a given historical place and time may actually induce the ruled to cling, despite themselves, to social and political forms already facing destruction in a long developmental cycle. Yet this objectified, "known past," the national identity to which men cling, which has now lost its congruence with social life, meant in its ascendancy a new and exhilarating sense of belonging; it was a great leap forward. "The evils of state" and "the evils of industry" (kokka aku, sangyō aku) that now torment the producing classes were at one time the implacable fist that over a century shattered the chains of feudal subjection in all areas of life and liberated the bourgeoisie. The English and French revolutions are eternal monuments to this smashing of fetters, no more, no less. Yesterday's progress, however, is today's misery; today's misery, tomorrow's progress. So it has gone and will go.[103]

But what is special about the state? It is the extraordinary degree to which it forces those whom it rules to live with this paradox:

> The present state of the state [*kokka genjō*] is such that without some sacrifice of humanity one cannot remain a member of the nation [*kokumin*]. It is a condition much lamented—so we are told—by representatives of the state who possess some modicum of conscience. And it is a condition that places the state in fundamental conflict with the natural and moral condition of humanity.[104]

The function of modern state ideology, therefore, is to make this situation palatable. It does this by denying the negative aspects of the reality of the state—its arbitrary use of force in the interest of the ruling class—and fostering the belief that the state is the proper arbiter, if not the very font, of all values, cultural, political, and social. Ideology, then, to substantiate its claim, must rely on what Nyozekan calls "metaphysics." For him this was a pejorative term. It connoted a manufactured "ideal" that served to hide what was real. This was, no doubt, a somewhat "outmoded" notion of ideology, just as his concept of "consciousness" is basically undialectical. But it is extremely powerful when used, as Nyozekan uses it, not to vindicate the ideological system of another state than his own, but to reflect, and prod, the consciousness of his own neighbors.

Ideology as an intellectual and emotional appeal seeks to reproduce the state's will in its subjects. Another name for this is patriotism, officially defined. This brand of patriotism, Nyozekan points out, is a modern phenomenon. It is not the same as rootedness, the profound feeling of attachment to a native land and its way of life. Granted that xenophobia has always been with us, modern state patriotism is new in that it turns the xenophobic impulse within, seeking to excise whatever deviant thought contradicts officially prescribed sentiments and the political position defined as consonant with those sentiments. The state is "like a jealous mother-in-law lording it over her son's bride" (society). It will tolerate no higher loyalties, and is thus in conflict with "scientific truth," [105] as well as with the moil that is social life. But it is ultimately in conflict with itself. The harder ideology is pushed, the stronger will be the reaction in the consciousness of the individuals who make up national society: Discontent can produce utopias. Combined with class hatred, it will lead to revolution.

Even if it is not employed in constant repression, a "metaphysical" concept of state" stands always in the wings. It is no accident, Nyozekan argues, that Hobhouse wrote on this theme in reference to Great Britain: given the right conditions, even Britain, whose system Nyozekan deeply admired, would not hesitate to adopt an ideology conducive to political repression; that is, an ideology vaunting a supposed ideal ("loyalty," "unity," etc.) embodied by the state. In the absence of such conditions—or at least of propaganda efforts to persuade the public that such crisis conditions existed—"metaphysical" state ideologies lose much of their force. Under "normal" conditions, after all, the state is, or should be, irrelevant. No modern state is immune from the "metaphysical" tendency; that is the point.[106]

The *Critique of the Modern State,* then, is an exposition of the paradox of modern political allegiance. It is *not* a negation of national or cultural identification. More important, it is an attempt to examine the social reality of the state. This brings us back to the "modern" of Nyozekan's title. We have seen a little of his specific analysis of then contemporary Japan. Let us now examine his views on what shape the state of the future may take, in Japan, and in the wider modern world.

> We should regard it as truly extraordinary if among the administrators of the state [*kokka*] today . . . someone could claim to possess a fair understanding of even one issue affecting it. The fact is that with the chaotic entanglements and vast size of the state, no one understands it correctly, administers it properly, or deals with it fairly. The state, to put it simply, is a bloody mess [*tada zawazawa gayagaya to sonzai shite iru*].[107]

As a life-form (*seikatsu yōshiki*) the state is subject to limitations that reflect the conditions of its emergence and growth, and to decline. The struggle against these limitations produces chaos, and it is out of this chaos that besets the state that those over whom it rules will wrest a new consciousness and find the power to transform the institution. This transformation, however, should not be seen as a single act of creation but as the result of irresistible and cumulative changes in society as a whole. In this process—especially in attempts at reform—limited meliorative measures are enacted as preservatives. At their worst, such measures only "cover up the bad breath" of a declining institution working at cross-purposes to society, and may even encourage reaction. At the same time, a needed reform may be the key to dramatic surges forward. Thus in evaluating a reform program, Nyozekan urges, the main thing is to *intuit* the potential for transformation that it contains. He took it as axiomatic, as we have seen, that the state cannot run ahead of society. His firm insistence on this point leads him to take some paradoxical stances. While identifying "interventionism" as the universal successor to laissez-faire among capitalist systems, Nyozekan asserts that new mechanisms such as the Kyōchōkai and "social policy" can be little more than "bribes thrown to the people" in the interest of preserving the intervening institution. This regardless of the "good intentions" underlying them. The same goes for the parties opening up to labor—a position, it will be recalled, that Nyozekan strongly supported.[108] How is one to sort this out?

Regardless of subjective intent, Nyozekan argues, institutions in fact cooperate in their own demise—or condemn themselves to violent overthrow. Thus passage of universal suffrage (still four years off when the *Critique* was published) would, along with the hoped-for liberal-labor alliance, lead to the "collapse of party government" as it had taken shape under Hara Kei. When and how, Nyozekan could not say. But he was confident for a number of reasons that the political future lay in this direction. Not, indeed, because the parties had evolved into institutions truly representative of society, but because their constituencies were still limited to the nonproducing classes. That is, their evolution had barely begun; they were still "under construction." When the parties began of their own accord to widen their constituencies, as had happened in Britain with the rise of Labour, the Japanese bourgeois parties could be said to have completed their evolution and to have entered the "self-destruction" cycle that was the prelude to further socialization.[109]

(In fact, the collapse did follow a decade later. But the "socialization" then barely under way was quickly coopted by elements within the parties themselves, the state and military, and transformed with mixed success into "nationalization" and preparation for war. The point that needs to be made, of course, is that as with individuals, institutions do not exist or act alone, but always in competition with others. The ends involved are seldom compatible. To predict the consequences of one development in a single institution—or a discrete group of them—is always risky because it invites so many imponderables from without and may end in demonstrating something quite other than what was intended.)

But what of the future? If the age of the ego—of Old Liberalism and laissez-faire, the nation and capital as little gods—was coming to an end, what form would a "socialized" political system take? Clearly, Nyozekan asserts, bureaucratic meliorism, parliamentarism, and "political" reform all represent transitional stages in a longer wave of evolution. "Utopia" would bring something different. Thus far (in 1921) the world had seen only one clear indication of what it might be—the Soviet Union. Nyozekan was not sanguine about the potential achievements of the Bolshevik regime. He had his doubts, first of all, about social planning in general: "The more practical the state's policies [i.e., the more they contrive to refashion society in accordance with an "ideal"], the greater the danger involved. Recall that after the French revolution destroyed the ancien régime, there followed the despotism of capital; and after the tsarist despotism in Russia, that of Lenin." [110]

Nyozekan's characterization of the Soviet regime is best understood in the context of his general typology of utopias. It is based on two intersecting analyses of the "new political movement," one based on the form of the state/society relation, the other on the mode (or "mood") of the regime. Thus there were, according to the formal analysis, four potential directions in which any state emerging from laissez-faire could go, depending on its history and current circumstances:

1. anarchism [*museifushugi*], which asserts the possibility of realizing genuine life-goals through the abolition of traditional state authority as we have known it;

2. national socialism, which acknowledges traditional state authority and would further endow it with total power in the administration of society;

3. syndicalism, which plans for the realization of new (social) organization based on producer control; and

4. guild socialism, which calls for the autonomy of industry through control by producers alone, in confrontation with the consumer state. [111]

Now, no one is in any position to predict which of these forms (ideal types?) will be adopted in Japan or in any other country. They represent in any case the necessary and possible ramifications of "socialization." Notice that Nyozekan uses neither "socialism" alone nor "communism" to describe these new political arrangements (a bow to the censor?); most likely he would place communism under "national socialism" as the category that most closely approximated, not the professed ideal of a given system, but its actual operation. Note also that "society" is synonymous with the producing classes. Nyozekan does not employ the concept of a "civil society" itself composed of a plurality of relations to the dominant mode of production. There is but one key relation, which is that of the social group actually performing the act of production. For Nyozekan, labor, as we shall see, meant life itself, and the condition of labor was the single most important problem in the social organization of the future.

The ideal political *form* assumed by the "new movement" in society does not of itself determine its relation to society. Of equal importance is the mode, or "mood" (*kokoromochi*), of rule. Nyozekan, rather than employing a right-left gradient, asserts that in day-to-day life, all the new regimes will manifest more or less anarchic or more or less dictatorial tendencies. These in turn represent "political thought—concepts of humanity expressed in political life"—characteristic of society at a given stage of culture/civilization (*bunmei*). Thus anarchism stands for social catabolism (*bunkai sayō*): the breakup of sociopolitical forms. It rests on an ultimately individualistic view of "natural" man. To the degree that he is left alone, he enjoys freedom in accordance with a natural propensity for self-restraint in the interest of the social good. An "anarchic" system lets (human) nature have its way, nature as expressed in the actual life (*jisseikatsu*) of work. Hence Nyozekan's sympathy for syndicalism to the extent that it sought to replace "antisocial" state power with that of producers' organizations. But in its insistence on the need for a strong "vanguard" authority—an elite party purporting to guide the process of socialization—syndicalism also exhibited dictatorial features that made it a threat to personal freedom.

"Dictatorship" seeks actively to sweep away all fetters of the old forms that hinder it. Since it regards the persistence of such vestiges as expressions of the "evil" in human nature, it tends inevitably toward despotism. Dictatorship, however, is "anabolic" in that its aim is to bind society to itself; it performs a "constructive" or "synthetic" function (*gōka sayō*). As with syndicalism, "national socialism" tends to dictatorship, but in the latter case, the *existing* state seeks to arrogate to itself all authority in the administration of society. The emergence of anarchic or dictatorial tendencies can hardly be fortuitous: again Nyozekan instances the Bolshevik regime. Despite the latter's plea that temporary necessity required dictatorial forms, Nyozekan remarks, "it is doubtful that these will be of short duration. No regime that has used dictatorship to establish itself will move away from it of its own accord; it has to be forced."[112]

The revolution, then, must be understood to have embodied the entire cycle. The actual destruction of the tsarist regime was its own work. Nyozekan viewed the predominantly "anarchist" intelligentsia—products of the nobility such as Tolstoy, Bakunin, and Kropotkin—as the articulation of a social consciousness in extremis. It reflected the separation of the cultural elite, not to mention state authority, from the masses whose sacrifice ensured their status. And it reflected the gulf between the few "advanced" cities and the trackless countryside. The empire was, culturally speaking, hopelessly overextended. Its autocracy was being eaten away from within by its "darling babes"—anarchist aristocrats who had recognized that the high culture of the elite had grown incomprehensible even to itself, quite apart from the unconscionable burden its maintenance placed on the lower orders. The power of "anarchist thinking," Nyozekan sums up, "is proportionate to the degree to which the anabolic function operates in civilization." [113] In this case, of course, autocracy (dictatorship) was the ideology—or mythology—of a ruling class in fast decline; anarchism as social consciousness reflected the actual condition of that civilization.

Nyozekan did not consider Japan to be facing the same situation. It was only in his cultural studies of Japan, written in the second half of the 1930s, that Nyozekan filled in the suggestion made in the *Critique* that the "high" and "mass" culture of Japan were to all intents and purposes mutually compatible and comprehensible. This was owing to the presence of integrating forces that served to maintain order in society, in the absence of which, Russia had broken apart. In the *Critique* Nyozekan limits himself to the observation that there had been no Japanese revolution at the end of the feudal period because the sovereign—the imperial *institution*—presented no actual obstacle to the "natural" process of transition from one social form to the other. For this reason, as we have seen, Nyozekan feared that efforts to foment revolution in Japan were fated to fail. The state could not, and need not, be destroyed so that the reconstruction he envisioned could take place. Of course Nyozekan never promoted a single program, much less enlisted in any effort to gain power. But in the *Critique of the Modern State,* he speaks hopefully of the potential of the last of the four modes of socialization mentioned earlier. Guild socialism recognized both the need for producer control and autonomy and the fact that industrial capitalism had created a national market—a "consumer state"—in Japan, with which the producing class could form a *modus vivendi.* Like all "socialisms" it was a mixture of anarchic and dictatorial elements, but it was the least lethal of all conceivable forms of the "new movement" in politics. [114]

We have seen on a number of occasions that Nyozekan's *Critique* calls for a scaling-down, shrinking—in evolutionary terms, further differentiation—in the role of the state vis-à-vis society. One must concur with the judgment of Rōyama Masamichi, an early *Warera* associate and later a New Order theorist, that the state/society relation in the *Critiques* remains hazy, and that Nyozekan's deepest inclination was to a "romanticism of daily life" (*seikatsuteki romanshugi*). Nyozekan, Rōyama argues, felt that the goodness and beauty of "daily life"—local, popular, and unpolitical—were of a greater value than national, collective, political life. It is true, as Rōyama claims, that Nyozekan is loath to recognize the state's function as the "regulator of collective life." [115] (But perhaps this says more about Rōyama than about Nyozekan!) The state does seem destined, in Nyozekan's eyes, to remain "an alienated presence" (*sogaitai*) in society. [116] Still, Nyozekan's anarchism was not anti-state. He recognized the necessary presence of the state. Recall that as against Felix Oppenheimer, who saw in the state only the abnormal expression of the "exploitative instinct" in human societies, Nyozekan identified two conflicting "instincts." An instinct to subjugate was, to be sure, always prominent in the state's behavior. And with the emergence of capitalism, the state had also come to represent the "possessive instinct" of the "haves" over the "have-nots." At the same time, Nyozekan had argued that the state was also "social" insofar as it protected society from external threat. [117] The danger, of course, came when these warlike instincts were turned (in the form of a "semifeudal" bureaucratic and military establishment) inward on society itself. The state, therefore, could not be dispensed with; it had to be "surrounded," used, controlled by society.

Nyozekan's critique of the state is a blowup of a crucial detail, but still a detail, of a greater whole. That whole is society: "the stage on which the struggle for existence among a myriad life-courses is played out." [118] The second of the *Critiques*, the *Gendai shakai hihan* of 1922, seeks to demonstrate the degree to which extra-state (*kokkagai*) institutions, whether cultural, economic, or sexual, were following their own evolutionary paths. Some of the major themes this *Critique* shares with its counterpart have been outlined above. The evolutionary nature of institutions, the repeated cycle of creation/destruction/creation by which evolution proceeds, have been made clear. Similarly, we saw that in the growth of industrial capitalism, Nyozekan identified a phenomenon of importance equal to the rise of the absolutist state. As the state developed a metaphysical raison d'être according to which it occupied the summit of human life, so the capitalist enterprise (*kigyō*) set itself up as a kind of mediator between society and a new divinity: wealth.[119] In the *Gendai shakai hihan,* Nyozekan follows the impact on social life of the incarnation of this new organizer of human energy.

With unbounded faith in the creative power of wealth (money and property), the enterprise, now a distinct social institution, assumed control over the processes of wealth-creation. Hitherto, in what is admittedly a drastic schematization, work, life, and thought had been organically related, as for example in the medieval guild. Here Nyozekan indulges in a little of the "romantic medievalism" of William Morris, but only a little.[120] The enterprise had destroyed that relation, substituting for it a nonproducing organ whose function was the exchange of externally created values. The capitalist enterprise, in short, robbed the worker of the vital sense of autonomy. Forced to "live his life within the thought categories of another," the worker became "a malleable apparatus attached to a machine."[121] The reward for service to the enterprise, Nyozekan writes, was "wretchedness, hunger, ignorance, and degradation."[122] And in the end, the humanity of both worker and capitalist—"the former through hunger and want, the latter through their satisfaction"—was spoiled.[123]

Nyozekan's *Critiques* treat ideology—the process of idealization—as inherent in institutional development. Thus we find an interesting parallel between the two works in the examination of state "science" and the so-called *rōdō no geijutsuka:* the transformation of labor into art. Under this heading Nyozekan attacks the work of early non-Marxist socialists, such as Edward Carpenter and William Morris in Britain, and the associated thesis of the "joy of labor"—labor as pleasure and as play—articulated in Japan by Morimoto Kōkichi and the philosopher Kuwaki Gen'yoku.[124] The pages Nyozekan devotes to this critique are among the most moving in his work. Not only does he make a fervent call for labor to be understood in its reality, and not as it *ought* to be; he uses the discussion as a point of departure to suggest a "labor theory of art." This in itself is only a partial articulation of Nyozekan's view of "humanity" as the impulse to create, born of the pain that is life.

What is labor? Labor is pain, the physical and psychic pain of yielding to material necessity. Labor is at once an individual and social act, the "interaction [*kōgo sayō*] of social necessity and individual impulse."[125] Labor is the basic condition of life; it is life itself. From this transhistorical set of definitions, Nyozekan examines the implications for the labor movement of the currents in it that spring from conceptions of labor as joy, play, or pleasure. Considering that Nyozekan pinned his hopes for social reconstruction in Japan on the labor movement, it is not difficult to understand the vehemence with which he rejected these views. His primary objection lay in the fact that any organized attempt to improve the condition of labor based on such premises amounted to a contradiction in terms. How could any good come of action based on a misreading of the reality of work? Though he did not question their sincerity, he could not help but find something dangerous, or at best obstructive, in these attempts to deny, to escape, what work was. Neither could work be made *into* something not of its own nature. It was axiomatic that misconception of reality played into the hands of those forces—capitalist enterprise—that sought to perpetuate it. Advocates of the labor as art/labor as pleasure thesis were of course no more satisfied with the status quo than Nyozekan. So the mystification in which they indulged was hardly intentional. It simply bore out a conviction that Nyozekan held apropos of politics: "Given the need to compel a majority, it becomes necessary, not to force its will mechanically, but instead to cause it to will what the despot itself wills." [126] So, too, in the realm of working-class consciousness. If the producing class can be convinced that it must escape from, rather than recognize, the force that dominates its life, the chance for advance now at hand will be lost. Thus "paternalistic" proposals "from above" for a shorter working day and improved conditions and treatment, though valid in themselves, can actually impede worker consciousness if they are thought to assist in the transformation of work back into what it was at some romantic time past, without any change in the relations of production. [127] This does not mean that Nyozekan, or *Warera,* denied their support to meliorative proposals or to one or another draft of a labor union bill. In fact, *Warera* editorialized in favor of the Home Ministry bill of 1920 (written by Nanbara Shigeru), rather than the version prepared by the Ministry of Agriculture and Commerce. [128] Work under capitalism, Nyozekan insists, can never be joy, never pleasure, never play. The acceptance of the contrary view amounts to an admission that the goal of life is to imitate Veblen's leisure class, to perpetuate the invidious division under capitalism of labor from life, thought, and pleasure—and from positions of power in society. [129] It takes little thought to see that "a society in which those who have the easiest life hold the most power is an absurdity. What we ought to have is a society in which those who bear the most suffering have the most power." [130]

Here, precisely, was the sickness of Japanese society, reflected, however innocently, in the slogan "transformation of work into art." Such an art would, of course, be a sham. The real imperative was the reverse, the "transformation of art into work." This does not mean simply the "proletarianization" of art in the sense of idealizing a proletarian subject, or setting up a false antinomy between "good" socialist and "evil" capitalist. Nyozekan meant rather that art, if it is to be real, cannot ignore the great cultural shift under way, from the age of the ego to that of society. And since for Nyozekan society *was* the world of work, art would perforce have to "reproduce" human toil and suffering. To the extent that it did so, it was genuinely creative.[131] The creative act and the act of work therefore shared this common spring—they were both, in a sense, sacrificial.

Could work itself then be creative? Was there no way in which it could be transformed? There was—given worker control over production. If the process of production were restored as far as possible to the control of those actually involved in it, the creative, spontaneous *element* in individual work could emerge. (It is an open question whether it was workers themselves, or the intellectuals attempting to organize them, who regarded producer control as the main issue. If, as has been suggested, recognition of their "right to benevolence" was the key worker demand in the early labor movement, where did Nyozekan get his ideas? He does not say.) But even with this element restored to certain kinds of labor, "no one can tell me that we ought to hope for the day when the coal diggers of the world will do their work with 'artistic feeling' or with the mechanical indifference of an ant."[132] In other words, certain kinds of work will remain, under any system, physically and psychologically painful. But the more work can be made to balance the primary social need for regularity and the individual (and still semiconscious) need to create, the more meaning the sacrifice that is daily toil will have.

Were there grounds for hoping that organized workers in Japan could bring about a "socialized," "humanized" world for themselves? Not in the short run. Thus Nyozekan counseled workers not to condemn the system in toto, but to win for themselves what legal gains they could, believing that "as sure as the hands of a clock turn," "socialization" was an eventual certainty.[133] But the steps were imperceptible. Frustrated hope could lead to thirst for revolution. This would fail. Perhaps, Nyozekan ventures, "by some miracle" the right laws could be passed and legal worker-based parties established.

But as long as the producing class must work through institutions controlled by the middle class, they will meet the same frustrating difficulty as if they were trying to grab hold of a snowball with red-hot tongs. A system in which such a reasonable goal can be achieved only through a miracle is not a good system. What of those unlucky souls who, no matter what they do, are unable to work their way free, and so search for the miracle? We dare not condemn them. Nor dare we laugh.[134]

Nyozekan viewed "present-day" society as being in transition. Modern times everywhere had in a sense "created" the individual as the core unit of all life—of all knowledge and action. Now, however, with the long-term development of institutions—political, economic, and social—the universal exaltation of the individual was giving way to a "social" perspective. This was not a regression to a closed or feudalistic pattern, but a new "sociality" of free (or "complete") individuals conscious of their interdependence and of the need for self-restraint in the interest of the whole. The individualist wave was now cresting on the undulating sea of the social.

It seems fitting, in this connection, to close this review of the *Critiques* with a look at Nyozekan's analysis of the evolution of sexuality. This is an area of special interest, also, because Nyozekan's critique itself provoked a counter-critique from feminist circles.

Nyozekan approaches the problem of sexuality along lines now probably familiar: as with the state vis-à-vis the *seimeitai* and the enterprise vis-à-vis the producing classes, this is an evolution of institutionalized power relations confronting the most basic and creative human impulses. Ever the functionalist, Nyozekan asserts that all culture is essentially a "refinement and sublimation" (*eibinka, junka*) of "unconscious" sexual feeling, whose purpose has, of course, been the reproduction of the species. This in no way diminishes the importance of conscious cultural transmission and creation; in fact, one characteristic of the age is the increasing "impingement of consciousness on the sphere of the unconscious." But there is no denying that real life will remain a sometimes volatile mixture, not wholly susceptible to manipulation, of both.[135]

Even in their current ego-oriented state, love and sex remain eminently social as well as individual. This accords, of course, with Nyozekan's thesis that "individual and social represent dual aspects of the same life." Now the "individualization" of sexuality, and the "divorce of sex from reproduction" are part of a larger socioeconomic phenomenon brought about by the Industrial Revolution, which has in turn had repercussions in many spheres. The institution of marriage, conceptions of pleasure and desire, and how these are to be pursued and satisfied, have all been affected. Prefiguring Ivan Illich by many decades, Nyozekan argues that with the development of industry over the course of the nineteenth century, gender roles—those sanctioned in the West by the church and in the East by "Confucian morality"—broke down in the face of the imperatives of the production process. Women could no longer expect to spend their lives as "reproductive specialists." Apart from the actual bearing of children, there was no qualitative difference in women's relation to a society dominated and defined by industrial production. That is, just as the male proletarian did not work for or with his family, but sold his labor as an "individual" on the "market," so too did women—with the burden of childbearing as an added, rather than definitive, role. The preindustrial (precapitalist) world—whose disappearance from Japan Nyozekan places in the first Meiji decades—had been one of "gender"; reproduction of the family the paradigm. In this world, Nyozekan argues, women can be said to have been far stronger than at present, even to have "dominated" existence. In common, conscious discourse, "sex" as an act has now been divorced from reproduction. In Illich's sense, "gender" has been overwhelmed by the atomizing abstraction of industrial work.[136] (One wonders what existential sources in Japan Nyozekan turned to in support of this assertion—literature? statistics?)

What effect has this combination of the "degendering of society" and the "refinement of love" had on the institution of marriage? Here (we may extrapolate) is where the potentially liberating contradiction arises. Marriage as *seido* has not kept up with the transformation of society into a market. It is dominated by feudal patterns that in some ways (for women) make life that much worse. Not only have they and the family been displaced in the market as the object of labor; the negative aspects of their former institutional position—absence of choice, legal subordination to the husband, practical serfdom—have been preserved. The social contract had yet to find its way into marriage. But "everything that lives, evolves." And the transitional phase of late-capitalist society, from the age of the ego to that of society, has prompted the development of "feminism" (Nyozekan uses this term). This is an attempt to overturn the persistent logic of subjection on two fronts. On the one hand, if there *is* no biological basis for women's *social* role, then there ought to be no legal-institutional barriers to its full exercise. There can be no scientific basis for the restriction, apart from biological necessity in childbearing, on what women do. In evolutionary terms, therefore, feminism is a necessary development. Nyozekan in fact makes the (at first sight reactionary) argument that just as the present system constitutes a male dictatorship, so might the future produce a female dictatorship. "Women just as men push their lives forward toward the infinite. They will not be confined by the stereotypes that take shape in the minds of our contemporaries."[137] However, Nyozekan makes this caution: for the feminist movement to seek liberation via the male rhetoric of "rights"—male because in actual fact males have set up the production process responsible for social contract theory—is to play with illusion.[138] Laws relating to sex, as with all other laws, will change only when it no longer serves the interest of dominant strata that they be preserved. Just as he had argued with respect to universal suffrage, Nyozekan supports the securing of women's *rights* as an admirable goal, but insists that without a transformation in the mode (and social relations) of production, the effort could easily end more in frustration than in creative change. And as with that earlier argument, Nyozekan seems to waver. He implies, despite his strictures against it, that only revolution will bring about the needed transformation, while yet arguing for "extremely gradual" development through piecemeal measures. These, backed by education in consciousness of the long-term end, will amount to qualitative change at some point.

The logic of subjection was open to challenge on another front. This involved the "sublimation [?] of romantic love" (*koi no junka*), as an expression of resistance to fossilization in the institution of marriage. Change in this sphere would decisively affect the lives of both men and women. It was no less important, and probably a better indication of the long wave of development, than reform of law:

As love in its increasing refinement and sublimation yields its dignity to individual sexuality, so too we see a similar tendency for political evolution to be grounded in the development of the individual. Modern man cannot endure a politics that does not take a strong individual as its key component. This arises from the fact that the end of society is seen to reside in the perfection [*kansei*] of the individual. We aspire to the refinement of love because it represents the perfection of our individuality. Modern society is bound to take as its purpose this perfection of individuality.

Herein lies the freedom of refined love. It is not limited by the institution of marriage. All institutions are subject to criticism. In some cases, they are trampled underfoot. This, however, is but the powerful expression of human emotion, before which all things lie subject. *Yet if this human emotion were not itself grounded in humankind's social consciousness, it would never enjoy the victories in our lives that it does.*

To attempt by main force to link such a basic emotion to a transient institution is a futile and impossible enterprise. Herein lies the failure of those who preach the conformity of love with the institution of marriage.

This is not to say that marriage as an institution does not stand in need of affirmation at present. But as with every other static institution, it is also bound to suffer the criticism of dynamic human emotion. Through the ceaseless stimulus of this criticism, the institution is spared sclerotic degeneration and is forced to follow a graduated and fluid evolution. Refined sexuality resists not only the particular institution of marriage per se, but all things that try to repress it. The public in applauding it is resisting the absurdity of man's present physical and mental life. From this resistance is born our continuing evolution.[139]

Nyozekan's conclusions about the social consequences of this "degendering" and "institutionalization" did not go uncontested. The feminist activist and historian Takamure Itsue (1894–1964), for example, took direct issue with Nyozekan on a number of basic points. Her critique, which appeared in the anarchist women's journal *Fujin sensen*, came in response to a lengthy article by Nyozekan serialized in the Tokyo *Asahi* early in 1929.[140]

In "Shakai mondai toshite no sei no goraku" (Sexual amusement as a social problem), Nyozekan had examined what he called the "hedonist culture" of the modern city; a culture in which sex had been divorced from reproduction and was pursued for its own sake in "institutions" (*kikan*) established for that purpose. One aspect of this culture was economic, as he sought to demonstrate in a discussion of legalized prostitution. Nyozekan regarded this as a kind of safety valve for the satisfaction of sexual desire by those incapable—primarily for financial reasons—of marriage in a bourgeois society. That is, prostitution was a social necessity in working-class life, with its many unattached men. It was—or, in modern, hedonist culture, had become—an index of poverty and the inability to form families.

Takamure refuted this argument. The truth, she asserted, was rather that, as had historically been the case, licensed prostitution was supported by men who had money, time, and desire. It was part of affluent life under a patriarchal system. Citing a survey of the clientele of a licensed quarter in Wakayama taken between 1915 and 1918, Takamure noted that "of the 166,000 and more customers, a mere 20.3 percent of the total number were thought to be between twenty-one and twenty-five years of age and unmarried; customers between the ages of twenty-six and forty-five were most numerous, and those above forty-six also appeared in no mean numbers." The licensed quarters, in short, catered to the married trade, to those able to pay. On the whole Takamure found that time—or boredom—and money among the propertied had led to hedonism. More fundamentally, Takamure questioned Nyozekan's deeply held (or at least frequently voiced) conviction that sexual desire, as an individual instinct, ought "naturally" to be subject to social constraint. In the most primitive societies, those who violated the boundary of institutionally licit sex were killed, Nyozekan had claimed, and "society" still establishes extreme sanctions against violations of sexual status norms. On the contrary, Takamure asserted, it is not "society" that abhors sexual license and disorder, but the privileged classes, fearful for the political and economic bases of their status:

> A society whose political and economic foundations are firmly set not for the ruling strata but for the good of all, will never find that freedom—of whatever kind—disturbs its good order. To the contrary, by allowing reproduction to take its natural course [*seishoku no shizen*]—and reproduction has an inherently proper direction and order—we promote the welfare of all humanity.[141]

Sexual taboos are therefore not natural or fated, but historical constructions aimed at guarding the interests of dominant strata. "Society" in the true sense, far from placing restraints on sex as natural (*sei no shizen*), understands, encourages, and provides for its development.

Takamure, then, was naturally bound to question Nyozekan's understanding of the aspirations of modern women. For her, sexual taboo and repression were a feature, not of the most primitive society, but of society *after* its division into ruling and ruled; after the emergence of social and economic exploitation. Far from being natural, they were historical and could be changed. To put it another way, Takamure was perhaps suspicious of the high valuation Nyozekan attached, on functional grounds, to "social" restraint. She seems to have found that here, concealed behind his otherwise radically critical language, lay a deep incomprehension of women's experience.

A final observation will bring this review to a close and open the way to what follows. This, too, has to do with Nyozekan's apparent radicalism. In her critique, Takamure identifies Nyozekan with Marxism. As we shall see, he in fact had a somewhat ambivalent attitude toward Marxism, while seeming to maintain close ties with its main Japanese theorists. Perhaps more interesting is the skepticism—if not contempt— Takamure reveals for Japanese Marxists and the Communist Party membership. The contradiction between their intellectual commitment to liberating revolution and their own day-to-day behavior and attitudes toward women was apparently quite flagrant. (And she adds, "Those who would excuse the sexual games of the Party membership should be aware just how reactionary they are.") It is to be noted, however, that she does not accuse Nyozekan in this regard; nor does she suggest any willing misogyny on his part.

Takamure closes her critique with a sharp parting shot, which reveals her skepticism of the liberating potential of the intellectualism of contemporary Marxists: "Hasegawa has of late become something of a Marxist. This is only right. Marxism is the sophism of our day; with its materialism and dialectics it is truly the heir of its distant Greek ancestor. And Hasegawa has shown his true colors as an unapologetic sophist."[142]

OF SHŌWA POLITICS BUT NOT IN IT

In an account of limited scope such as this one, some injustice to the subject and his concerns is unavoidable. Nuances are missed, insights overlooked. I have not, unfortunately, been able to capture the rich variety of voices with which *Warera* articulated its criticisms and program for social reconstruction. True, Nyozekan *was Warera:* but both were more than synonyms for each other, and both changed. At the risk of schematizing too much, I must now try to put Nyozekan in some kind of perspective by considering his work in the light of the diverging paths taken by three major contributors to the journal, Nyozekan himself, Ōyama Ikuo, and Kawakami Hajime. The latter two had been associated with Nyozekan at the Osaka *Asahi.* Kawakami's reports of prewar London, and his enormously famous *Binbō monogatari* (Tales of poverty) had appeared on its pages. Ōyama, whose career up to 1932 in many ways parallels that of Hobhouse, had despite student protests been forced to resign his post at Waseda University in the wake of the violent "Waseda Incident" of 1917, and joined the *Asahi*'s editorial staff.[143] Along with Nyozekan, he had left the paper at the time of the "White Rainbow" trial and was prominent among the founders of *Warera.* Each of the three men used the journal as a home base from which to pursue their linked, but increasingly divergent, destinies. In the decade between 1922 and 1932, each of the three made a choice of weapons in the social struggle that drove them apart, never, to be sure, into mutual hostility, but nonetheless apart.

This was the period punctuated, in 1925, by the enactment of universal male suffrage and the Peace Preservation Law. While the former virtually guaranteed the mushroomlike growth of legal "proletarian" parties, the latter sought to ensure that none of their programs could ever become reality. In this sense, we may say that the left hand knew what the right hand was doing, and vice versa. By 1925 Ōyama, having been reinstated at Waseda, was regarded as the opinion leader among progressives. He was as ever idolized by his students. He and Kawakami, professor of economics at Kyoto University, reigned as the "Twin Bulwarks of the East and West" (*Tōzai no sōheki*) among publicists of the left social movement. Between 1921 and 1925 Kawakami had "drawn close" to Marxism. Along with his monthly, *Shakai mondai kenkyū* (Studies in social problems), Kawakami published a translation of Marx's *Wage Labor and Capital* and authored *Yuibutsu shikan ryakkai* (An outline of the materialist view of history) and *Shihonshugi keizaigaku no shiteki hatten* (The historical development of capitalist economics). The latter work was criticized by Kushida Tamizō, Kawakami's student and a *Warera* contributor, for its moral idealization of the proletariat. This and other criticism—notably that of Fukumoto Kazuo that Kawakami's work had an inconsistent and deficient theoretical foundation—prompted Kawakami to embark on an intensive and self-critical examination of his Marxism.

The enactment, meanwhile, of universal male suffrage and the political organization of the proletariat was in the eyes of both Ōyama and Kawakami a signal opportunity. Ōyama, with Nyozekan's support, was the first to take the plunge, when in 1926 he accepted the chairmanship of the newly formed Worker-Farmer Party (Rōdō Nōmin Tō, or Rōnōtō). Compelled on this account to resign once again from Waseda, Ōyama stood for election to the Diet from Kagawa. True, the Rōnōtō was regarded as the legal arm of the Communist Party. On the other hand, Ōyama had the support of the local peasant movement. Admittedly, the association with Bolshevism was dangerous, but Ōyama was probably not prepared for the viciousness of the Tanaka government's repression of the party. He was, needless to say, defeated. Nyozekan commented mordantly that "If Ōyama could have gotten elected, so could have one of the stone lanterns at the [nearby] Kotohira Shrine."[144] (Ōyama's dramatic campaign slogan turned out to be prophetic. "In this election," he proclaimed, "we are headed to a battleground—and to our graves." Two years later, Yamamoto Senji, a Kyoto University biologist elected on the Rōnōtō ticket, was stabbed to death by a right-wing terrorist.) Ōyama was soon pushed to the forefront of the legal left. He weathered the dissolution of the Rōnōtō by official order following the mass arrest of Communists and their sympathizers in March 1928. And despite "blistering" criticism by the Communist Party (which followed the lead of the Comintern), Ōyama was among the founders of the Shin Rōnōtō in 1929, and finally elected to the Diet in 1930 as a representative from Tokyo's fifth electoral district. After the Manchurian Incident, however, Ōyama felt that the tide of reaction had made his political activity both futile and dangerous. On the advice of Nyozekan, Maruyama Kanji, and others, Ōyama and his wife left Japan for the United States in February 1932. They returned sixteen years later.

The formation of the Shin Rōnōtō proved to be the parting of the ways for Kawakami and Ōyama. The former, along with Hososako Kanemitsu, had been intimately involved in founding the party as a transitional organ in anticipation of a resurrected JCP. But the Party, now underground, regarded the new organization as a rightist-deviant betrayal, and vilified it from the first. Before long Kawakami and Hososako adopted this line. From this point onward Ōyama, already considered a Communist and sellout to Russia by the bourgeois parties, was enrolled among the "betrayers" of the left. As for Kawakami, he had already been expelled from the university following the March 1928 arrests. Returning to journalism and translation, he wrote a "Leninist" *Tales of Poverty: II,* began translating *Capital* in 1931, translated the Comintern's 1932 Theses for *Akahata,* and finally joined the Party later that year. After this "supreme moment" in his life, Kawakami went underground, but he was arrested in January 1933. Although he foreswore any further active involvement in the movement, Kawakami never repudiated the ends or means adopted by the Party: he remained a "theoretical" non-apostate. Kawakami's subsequent career need not detain us here. Let us merely take stock of what became of Nyozekan's *Warera* colleagues. Ōyama went into politics, though to Nyozekan's mind he did not possess the necessary ambition, guile, or sangfroid, eventually finding exile the only logical step to take. Kawakami moved from legal to illegal political activity, was arrested, and spent five long years in prison. The point is that both men did what Nyozekan would not and could not: joined the organized struggle for political power. Nyozekan's personal motto, it will be recalled, was *danjite okonawazu:* "[Be] resolute in not taking action." With the passage of suffrage in 1925, this position obviously took on new meaning. Not that Nyozekan's contribution would have been greater had he chosen to *okonau,* to act. The point is that the political fates of Ōyama and Kawakami clearly suggest what might have happened if he had.

Nyozekan, Ōyama, and Kawakami were all three of them consistent. But we come now to a point in the story where drastic shifts in direction became the order of the day as the left responded to the reactionary political situation. Aside from complete submersion in unpolitical life (the "cocoon" option), one choice open to public outsiders was repudiation of the left and some degree of active involvement in rightist politics. This was *tenkō* in the "classic" sense of Sano Manabu, Nabeyama Sadachika, Hayashi Fusao, and Akamatsu Katsumaro. But this is to view the matter too narrowly. The broader question, beyond the organizational impact of mass defection from the JCP, concerns the generalized "return to Japan" (*Nihon e no kaiki*) by leftist intellectuals after 1933. Here, unlike Ōyama and Kawakami, Nyozekan was involved. However, we can treat his "return"—the issue of *tenkō* broadly conceived—only after considering the crisis that engendered it. We must, in short, place Nyozekan and ourselves amidst the cross-currents of Japanese fascism.

By the last years of the 1920s *Warera* was on its way to becoming a financial basket case. Loss of revenue through periodic run-ins with the censors and postal authorities, fires, and the death of a long-time patron in 1929 all took their toll. The whole tenor of the times seemed to militate against *Warera*'s survival. The "rise of the military" and right-wing terror against the backdrop of depression needs no rehearsal here.

Overall, *Warera* in its last years continued along the lines suggested in the two *Critiques*. But now certain problems only adumbrated there— because as social developments they were present then only in germ— came to the fore. A good deal of attention is given to the Japanese role in Manchuria, especially that played by the army and the South Manchurian Railroad (Mantetsu). Nyozekan's concern was not the autonomous function of these organizations. He asked, rather, how they fit into the larger dynamic of the expansion of Japanese capitalism, and how this dynamic in turn was tied into the mutual relations of the Japanese bourgeoisie in the state and political parties. That is, Nyozekan, though he would not have used the term, was moving toward an analysis of "superstructural" problems as such in Japanese capitalism. It is intriguing to note in this connection that in 1926 and 1928 Nyozekan made month-long speaking tours of Manchuria and North China, both at the invitation of Mantetsu itself.

At the same time, Nyozekan continued to write on the related problems of ideology and consciousness. In 1932 Iwanami published a long article by Nyozekan on the production of ideology, which dealt with art in its relation to the "reality" of social movement, a theme he had treated a decade earlier. By this time, however, Nyozekan found himself sharing the current with such Marxist literary critics as Kobori Jinji and Kurahara Korehito.[145] But it is well to remember that inevitable and "conscious" evolution, not a vanguard-directed social revolution, remained Nyozekan's chief value position, despite their shared categories of analysis.

As the earlier sketches of the careers of Ōyama and Kawakami show, the late 1920s and early 1930s marked a final act in the "late Taishō" discovery of society. The logic of radicalization was playing itself out: *Warera* published its final issue, the 128th since 1919, in March 1930. Included in its pages was a short announcement of a change in title, to *Hihan*—Criticism. For twelve years, *Warera* had "put the whip" to society and history; the contrivances of the mind, conscious and unconscious, had about run their course, while "like a mule that has overeaten," society would seem to have stood stock still. That is, the problem remained a problem, and now "new energy, new weapons, new methods" were needed to "kick" society in the mind and force it to move.[146] *Hihan* made its first appearance in May 1930. With the Esperanto subtitle *La Kritiko Socialista* (later just *La Kritiko*) the journal ran for four years, publishing forty-two issues, of which two were banned, others censored so severely as to be illegible.[147]

Ōyama Ikuo had been insisting since 1925 that the proper role for *Warera* was as the "theoretical organ" of the working class, an explicit link between the proletariat's theory and practice.[148] Nyozekan had demurred, first because he did not want to set the journal up as an arm of the "vanguard" within the organized revolutionary struggle. As Rōyama Masamichi points out, Nyozekan regarded the Bolshevik idea of a vanguard party as an anachronism and a weapon specific to the far more backward conditions Lenin had faced in Russia.[149] We saw earlier that Nyozekan regarded revolution as historically and socially unnecessary for Japan. Yet he speaks of the need for "new energy, new weapons, new methods" to "kick" society and "make it move." All very vague and allusive language, to be sure. Clearly Nyozekan is signaling a break from the counsels of patience in the earlier *Critiques*. As Tanaka Hiroshi remarks, Nyozekan had replaced *Warera*'s essentially moral critique of the state as an abuser of power with analysis and critique of the state as the instrument of a late-capitalist ruling class. In this respect, the earlier *Critiques* are transitional, since the link between change in the social relations of production and in social consciousness is clearly made. Tanaka is careful to point out that if anything, the change from *Warera* to *Hihan* represents an intensification of critical *focus* rather than an embrace of "the unity of theory and practice."[150] Nevertheless, one senses a drop of despair in *Hihan*. The confidence that had animated *Warera*, that change would come "as surely as the hands of a clock turn" is missing. Had Nyozekan misjudged the volume and force of the reactionary tide he had identified a decade before? *Hihan* vibrates with the perception that "something" had happened, a qualitative change in world (and hence Japanese) politics and society, ominous in nature and not soon to disappear. Japan, in short, was turning fascist.

Hihan, with some hints in the last issues of *Warera*, can be read as an attempt to analyze and counter the threat of fascism theoretically. Nyozekan's articles on the subject were in short order prepared for publication as a book. Appearing on 20 November 1932, *Nihon fuashizumu hihan* (Critique of Japanese fascism) was banned the same day, and reissued in heavily censored form on 12 December.[151]

How and when did Nyozekan come to view Japanese fascism as a possibility? At what point did the development of Japanese politics and society seem to him congruent with what contemporary European and Soviet analysts described as fascism? To what degree, and with what differences? For a public outsider with Nyozekan's background to broach this issue in print was clearly a risk. Vis-à-vis not only the state, but also the Japanese left, he was walking a tightrope. Hence the second strand of our discussion: Where did Nyozekan's critique situate him? To what consequences did the *Critique* and his other activities during these years lead? What, in other words, were the personal consequences of his public stance? Finally, what legacy did Nyozekan's experience leave for other, later public outsiders?

Limitations of space permit only a rough outline of how these two strands are woven together in the *Critique*. The "imported" theories of fascism that inform Nyozekan's analysis all shared the perception that fascism was a form of counterrevolution. Thus its definition and analysis were of greatest concern to the revolutionary forces, for whom the fight against it was an urgent theoretical and practical necessity. It was not until 1933 (with some exceptions) that non-Marxists began to direct their critical attention to fascism. Nyozekan's work, since it dates from 1928–31, naturally reflects the viewpoints and concerns of revolutionary Marxist writers, both those working within Comintern orthodoxy and others who formed the various "side currents" of the debate.

The identification of a tide of reaction after the events of 1917–18 was, of course, common to all parties. The first wave had come with the attempt by the West (and Japan) to encircle and destroy the Soviet Union; next, there was the role of social democracy in the collapse of socialist revolutions in Germany, Hungary, and Austria; and, third, the assumption by Mussolini of power in Italy. This wave of counterrevolution appeared to most analysts in the revolutionary camp as an attempt by parliamentary regimes in late-developing capitalist states to shore up a declining finance capital by means of petty bourgeois (in some cases social democratic) shock troops. Thus between 1922 and 1931 the Comintern was led to define fascism as (in 1924) "one of the classic forms of counterrevolution in the epoch when capitalist society is decaying." As Stalin put it, fascism was "the bourgeoisie's fighting organization" and relied "on the active support of Social Democracy."[152] It is beyond my purpose to examine the consequences for the left—widely acknowledged to have been catastrophic—of the Comintern's identification of "social fascism" as the greatest enemy of the proletariat. In any case, when after 1928 Stalinism "fell like a hood" over Soviet culture,[153] potentially fruitful and liberating debate on fascism was an early victim, bringing with it "a widening divorce between the Comintern's policy and the actual situation, internationally and within each country."[154]

Now although the concept of fascism rested on the "economic" assumption that capitalism had entered its final crisis, it is important to keep in mind that the crisis itself, while springing from wartime destruction and economic dislocation throughout the 1920s, was also social and political in expression. Indeed one of the egregious failures of the Comintern theses on fascism was the neglect both of the interclass (social) and cultural (ideological) aspects of counterrevolution. Although the 1929 crash and Hitler's rise to power in 1933 did force a tactical shift—the call for communist parties to join with social democracy in an antifascist "Popular Front"—this "did not reflect," one critic notes, "any significant advance in comprehension."[155]

These developments, of course, came after Nyozekan had published his analyses. For him, late 1931—the aftermath of the Manchurian Incident—represented the climax of the process up to that point. Thus it is all the more interesting to note the similarities between Nyozekan's ideas and those generated from among the "side currents" of the contemporary European debate on fascism. Indeed, it was only here that attempts were made to flesh out the phenomenon's social and cultural dimensions. None denied what Gavan McCormack calls the "capitalist essence" of fascism. But its contradictory ideological tendencies, strength among the petty bourgeoisie *and* the proletariat, and the mechanisms by which the fascist movement articulated with capitalist states would have lain virtually unexamined were it not for such unorthodox commentators as Karl Radek, Clara Zetkin, and August Thalheimer. One can see in their insights strands of thought shared with Nyozekan. How this is so will become clear in due course. The question of influence is impossible to resolve and may be irrelevant. But the congruence in certain areas is not.

Nyozekan did not consider his *Critique* a work of "abstract theory." Rather it aimed at understanding "concrete political phenomena" in Japan. And although not meant as prophecy, Nyozekan felt that the course taken by Japanese politics—the end of party cabinets and the final turn toward open military aggression—had borne out his analyses.[156] They are a blend of close reading of political developments in Japan from 1929 to 1932, and comparative "social science"; that is, a class analysis of "Japanese" fascism that, while it employs Marxist formulations, comes to conclusions quite different from the Comintern and contemporary Kōza-ha positions. In fact the term "emperor-system absolutism" (*tennōsei zettaishugi*), the linchpin of the prewar Kōza-ha characterization of the modern Japanese state, is conspicuous in Nyozekan's *Critique* by its absence, even in disguised form.

The *Critique* embraces two theses. First, fascism as a potentially dominant political form emerges preeminently in "late-developing" capitalist states such as Italy and Japan, where bourgeois social power has historically been weak, and where the postwar economic crisis has shaken an already exclusivist, "oligarchic" parliamentary system. (The case of Germany, with its powerful Social Democratic Party, comes immediately to mind as a counterexample to the type of parliamentary system dominant in a potentially fascist regime. At the time Nyozekan wrote, of course, the Nazi takeover was only a speculative possibility.) Ultimately, fascism serves to reinforce capitalism and its "bourgeois dictatorship" by the elimination of all organized legal opposition, especially that of the working class. Thus fascism need not mean the dismantling of parliamentary institutions per se, only the removal from them of working-class representation.[157]

Here we come to the second and larger thesis, which revolves around the role of social classes and groups in the achievement of fascist ends. We must understand that no concept of an all-pervasive rationality is at work in the idea that one class can achieve its ends through the manipulation of another. The sense is closer to the "playing out" or expression of a "nature" determined by the total social being of a given class—its relation to other classes and to the national past.[158] Members of a class cannot but be what they are, and in doing so can serve two masters without being conscious of the fact. Thus, in explaining fascism, Nyozekan joins with Radek and Zetkin, who "recognized as early as 1923" its petty bourgeois roots and appeal, and admitted that the appeal "extended through broad social groups, large masses which reach far into the proletariat." Zetkin, addressing the executive committee of the Comintern in the same year, reminded her audience that fascism was a "movement of the hungry, the suffering, the poverty-stricken, the frustrated."[159] That is, fascism as a movement depended on the mobilization of petty bourgeois fears of displacement, especially by the working class from below. It was a mistake, therefore, to make an enemy of social democracy at a time when, on the contrary, an alliance against capitalism and (though Nyozekan could not have said so) for the overthrow of the capitalist state was necessary.[160] This was not to deny petty bourgeois hostility to the working class; and that the petty bourgeoisie was (in theory) susceptible to mobilization/manipulation from either side. It played, as Nyozekan put it, a "pendulum" role. Lacking a clear "class attitude" of their own, the groups that make up the "middle stratum" ("small landowners and shopkeepers," etc.) are driven back into reactionary chauvinistic nationalism—the defensiveness of the tribe under attack.[161] This chauvinism took as its prime target the parliamentary status quo, its attack taking shape as a call for order and justice for the little man, and for an end to the anarchic internationalism and "liberalism" of big capital. It is similarly opposed to the true internationalist socialism of the working class—the internationalism so decisively rejected by the majority of social democratic parties in 1914, which is the only possible defense against fascism.[162]

Nyozekan's point, however, is not to idealize an existing hero-class but to expose the political tendencies of the middle stratum under certain conditions: the greater the development of bourgeois democracy in a society, and the greater the representation enjoyed by the working class, the smaller the chances of fascism developing when capitalism experiences a serious crisis. However, the obverse is also true; even a democratic society long accustomed to political stability will face, as Britain did after 1929, the internal threat of fascistization in the name of order. This was the lesson Nyozekan drew from Oswald Moseley's breakaway from the Labour Party and his creation of the British Union of Fascists.[163] Nyozekan does not deal in absolutes, but rather in terms of degree and extent. Fascism was not a ready-made article that could be imposed on a social and political system by a determined enemy, whether internal or external. It was to some degree an "organic" development. Though vitally affected by and transforming that system's relations with the outside, fascism was essentially domestic in its genesis. Its growth (from movement to state?) could be gradual and legal, or violent and illegal. The removal of a fascist regime was of course another matter. Writing in the aftermath of the Manchurian Incident, Nyozekan contemplated the prospect of a second "World War" between fascist and bourgeois democratic (and socialist) regimes. The cure for fascism was sure to be violent.[164]

Let us consider how Nyozekan applies his argument to Japan. His first thesis, as we saw, concerned the general function of fascism. The second outlined the petty bourgeois roots of the phenomenon but stressed, on the basis of the Italian example, the cooptation of "primitive" fascism as the regime made its peace with capitalism. In discussing Japan, Nyozekan arrived at a formula that was to see lasting service. This was "cool fascism" (sometimes "cold" or "legal" fascism): the idea that, in Japan at least, with the petty bourgeois "movement" too fragmented to coalesce into a single political force, but too strong to ignore, fascism would come about not only without the destruction of, but indeed through, the existing institutions of government. That is, elements within the state and political parties would gradually make it their purpose to destroy independent working-class organizations and blunt, in the name of national unity and harmony, all opposition from within the bourgeois camp.[165] Thus: "I believe that in Japan, too, it is not violent, but legal, cool fascism now preeminently taking shape. Before long middle-class fascism will be absorbed [gōryū seshimerareru] into cool fascism. If we consider Japan an advanced capitalist nation, that, in formal terms, is the course fascism will take."[166]

In the realization of cool fascism, it is the petty bourgeois movement that provides the necessary *destabilization* as it seeks by its own violence to counteract the threat to the system from the radicalized working class. That is, it creates the desire for order, and having done so, it is to be "melted into the furnace" of the "cool fascist" dictatorship of the bourgeoisie (an odd mixture of metaphors).[167] In the economic realm, fascism serves capitalism in analogous fashion: "it erects a bulwark against collapse using the [ideology] of small and middling industry and commerce."[168] After 1929, of course, this bulwark, far from having been strengthened, was all the more easily absorbed through the process of the concentration of capital.

Nyozekan does not seem to have regarded Japanese "cool fascism" as a kind of Bonapartism. That is, he did not accept the idea of "class equilibrium" maintained, or a power vacuum filled, by an autonomous fascist state.[169] Rather, he took the opposite, eclectic tack of trying to subsume the increasingly powerful influence of segments of the military *within* the category of the middle stratum. Assuming a correspondence between the upper stratum of the bourgeoisie and that of the military, and between the middle stratum (petty bourgeoisie) and middle echelons of the military, Nyozekan argues that in fact the conflict emerging between the "Young Officers" (he does not use this term) and their civilian allies on the one hand and the entrenched bureaucrats of the upper echelon of the army on the other was one of class.[170] And just as the ideology of the middle differs from that of the upper stratum in society as a whole, so, too, within the military. Just as the petty bourgeoisie's construction of social reality, when threatened, resorted to irrationalist chauvinism—as was proven, to the profound shock and disgust of many progressives at the time of the Great Kanto Earthquake—so, too, the middle ranks of the military were the most determined to impel Japan toward aggressive territorial expansion as a solution to overpopulation and rural poverty. Both, finally, were the first to resort to violent methods in domestic politics.[171] The question becomes, how is this petty bourgeois front to be absorbed into the ranks of cool fascism? Is this a *conditio sine qua non* for any development of fascism in Japan? It is difficult, in Nyozekan's *Critique*, to see what the mechanism of absorption (or de-fanging) is to be. And it is not surprising to find that contemporary Marxist commentators, like Shinomura Satoshi, found the assumption that fascism in Japan would ultimately triumph through existing institutions to reflect an "undialectical grasp" of the problem: "So long as the soil for the cultivation of fascism exists, we must account it a crucial error to recognize in it only the growth of 'cool' or 'legal' fascism while denying that of fascism proper (*honrai no*)." There is a "practical [*jissenteki*] danger" that "by confining the emergence of fascism to one or the other type, our [the party's] praxis will fall completely into the clutches of the bourgeoisie's maneuvers."[172]

However, Nyozekan does at least try to outline the process of absorption. He hints, first, that in the case of the military (in regard to which censorship must have been extraordinarily rigorous) it will be violent. Here, of course, Nyozekan was right. He also shows, through an examination of contemporary Japanist groups and their platforms, that "fascist" organizations in Japan's rural districts and towns, while avowedly anticapitalist, were frequently under the control of local bigwigs with connections to the major parties. These organizations in fact gloried in their service to counterrevolution. Anticommunism, rather than anticapitalism, was their great point of pride.[173] (Thus Nyozekan was probably not surprised that such groups went over to the cause of capital [= the state] once the final attempt by officers of the Imperial Way faction at a coup d'état failed. They had lost their only focus of activity outside the state itself.) But what of the relation between *zaibatsu* capital, state bureaucracy, and the parties as a whole? How did Nyozekan envision their eventual role in the development of a fascist regime in Japan?

As of mid 1932, portents of the development of cool fascism were coming, in Nyozekan's view, from the parties. These signs, of course, came after the government's apparent acquiescence in the army's moves in Manchuria, after the March coup d'état attempt, and after the open repression of the left, beginning in 1928. Nyozekan had in mind particularly the activities of Home Minister Adachi Kenzō (1864–1948), whose "boycott" of cabinet business and call for a government of "national unity" had brought down the Minseitō cabinet of Wakatsuki Reijirō at the end of 1931. Having caused the collapse of the government (and of a cabinet led by his own party), Adachi bolted from the Minseitō and, with the famous "Shōwa Restorationist" Nakano Seigō, formed the Kokumin Dōmei. How did Nyozekan interpret these moves? To better understand his position, we must take a small detour and fill in the background, with which Nyozekan must have felt his readers already quite familiar.

It is interesting to note that Adachi had long been known as a maker and breaker of party fortunes. From his beginnings as an organizer of right-wing terror gangs under the direction of Tōyama Mitsuru and Uchida Ryōhei (leaders of the "classic" radical-right Genyōsha), Adachi had gone on to become the "giant killer" in the smashing election victories of the Rikken Dōshikai in 1915. (Formed in 1913, the Dōshikai combined with two other groups in 1916 to form the Kenseikai, and then in 1927 with the Seiyū Hontō to create the Minseitō.) A consistent advocate of a "hard"—pro-military—line in China, Adachi was joined in his efforts to forge a "national unity" coalition by other friends of the army, notably the "new *zaibatsu*" magnate and Seiyūkai chairman

Kuhara Fusanosuke. Indeed, elements of the Seiyūkai had on their own sought "army cooperation to bring down the Wakatsuki cabinet."[174] To be sure, the ultimate aim of all these efforts, a one-party government that enjoyed the blessing of the military, was not shared by all the elders of the Seiyūkai or the Minseitō. This much is clear from the defense of the principle of parliamentary government mounted by Inukai Tsuyoshi and Wakatsuki Reijirō in the wake of the assassination in February 1932 of Inoue Junnosuke, the Minseitō leader and a former finance minister. Inukai had reaffirmed his belief in the "beneficial effects" of parliamentary government, while Wakatsuki denounced the trend toward fascism in Japanese politics and the rule of terror certain to result if Japan were to follow the lead of "Russia, China, and Italy" in establishing a one-party state. With Inukai's own assassination in May, however, "the era of party cabinets came to an end."[175]

There is little question, then, as to Adachi's antipluralist proclivities. At the same time, it would be wrong, as we have seen, to imagine that he or Kuhara desired the establishment of an outright *military* dictatorship; certainly they did not relish the prospect of rule by those who had assassinated Inukai. Nevertheless, it is equally obvious that Adachi—and not only for Nyozekan—was a symbol of the powerful trend toward accommodation with the military that was permeating the parties. But what sort of accommodation was this to be? What could a man such as Adachi have hoped to achieve through a "national unity" cabinet—the type of cabinet that did, of course, predominate in the years after 1932, and under whose aegis actual party influence within the cabinet drained steadily away?

In Nyozekan's view—to return now to the *Critique*—Adachi was concerned to guarantee that the interests of industrial and finance capital represented by the parties would still be served despite the "new situation" in Manchuria. This meant winning control for big capital over the South Manchurian Railroad and its allied enterprises. These had become a zone of special privilege for bureaucrats and military figures, and as such were insufficiently flexible as tools in the expansion of private Japanese capital.[176] Although the two-party system had seemed to promise a stable domestic political arrangement for this expansion, too many destabilizing elements were surfacing: abroad, the Western and Soviet threats, intensified now since the overrunning of Manchuria, and Chinese nationalism and capital in North China; at home military insubordination and working class and peasant agitation, not to mention (for Adachi) the immediate problems of strategy vis-à-vis the Seiyūkai.[177] Adachi thus felt it expedient to "unify" the parties under retired military figures beyond accusation of partisanship, and to accommodate rather than antagonize the military. (Inukai Tsuyoshi had of course taken the opposite tack.) In short, cabinet power had to be single, not in order to prevent further military outrages in Manchuria or North China, but so that the parties' constituencies could begin to reap the benefits of "acquiescence."

The real issue, as Nyozekan saw it, was not civilians versus the military, but upper versus middle/petty bourgeoisie. (The fact that in their efforts to secure military favor for coalition, Seiyūkai officials had approached the army general staff and ministry officials, would seem to bear this out.) Adachi was this upper stratum personified, looking ahead to the time when it would be necessary to bring its minions—the line officers of the Kwantung Army and their domestic allies—to heel. Whether this would be possible was, as Nyozekan points out, quite another question. There was always the danger that the petty bourgeois "horse," while still "bridled" by the institutions of the bourgeois state, would grow too strong and throw its rider.[178] Thus Adachi's moves, as Wakatsuki himself had hinted, could be seen as the "fascistization" of the parties themselves, through fear not so much of direct revolution as of loss of their dominant position in the state as then constituted.

Nyozekan thus locates the engine of cool fascism, as of 1932, in the parties, and ties it directly to the interests of Japanese capitalism in Manchuria. At this point, bureaucracy in Nyozekan's view remained, like the military, divided in itself, at "heart" a semifeudal and guildlike province, and allied in its rank and file with the petty bourgeoisie. (This is not to imply that there was any sort of "Luddite" mentality involved. Bureaucracy was never antimodern in the sense that it resisted technological innovation. Quite the contrary. The question was rather one of control.) The parties had clearly established their dominance over the political system, but only on the condition that bureaucratic influence remain as a structural and ideological brake on big capital. Abroad, the anti-*zaibatsu* policy of the government in Manchukuo seemed to bear this out; similarly bureaucratic sponsorship of "social policy" as a means of class conciliation was evidence of this same influence. For while it might seem to reflect the rising influence of the proletariat, it sprang in fact from the "petty bourgeois" origins and consciousness of bureaucracy itself. Nyozekan traces this lineage back to the "middle stratum force of the feudal warrior class," which was itself responsible for the Meiji Restoration. Bureaucracy had served as the technician of the hurried transition from feudal to (industrial) capitalist production and still harbored the territorializing impulse characteristic of the former condition of society. This was evident in the frequent attacks on giant industrialists and financial combines as "antinational." The parties in turn were compelled to go after petty bourgeois support and to acquiesce in continuing bureaucratic influence. In this sense—in its partial orientation to petty bourgeois interests and consciousness as Nyozekan very broadly construes them—Japan was *ab origine* "fascist." [179] Within five years, of course, the center of gravity was to shift, as Nyozekan had predicted, from this "aboriginal" to a "legal" fascism. One may perhaps infer that the technical side of bureaucratic personality, following the collapse of the radical petty bourgeois front in 1936, finally came into its own, overcoming its "guild" consciousness sufficiently to supplant the parties as the dominant institution, along with the army, in political society.

Nyozekan's account of Japanese fascism is necessarily truncated. Its categories seem eclectic and arbitrary at times. The membership of the middle stratum is only vaguely indicated; there is not a single economic statistic in the entire work. Nyozekan obviously had heavy censorship to contend with. And while he did believe that fascism could be understood through class analysis, one could not pin down the author of the *Critique* as an adherent of any organized ideological movement or party. These factors may account for some of the vagueness and imprecision. Despite these limitations, *Nihon fuashizumu hihan* can claim to be the first attempt to clarify the interclass dynamics of fascism in Japan. It has the immediacy of a work wrestling with an immense and present danger.

One point of particular interest in the *Critique* is its powerful treatment of fascist ideology and art. For Nyozekan art becomes fascist when its producers make use of obscurantist traditionalism not out of principle, but for purely commercial motives. Such, Nyozekan contends, is the nature of much of the contemporary "mass art." Fascist because it plays on the emotions of the masses while mobilizing them against (unexamined) "forces" that threaten the national essence, such work is also pure nihilism. Its producers are, of course, pawns in the bourgeoisie's campaign of cultural imperialism. What is important is that "art" hide reality from its consumers. To the extent that the producers of such work are unaware of their political role, they are to be pitied and awakened. To the extent that they *are* aware, they are vultures to be unmasked. Yet this is in fact the dilemma of the whole petty bourgeoisie. Inescapably bound to a capitalist system of production (including artistic production), its particularism cannot but be compromised by the "universal" quest for profit. Unable to see its own liberation in the struggle of the proletariat, the middle stratum turns against it. But in whose cause? The petty bourgeoisie have none of their own. They condemn the corruption of bourgeois politics not (despite the rhetoric) because it is corrupt, but because it is not *theirs*. The middle stratum is the big loser.[180]

The *Critique,* finally, seems to have been the first work to expose the "timelessness," social ubiquity, conceptual emptiness—and supreme usefulness—of contemporary Japanism.[181] It was this ideological feature of Japanese society that implicitly linked mass and elite: though the elite version of Japanism was more refined, it helped in its own way to integrate the intelligentsia into the ideological superstructure of the state. Indeed, it was debate over how to counteract this kind of integrating force that divided the Japanese left. And for the JCP in particular, it was a major stumbling block, not least because the Comintern could not grasp such a situation.

However, between the intelligentsia and mass there was, according to Nyozekan, a major difference in degree of consciousness. Like big capital, Nyozekan argues, the *interi* knew what they were about. They were conscious of their social role,[182] whether in support of or opposition to the system. Scholar-functionaries (who, according to Maruyama, must be considered members par excellence of the *interi*)[183] had explicit knowledge of their purpose: to legitimate capitalism under the Meiji constitutional system. One dimension of this task was the attempt to link the "timeless" idea of the *kokutai* with the current system that professed to protect it. This was the purpose, for example, of works such as the *Kokutai ron shi* (History of theories of the national polity), compiled by the Shrine Bureau of the Home Ministry in 1919. The volume contained articles by such established academics as Kakehi Katsuhiko, a constitutional law scholar, and the historian of religions Anesaki Masaharu—both of Tokyo Imperial. (Admittedly, Nyozekan remarks, Kakehi is a "crank [*kijin*] who claps his hands in supplication when he mounts the rostrum and dances strange dances." But Anesaki is a "sound scholar.")[184] Whatever the differences in tone, they are in agreement on the unchanging nature of the *kokutai.*

In this respect, the work of figures such as Yoshino and Minobe can be understood as attempts from within to reformulate the argument for the system's legitimacy under changing conditions. But what happens when the impingement of society on politics forces the *interi* to seek not a new formula but a new system? Here Nyozekan's argument on the dynamics of *seido* comes to mind: the existing institution reacts to protect itself; the means it chose in the early 1930s were fascist. For the *interi* as for the mass, the line between tolerable dissent and heresy had been drawn in 1925. Now, in the early 1930s, the space given over to legitimate dissent was narrowing drastically. Nyozekan, it will be recalled, regarded a self-conscious proletariat as the only real answer to fascism. It did not materialize, and we may assume that he took for granted the absorption of the masses into a "fascist" system. But what of the *interi* themselves? Until the advent of the "national emergency" (*hijōji*) around 1933, there had been no obvious connection between the *interi* and fascism. Indeed, their sentiments, if Nyozekan is any indication, seemed genuinely hostile to it. But by the last years of the decade, after the mass *tenkō* of the JCP leadership and rank and file, the campaign against Minobe Tatsukichi and the university purge of 1938–39, the hostility seems to have softened considerably. With the triumph of "cool fascism," many among the *interi* were hewing to the state. Some, like Rōyama Masamichi, Kaji Ryūichi, and the journalist Matsumoto Shigeharu, were followers of Nyozekan who had come to see such service as the cutting edge of social renovation. Rōyama, indeed, spoke the language of a refined fascism. Nyozekan could not have forecast this development, and both he and others were hesitant (after 1945) to examine it. Nonetheless, the involvement of Japanese intellectuals in the country's mobilization for struggle against the West can be seen as the extension of a problem implicit in Nyozekan's *Critique*. More to the point, it is implicit in his *life*. To this problem, that of *tenkō* broadly conceived, we now turn our attention.

RETURN TO THE WOMB

Beginning in the year 1933 the reel of Nyozekan's life seems to turn back on itself and begin to unwind. After this point, Nyozekan repudiated any associations that could possibly link him, in official minds, with the illegal Communist Party. The rhetoric of class struggle drops away from his texts, to be replaced, within two years at most, by that of national integration and communitarian harmony. Themes of remembered childhood and youth reemerge in his writing (he had in fact begun to publish a serial autobiography as early as 1921).[185] The *seimeitai* reasserted itself. Nyozekan, in short, "returned to Japan." But this time the cause of the state *was* the cause of the life-world. The two, once separate, were now bound together in Nyozekan's thinking as Japan moved closer and closer to war.

This thumbnail sketch, though it captures the salient features of Nyozekan's reorientation after 1933, still does not explain very much. We may not accept the judgment of Yamaryō Kenji, the senior scholar of Nyozekan's work, that Hasegawa Nyozekan "committed" *tenkō* after 1933. But it is impossible to dispute the reorientation, or its comprehensibility in the context of Nyozekan's own experience. In "returning to Japan," he at least was returning to a world he professed to have known in reality. Yamaryō was not perverse in describing Nyozekan's *tenkō* as a *nashikuzushi no tenkō: tenkō* on the installment plan; deliberated *tenkō; tenkō* sans crisis. One problem comes immediately to mind, however. Yamaryō seems to begin with a postwar concept of *tenkō* that has two implications: betrayal of the left (in practical terms, the Communist Party) sometime before 1945, and (what is crucial but left unstated) a second "reorientation" to the left, at least in the sense of a self-critical examination of the first *tenkō,* after 1945. Room for argument about Nyozekan's change of position after 1933 does exist. On the second point, not so much. Nyozekan made no return to the left that even approximated his position up to 1933. These questions aside, it seems to me that Yamaryō so tailors the category to fit his client that his argument is reduced to a tautology. Nyozekan's *tenkō* equals Nyozekan's experience defined as *tenkō.* I feel it is better to examine Nyozekan's thinking after 1933 without recourse to the *postwar* use of the term. Instead, let us for now take as a point of departure an observation made by the Polish historian Andrzej Walicki apropos of Tolstoy's spiritual crisis and "sudden change" in the late 1870s: "In sum, we may say that whereas [this crisis] was only a stage in the evolution of Tolstoy's *ideas,* it did mark a real turning point in his *life.*" [186]

At what point did the pressure of his situation on his ideas and vice versa compel a conscious change in Nyozekan's life? What ideas? What sort of change? And how did this change react in turn on his ideas?

Hihan, the successor to *Warera,* was short-lived. Its last issue appeared on 1 February 1934. At that point, Nyozekan's reorientation was still in its initial stage—that of cutting old ties. With *Hihan* no longer being published, Nyozekan gave up the means he had employed since 1919 of making his criticisms heard on as close to his own terms as possible. Thenceforth he would publish frequently (until late in the war), but now mainly in the mass circulation dailies, especially the *Yomiuri,* and in books. Still, demand for his essays and *Zeitkritik* remained, and Nyozekan published in such "highbrow" monthlies as *Bungei shunjū* and *Shisō,* as before in high-powered opinion journals like *Chūō kōron* and *Kaizō,* and later in *Nihon hyōron.*[187] Unlike a number of well-known liberals of the 1930s and early 1940s, Nyozekan never chose to publish a purely personal "mini-journal."[188] He continued to speak in public on panels, gave lectures, made addresses, and so forth. In point of fact, 1934 as compared to the previous year was spent in relative silence and privacy, with the exception of a short daily column in the *Yomiuri.* When Nyozekan began to resume a more typical public life, it was clear that the "critical period" was over.

Its last years had been marked by impeccable progressive politics. In September 1931 Nyozekan had been named chairman of the Sovieto Tomo no Kai (Friends of the Soviet Union) at the time of its reorganization into the Nisso Bunka Kyōkai (Japan-Soviet Cultural Society).[189] His article in the December *Hihan* on the Manchurian Incident prompted the authorities to ban the issue on the grounds that it subverted public order. The May 1932 issue of *Hihan* was banned for "suggestions of antimilitary and antiwar sentiment." In September and October of that year, Nyozekan presided over the founding and organizational meetings of the Yuibutsuron Kenkyūkai (Society for the Study of Materialism), or Yuiken, and he continued as chairman—some say as a figurehead—for a brief period.

Early 1933 brought the deaths of Sakai Toshihiko and Yoshino Sakuzō, and the murder by police of the proletarian writer Kobayashi Takiji. In May Nyozekan, at the urging of the critic Nii Itaru, joined the philosophers Miki Kiyoshi and Tanabe Kōichi in founding a group to protest the burning of books throughout Germany under the aegis of the newly installed Nazi government. The next month Nyozekan joined some three hundred artists and literary figures at an anti-Nazi protest meeting. He was among the organizers, also, of the antifascist Gakugei Jiyū Dōmei (Arts and Sciences Freedom League). And so on: in short, Nyozekan at fifty-eight was one of the grand old men of the *interi* who lent their names, energy, and sympathy to the antifascist movement on the Japanese left.

But it was Nyozekan's association with Yuiken and the remaining micro-organizations associated with the JCP that figure more closely in his ostensible *tenkō*. We have already mentioned his chairmanship of Yuiken. In the eyes of the Home Ministry the organization (which had an initial membership of about forty) was designed to "contribute to the expansion and strengthening of the Japanese Communist Party and the Comintern." Thus the claim of its chairman that it was "purely scholarly" in its concern for materialism was "deeply suspect" and the organization's movements were needful of the authorities' "closest attention." This Yuiken received. It is worth noting that the Marxist philosopher Kozai Yoshishige, a Yuiken and Party member, considers that by the time of Yuiken's founding, the Party had been so decimated that it had neither the personnel nor the organization to support the luxury of a "cultural policy." "The Party did agree," however, "that such an organization was necessary," and Communists such as Tosaka Jun and Hattori Shisō were indeed among Yuiken's founders and driving figures. Still, Nyozekan was undoubtedly sincere in his statement that the society's study of materialism was meant to be purely scientific. But it was not long before ideological disputes arose, even among the Communists themselves. These were serious enough that non-Marxist members such as Nyozekan ("I don't really 'get' Marxism. Especially dialectical materialism: that I can't swallow whole."),[190] and unorthodox Marxists like Miki soon felt alienated. Despite Tosaka Jun's "asceticism"—his efforts to preserve Yuiken's intellectual autonomy and hence ensure its survival—the organization was so split internally, and police harassment so severe, that it became insupportable. It is difficult to say what Nyozekan's contribution to Yuiken was exactly, apart from the figurehead value of his name, and possibly a role as gadfly; he was, after all, a materialist of a kind. The society's genuine advances in the dissection of Japanese ideology and in formulating a Marxist theory of technology cannot be denied. But since Nyozekan's direct involvement in the *theoretical* debates seems to have been slight, we shall, regretfully, pass over them here. Yuiken disbanded voluntarily in 1938, just as "academic Marxists" such as Ōuchi Hyōe, Arisawa Hiromi, and Wakimura Yoshitarō found themselves arrested and headed for prison in the second "Popular Front" incident in February of that year. Nyozekan, of course, along with Miki and many others (whose names will soon reappear) had long since ceased to have any association with Yuiken.[191]

One indication of the atmosphere in which Yuiken operated from the beginning ought to suffice. In March 1933 Nyozekan spoke at a public lecture meeting called to commemorate Yuiken's founding six months earlier. Held at the Bukkyō Seinenkan (Buddhist Youth Hall) in Hongō, the meeting was attended by a number of university and higher school students. One of these was Maruyama Masao:

> I was just finishing my sophomore year at Ichikō, and went to the meeting from my dormitory. Hasegawa Nyozekan, who was chairman of the society, addressed the gathering. He began with a statement of Yuiken's purpose as an organization. "[The members of Yuiken] strive constantly to undertake the scholarly study of materialism, and as such neither take any political action nor hold to any fixed political purpose." What he said—or more accurately tried to say—next is interesting. "Rather it seems these days that it is those who speak from 'idealist' or 'spiritual' standpoints that have taken on a distinct political coloring—." The instant Mr. Hasegawa delivered himself of this statement, the commander of the Motofuji Police Station, who had been seated, in uniform, to the left of the rostrum, picked up the sword he had propped between his legs, and pounding it on the floor, shouted that the meeting was over. At the same moment a contingent of chin-strapped police—there were so many of them you had to wonder where they had all come from—rose abruptly from their seats scattered throughout the hall, and glowered at the audience. The commander strode up to the rostrum, moved Mr. Hasegawa aside, and in severe tones declared, "I hereby order this assembly to disperse." People were stunned; the meeting had barely gotten under way! Still they had little choice but to make their way to the exit. As they streamed out, plainclothes officers of the Special Higher Police [Tokkō] who had been waiting there for them began to direct the police in making arrests. "Take this man. That one." I had the honor at this time of being pointed out for arrest.[192]

The second half of 1933 brought the *tenkō* declarations of Sano Manabu and Nabeyama Sadachika. The Party, already laboring under the direction of a Comintern that "understood nothing of conditions in Japan,"[193] now lost its domestic leadership. The "moderate" 1927 theses of Bukharin had been superseded in 1932 by new theses that, while reaffirming the need for a bourgeois democratic revolution first (the *tennōsei*, in other words, was acknowledged to be "absolutist"), also prescribed illegal methods as the key to shaking the imperialist regime. Remember that the USSR's heightened fears of a Japanese threat in the wake of the occupation of Manchuria were being translated into the Comintern's instructions to its client Party. And, as E. H. Carr points out, while direct communication between the Comintern and the "struggling rump" of the JCP was virtually nil after 1933, the 1932 theses had been widely disseminated. The stand members of the left took on the issue of legality versus illegality of Party methods was thus a key indication of allegiance in the eyes of both the Party and the police. The issue had come to a head in the Ōmori Bank Robbery Incident of 6 October 1932. Three khaki-clad Party members—initially thought to be army officers—stole 32,000 yen from the Kawasaki Daiichi Bank in a desperate attempt to obtain funds for Party operations. (The plan was unknown to all but one member of the Central Committee.) The robbery "badly discredited the . . . Party in the eyes of the public and seriously damaged its prestige among its own members," notably Sano Manabu. The government took full advantage of the incident and subsequent trial to portray the Party as a nest of gangsters. Beginning that same October, and continuing throughout 1933, police arrested the leadership, displaying stunning brutality in the treatment of its prisoners. By fall 1934 the authorities had demolished the Party's professional revolutionary core[194] and were free to concentrate on theoreticians, and, increasingly, on non-Marxist sympathizers. Noro Eitarō (an example of the former) was a leading Kōza-ha theorist and historian who had been the guiding figure in the debates on Japanese capitalism during these years. He was arrested at the end of November 1933, and died in custody the following February. He was thirty-four.

This was the situation when Nyozekan's number came up. One morning during the same week in November, Nyozekan was taken in custody to the Nakano Police Station (he had moved to Nakano from Yotsuya in 1926). There he was interrogated by a detective dispatched by the Tokkō for that purpose. Nyozekan was suspected of having paid, through Hosos̲ᷢ o Kanemitsu (former chairman of the Rōnōtō) some hundred yen to MOPR (Mezhdunarodnaya Organizatsiya Pomoshchi Revolutsioneram)—International Red Aid.[195] Blankets and personal belongings were brought. Nyozekan was released sometime after midnight. The major papers carried the story of the arrest, since Nyozekan (according to the Tokyo *Nichinichi*) was a "central figure" in Yuiken. Other arrests of Yuiken associates followed: Funaki Shigenobu, Ōya Sōichi, Tosaka Jun, Kaji Ryūichi, Oka Kunio. Thus it was not Nyozekan the individual, not the liberal, but the Yuiken associate and "communist sympathizer" whose activities the authorities sought to interdict.[196]

The details of the Tokkō's investigation, which concluded some three weeks later, are unavailable. But the result was public. On 15 December the Tokyo *Nichinichi* announced: "All Suspicions Cleared Up: Nyozekan Quietly Tells His Story."

> I have always respected the law. In the past I have acted, and [I] expect to continue to act in the future, in accordance with my motto: Never break the law. If you break it, pay the penalty. Of course, being human I cannot guar-

antee that I will never break the law, but if I did I would never ask the authorities to look the other way. I would be prepared to accept a fair judgment. As a social critic I could not preserve my critical conscience without an attitude toward daily life of an almost too rigorous self-regulation. These days society has grown altogether too lax. People seem to make no effort to apply discipline in their actions. So it happens that even opponents of the Communist Party tend to find themselves playing the role of sympathizer. For the sake of ideology [*shugi*], friend leads friend into error; the young deceive those who came before them. Outrageous behavior of this sort has grown all too common. What will become of our society if friends can no longer trust each other and neighbors come to suspect one another? We Japanese still enjoy cohesion as a people, but will we be able to [continue to do so] the way things are going? This is a fundamental problem, greater than that of the Party or any other issue! Where does responsibility lie for this state of affairs? It lies in particular with the flaws in our moral education up to the present. This is what thinking people [*shikisha*] ought to pay heed to.[197]

It is hard not to smile at this statement. Here is Nyozekan the "elder" blaming the system for his being trapped into "playing the role" of communist sympathizer—not that this was the real issue, of course. One wonders who is accusing whom. The statement is characteristic in its indirection, its deflection of responsibility. Nyozekan was anxious to portray his action as that of a generalized subject (I the people?), responding to institutional ills: the state pounding its mailed fist, the Party forcing its adherents to degrade human ties in the name of ideology. Nevertheless, the statement does mark a turning point in Nyozekan's life. Despite its artfulness, the statement contains a clear repudiation of the illegal JCP and its methods and purpose. Nyozekan's declaration of fidelity to the law was, I believe, sincere. He was not bending over backward completely, though he did wish to mollify the police. He owed nothing to the Party—quite the contrary. And his long-standing doubts about vanguard activity were a matter of record. In any case, Nyozekan's memberships in leftist organizations lapsed. A planned contribution to the *Nihon shihonshugi hattatsushi kōza* (Lectures on the history of the development of Japanese capitalism, 1932)—on the influence of the Restoration on later social thought—was left unrealized.[198] At the same time, Nyozekan did not embrace the official Japanism. He wrote no self-criticism beyond the statement quoted above. Most important, he never denounced his associates. All in all, one may say that Nyozekan, at the moment of his arrest, faced an unappetizing choice: cut loose from any association with illegality, make a feint to the right, or not play the public game at all. But was it possible to make a mere "feint" to the right?

Is Yamaryō correct in saying that public repudiation of the JCP was, psychologically and symbolically, a permanently debilitating blow to Nyozekan's critical capacity? As of late 1933–early 1934, it was still impossible to say. But one can agree with Yamaryō that Nyozekan did make a "proto"-*tenkō,* in the sense that his renunciation of the left was permanent. The ties were cut.

But as Yamaryō himself points out, Nyozekan's reorientation was a drawn-out process. And obviously no single text can stand as "proof" of *tenkō* (assuming that one accepts the implied problematic). It is rather a question of a total life-text. Let us approach the matter from a different angle. How did Nyozekan understand the concept of *tenkō* at the time? What sort of process did he think it was? Now admittedly, with his tendency to generalize the subject, it is sometimes difficult to tell where "Nyozekan" begins and ends. When is it legitimate to infer that he is referring (obliquely) to himself and his convictions? Always? Never?

The July 1933 issue of *Hihan* contained a collection of short "self-tributes" to the journal from its writer-readership. In large part they lionized Nyozekan himself. As one contributor put it, he was "an oasis in a time of emergency," a bastion of sanity, critical sense, and so on. In the same issue, Nyozekan published a mini-essay on the subject of *tenkō* (this in the aftermath of the Sano-Nabeyama bombshell). Here Nyozekan argues that nations, not individuals, undergo *tenkō:* the entire history of Japan is a series of *tenkō,* necessary steps back prior to a vault forward. Note where Nyozekan lays the stress. While he sees clearly that *tenkō* represents a drawing back (as of a bow string), his interest lies with the vault forward that ultimately results from *tenkō.* Thus, the importation by the Soga of continental systems of thought and government for "Westernization" that later culminated in the Taika Reforms had been preceded by the Shintoist reaction of the Mononobe to the introduction of Buddhism. The efflorescence of the early Meiji period had been preceded and made possible by the *sonnō jōi* movement. Proposals for a modern constitutional system came only after the defeat of reaction in the 1873 debate over whether to "chastize" Korea—and from within the defeated party. These three movements, each of vital importance in the nation's history, represent three *tenkō.* And now after the invasion of Manchuria, another was at hand:

> The Japanese capitalist form of state, now approaching completion [*kansei*] has in this worldwide final phase [of capitalism] arrived at the point where to

support itself it must make a further capitalist leap. This has, as was to be
expected, required an "anticapitalist" reaction. The present-day Mononobe
have not been content to insist that all images of Buddha be cast into the
canals of Naniwa. They have taken up arms themselves [*gunjiteki seiryoku o
katsudō seshimeta*].

Will the history of Japanese capitalism, with this reaction, now shrink
back into feudalism, or will it by a "turnabout" [*tenkō*] to imperialism make
a great leap forward? The matter is now "under consideration."[199]

Leaving aside the particular, and pressing, question Nyozekan is addressing here, let us note again the key point in his concept of *tenkō*
The main thing is not to look back at what has been renounced, but at
the—partly unintended—progressive consequences. "The significance
of conservatism," Nyozekan had written many years earlier, "lies in the
fact that it creates the primary condition for progress." His argument
about *tenkō* is a refinement of this position.

Let us now take a leaf from Nyozekan's book and "degeneralize" the
subject from nation to individual: Nyozekan had, after all, argued that
the *interi* were fully conscious of their social role. They must, then, be
prepared to take a stand. If Nyozekan left the left behind, to what "reaction" did he ally himself? And if that alliance was to serve as pressure
on the springboard to progress, what sort of progress did he envision?

The "reaction," it is fair to say, was the cause of the *seimeitai*, the
unpolitical world of everyday life. Nyozekan for a time stepped back
from the explicitly public world. He signaled this opting out with a
translation, in the final issue of *Hihan*, of a telling passage from the
Analects:

Tzu-lu, Tseng Hsi, Jan Yu, and Kung-hsi Hua were in attendance. Confucius
said, "You think that I am a day or two older than you are. But do not think
so. At present you are out of office and think that you are denied recognition. Suppose you were given recognition. What would you prefer?" Tzu-lu
promptly replied, "Suppose there is a state of a thousand chariots, hemmed
in by great powers, in addition invaded by armies, and as a result drought
and famine prevail. Let me administer that state. In three years' time I can
endow the people with courage and furthermore enable them to know the
correct principles." Confucius smiled at him as if flattered.

"Ch'iu, how about you?" Jan Yu replied, "Suppose there is a state the
sides of which are sixty or seventy *li* wide, or of fifty or sixty *li*. Let me administer that state. In three years' time I can enable the people to be sufficient
in their livelihood. As to the promotion of ceremonies and music, however, I
shall have to wait for the superior man."

"How about you, Ch'ih?" Kung-hsi Hua replied, "I do not say I can do it
but I should like to learn to do so. At the services of the royal ancestral

temple, and at the conferences of the feudal lords, I should like to wear the dark robe and black cap [symbols of correctness] and be a junior assistant."

[Turning to Tseng Hsi,] Confucius said, "How about you, Tien?" Tseng Hsi was then softly playing the zither. With a bang he laid down the instrument, rose, and said, "My wishes are different from what the gentlemen want to do." Confucius said, "What harm is there? After all, we want each to tell his ambition." Tseng Hsi said, "In the late spring, when the spring dress is ready, I would like to go with five or six grownups and six or seven young boys to bathe in the I river, enjoy the breeze on the Rain Dance Altar, and then return home singing." Confucius heaved a sigh and said, "I agree with Tien."[200]

This was not mere nostalgia. Nyozekan was tired. It must not be forgotten that he had spent the years since 1918 in a running battle with censors, police, and financial ruin. Despite all the efforts of *Warera* and *Hihan,* of the dissident *interi,* the forces of armed reaction at home and abroad seemed everywhere to have triumphed. The philosopher Miki Kiyoshi, with whom Nyozekan was soon to be associated in new circumstances, described the situation in contemporary terms: "Those who have been crushed by the political pressure of the fascism now current withdraw from reality and return to themselves. Just as a man, after enduring the struggle that is city life, returns beaten and wounded, fed up and weary, even disconsolate, to his home village."[201] But "home" for Nyozekan no longer meant Fukagawa or Tokyo. He had so thoroughly generalized himself that "home" meant Japan itself. Nyozekan the public man returned to a public womb: he immersed himself in cultural studies. The shift from "criticism"—read dissent—was decisive. It was also latent. Nyozekan was, of course, conscious of the change, remarking that he felt as if a "great rock" long hidden from view had been uncovered.[202] Indeed, no one so long under the influence of Seikyōsha thinking could have failed to form an intense concern for an integrated national character and identity. Nyozekan's earliest sensibilities (as he later portrayed them) were colored by chronological and geographical out-of-jointedness; and nothing makes for an acute sense of identity like standing "alone together." In short, Nyozekan's "return to Japan" was personally authentic. Recall his huffy defense against accusations of *arrivisme:* "My preference for things Japanese is not new."

Its personal genuineness does not mean that Nyozekan's embrace of "home" was unproblematic. He could hardly accept the monopoly on national identity claimed by "idealists" and "spiritualists." His contempt for those who capitalized on Japaneseness for purposes of political reaction never abated. This much is implicit in the major expression of Nyozekan's reflections on the national character, *Nihonteki seikaku*, a collection of essays written between 1935 and 1938 and published in that year by Iwanami. The work was clearly meant to be controversial, and, coincidentally or not, sold 112,000 copies by 1941. (To this we might contrast the 5,000 copies sold of the first [1942] printing of Nanbara's *Kokka to shūkyō*. The latter figure, however, represents the total available at a time when paper was in exceedingly short supply, especially for academic books. Nanbara's work, in any event, was a sell-out, and it appeared in at least three postwar editions.)

The Japanese national character depicted in *Nihonteki seikaku*, while dynamic and evolving, still manifested certain traits conspicuous for their "modernity": realism, pragmatism, restraint, rationalism (not abstractionism), and tolerance. Futhermore, Nyozekan argues, in each period of Japanese history, constructive popular energy has been the dynamic force in the growth of culture. For this popular life, the imperial institution has been, until modern times, virtually irrelevant.[203] In 1938 Nyozekan chooses to imply this irrelevance through omission rather than declare it openly. But it is not hard to find more explicit hints at the point in his earlier writings: his debunking, for example, of patriotism in the *Critique of Modern Society,* or the treatment of *kokutai* in the *Critique of Japanese Fascism.* It is this aspect of Nyozekan's exploration of the national character that has led some critics to reject Yamaryō Kenji's thesis that Nyozekan "committed" *tenkō*. Iida Taizō, for example, finds in Nyozekan's public valorization of a "stateless" Japanese society a valid expression of "resistance" to the overweening presence of bureaucracy and military power. He suggests further that this tendency in Nyozekan's thought can be traced back to the period immediately following the Kanto earthquake. The mob violence and massacre of Koreans in Tokyo and Yokohama came as a deep shock and disillusionment to Nyozekan. The disillusionment and shock were double: the violence was the work of everyday people, and the government did nothing to prevent it, in fact took advantage of it in order to murder a number of socialists and anarchists. But, rather than convincing Nyozekan of the need for a genuine social revolution, the terror drove him to idealization of a free and natural *communitas* uncorrupted by tribalism and the will to power. However, as Iida stresses, the change was gradual and revealed itself only in subtle ways. And it certainly did not lead Nyozekan into apoliticism.[204]

So far, so good. But how long could this "passive" resistance last? Had not Nyozekan, through his audacious choice of problem, made himself vulnerable to those forces he sought to counteract? Nyozekan's choice of problem, as Yamaryō says, is a problem in itself. Yamaryō cannot have meant that the choice of "Japan" was ipso facto a problem: The work of Tosaka Jun (*Nihon ideorogii ron*, 1937); Nagata Hiroshi, (*Nihon hōkensei ideorogii* and *Nihon tetsugaku shisōshi*, both published in 1938); Hani Gorō's studies of the Restoration; and of course Maruyama Masao's essays, written between 1940 and 1944, in *Nihon seiji shisōshi kenkyū* (1952) all come to mind as evidence to the contrary. Perhaps it was Nyozekan's conceptualization that caused the difficulty. Why Japanese "character"? Did not this approach reflect some deep conservatism? Still, if we isolate *Nihonteki seikaku*, we can agree with Iida that Nyozekan remained the cagey urbanite, mocking the exceptionalist orthodoxy in its own language. But Nyozekan does not equal this single text: if we consider also his organizational affiliations of the same period, we can clearly see that Nyozekan's "urbanity" and critical detachment were themselves mobilized as Japanese society was prepared for an East Asian war after the China Incident. So the real question becomes: *given* mobilization, how much or how little?

In *Nihonteki seikaku*, Nyozekan embraced a "modern"—rational, tolerant, realistic—Japan, one very much of a piece with his long-standing position on the basically more humane tenor of life in a society free of ideology. At the same time, however, Nyozekan had put on the "flip side" of the *Nihon fuashizumu hihan*. For in his writing after 1938, Japan has (or *is*) a cause. It is one needful of rational criticism to be sure, but primary; needful of tolerance and realism, yes, but primary. He had taken a crucial step. "Japan" had been a nation woven into an international society whose members were all subject in one way or another to capitalist production. Each nation had taken its own path, but in a broad sense all faced the same task: to restructure the production and distribution of wealth so as to place control in the hands of those who actually produced, who sacrificed themselves. But now the international task had become the national cause. It began as an effort to make Japan "understood." But Nyozekan went further, seeking to be among those who actually defined the cultural dimension of the cause. Japan was to be the subject of action. The question was no longer "What should be done about Japan?" Now it was, "What should Japan do—in China, in East Asia, in the world?"

Ironically, Nyozekan's very openness must have led him into mobilization. He came to emphasize the virtually innate harmony of the Japanese, the absence of cultural divisions and class conflict—indeed even of class itself. Five years earlier he might have attempted to expose the ideological genesis of such an assumption. But no longer. One corollary of the emphasis on the realism and rationalism of Japanese culture, found also in *Nihonteki seikaku,* is identification of the two. Because the Japanese are a realistic and rational people, things are the way they should be and vice versa. Hitherto, such a claim might have reflected Nyozekan's clear sympathy for a "humane anarchy"[205] in society. The *seimeitai* was best left to itself. The state in particular had no business fooling with the "real" world. But in what is perhaps the key shift, or deemphasis, in Nyozekan's writing after 1938, this perception of the state as extrinsic, even dangerous, begins to waver. This is not a matter of the printed word alone. In this respect, the record up to 1945 is equivocal. Less so was Nyozekan's association with the Shōwa Kenkyūkai (Shōwa Research Association).[206]

The Shōwa Kenkyūkai was nothing if not an attempt to wed the social consciousness of the *interi* with a concomitant desire to exercise actual authority in the state. Konoe Fumimaro's brain trust, founded in 1936, sought to provide the prince and the reformist technocrats and military figures associated with him with a workable plan for a way out of the China quagmire, for the "reintegration" of the Japanese economy and broader economic development in East Asia, and for the mobilization of the Japanese people in the service of these ends. In part this was a last-ditch attempt to channel state authority into a new center, one that could prevent the fruitless dispersion and contention for power among upper- and lower-echelon civil and military officials, party men, and extraconstitutional figures. Some way of "rationalizing" Japan's widening aggression abroad, in the context of attempts to resolve the entrenched problems (especially in agriculture) of the nation's dual-structured economy, was obviously necessary. At the same time, involvement in the association did not preclude a desire among some members to work for "creditable . . . and humane" ends through a revitalized state.[207] As *organizations,* after all, the parties were no longer a factor.

The failure of the association in all these aspects has been analyzed by Japanese and foreign experts and need not detain us here. But it is important for our purposes to note that the association was widely suspect from the start owing to the leftist background of its most brilliant members. Miki Kiyoshi, whose attempts to place Japan's aggression in China in a legitimate philosophical and world-historical framework formed the nucleus of the New Order's cultural policy, is only one prominent example. And it is significant, though not surprising, to find that with Konoe in eclipse after 1941, Miki soon fell out of favor. He resumed contact with the left. Arrested for harboring a suspected communist, Miki died in prison shortly after the end of the war.[208] His death, coming when it did, crystalizes the dilemma of public outsiders who were drawn into state service after the left had been decimated.

Nyozekan's case is similar to Miki's in that for the first time in his life, he found himself a servant of power—or would-be power. His activity in the association centered on cultural policy. As a member of the Bunka Mondai Kenkyūkai (Research Committee on Cultural Problems), a suborganization of the association, Nyozekan seems to have served as a "generalist." And, since he was a close observer of Chinese politics, his opinions were particularly valued. Nothing published or circulated by the association bears Nyozekan's name as chief author, but it is a fact that he contributed to the synthesis of cultural principles designed to guide the New Order, Miki Kiyoshi's *Shin Nihon no shisō genri* (1939).[209] Articles by Nyozekan published in *Kaizō* and elsewhere somewhat earlier are in any case congruent with the general thesis of the *Principles*. This held that Japan, as the only successful modern power in Asia, had ipso facto the opportunity, right, and duty to use its unique position to force subject peoples out of their Western captivity; to create a postcapitalist "cooperativist" order with Japan as the natural nucleus and source of industrial, political, and cultural expertise. To be sure, Nyozekan was aware of the issue of Chinese nationalism, but he seems to tie it in with the expansion of Chinese capitalism rather than to recognize in it a broader phenomenon. Indeed, for him, regionalism and geographically differential modernization ("China is a Commonwealth without an England"), rather than external interference, were the greatest problems facing China. Thus he discounts the possibility that Japan might be a factor in unifying China in a way permanently disadvantageous to itself.[210] A modern aggressor must believe that if successful it will convince those it has conquered that it rules in obedience to some higher principle. Nyozekan had to have accepted this myopia, at least enough to have joined in synthesizing the association's cultural program. (He did not have the heart of a saboteur.) And that meant accepting the corollary, that an activist state was needed at home to mold the masses to the ends that inspired the association's formation. Nyozekan was also a member of the Shōwajuku (Shōwa Academy). Founded in 1938, the academy (according to its statutes) sought "to contribute to the formation of leading figures [*shidōteki jinkaku*] equipped with [the] spirit, knowledge, and experience necessary for the total fulfillment of

the historical mission, now in process of realization, of the New Japan."
At the same time, genuine chauvinists at the fringe of both organizations
found Nyozekan—in fact all the "ex-leftists"—to be undesirable; this
we know from the diary of that quintessential servant of power, Yabe
Teiji.[211] The point, however, is not the impact Nyozekan had or did not
have, but that he, like Miki, Sassa Hiroo, and Saigusa Hiroto—all early
departees from Yuiken and association members—was mobilized. If
others found him questionable, so be it. Nyozekan was prepared to
serve, and in a limited capacity, he did.

In addition to his involvement in the association, Nyozekan took
part in two other organizations. Here he was more prominent, and his
tenure of greater duration. To take the latter first: in June 1942 Nyozekan
joined the Bungaku Hōkokukai (Society for Patriotism through Literature), as honorary chairman of the Criticism and Essay section. He
had been recommended for this position by Kuwaki Gen'yoku and
the venerable Min'yūsha historian Takekoshi Yosaburō. In April 1944
Nyozekan was named chairman, in which capacity he remained, presumably until the organization's dissolution. It seems to me that Nyozekan's membership in the society means comparatively little: one must
consider the date. It was probably incumbent on anyone without independent wealth or patronage to join in order to keep publishing. It may
not be unfair to regard joining the society as akin, mutatis mutandis, to
joining the Soviet Writers' Union. For some Japanese it may even have
been a kind of professional lifesaver, not unlike the Federal Writers'
Project during the New Deal, again mutatis mutandis.

The other affiliation is more revealing, since it was unofficial and
wholly voluntary. In mid 1939 Nyozekan helped to found the Kokumin
Gakujutsu Kyōkai (League for the National Arts and Sciences).[212] Conceived by Shimanaka Yūsaku, president of the prestigious Chūō Kōronsha, the league numbered among its charter members some twenty-
six luminaries of the Japanese intelligentsia. The group's intent was to
promote "cultural science"—read internationalism, objectivity, and free
inquiry—from a refined "national" (kokuminteki) standpoint. With its
appeal to the "masses" (via the state) on the one hand, and on the other
to the interi as dispensers of Western (cosmopolitan) enlightenment, the
organization managed to bring together under its aegis a varied cast.
There were former members of Yuiken (just as in the Shōwa Kenkyūkai)
such as Miki Kiyoshi and the mathematician Ogura Kinnosuke; journalists such as Kiyosawa Kiyoshi, Abe Ken'ichi, and Ryū Shintarō (Ryū,
of course, had authored the association's economic "bible," *Nihon Kei-*

zai no saihensei, and was an admirer of the theory of Italian fascism); and eminent philosophers and scholars such as Watsuji Tetsurō, Nishida Kitarō, Kuwaki Gen'yoku, Tsuda Sōkichi, Yanagida Kunio, and Koizumi Shinzō. Creative writers such as Shimazaki Tōson and Masamune Hakuchō were also enrolled. And so on. Clearly no such mélange of personalities and approaches could be brought together to serve a single, clearly articulated principle. The tension was implicit in the league's statement of purpose, and by and large the "internationalist" impulse suffered. But this was owing in no small measure to attacks from without, first from rightists led by Minoda Muneki, on Tsuda Sōkichi; and later, in 1943, from the army, which was alarmed at the presence of Miki Kiyoshi on the membership rolls.

The league managed, nevertheless, to meet regularly until 1945, and to hold lectures and publish a series of monographs. Some of these works, like Ogura Kinnosuke's *Senjika no sūgaku* (Mathematics in wartime), were repudiated by their authors after 1945: "It speaks all too clearly to my abject submission to the powers-that-be."[213] Alone among its members, Nyozekan was (according to Yamaryō) catholic enough in his background, interests, and talents to embody the group's purpose and enjoy the confidence of all involved. It is characteristic of him that he remained enthusiastic until the end, and certainly had no cause after 1945 to regret any of his public acts as a member.

There was, to be sure, a range of feeling among the members as to the eventual outcome of the war. The journalist Baba Tsunego was possibly the most pessimistic. Next came Kiyosawa Kiyoshi, forced to confine his forebodings to private conversations and to his now famous diary, *Ankoku nikki.* What Kiyosawa had to say about Koizumi Shinzō, whom he found hopelessly sanguine about Japan's prospect, probably would apply to many among his confreres. "I had thought him a harder-headed liberal. Instead," Kiyosawa wrote, "he seems to be afraid to think things through to the end."[214]

As for Nyozekan, we might rather say, following Yamaryō, that *living* the situation, the here-and-now of war everywhere, was all. Though he was invariably acute in discerning the contradictions and stupidity of that situation—not, significantly, its tragedy—Nyozekan was not given to prediction or to dramatic shifts in temperament or opinion. This was characteristic, perhaps, of a man who viewed words and ideas as following after and looking at, rather than creating or changing, reality. This quality of hanging back is evident even in Nyozekan's most propagandistic and programmatic writing of the middle years of the Pacific

war. Even here, one finds the distinct and complex layering of voices
that reflects his development; the inability to yield entirely to an irrational "ideal" or a conviction unsupported by the evidence of "life."
I shall close my account with a brief consideration of two of these wartime texts.

"The Greater East Asia War," Nyozekan proclaimed in April 1942,
"has as nothing else caused the whole world to recognize anew the
national [*minzokuteki*] superiority of the Japanese."[215] The immediate
cause of Japan's crusade lay not in any inherent aggressiveness on the
nation's part. Far from it: after long efforts at what Nyozekan calls
"Amaterasu diplomacy"—"to assuage with words"—the nation found
to its dismay that its pacific character remained misunderstood and be-
littled by the Western powers. Japan had no choice now but "to pluck
up [its enemies] like young reeds, crush them, and send them flying in
the wind."[216]

Nyozekan assumed the task, in this connection, of setting forth the
true, and obviously unappreciated, source of the nation's superiority.
This lay not in weaponry or machines but in its dynamic character—a
theme common to, but hardly the exclusive domain of, Japan's war
propaganda. Indeed, it seems very much a part of present-day *Nihonjin
ron*. The main lines of argument have been introduced earlier, in the discussion of *Nihonteki seikaku*. We may note here one major, though un-
surprising, difference in the argument. In the earlier work, Nyozekan
had conspicuously avoided reference to the imperial house, or to politics
in general, as a central concern of, and spur to development in, Japanese
ethics and intellectual life. Now, with the entire nation (*minzoku*) involved, and to all appearances headed for victory in, a world war,
Nyozekan feels compelled to identify the continuity of the imperial
presence as the dynamic core of the nation's political being. It is this
presence that distinguishes the modern Japanese from all other constitutional systems. Characteristically, Nyozekan quotes Kuga Katsunan's
Kinji kenpō kō (1888) to make the point. This saves him from having to
rely on any of the current highly illiberal and antiparliamentary "theorists" of the *kokutai* in making his pledge of allegiance. Furthermore,
Nyozekan's gesture to orthodoxy is deliberately kept within political
bounds. The "imperial prerogative from which the constitutional system proceeds" (Katsunan) is used in a "liberal" manner. It is not the
font of value or coeval with all that is Japanese. Rather, the imperial
institution is used as an analogy for the constant self-renewal of Japanese culture. Japan has not discarded its past, political, social, or aes-

thetic. But "pastness" is not its own justification. Rather, it is their continuing and immediate contribution to the national life and character that has guaranteed the vigor of past cultural products. Japan is not an antiquarian nation. In fact (as Fukuzawa had first argued) Japan has always been modern in the sense that the products and spirit of the past have never been "idealized" or frozen, but have served—the past-as-present—to make Japanese society a single evolving whole.[217]

However, Nyozekan avers, the single evolution of Japan (mandated in large part by ethnic homogeneity and geography) has never meant the repression of natural human complexity. Here we see the Spencerian moment in his thought, healthy as ever. Nyozekan does not deny the presence in Japanese history of sometimes severe conflict. But this conflict—such as that which caused the fall of the Tokugawa—has taken place within the context of a long, upward evolutionary development toward harmony through complexity. No political or social strife in Japanese history has ever been severe enough to shatter the underlying unity of the people; this is a point of tremendous pride for Nyozekan. In fact, the national character may be said to be "nuclear," and hence extremely conservative. That is, each period of emerging differentiation resolves into integration through a renewal of the springs of identity. In what Yamaryō Kenji calls the "spatialization of history"—understandable in Japan's case, where the geographical determinant is so powerful—Nyozekan alludes constantly to a return to national self-as-place. To be Japanese means to live as Japanese. Nyozekan asserts that no abstract "human being" can exist in Japan: "For a Japanese, all [other] Japanese are part of the Japanese *ethnos* [*minzoku*], that is, of the Japanese nation, the clan [*shizoku*], the family; whether as sovereign or subject, parent or child. He cannot conceive of them otherwise than as actual human beings living their lives within the territory of Japan."[218] Japanese mythology and philosophy support this sense of belonging. They are entirely specific. Indeed, Nyozekan adds, the great universal philosophizing nations—Greece and India—have "died out." Specificity is strength. Science (i.e, abstract thinking), too, is pursued in Japan not for its own sake but for practical purposes. For this reason it serves, as does the quotidian art of the *shokunin*, to integrate the people rather than to divide them. The summit of Japanese creativity is reached in the realm of the intuitive and practical.[219] Art is life; life is to be "crafted." With this spirit (Nyozekan uses the word *seishin*) Japan has embarked, unwillingly, but now with total dedication, on an effort to display its character.

The second and final text to be considered comes from late 1943. *Nihon kyōiku no dentō* (The tradition of Japanese education)[220] merits our attention for one chief reason, its equivocal attitude toward the state. In part the work was a contribution to the wartime effort to create a more efficient educational system. It was time, Nyozekan felt, to counteract the "Western" tendency toward "useless" abstraction and overspecialization, and, by implication, the invidious separation of mass from elite in society. Nyozekan proposed that Japanese society be "de-schooled" (to use Ivan Illich's term). Education happens not only in school, but in life. And life meant work and home. All of life's "places" (*ba*) should be transformed into sources of social education. This is not only a matter of changing perceptions, but of institutional mobilization and decentralization. Nyozekan never denies the need for a requisite degree of specialized training, or for the analytical frame of mind that supports it (true for any industrial society, whether at war or not). But, he suggests, the Education and Armed Service Ministries need not be the only dispensers of education. Indeed, he implies, such education as they do dispense may even obstruct genuine "social" learning. Every ministry—Agriculture, Commerce and Construction, Welfare—and organization, public and private, ought to involve itself. The responsibility should be shared, diffused.[221]

What appears on the one hand a proposal to save the state's resources by redistributing the cost of cannon fodder, and to expand the role of the state to boot, can also be seen as a criticism of the institutions that have created the need for cannon fodder in the first place. "Social" education could not help but be more pacific; the more deeply rooted learning is in society, the less inclined young minds should be to an uncritical acceptance of official and military indoctrination.

Given the context, one must seem to bend over pretty far to make such a reading. Still, virtually all of Nyozekan's writing on state and society up to that point suggests that he took advantage of the forum offered to try and take back even a little of what the state had commandeered.

It is not my purpose at present to follow Nyozekan's public life into the postwar years. One comment here will have to suffice. Only remove references to the particular cause—or rather the means—chosen by Japan in 1941, and one finds that virtually nothing changes in Nyozekan's subsequent presentations of the national character. Indeed, Kuwabara Takeo regarded Nyozekan as basically conservative in his thinking for having clung to the concept itself. And so he was. After 1945 he remained what he had become after 1935, a conservative (but not even remotely reactionary) "man of culture" (*bunkajin*). Nyozekan never ceased to regard a deliberate caution, living from and with the past, as the trait most dominant in the Japanese national character. He continued to identify his own life with that of his fellow Japanese to an extraordinary degree. What he idealized in his own past-as-present, he idealized in that of the nation as a whole. Although we are assured by Ōuchi Hyōe that Nyozekan was a "very private person," his projected personality assumed a direct continuity between self and the society he represented as a public man. Nyozekan's shift after 1938 from outsider to insider meant an ever stronger identification of society and nation. And though his period of state involvement was brief, the identification was permanent: there was no *tenkō*, no return to dissent, after 1945.

Recall the embarrassment Nyozekan admitted when in 1937 he "discovered" in himself a visceral chauvinism. This aspect of "national" (indeed, not only Japanese) character—the explosive, state-sponsored xenophobia that has made of nationalism "the starkest political shame of the twentieth century"[222]—seems to have merited but little of Nyozekan's attention after 1945. True, he threw himself into the "reconstruction" (*saiken*) of the national psyche along peaceful lines after Japan's defeat. But it is a pity that Nyozekan forsook the darkness so soon. For only in its immediate aftermath, and then for the first time, could that darkness be spoken of openly. To do so, Nyozekan would have had to expose the unexcised, violent "petty bourgeois" element in his own and the "Japanese character." He would have had to "spit on himself," as (he said) any critic worthy of the name had to. But did he?

Perhaps this is unfair. Nyozekan did not, even in his propaganda, write words he did not believe. In the essay on national superiority written in 1942, and in other writings after 1945, Nyozekan recognized the absence from the "Japanese mentality" of a universalizing or transcendent impulse able to place the subject of thought outside its object.[223] Where once he had gloried in the specificity of Japanese culture, he now lamented its tenacious grip. And he blamed the *interi* (himself included, says Yamaryō) for never having developed "eyes for the universal." Thus, the Japanese reality persisted: life and place "produced" thought. Being—being Japanese?—produced consciousness. Neither before 1945 nor after did Nyozekan's worldview recognize an encompassing, immaterial "outside." He saw only coexisting material universes with distinct experiences.

Nyozekan came closest to identifying a "universal" in the Spencerian developmental premises of his early *Critiques*. His exposure to Marx's analysis of nineteenth-century capitalist production allowed Nyozekan to distinguish the spurious cosmopolitanism of the bourgeoisie from the genuine international solidarity of the working class. The new capitalist powers of the twentieth century reacted to both of these phenomena with a massive display of armed nationalism. Nyozekan began a critique of this process—an effort recognized and praised by Marxists such as Sakai Toshihiko. But Nyozekan, rejecting the Soviet alternative both as a model and critical vantage point, was drawn into the reaction itself. Unable to yield to the violence it entailed, however, he sought to tease a stateless society out of Japanese history: remember that according to Iida Taizō, Nyozekan was propelled in this direction by the shocking aftermath of the Kanto earthquake. Nyozekan created a personal myth and shared it generously. As public man, it was the least he could do. As a critic, it was the most.

Conclusion: Notes on the "Public" in Postwar Japan

Sketch of Hasegawa Nyozekan by Yanase Masamu,
1935. Courtesy of Chūō University.

What, in sum, are we to say of these two political thinkers? Nanbara Shigeru combined a philosopher's concept of state with an administrator's view of society. Hasegawa Nyozekan had empiricist concepts of both society and the state, but the two were never integrated. Nanbara's idealist philosophy of political value was a constant shield against cooptation at a time of awful pressure to conform. For this one may, as I do, admire him deeply. The significance of his thought, however, is specific and contingent; first in that Nanbara worked in an anomalous institutional setting, second in that its neo-Kantian philosophical underpinnings ceased, except in the indirect ways already noted, to be salient in political discourse after 1945. It was above all a successful intermediate strategy. With Hasegawa Nyozekan matters are less clear. His *communitas* did not produce a theory of resistance to state authority, or even an escape from it. Nyozekan recreated a good world. But in the existential moment of its creation, it was stripped by its author of any explicit political purpose. Nyozekan was a tragic optimist. Both men shared the inability to withdraw from the "national life" concomitant with publicness in imperial Japan. Publicness, therefore, was their crucible. But that world is gone.

Does this mean that no contemporary significance is to be attached to Nanbara or Nyozekan? Certainly their postwar careers have their interest. Nanbara served in a number of characteristically elite positions: for example, in the House of Peers, where he participated in deliberations on constitutional revision; twice as president of Tokyo University; and as head of the first Japanese educational mission to the United States in 1949. Let us glance at one representative instance: Nanbara was named to the House of Peers in March 1946. This was a position he shared with a number of "organ theory" adherents, notably Miyazawa Toshiyoshi, who were appointed to fill vacancies occasioned by the purge. Nanbara was among those who argued that the new Imperial House Law, which was presented to the Ninety-first Diet at the end of 1946, should provide for the possibility of abdication. While the emperor, Nanbara said, bore no legal or political responsibility, he did bear "moral responsibility" to the people (*kokumin*) and to the imperial ancestors for "plunging the people into such misery with this first total defeat since the founding of the empire." Abdication, it seemed to Nanbara, was the appropriate expression of such responsibility. Owing to the combined opposition of Allied GHQ and Prime Minister Shidehara Kijūrō, however, the law was written without this explicit provision. The immediate issue, of course, was the constitutional fate of the *koku-*

tai: How had it been affected by the surrender (specifically by the acceptance of the Potsdam Declaration)? Miyazawa and Nanbara argued that in fact, after 15 August, the *kokutai* as defined by the Peace Preservation Law was dead. Imperial sovereignty, after all, had been denied in the acceptance of the declaration. A "new *kokutai*" had been born, in which the emperor (in the words of the new constitution) was a "symbol of the unity of the people." As Nezu Masashi has remarked, it was in part because of rigorous interpellations, by Nanbara among others, in the House of Peers that the government was forced to yield in its determination to make "retention [*goji*] of the emperor system" the purpose of the new constitution.[1]

Hasegawa Nyozekan, who was seventy in 1945, took his place with Yanagida Kunio, Tsuda Sōkichi, and Watsuji Tetsurō as grey eminences in the "reconstruction" of Japanese culture after the defeat. But it cannot be said that his contributions brought out any new themes. With a combination, one imagines, of urgency and a sense of déjà vu, he restated the positions he had taken on rationality and restraint in *Nihonteki seikaku* and other contemporaneous works. As was noted earlier, Nyozekan never took a radical stance after his repudiation of illegality in 1933. He "returned" to what he claimed he had always been. So much is this the case that Maruyama even speaks of Nyozekan's radicalism as "unnatural"! A final anecdote will underscore the point: In 1961 Nyozekan (at eighty-six) was nominated by the Liberal Democratic Party head, Ikeda Hayato, for the chairmanship of the Kokumin Kyōkai, a party fund-raising organ then in the planning stages. Nyozekan declined.[2]

As noted at the outset, this study has aimed primarily to describe and explain the dilemmas of public life in imperial Japan, and not to write complete intellectual biographies of its two main subjects. As such, its contribution must be judged independently of its secondary purpose, which is to sketch out, in part, the "prehistory" of certain postwar trends and figures. In fact, the two come together. For in trying to describe the long-term significance of Nanbara and Nyozekan, it becomes apparent that it is less their personal achievement after 1945 than the patterns of thinking and certain key ideas, as taken up by others, that matter. The best example, as I suggested in the Preface and elsewhere, may be found in Maruyama Masao himself. I leave for a later work the full exposition in its own context of Maruyama's thinking as it has developed since the late 1930s. Yet here, too, my interest is not—and will not be—in Maruyama alone. He is representative of the generation educated at the apex of the academic hierarchy while the imperial system faced its deepest crisis, which took it upon itself to "decode" the imperial system and to define the meaning of *postwar* for a defeated and occupied country. This decoding and definition was not to be the work of Nanbara or Nyozekan—or indeed of any public man of their vintage. It would fall instead to those nourished on crisis, and, more important, on systems of thought explicitly proscribed until 1945. For this reason, rather than simply continuing the story with a focus, perhaps misplaced, on Nanbara and Nyozekan, I have thought that a slightly detached conclusion that attempts a preliminary setting out of "postwar" themes would be truer to my present and future intentions.

"It is my view," the novelist Ōe Kenzaburō has written, "that the concept 'postwar' struck the mind and imagination of the Japanese people with utter clarity the moment the war ended."[3] This "utter clarity" was a matter of both light and space. It was linked, literally and metaphorically, not only to the "blinding flash" that laid waste Hiroshima and Nagasaki, but to the steadily widening circle of urban desolation caused by many months of Allied bombings. This spawned one of the great migrations of history—from Japan's cities to the countryside—and left the nation's population stunned and prostrate in anticipation of an occupation as brutal as that carried out by their own forces on the Asian continent. The fact that the American occupation was not as violent and vengeful as expected needs to be understood in the context of the long period of physical and psychological violence—capped by the bombings of Hiroshima and Nagasaki—let loose upon the Japanese people beginning in the last year of the war. The population had been beaten into passivity, and the economy of violence dictated that further bloodshed was unnecessary. In this context the virtual absence of post-surrender resistance by Japanese, and of wholesale violence by Occupation forces is perhaps less difficult to explain.

Abject defeat, in any case, threw into glaring relief the hollow fantasy both of the New Order at home and of the "extension of the imperial virtue" to the peoples of Asia. The former was a "mangled caricature"[4] of state and national community that exhausted the energies and loyalty of its people. The latter was a misbegotten, unwelcome, and tragic campaign for the "liberation" of Asian peoples who (with a few exceptions) found unbelievable Japan's claims to have undertaken such a mission.

It has been argued that Japanese occupation ended Western colonialism in Asia and was therefore a progressive force. So said Ba Maw of Burma, whose country, under British control was (as J. S. Furnivall put it) "not a human society but a business concern." But even Ba Maw was forced to admit that Japan had betrayed "her Asian instincts."[5] So be it, then: history is cunning. Japan cannot be called a conscious (or even knowledgeable) liberator. Its concerns were military and geopolitical, and it exploited nationalist sentiment where local hostility to prior Western colonial authority, and its own strategic aims, made such a policy advantageous. In most other cases—formal colonies such as Korea and Taiwan, objects of attempted and actual control such as China, and later Indochina, the Philippines, and Indonesia—nationalism was as dangerous to Japan as it had been to the Western powers it displaced. It was for this reason that Japan—here, too, offering a lesson still unlearned by later arrivals—claimed to Western audiences to be fighting against communism in Asia. No colonial power was credulous enough to believe that Japan sought anything better for the subject peoples of Asia than they had already endured. Here Japan and the West stood on, and fought over, common ground. Liberation by Japan brought bitterness to Asian peoples, many of whom also sought liberation from Japan.

This point—Japan's appeal to the threat of hostile ideologies as justification for its imperialist campaigns—brings us back to the collapse of the imperial system at home. Within Japan the ideological threat was taken seriously and used effectively against critics of the regime. The "national community" (*kokumin kyōdōtai*) in the name of which Japan's population was mobilized for and participated in total war was an ideological construct with an emotional appeal and intellectual legitimacy incomprehensible to those who were not members of that "community." The "magnetic" power of the emperor at the zenith of the imperial system, with his ministers and officials and soldiers arrayed beneath, along with the masses of imperial subjects all giving "assistance" (*yokusan*) to his rule, drew upon long-inculcated sentiments of political, ethnic/national, and moral identity of the utmost validity. Only objective physical defeat, accompanied by the self-denial of its own enabling ideology of *kokutai*, could bring the system down. And down it came, leaving the nation in a moral as well as ideological vacuum. But a nation—even Japan with its dominance of political values—is more than its political system, and the Japanese people survived and struggled to make sense of the new, postimperial world.

In the political realm especially, the postwar "moment" opened up vast, uncharted possibilities. The destruction of the empire and negation of its premises meant that ideologies and worldviews formerly held to be inimical to the *kokutai* were no longer so; socialism, liberalism, and democracy (as models for a political system and for society as a whole) were permitted to reenter the public discourse from which the imperial state had long sought to excise them as unhealthy and dangerous to the spiritual constitution of the nation.

The alacrity with which Japanese intellectuals took up this new (or renewed) discourse has been amply documented and in any case is beyond the scope of this discussion to recapitulate.[6] Here I wish only to ask the questions, to help set the agenda. What has this renewed public discourse meant, and how has it functioned in postwar Japan? What role have public men played in shaping the political and social consciousness of the country? More specifically, how has participation in the public changed since 1945?

The ideological transformation to postwar has been described by Maruyama Masao as a third "opening of the country" (*kaikoku*) to the world—and to "universal" ideas, philosophies, and worldviews. This was a process accompanied by cultural experiment and uncertainty, sexual and moral license, economic chaos and physical deprivation. The productive capacity of the country was virtually wiped out, hunger rampant, the people massively displaced and thrown back upon their own resources and imaginations. This negation, this new horizon brought by desolation, also pointed the way toward reconstruction. Defeat for the Japanese brought a bitter trial, recrimination, and (some) well-deserved guilt. But it also created a still unknown future and a mandate to transform self and nation along humane and democratic, perhaps revolutionary, lines. For participants in public discourse, this meant a chance to explore freely and with undisguised passion ideas whose expression (since it was hard to distinguish it from advocacy) had been obstructed or closed off entirely.

Freedom could not mean historical amnesia, however.[7] For as we have seen, the sense among public men of identification with the nation—and therefore with the state—was not entirely the result of coercion. It was not to be uprooted through "liberation" from without in an institutional, let alone military, sense; this to be followed by a return to some imagined "liberal" status quo ante 1931. For Japan as a state, society, and culture, the war and all it represented was not simply an aberration that could be repudiated and wiped from memory. This would seem to be true especially for those who lived through the communication of ideas and experience to others—here their credibility and intellectual legitimacy would stand or fall. However, some public men fell strangely silent after 1945 about their experience of war and national emergency. I shall try to explain why this happened.

An entire generation of public men had come to maturity during the years of the national emergency that was proclaimed in 1933, and it was precisely from among them that the intellectual leaders of the early postwar years would emerge. They had lived through the greatest crisis ever faced by Japan, knowing that in large part Japan itself had brought that crisis to birth. Thus their identity and intellectual formation, their sense of personal role, their values and morality, reflected a basic existential engagement (acknowledged or not) with the imperial system; that is, with the modes and structures of thought that had developed within, both in support of and in opposition to, that system.

The generation with which I am here concerned never knew "traditional" Japan. They could not claim, as Hasegawa Nyozekan did, to have known a world unaffected by the Meiji Restoration. And the imperial Japan that formed them had undergone a cataclysmic defeat. (Indeed, for true believers like Minoda Muneki, a defeat of cosmic proportions, to which the only possible response was suicide.) Until August 1945, no one of them, nor any public man, could claim membership in the political or national community except by rejecting, or integrating into the framework of the "national community," universalistic beliefs that officially defined public discourse would otherwise deem unacceptable. After the decimation of the organized left began in 1928, the sphere of orthodoxy had expanded but flattened; modes of participation in the "national life" had become more explicit, the costs of *inclusion* more prohibitive. Paying one's dues—remaining within the pale—could be deeply demoralizing. We have seen how profoundly this was so for Miki Kiyoshi and for Tanabe Hajime. The intellectual illegitimacy of the national cause had become a source of anguish for them. Others with similar sentiments had responded with debilitating or defiant silence, public but coded criticism, private anger, and despair. There was no neutral ground.

Nor was there any transcendent space or universal sphere of values

unmediated by the "nation" (*minzoku*) or the "national community."
Indeed, as Hashimoto Mitsuru has noted, for Japanese intellectuals
minzoku was a category that "overcame universality" and itself became
"absolute." In Ishida Takeshi's words, "community [*kyōdōtai*] was the
Achilles' heel of Japanese social science."[8] Not every public man was
willing to perform this exaltation unconditionally, of course. Thus the
struggle and challenge of publicness lay in the definition of *minzoku*. To
what extent could it include "universal" characteristics? Was it entirely
particularistic? Needless to say, the state's fissured hegemony over the
discourse meant that dissent was muted and seldom directly ideological;
the *self-acknowledged* audience for dissent was small, the intellectual
surface suffocatingly uniform. And though there was much movement
beneath that surface, the ideological hegemony of the "national community" was maintained.

With the collapse of the old order, however, this hegemony disinte-
grated. Within the limits set by Occupation censors—which, *pace* Etō
Jun, allowed a quality, and not only a quantity of freedom—the key assumption of orthodoxy was overthrown. This had held that "universal"
equaled Western equaled alien and dangerous. The vaunted claim of the
"overcoming the modern" theorists, that rationalism, liberalism, and
materialism (whether individualist or collectivist) had been sublated
(*aufgehoben*) into a higher communal and spiritual unity was exposed
as a sham. This is not to deny (as Maruyama Masao, for example, does
not) the cogency of certain aspects of the "overcomers'" critique. But
whether that critique can be detached from its historical context of out-
and-out cooptation and manipulation, and thus contribute to the current debate about the "postmodern," is another matter. It is clearly
related, in ways that need careful elucidation, to the critique of Enlightenment thought, to postsubjectivist theories of politics, and to the
posthumanist discourse that continental thinkers have done so much to
make salient in contemporary intellectual life. But all this, save for a few
comments at the end of the present work, must await later treatment.[9]

How, then, did a wartime generation conceptualize the postwar "moment"? And with what consequences for those who knew nothing of
war and little (and frequently nothing) of postwar privation and uncertainty? Here I wish only to suggest the main lines along which this conceptualization took shape—the Marxist and the "modernist"; or, in
Shōji Kōkichi's terms, "socialist" and "humanist." Focusing particularly on the latter, I shall try to indicate how these lines are interwoven,
and make a number of observations about the fate of what Victor

Koschmann calls the "modernist" project as it concerns the general problem of the "public" in contemporary Japan.[10]

At the core of the postwar emancipation of public discourse lay a twofold mandate: reconnection with "universality" and with "subjectivity." Social theory and practice would henceforth have to embrace these categories. Obviously, neither the meaning nor the consequences of this avid embrace were clear in 1945. Like everything else in the years immediately after the defeat, concepts and positions were fluid, owing to the uncertain ideological orientation and policies of the Occupation authorities, associated developments within Japanese politics and society, and changes in the international situation. In particular, the legal reemergence not only of hitherto "dangerous thought" (*kiken shisō*) but of proscribed organizations meant that intellectual and political life would be related with a sensitivity and dynamism never before experienced in modern Japan.

Thus the universal concepts to which virtually all public men swore allegiance—"universality" itself, "reason," "science," "progress," "democracy," "modernity," "subjectivity," and so on—became potent signs and symbols in a public discourse undergoing rapid and concentrated development after 1945. The key here is the great impact, for good or ill, of "external" social and political forces upon that discourse. This is another way, perhaps, of saying that it was "public" rather than the preserve of an out-of-touch academy or other elite. At least this was the case for the years up to 1960: As is well known, fragmentation, disillusionment, and violence plagued the Japanese left as the succeeding decade neared an end. The established (or establishment) opposition was only one of a number of canalized or segmented institutions (universities were obviously another) by then inadequately equipped to deal with public questions. Over this same period—one of "miraculous" economic growth at home and vast expansion of Japanese economic interests overseas—the "public" in Japan came to represent an *object* to be administered rather than a self-conscious social entity. Ideologically, this administration is often clothed in an essentialism of national character (symbolized by the so-called *Nihonjin ron*), and complemented by an "internationalist" projection.

This is all very different from the ardent embrace of universal ideas and ideals by public men of the early postwar years. *That* embrace was not without its own pitfalls and serious fallacies, as we shall see. And the reasons for the shift to essentialism can only be suggested here. High economic growth, a political system dominated by a bureaucratic/single party complex, rapid specialization, and concentration of commercial communications media all seem to have worked to bring this about. Underlying the process, I think, was the historical power of the cult of public *authority* over association for open public *discussion,* which simultaneously dampens the popular desire for participation in politics, and perpetuates the condition of tutelage. This hobbles attempts to transform popular discontent and aspirations into a continuing, affirmative public movement.

While not denying the importance of these recent developments in any way, however, I believe that in fact, the Occupation itself, especially the years from 1945 to 1950, was decisive for the subsequent shape of public discourse in Japan.

I suggested above that Marxism and "modernism" formed the two main lines of development in public discourse after 1945, one proceeding along "socialist" lines and concerned with establishing the conditions for an assertion of class subjectivity by the proletariat; the other along "humanist" lines and striving for the "establishment of the modern self" (*kindaiteki jiga no kakuritsu*) in Japan.

The impression is sometimes given in schematic accounts that Marxism simply "took over" among Japanese intellectuals after the war. No doubt this must have seemed the case to American scholars; whose military language training and growing diet of Cold War rhetoric did little to prepare them for well-informed involvement in Japanese intellectual life, at least in its immediate postwar incarnation. It is also true that the legalization of the long-suppressed Communist Party under the orders of occupation authorities came as a shock—and not only to those hostile to the left—and that Marxism as a Weltanschauung had posed the most comprehensive and compelling intellectual challenge to the prewar system. But we simply cannot understand postwar Japanese public discourse by calling it "Marxist-dominated." Let me try then to indicate something of the significance of prewar Marxism to the postwar situation.

In the exhaustive analysis by participants in the "debate on Japanese capitalism" of the transition from feudal to absolutist (or bourgeois) society, the position of the Kōza (or Lectures) faction of the Party, which tended to follow closely the theses worked out within the Comintern, was dominant. This held that Japan remained "feudal" in certain crucial respects, such as social relations of production in agriculture and the makeup of the ruling alliance. The position is significant for two reasons. First, it determined revolutionary strategy (after the promulgation of the 1932 theses) in treating a bourgeois revolution as still necessary before any transition to socialism could be possible. Second, and more important in terms of postwar public discourse, it drew attention to the continued power of "feudal" forces in the as yet unreformed system of land tenure. This basic position was easily transposed into non-Marxist terms to read that Japan was not yet fully *modern*. Leaving aside the question of means and priorities in the desired transformation, this was in substance the position taken by "modernists" such as Maruyama Masao, Ōtsuka Hisao, and Fukutake Tadashi.

It cannot be said, however, that prewar Marxists (or anyone else) had been able to give sufficient attention to the particular problems of ideology and consciousness under the imperial system—to the whole problem of the mobilization of an "irrational" tradition in support of absolutism. In this respect, as Shōji argues, the economistic approach of the dissident Rōnō (or Labor-Farmer) faction was probably more deficient than the politicist Kōza argument in "grasping the totality" of Japanese society under the imperial system.[11] In any case, the way was open for (relatively) untrammeled analysis of that totality only after 1945. But the practice of "social science" must be recognized to rest on a Marxist foundation.

In the political arena, the Party claimed a history of "resistance" as an organized body to the imperial system and won a legitimate place in the ideological spectrum. Its star rose quickly in the newly legalized and officially sanctioned movement to organize Japanese workers, for example. And it shone just as brightly over the scarred intellectual landscape as well. The internationalist faithful remnant that remained after the leadership had recanted and gone over to a chauvinistic Japanism in 1933 had been released from a decade and more of imprisonment, or had returned from exile. Their impact was immediate; they appeared now as "mirrors which in their brilliance shed glaring light on the weakness that haunted the innermost hearts" of intellectuals who had sung hosannas to the New Order.[12]

Thus Marxism rightfully played a powerful role in public discourse, and its definitions of key words such as *democracy, people, science,* and *subjectivity* received wide and respectful attention. However, the transformation of that discourse after 1945 is by no means reducible to an exchange of hegemonies; *kokutai* did not simply yield to *Capital* or to the Party's theoreticians. Indeed, the philosopher Nakamura Yūjirō goes so far as to argue that Marxism did not even constitute the "mainstream" in postwar thought.[13] Rather, we need to consider Marxism as one fertile source of theory and critique, which had to compete and engage in debate with other emancipated, but less systematic, approaches to public questions.

Among the latter, one is of particular interest to us here: the group of academics (many from imperial universities), critics, and writers known collectively as the "modernists" (*kindaishugisha*). Most prominent among them were Maruyama Masao (b. 1914), a specialist in political thought; the economic historian Ōtsuka Hisao (b. 1907); Kawashima Takeyoshi (b. 1909), a legal scholar; the literary critic Kuwabara Takeo (b. 1904); and the sociologists Fukutake Tadashi (b. 1914) and Shimizu Ikutarō (b. 1907).

As is frequently noted, this loose association of public men did not take the name "modernist" for themselves. It was attached to them by their Marxist counterparts in cultural and ideological debate, who pointed to their more or less uniform insistence that Japan had yet to achieve "true" modernity. This was a "not yet" to be struggled *for,* and hardly something that Japan had "overcome". The attainment of this true modernity was to entail a transformation not only of the structure of society (though Maruyama and Fukutake lay considerable stress here) but of the spirit or mentality of the people. The modernists broke with the historical materialists in rejecting any one-way causality from being to consciousness, arguing that these constituted a totality of semiautonomous elements rather than phenomenon and epiphenomenon. The exact formulation varied, of course. But all were self-conscious heirs of the Enlightenment. Maruyama, whose brilliance was said (somewhat formulaically) to have illuminated the darkened skies of the defeated nation "like a comet," sought to overcome the "irrational" and feudalistic spiritual subservience of the people under the former regime and to foster among the Japanese a modern ethos of politically engaged subjectivity. He sought, in short, to create citizens. Maruyama was skeptical of the transformative potential of sensually based subjectivity ("only the flesh is true"), insisting that ultimately a leap from "carnal literature" to "carnal politics" would have to be made if modernity were to be achieved.

In focusing upon the modern ethos, Maruyama followed Ōtsuka, with whom he shared the decisive influence of Max Weber. Maruyama's commitment to modernity, as is well known, dates from the interwar years and found its first and perhaps most powerful expression in his essays on Tokugawa Confucianism. Written in the midst of war (the later ones under the Damocles' sword of the military draft), the essays uncovered a "modern" political rationality—specifically, a Hobbesian theory of social contract—in the "logic of invention" that drove the philosophy of Ogyū Sorai (1666–1728). Here it must be understood, however, that a historical paradox lies at the core of this logic. Sorai's "modern" logic of invention had been exercised in an attempt to restore the Tokugawa system to a pristine feudalism. His articulation of what was a "modern" concept of politics was an unintended consequence of this attempt. Deeply influenced as he was by Hegel *and* Marx, Maruyama could not be satisfied with the exposition of the thought of a single thinker, except insofar as the mode of thought it revealed could be linked to shifts in the political and economic base of society. While he came to modify his base/superstructure approach, the commitment to subjectivity remained to animate his later work. In context, the wartime essays represent a powerful *insider* protest of an unfree present and defense of rationality already present within Japanese political thought. Having shown that the "demon" of modernity was deeply insinuated within the native tradition, Maruyama set out after 1945 to reconstitute Japanese politics by tapping that latent rationality, making it explicit and empowering it to transform contemporary consciousness. Indeed, that transformation was the key; the target was the "tenacious familial social structure—the hothouse of traditional Japanese nationalism—and of the ideology that perpetuated this structure." [14]

Maruyama's modernism clearly flowed from deep and long-standing conviction rather than an unreflective acceptance of a new hegemony. At the same time, the fact that Maruyama absorbed the national perspective of his mentors (both Nanbara the insider and outsiders such as Hasegawa Nyozekan and his own journalist father), and that he made it the critical concern of his entire intellectual life illuminates the difficulty of distancing oneself even from a political ideology and culture perceived as pathological. Maruyama remained critical of unreflective claims for or against "universality." Subjectivity—the exercise of *transcendent* critical faculty in a *particular* social and cultural nexus—was (and is) for Maruyama nothing if not a struggle to be both/and rather than either/or. It is a critical standpoint, not a national perspective, which Maruyama has privileged and sought to make a "mobile constant."

Another unfolding of modernism may be noted briefly here. This we encounter in the work of Shimizu Ikutarō. A pioneer of social psychology in the early 1940s (his chief work being *Shakaiteki ningenron*—On social man), and an adept in pragmatic philosophy, Shimizu called after the war for the subjugation of "irrational" blind desires through rational instrumentalities to create a constructive new social type. Unlike Maruyama, who had discerned the development of modern political rationality within the feudal womb; and unlike Ōtsuka, for whom (as for Nanbara) the transcendent—but still nonrational—realm of faith could vivify a modern rationality, Shimizu conceived of nothing beyond instrumental rationality itself. And that rationality had as yet no part in Japanese society, but had to be mediated to it by a community of enlightened democratizers. Rationality, introduced from without, would have to wage a constant battle with "explosions" of blind, and presumably reactionary, impulses. After the anti–Security Treaty demonstrations in 1960, however, Shimizu's basic position changed. He denied the need to subdue the blind impulses of the mass, instead insisting that the desires and mentality of "everyday" people, in the context of the existing social structure, "already revealed the values necessary to democracy." [15] Shimizu's shift in perspective may have prefigured the critique by younger thinkers, such as Yoshimoto Takaaki and Irokawa Daikichi, of modernist "elitism," and as such had some merit. (One might even call attention to the echoes in Shimizu's position of a work like Nyozekan's *Nihonteki seikaku*.) On the other hand, it seems to me that Shimizu's post-1960 approach fits more easily than Maruyama's into the ideology of an "administered" society that emerged in the 1960s. This is because it basically considers popular consciousness unchangeable; once a lamentable failing, it is inverted to become a strength. It also leaves in place structures of power and communication to perform the procedures of administration. Maruyama's position, with its negative valuation of Japanese social structure and call to complete the bourgeois revolution, may seem discordant amidst Japan's economic dynamism and political stability. Shimizu's social psychologism, on the other hand, while perhaps better in touch with "reality," bears the taint of thorough cooptation. This suggests, among other things, that the problem lay not so much with the masses as with the intellectual elite. Shimizu particularly wants to affirm the basic congruence of his thought with the "democratic" status quo *and* remain an opinion leader; to have his cake and eat it too. But might it not be the case that without *some* degree of tension with, and separation from, the "audience" and the status quo, really creative thinking and the intellectual power necessary for leadership simply run dry?

"Modernism" clearly contained seeds of internal division. But let us remind ourselves of the basic situation of public discourse in the years following Japan's defeat: the old "paradigm" of *kokutai* and "national community" suddenly and violently collapsed, to be replaced through intellectual contestation—carried out on a far broader scale than hitherto, involving multiple social strata—by a series of overlapping, sometimes conflicting, versions of a new publicness.

As Hashimoto Mitsuru noted, public discourse during the "national emergency" was virtually hegemonized by an exalted, even "absolutized," concept of *minzoku* intended to "overcome" a hostile "universality." With the new dispensation and the renewed embrace of universality, are we not simply talking about a recolonization of public discourse by Western categories congruent with Japan's subservience to U.S. interests and the reintegration of Japan into a U.S.-dominated "Free World"—or, in the case of leftists, by a mere self-referential utopianism? Alternatively, was it not simply a rewriting of the equation "universal equals Western equals alien and dangerous" to read "universal equals Western equals liberating and politically correct"?

Clearly there were ambiguities in the situation. Perhaps the best way to answer the question is first to glance at the political history of the early Occupation as it concerned intellectuals. In its initial objectives, as is well known, occupation policy was viewed as a liberating force by many who had chafed or been persecuted under the old regime. The new Constitution, legalization of the Communist and other opposition parties, encouragement of labor organization, enfranchisement of women, and reform of family law and land tenure were hailed as measures symbolic of a democratic and peaceful Japan. Postfeudal, postimperial Japan was to be open to the world, capitalist and socialist. It was a roseate vision. But the conditions that made it credible—foreign military occupation and loss of sovereignty—also ensured that nationalism, the appeal to *kyōdōtai,* would remain a powerful political weapon. This, indeed, was a point lost on neither the left nor the right. Nor has it been lost today, as the presumptive harmony of the people is used as a rationale for legislative retrenchment and ideological regimentation in education.

A number of public men became uncomfortable in this world of "rationed freedom" (which was nevertheless real, just as rationed food was still real food). Partly this had to do with the issues of nationalism and sovereignty just alluded to. But it had equally to do with the inevitable debate on the question of war responsibility. This was not, as many realized, an issue that could be settled by a purge of "ultranationalists." For, leaving aside legal questions of the "right to judge" and the validity of "victor's justice," the execution of the purge, when not halfhearted and inept, was hasty and allowed numerous loopholes. We cannot deal with particular cases; it is a matter of record that for political and practical reasons the official bureaucracy emerged largely untouched below the very highest levels. As far as academics, journalists, and writers—public men—were concerned, the abstraction and allusiveness common to much of their wartime production saved many a career. (There were also cases of voluntary withdrawal from public work—Yabe Teiji being but one example.) The issue of how public men treated their own immediate past was, therefore, one that had to be addressed not *officially* but *publicly;* that is, in open, transparent discussion.

It is Maruyama Masao's claim that something like this happened; that the majority of Japanese intellectuals formed what he calls a "community of contrition" (*kaikon kyōdōtai*).[16] He sees this community as functioning through 1960—breaking up after the anti–Security Treaty demonstrations that brought down Kishi Nobusuke but failed to prevent the treaty from taking effect. This, Maruyama seems to feel, was the last act of engaged and organized political subjectivity, and the (premature?) end, of the "community of contrition."

In another sense, the community of contrition came to an end sooner, perhaps by 1952. To put it another way, its internal contradictions combined with the rightward shift in Occupation policy to prevent its full potential from being realized. How was this so? We have already seen that the "community"—what we have termed postwar public discourse—was composed of two separable groups. On the one hand were Marxists, some of them Party members, many sympathizers; and on the other "modernists," who, while they incorporated and built upon Marxist categories and insights, were not historical materialists and felt no political bond to the Party or to the USSR. (This is not to deny the sense of moral identification many modernists felt with the cause of the left to combat counterrevolution, as witness the extensive discussion of contemporary fascism in journals such as *Shisō* and *Sekai*.)

These constituencies, indeed Japan as a whole, were immediately and profoundly affected by the great political movements of the second half of the 1940s: the coming to power of Stalinist regimes in Eastern Europe and, under vastly different circumstances, of Mao Zedong in mainland China, along with the reintegration of the "Free" or capitalist world order under the domination of the United States. First of all, occupation authorities had begun to issue warning signs even in 1946 that they would not tolerate what they regarded as a communist-controlled labor movement. Indeed, the banning of the general strike in early 1947, amidst a still desperate economic situation, was a body blow to the entire left.[17] Continuing with its "lovable Party" line (first enunciated by Nozaka Sanzō), the Party struggled to remain at the head of the democratic labor movement. But with mounting repression after 1948, culminating in the "Red Purge" of 1950, this became problematic in the extreme. (Indeed, MacArthur sought to make the Party once more illegal.) More telling, however, was the fragmentation of the leadership and the Party generally brought about when in 1950 the Cominform condemned Nozaka's "lovable Party" deviationism and demanded a more militant confrontation with the occupying powers and the Japanese state. The Party officially accepted the criticism, and followed it up with a period of attempted terrorism. This cost it much mass support, and the end of the Occupation found the Party in tatters, its leadership underground and its policies discredited. The Party had moreover presented to the public a most unedifying example of Stalinism in action by truckling to every instruction emanating from Moscow.

This harsh judgment is mitigated somewhat when we consider just how dramatically the political climate changed after 1947. The entire period from 1947 to 1952 was stamped by SCAP's definitive renunciation of some of its earliest, and in context most radical, reforms. This was particularly the case with labor organization. Communists, as we have noted, were expelled from public and private sector unions, and the Party as a whole was driven from public life by 1950. But much more was at stake: experiments in production control and with worker councils were halted as capital regained the initiative. *Zaibatsu* dissolution was, of course, abandoned as harmful to capitalist reconstruction. Conservatives in Japan were no doubt relieved to be able to identify themselves as "liberals" and observe that radical policies that had "gone too far" were now being reversed. Indeed, the "logic of capital" had by the early 1950s fully displaced the "logic of labor." Especially symbolic in this regard was the vastly expanded influence of two organizations: Keidanren—the Federation of Economic Organizations, and Nikkeiren—the Federation of Japanese Employers' Associations. The former was founded in 1946, but its functions were restricted to liaisons between individual economic organizations. In time, and particularly after 1952, it became the chief means by which industry and business articulated with the Diet and official bureaucracy. In this role it far overshadowed the labor organizations that had once found favor with Mac-

Arthur. The story of Nikkeiren is similar. American authorities would
not at first permit even the formation of such a body. By 1947 it had
reversed this policy, and Nikkeiren soon came to represent "virtually all
major Japanese enterprises." Under its leadership, and with the full cooperation of the government, Nikkeiren in 1948 spearheaded a drive to
"Secure Management Authority," and in 1949 followed with a call to
"Establish New Labor Relations." Union authority within the workplace was severely compromised in the name of worker "independence"
from "outside" control, and at the national level, a revision of the 1945
Labor Union Law ratified the inversion of power relations between
labor and capital.[18]

Just as the "reverse course" was not as sudden as it is sometimes described, so, too, its meaning is not clear-cut. We have already seen that
the left was divided between Marxists (Communists, left-wing Socialists) and "modernists," and that each constituency was itself composed
of overlapping groups representing different perspectives. Its unity was
tenuous enough to begin with. We may say that the "reverse course"
that unfolded after 1947 and reached its peak in 1950 meant not so
much (or not only) that socialist revolution was made impossible, but
that in general a strong, politically conscious, labor-based democratic
opposition was blunted and canalized along enterprise lines. This was
not inevitable. It was the result of conscious policy decisions within Allied GHQ, the Japanese government, and business circles. In industry,
capitalism was to take precedence over democracy.

The unquestioned success of the land reform, meanwhile, created for
the post-Occupation government a strong rural base, maintained without great difficulty in political tutelage once economic growth allowed
some rechanneling of largesse to rural districts. This payoff constitutes
one of the great successes of the postwar reforms, in terms both of social
and economic equity and long-term political benefit.

The significance of the "reverse course" is greater still, for it is by no
means certain that the basic task of "democratization" was complete by
1950. Contemporary accounts—not always sympathetic—suggest that
after 1945, as at no other time, there was among the Japanese people a
pervasive concern, almost a hunger, to explore questions of ideology
and to participate in politics. Images of "students with empty bellies
lined up in bookstores to buy works of philosophy and social science"[19]
come to mind here, along with the names of a myriad of groups seeking

to try out their vocal chords in public: one thinks of the Seinen Bunka Kaigi (Youth Culture Conference), the Jiyū Konwa Kai (Society for Free Discussion), smaller groups such as the Jinmin Bunka Dōmei (People's Culture League) and the Nihon Bunkajin Renmei (League of Japanese Men of Culture). Particularly emblematic are the Minshushugi Kagakusha Kyōkai, or Minka (Association of Democratic Scientists), which drew members from prewar Marxist intellectual groups and metamorphosed into a Party front organization; the 20-seiki Kenkyūjo (20th Century Research Institute) and Shisō no Kagaku Kenkyūkai (Association for Research into the Science of Thought), which (via certain segments of their membership) helped to introduce postwar American social science, especially social psychology and its underlying pragmatic philosophy, to a receptive Japanese audience.[20] We have already seen that intellectual lines and positions tended to overlap rather regularly at this point. It ought not to cause great surprise, then, to find on the roster of the Minka the name of Hayashi Kentarō, later to become one of the staunchest of Japan's intellectual cold warriors. But we should not miss the larger point here, which is not the sometimes short life or confused political orientation of such organizations, but the impulse that gave them birth: "contrition" and the democratization of knowledge. These were the intertwined sentiments that gave public discourse its vitality. The real damage that may have been done by the hard rightward swing of the Occupation, and by the left to itself through its Stalinist tendencies, was to prevent the full realization of a profound popular desire to join the public world—even if, as for many, it meant missing a meal.

Yet neither GHQ, the subsequent Japanese governments, nor the Party—none of these organizations, however powerful—can alone be held responsible for this unrealized potential. In saying this I do not mean to imply that the armed force of an occupying power was something that could have been overcome, for example, in a "February Revolution" in 1947. (Indeed, it could legally have been mobilized to crush any popular insurrection until 1960.) But there are areas, less tangible to be sure, for which public men and the "community of contrition" were responsible, and that bear some consideration here.

I have in mind two problems: the extent and quality of "contrition," and a broader claim, differently expressed and with differing political implications, that Japanese intellectuals are somehow unable or unwilling to put their theory into "practice"; that they live vicariously in a world of imported concepts that bear little relation to the social reality around them and are therefore easily replaceable when their dissonance with reality becomes (politically) inconvenient, suspect, or otherwise unacceptable.

Clearly the two problems are bound up with each other. As we have seen, postwar public discourse began with "contrition" for the excesses of an absolutized ideology of national community, and with a corresponding embrace of universal values. The forms of contrition and embrace were, of course, not uniform. "Contrition" and the embrace of "universal" values seemed frequently to involve discrete gestures and organizations. Partly this had to do with the "Red Purge" and the assault on labor unions thought to be controlled by the Party. But there were also internal dynamics—ideological and political conflict—that acted as a brake on long-term unity. Thus the opposition parties came to sponsor their own forces in the labor and peace movements separately; within these movements, too, forces seeking independence of the parties also emerged. The idea of forming loose, self-sustaining networks for social and political action was not powerful—at least until the advent of Beheiren in the late 1960s. Thereafter, too, the citizens' and antipollution movements have had to contend with the problem of fragmentation and narrowness of perspective.

But let us return to the expression of "contrition" in the early postwar years. More characteristic of early "contrition" was the exaltation by fallen leftists of the Communist Party to the exclusion of any criticism. They would not fall again! Alternatively there was the call for sōzange, a collective/summary metanoia or confession in which the *entire* nation would unite as one in repentance of its sins and dedicate itself to the promotion of peace.

We must be careful here, however. On religious and philosophical grounds, there were serious attempts to confront the implications many intellectuals drew from Japan's brutal aggression and defeat, and from their own self-acknowledged involvement in, or impotence to prevent, what had happened. One such is Tanabe Hajime's *Zangedō toshite no tetsugaku* (Philosophy as metanoetics), a work published in 1946 but completed in 1944, "as the nation [sank] deeper and deeper into hell." Certainly the issue of a philosopher's responsibility for the implications, not to mention the distortion and misappropriation, of his thought is extremely contentious. In this case the difficulty lies in Tanabe's concept of the "logic of species" (*shu no ronri*), which Nanbara Shigeru—in *Kokka to shūkyō*—and a number of postwar critics charged was an elaborate rationalization for Japanese statolatry. Beginning in 1935, Tanabe wrote of "species"—as opposed to genus or individual—as "the most immediate ground of being . . . a concrete substrate in terms of which the individual formally actualizes its genus in history." As such, "species" represented the "radical irrationality of pure desire for life at the core of human consciousness, a desire defined by social conditions, . . . a social archetype." Here, it should be emphasized, social meant national; and as with Nishida Kitarō, Tanabe came to see "a positive significance in acknowledging the emperor of Japan as a symbol of the sacredness of the nation." On the basis of this "logic of species," Tanabe went on to discuss, in terms of Henri Bergson's *Two Sources of Morality and Religion,* "how only an 'opening of species' to genus through the dialectical mediation of rationality has any hope of promoting freedom in history." In *Zangedō toshite no tetsugaku,* Tanabe attempted to provide an existential ground for the confrontation by the individuals making up the species (i.e., himself and his fellow Japanese) of its collective sin, and in so doing, simultaneously to use philosophy to get "beyond philosophy." This, Tanabe was convinced, was his duty, as a philosopher, to the nation. Despite the inference—drawn by ultranationalists and their critics alike—that such notions as the logic of species reflected his espousal of aggressive, imperialist war, Tanabe's intent was quite otherwise. He had in fact sought to articulate a *critique* of "blind nationalism." Thus Tanabe did not regard his entire philosophical project as tainted, but believed it to contain the potential for its own transfiguration in confrontation with history. And he was willing, where Heidegger never was, to face the issue of the moral, social, and political meaning of his own act of philosophizing in the context of a malevolent particularism. Tanabe never intended the logic of species to mean the yielding of the individual moral sense or subjectivity to the state-as-nation, but seems to have realized that, in minds other than his own, it did foster precisely such abdication.[21]

So, too, ironically, for the *sō-zange* Tanabe enjoined on the Japanese people in his first postwar work. We have already seen that the need to face the reality of moral failure was apparent to him by 1944, and that any confrontation with it would be undertaken by individuals on the basis of the logic of species. But in its officially sponsored form, the call to repentance seems to have assumed the character of unconditional collective absolution. As Maruyama Masao noted in 1956, "There can be no doubt whatsoever that the 'collective repentance of 100,000,000' [i.e., national repentance] was in reality no more than a squid's jet of black ink released by a ruling group facing a desperate situation."[22] *Sō-zange* became a "blackwash" to evade the issue Tanabe sought to face. It dissolved all individual responsibility in a collective gesture meant more to foster domestic tranquility than to face the painful question of why the war was begun and how human beings act in wartime.

Softening American attitudes toward the whole question of war responsibility also had a role to play. The "reverse course" brought back into public life many who had been purged for their wartime activities. It became possible for certain intellectuals, uncomfortable with their past actions, to retreat into a practical collectivism in the interest of national reconstruction, to talk grandly about problems of "peace" and "democracy" without ever considering how their past and present were related. As I have said, neither official acts by the U.S. authorities nor any institutional approach would have been sufficient to sustain an inner compulsion among Japanese public men to face the past. Not sufficient—but they were necessary. It is my feeling that public forgetfulness, sometimes masked in confessional, sometimes practical, "get-on-with-life" terms, was countenanced for political reasons before the full dimensions of the issue were revealed. The atmosphere of "contrition" could not survive cooptation and repudiation by the highest authorities of state. In this respect the interests of conservative Japanese officials and those of the United States were identical.

———

This brings us finally to the connection between "contrition" and the dual problems of intellectual vicariousness and the failure of praxis on the part of public men. Unquestionably, certain long-term factors are at work here: these are the external origins of the infrastructure of the modern state in Japan and its political and intellectual "technology," and the position of public men as nationalizers of foreign models. One result of this nexus, as we have seen, is a vulnerability to appeals made by the state in the name of the national community, and a general tendency to reject positions of organized and confrontational "outsideness." This is not to deny that public outsiders have spoken passionately and persuasively on behalf of the good and decent life—one threatened by state incursions—of "everyday" people. In this sense, the "Nyozekan model" (if I may be forgiven the phrase) is very much alive. But whatever its virtues, this is a now nonconfrontational strategy that frequently, and explicitly, abjures any political intent. More specifically, publicness has tended to ramify with a bias toward the state. Liberalism, in the sense of a "doubt that seeks to build fences around those in power, rather than bridges for them," [23] has historically been weak in Japan. And it has not been easy for public men to maintain the independence of perspective that is vital to their work. My suspicion is that this difficulty has a great deal to do with the conditions under which Japan entered the modern world—rapidly, under external pressure, and driven by the state. I also suspect that Japan is not alone in this, and that something like the experience of its public men has been shared by others in similar societies. The weakness of the public sphere can be dangerous to any nation.

But will it always be such a struggle to support an independent public sphere? Will Japanese public men always shrink from confrontation with the state and "unauthorized" social practice, and therefore condemn themselves to intellectual vicariousness? Skepticism in this regard is not hard to understand. Consider the tempting symmetry of Takeuchi Yoshimi's sardonic observation, made in 1948:

> In Japan, when ideas are out of line with reality we start afresh by abandoning our former principles and searching for others. Concepts are left high and dry, principles abandoned. . . . With increasing speed and intensity we junk what is old and adopt what is new. If liberalism doesn't work we try totalism [zentaishugi]; if that doesn't work we turn to communism, and so on. We are bound to fail, but failure itself never fails. It is the mother of success. . . . Japanese ideology, in this sense, never fails. It is eternally successful by eternally failing. This is repeated ad infinitum. And that we call progress.[24]

I confess that I am not prepared here to defend or reject Takeuchi's sweeping claim as a whole. Maruyama Masao and Fujita Shōzō, among others, have in their own way voiced similar ideas: that the essence of the "Japanese spirit" is its emptiness; that it is the contentless "something that remains" when external, universal elements are (analytically) removed; a "logic" of eternal renewability, and so on.[25]

However, I am not persuaded that such a phenomenological observation captures the specificity of intellectual experience. It does not explain the "failure." I have tried to capture some of the specificity and explain some of the "failure" here, using the example of the modernists to suggest the sense of vacuousness of past values, the hope of future empowerment, and how that hope was defeated. I do not think that the fragmentation and subversion of the postwar public discourse represents simply a resurgent particularism. It was encouraged for political and other reasons by those who controlled Japan, was consonant with conservative sentiment outside the ruling circles, and afforded an easy way out of a still unresolved moral dilemma.

Who then stands as the "representative" public man? It seems that in terms of content, publicness in Japan continues to entail some attempt to mediate "universality" to the particular political and social nexus of Japan, but that the public sense has been weakened by its burden of bureaucratism and statism. I believe, following Ishida Takeshi, that the links of private individuals and groups to each other have grown tighter, but that this remains a "corporate privatism," exclusive rather than inclusive. The links of *society* to the *public* remain tenuous.[26] I would argue that this is true to a surprising degree even among the academic (and literary) "counterestablishment." Here, too, one must recognize important exceptions such as Ōe Kenzaburō, Oda Makoto, Takeuchi Yoshimi, and Takahashi Kazumi. The latter two, interestingly enough, were specialists in Chinese literature and admirers of Lu Xun.

The overall situation, however, fits well with the "administered society" (*kanri shakai*) Japan has become. It is no accident that sophisticated administration, under the now four-decade long dominance of the bureaucratic/single-party complex, and stunning corporate prosperity since the late 1950s have brought Japan remarkable political stability. There is even a democratic glitter and playfulness in the accessibility in "hyper-urban" places like Tokyo, of safe, short-term escape from company, school, and family. There is "information" and all manner of intellectual and physical stimulation available everywhere. The Japanese are thoroughly "informed" about the world through highly centralized sources. The countryside, except for truly remote areas and others dependent on declining industries like coal mining (Yūbari in Hokkaidō, for example) is scarcely less wired. Perhaps, as Ishida notes, the democratic system, with its "peace constitution" and guaranteed rights, no longer appears as a "gift of the Occupation."[27] Indeed, the administrative (or in Robert Bellah's terms) "schoolmaster" state[28] is thoroughly *atarimae*. It is "deserved"; it is "obvious," as are the prosperity and stability it has brought. This is no mean achievement.

But in trying to answer our question, "Who is the representative public man?" we are faced with the fact that, in terms of what Ralf Dahrendorf calls "representative" (read "public," as opposed to "legitimative" activities), there is a singular sterility about the contemporary situation. One may cite the work of the antipollution activist Ui Jun as an example of genuine representative action: performed on behalf of others and contributing to the "reservoir of possible futures."[29] There must be local examples many times over of such individuals—indeed, real public vitality may depend on movement below the national level. But this in a way proves the larger point: Ui must confront the system as a representative of its *victims*. He cannot claim to be part of a transparent public discourse. Yet this, if nothing else, was the promise of the "community of contrition."

Not so long ago the phrase *datsu seiji*—"connoting a trend toward 'depolitical' apathy"—came to the fore. It has remained apt.[30] Politically the country seems to be spinning its wheels, waiting on the one hand for the final triumph of the right, in the form of constitutional revision to renounce the renunciation of war, and on the other for the fragmented opposition to find some way out of its semiexile within the system. (I am not overlooking the important role played by opposition parties in keeping the LDP "in line," and preventing egregious abuses of its—as of 1986—commanding majority in the Diet.) The claim has been made that the Socialists are at work formulating a correct practical response, in the light of stepped-up and assiduous theoretical work, to the long series of electoral defeats that has marked the party's recent history.[31] Perhaps this may lead to something. For the moment, I cannot say from what quarter a renewal of the public sense in Japan will come. Perhaps it is always destined to be ephemeral, some kind of Durkheimian "collective effervescence." Perhaps we ought not to wish for the conditions that initially brought forth the "community of contrition" to emerge again. On reflection, however, it is precisely such thinking—and the inclination to "leave things to the august authorities" (*okami makase*)—that led to disaster in the first place.

In the light of these observations, I would propose that we may view two public men as representative of the postwar period. I begin with the majority report. This would be the ex-Marxist, long-time pragmatist Shimizu Ikutarō, who as an insider at Tokyo Imperial tapped the mobilized intellectual energies of the "national emergency" to pioneer social psychology; as an opinion-leading journalist was heavily influential in discussions of the problems of "peace" and "democracy" in the immediate postwar years; ushered in the theory of mass society in the 1950s, and Daniel Bell's "end of ideology" somewhat later; finally turning after the mass demonstrations against the U.S.-Japan Security Treaty of 1960 to the explicit defense of the democratic system that was and is the status quo. At first glance, Shimizu seems to embody the eternally renewable "Japanese ideology" criticized by Takeuchi Yoshimi. But where is the failure? Shimizu has been a trendsetter. One would have little difficulty in showing, furthermore, that Shimizu's intellectual peripeties are not fundamentally different from those, say, of Sidney Hook, Norman

Podhoretz, Michael Novak, or any of a number of neoconservative thinkers in the United States. Perhaps "Japanese ideology" here means a capacity to see the virtues of corporate and multinational capitalism and consumerism without (as yet) any overt official militarism—although Shimizu has leanings in this direction as well.[32] In any case, in his moves back and forth between representative and legitimative activities, and his apparent settlement on the latter, Shimizu seems one effective symbol of public discourse in Japan as it has developed over the past four decades.

I close with a somewhat longer minority report. This comes best, I believe, from Maruyama Masao. We have already glimpsed something of his chief problematic, which differed from Shimizu's in a number of respects even as they cooperated in such groups as the 20th Century Research Institute. Let me say something about what makes Maruyama a "minority," though certainly not a "minor," thinker.[33]

Maruyama owed his once commanding position in the social science firmament to his consistent, intellectually informed commitment to the inculcation of political subjectivity in Japan, and to the explosive creativity of his conceptual formulations. His 1946 essay on the "theory and psychology of ultranationalism" was virtually physical in its impact on readers as it overturned everyday reality by breaking the code in which all discourse on the emperor system had been conducted for so long. In seeking to expose the "pathology" of Japan's ideological "slavery" under that system, Maruyama's text employed (as Victor Koschmann notes)[34] an almost coercive irony. In a sense, this irony, and an insistence on the ubiquity of spiritual subservience among the Japanese people, placed an unbridgeable gulf between Maruyama and his audience. This was a source of great strength. He was ever the *magister*. He exploited (and I mean no cheap criticism here) his insideness to the hilt. Maruyama the enlightener met the hunger for empowering knowledge—not just for "information" as in later decades—in a way few others in the early postwar years could emulate.

A good deal of Maruyama's credibility, I think, stemmed from the fact that he was not a "pure" insider à la Nanbara. His father, Maruyama Kanji, was a prominent liberal journalist and close associate of Hasegawa Nyozekan. Along with the influence of his father, Hasegawa Nyozekan's attitude toward the state, his ability to draw out the significance of a detail or episode, and, concretely, his analysis of "Japanese fascism"—all these informed Maruyama's outlook. It is not an indifferent piece of *petite histoire*, then, that Maruyama, at a crucial moment, combined in his own work the two streams of "insider" and "out-sider" publicness represented by Nanbara and Hasegawa Nyozekan respectively. This is what gave his texts their appeal, and explains why the gulf that he (like Nanbara and unlike Hasegawa) created, worked in his favor. Maruyama portrayed himself as an intellectual, a public man, who was in the system but not of it.

And here precisely was the problem. Could that really be true? Could he really be so involved and so distant at the same time? (No wonder he was dubbed "Maruyama Tennō".) It seems that he could not. Maru-yama reacted defensively and only piecemeal to the criticism that he was slow to acknowledge the deep implication of public men in Japan's mo-bilization for, and execution of, total war. There seemed to be a blind spot in his analyses of "Japanese fascism." He alluded only briefly and obliquely, for example, to the roles of his senior colleagues Rōyama Masamichi and Yabe Teiji as "theorists" of the New Order. He scarcely acknowledged the existence of the Shōwa Kenkyūkai. One reason may be that attacks on intellectuals were motivated by a desire, or at least served, to deflect attention away from others who were more "respon-sible"—members of the ruling elite on the one hand, prewar Commu-nists on the other. Although "responsibility" did not mean the same thing in these cases—one involving execution, the other failure to fore-see and prevent—Maruyama claimed that there was more to be said on this score before the war responsibility of intellectuals became a central issue. The evasive tone (at least for this reader) is inescapable.[35]

Over the years, Maruyama has made an effort to address this ques-tion. But it has come in the context of a broader discussion of the intel-lectual as "organization man" (as Koschmann puts it), and much read-ing between the lines must be done. I would not expect anything on the order of his early postwar analyses to emerge. The larger point seems to be that in modern, technologically capable societies, public men will in one way or another be involved professionally in any undertaking that requires a massive mobilization of a nation's resources. In future total wars, victory and defeat may become indistinguishable. But until now, defeat in such conflicts has for the vanquished meant the repudiation and transformation (sometimes through domestic revolution) of entire political, social, and cultural systems. Certainly this was the case for Japan in 1945. Defeat and occupation became the occasion for a radical self-questioning that took on a significance of its own, raising historical and moral questions of unparalleled urgency.

It is for this reason that one looks at the blank spot in Maruyama's work with regret. "Who, in later times, will be able to understand that we had to fall again into the darkness after we had once known the light?"[36]

Some brief reflection, in the light of Maruyama's work, on the question of whether *public man* is synonymous with *organization man* seems fitting here. Maruyama has restricted much of his analysis to Japan, insisting that there remains unsolved for Japan a special problem of detaching from *universal* its persistent identification with what is foreign to Japan. I do not wish to refute this point, which seems quite valid. But one may still ask whether Maruyama is not to be numbered among those who would subscribe to Peter Nettl's dictum: "As modernity advances, the intellectual retreats."[37] This is not, I think, a moral judgment so much as a lament and call to arms. Maruyama seems to me to have responded to that call at a time when many others in Japan, knowingly or not, were retreating. Valid criticisms can and should be made of Maruyama, as of all public men. But they should be made in recognition of his special "minority" status as a defender of what was most valuable in postwar public discourse: the commitment to open political process, to clarity in public matters, to freedom of thought and action.

Modern societies have been marked by the great, if contested, incorporation of public men into highly sophisticated structures of power, administration, and communication. This has not meant subservience only. Vast potential for the sharing and actualization of knowledge awaits participants in public discourse. But this will demand an independence of perspective and a commitment to free activity. It is not clear that we understand how this independence is to be preserved.

Abbreviations

GKH	Hasegawa Nyozekan. *Gendai kokka hihan*. 1921. In *HNSS*, vol. 2.
GKS	Nanbara Shigeru. *Gakumon, kyōyō, shinkō*. Tokyo: Kondō Shoten, 1946.
GSH	Hasegawa Nyozekan. *Gendai shakai hihan*. 1922. In *HNSS*, vol. 3.
HNSS	Hasegawa Nyozekan. *Hasegawa Nyozekan senshū*. 7 vols. Tokyo: Kurita Shuppankai, 1970.
KGZ	*Kokka Gakkai zasshi*.
KTS	Nanbara Shigeru. *Kokka to shūkyō*. Tokyo: Iwanami Shoten, 1942.
NFH	Hasegawa Nyozekan. *Nihon fuashizumu hihan*. Tokyo: Ōhata Shoten, 1932.
NSCS	Nanbara Shigeru. *Nanbara Shigeru chosakushū*. 10 vols. Tokyo: Iwanami Shoten, 1974.
OA	Osaka *Asahi shinbun*.
YTN	*Yabe Teiji nikki*, vol. 1. Tokyo: Yomiuri Shinbunsha, 1974.

Notes

PREFACE

1. Over the years, Maruyama has published a number of reminiscences and reflections on his work. Some are in the form of round-table discussions; a few are transcribed lectures or essays. For the period prior to 1963, the indispensable bibliographical source is Imai Juichirō, *Maruyama Masao chosaku nōto* (Tokyo: Tosho Shinbunsha, 1964). For later periods, see inter alia Maruyama Masao and Kozai Yoshishige, "Ichi tetsugakuto no kunan no michi," in *Shōwa shisōshi e no shōgen* (Tokyo: Mainichi Shinbunsha, 1968), 1–102, and "Nyozekan san to chichi to watakushi," in *Hasegawa Nyozekan: Hito; jidai; shisō to chosaku mokuroku,* ed. Sera Masatoshi et al. (Tokyo: Chūō Daigaku, 1986), 267–317. Recent discussions of the evolution of his methodology include "Shisōshi no hōhō o mosaku shite—hitotsu no kaisō," in *Nagoya Daigaku hōsei ronbunshū,* no. 77 (September 1978): 1–31, and "Genkei; kosō; shitsuyō tei'on—Nihon shisōshi hōhōron ni tsuite no watakushi no ayumi," in *Nihon bunka no kakureta kata,* ed. Takeda Kiyoko (Tokyo: Iwanami Shoten, 1984), 87–152. See also n. 6 to Conclusion for a number of recent essays on Maruyama and his work.

2. Robert N. Bellah, *Beyond Belief* (New York: Harper & Row, 1970), xvi.

3. Simone Weil, "The Power of Words" (1937), in *Selected Essays,* ed. Richard Rees (Oxford: Oxford University Press, 1963), 154–75, esp. 157; *The Need for Roots* (1943) (Boston: Beacon Press, 1952); "East and West: Thoughts on the Colonial Problem" (1943) in *Selected Essays,* 195–210.

4. Maruyama Masao, "The Ideology and Dynamics of Japanese Fascism" (1947), in *Thought and Behaviour in Modern Japanese Politics* (New York: Oxford University Press, 1969), 60–61.

5. John Dunn, *Western Political Theory in the Face of the Future* (Cambridge: Cambridge University Press, 1979), 1.

6. Hasegawa Nyozekan, *Gendai kokka hihan* (1921), in *Hasegawa Nyoze-kan senshū* (*HNSS*) (Tokyo: Kurita Shuppankai, 1970), 2:39.

7. In Maruyama, *Thought and Behaviour*, 321–48, esp. 332–33. His discussion draws on the work of Milton Mayer, *They Thought They Were Free: The Germans, 1933–1945* (Chicago: University of Chicago Press, 1955).

INTRODUCTION

1. See Maruyama, "Kindai Nihon ni okeru shisōshiteki hōhō no keisei," in *Seiji shisō ni okeru Seiyō to Nihon: Nanbara Shigeru sensei koki kinen,* ed. Fukuda Kan'ichi (Tokyo: Tokyo Daigaku Shuppankai, 1961), 2:265–90.

2. Makoto Itoh, *Value and Crisis: Essays on Marxian Economics in Japan* (New York: Monthly Review Press, 1980), 13.

3. See Ishida Takeshi, *Meiji seiji shisōshi kenkyū* (Tokyo: Miraisha, 1966), pt. 1; Joseph Pittau, *Political Thought in Early Meiji Japan, 1868–1889* (Cambridge, Mass.: Harvard University Press, 1967; Fujita Shōzō, *Tennōsei kokka no shihai genri,* 2d ed. (Tokyo: Miraisha, 1979), discusses the contradiction that surfaced between family and individual, and between family and family-state, under conditions of depression and total war. In this sense, his work is a discussion of the process of "deracination" in Japan.

4. Pittau, *Political Thought,* 11–17.

5. See the relevant entries in Morohashi Tetsuji, *Dai kanwa jiten* (Tokyo: Taishūkan Shoten, 1955–60), 2:1108–27.

6. See B. Schwartz, *In Search of Wealth and Power: Yen Fu and the West* (Cambridge, Mass.: Harvard University Press, 1964), 69–73; Hao Chang, Liang Ch'i-ch'ao and Intellectual Transition in China, 1890–1907 (Cambridge, Mass.: Harvard University Press, 1971).

7. On this point, see the new and important work by Carol Gluck, *Japan's Modern Myths: Ideology in the Late Meiji Period* (Princeton: Princeton University Press, 1985). As will become clear, my own view of the ideological situation of imperial Japan differs somewhat from Gluck's.

8. See Fukuzawa's editorials in *Jiji shinpō,* esp. "Jiji taisei ron" (1882), "Hanbatsu kajin seifu ron" (1881), "Kokkai no zento" (1890), "Teishitsu ron" (1882), all in *Fukuzawa Yukichi senshū* (Tokyo: Iwanami Shoten, 1981), vol. 6; *Meiroku Zasshi: Journal of the Japanese Enlightenment,* trans. D. Braisted (Cambridge, Mass.: Harvard University Press, 1976), intro., xi–xiv.

9. On the Tokugawa origins of the "new political space" see, inter alia, H. D. Harootunian, *Toward Restoration: The Growth of Political Consciousness in Tokugawa Japan* (Berkeley and Los Angeles: University of California Press, 1970); Matsumoto Sannosuke, "The Idea of Heaven: A Tokugawa Foundation for Natural Rights Theory," in *Japanese Political Thought in the Tokugawa Period,* ed. Tetsuo Najita and Irwin Scheiner (Chicago: University of Chicago Press, 1978), 181–99, esp. 189–91; and the *locus classicus* in Maruyama Masao, *Studies in the Intellectual History of Tokugawa Japan* (Princeton: Princeton University Press, 1979).

10. See I. Scheiner, *Christian Converts and Social Protest in Meiji Japan*

(Berkeley and Los Angeles: University of California Press, 1970), 194–208, for an incisive contrast of Fukuzawa's and the various Christian perspectives.

11. See Irokawa Daikichi, *Shinpen Meiji seishinshi* (Tokyo: Chūō Kōronsha, 1976), 218–44; Kano Masanao, "The Changing Concept of Modernization: From a Historian's Viewpoint," *Japan Quarterly* 32, no. 1 (January–March 1976): 28–35.

12. See Byron Marshall, *Capitalism and Nationalism in Prewar Japan* (Stanford: Stanford University Press, 1967); M. Y. Yoshino, *Japan's Managerial System: Tradition and Innovation* (Cambridge, Mass.: MIT Press, 1968), 19–28.

13. On Meiji and Taishō socialism, see Matsuzawa Hiroaki, *Nihon shakaishugi no shisō* (Tokyo: Chikuma Shobō, 1976), pt. 1, passim; I. Scheiner, "Meiji Socialists: The Moral Minority" and "Taishō and Shōwa Marxism," forthcoming in the *Cambridge History of Japan*.

14. Max Weber's observation is germane here: "In addition to the direct and material interests . . . there are the indirectly material as well as ideological interests of strata that are in various ways privileged within a polity and, indeed, privileged by its very existence. They comprise especially all those who think of themselves as being the specific 'partners' of a specific 'culture' diffused among the members of the polity. Under the influence of these circles, the naked prestige of 'power' is unavoidably transformed into other special forms of prestige and especially into the idea of 'nation'" (*Economy and Society* [Berkeley and Los Angeles: University of California Press, 1978], 2:922).

15. Fukuzawa, "Teishitsu ron."

16. Kano Masanao, *Taishō demokurashii no teiryū* (Tokyo: NHK, 1978).

17. Oka Yoshitake, *Konoe Fumimaro: A Political Biography* (Tokyo: Tokyo University Press, 1983), 107–15.

18. Pittau, *Political Thought*, 159–201.

19. See Gustav Ranis, "The Community Centered Entrepreneur in Japanese Development," *Explorations in Entrepreneurial History* 8, no. 2 (December 1955), cited in Marshall, *Capitalism and Nationalism in Japan*, 117.

20. Maruyama, "Kindai Nihon no chishikijin," in id., *Kōei no ichi kara* (Tokyo: Miraisha, 1982), 124.

21. Ibid., 98.

22. Ibid., 101, where Aizan is also quoted.

23. See Earl Kinmonth, *The Self-Made Man in Meiji Japanese Thought* (Berkeley and Los Angeles: University of California Press, 1981), for a stimulating but unsuccessful attempt to reduce the psychic strains of the success ethic to frustrated self-interest. The idea of the "rewards of insideness" (in this case deference from outsiders) is drawn in part from Thomas Huber's suggestive discussion of the ethos of the lower samurai "service intelligentsia," which he identifies as the revolutionary class in the destruction of the Tokugawa system. See Huber, *The Revolutionary Origins of Modern Japan* (Stanford: Stanford University Press, 1981).

24. I wish to thank Takashi Fujitani (University of California, Santa Cruz) and Nimura Kazuo (Hōsei University) for these references.

25. Maruyama, "Chishikijin," 88–92.

26. Ralf Dahrendorf, *Society and Democracy in Germany* (New York: Norton, 1979), 267.

27. Maruyama, "Meiji kokka no shisō" (1946), in id., *Senchū to sengo no aida* (Tokyo: Misuzu Shobō, 1976), 215, 239.

28. See Kobayashi Hajime, "Nihon riberarizumu no dentō to marukusushugi," *Shakaigaku hyōron* 23, no. 4 (April 1973): 2–27. Kobayashi sees the "modernists" as combining "Meiji consciousness" (= nationalism) with "Shōwa method" (= social science), and stresses their interwar roots in the thinking, for example, of Hasegawa Nyozekan and Maruyama Kanji.

29. See Arakawa Ikuo, "1930-nendai to chishikijin no mondai: Chishiki kanryō ruikei ni tsuite," *Shisō*, no. 624 (June 1976): 2–14, esp. 9–13; also see Chalmers Johnson, *MITI and the Japanese Miracle* (Stanford: Stanford University Press, 1982), 3–197 passim. It is interesting to note Yoshino Shinji's comment: "It would not be wrong to call [industrial rationalization] an intellectual movement" (quoted in Arakawa, 12).

30. See C. Wright Mills, "The Cultural Apparatus," in id., *Power, Politics and People* (New York: Oxford University Press, 1963), 405–7.

31. Ralf Dahrendorf, "Representative Activities," in id., *Life Chances* (Chicago: University of Chicago Press, 1979), 141–63, esp. 150, 153, 159–63.

32. For an example, see Nanbara Shigeru, *Kokka to shūkyō* (Tokyo: Iwanami Shoten, 1942), 27.

33. Tsuji Kiyoaki, *Nihon kanryō no kenkyū* (Tokyo: Tokyo Daigaku Shuppankai, 1974), esp. "Nihon fuashizumu ni okeru tōchi no kōzō," 206–41.

34. See T. Najita, *Hara Kei in the Politics of Compromise* (Cambridge, Mass.: Harvard University Press, 1967).

35. See the special issue of *Chūō kōron*, "Tenraku jiyūshugi no kentō" (May 1935), and the discussion in Ishida Takeshi, "Waga kuni ni okeru jiyūshugi no issokumen," in id., *Nihon kindai shisōshi ni okeru hō to seiji* (Tokyo: Iwanami Shoten, 1976), 221–61.

36. Oka Yoshitake, *Konoe Fumimaro,* 111.

37. See Ishida Takeshi, *Nihon no shakai kagaku* (Tokyo: Tokyo Daigaku Shuppankai, 1984), esp. 125–60.

38. Forster is quoted in Thomas Merton, *Conjectures of a Guilty Bystander* (New York: Image, 1968), 162; for accusations of hubris (directed at liberals in the Law and Economics Faculties at Tōdai by one of their own colleagues) see Hon'iden Yoshio, "Daigaku no kakushin," *Nihon hyōron* 13, no. 5 (April 1938).

39. James Crowley, "Intellectuals as Visionaries of the New Asian Order," in *Dilemmas of Growth in Prewar Japan*, ed. J. Morley (Princeton: Princeton University Press, 1971), 319–73; Miles Fletcher, *The Search for a New Order: Intellectuals and Fascism in Prewar Japan* (Chapel Hill: University of North Carolina Press, 1982); Sakai Saburō, *Shōwa Kenkyūkai: Aru chishikijin shūdan no kiseki* (Tokyo: TBS Britannica, 1979); Muroga Sadanobu, *Shōwa Juku* (Tokyo: Nihon Keizai Shinbunsha, 1978); Itō Takashi, *Shōwa jūnendaishi danshō* (Tokyo: Tōkyō Daigaku Shuppankai, 1981).

40. Fletcher, *Search,* 5.

41. Rōyama Masamichi, "Kokumin kyōdōtai no keisei," *Kaizō* 21, no. 5 (May 1939), 15; also discussed in Ishida, *Nihon kindai shisōshi,* 229–30.

42. This discussion draws on Fletcher, *Search*, 121–33, esp. 127–33.

43. Miki's clearest statement of this thesis appears in his *Shin Nihon no shisō genri* (1939), reprinted in *Miki Kiyoshi zenshū* (Tokyo: Iwanami Shoten, 1967), 17:507–88. See also John H. Boyle, *China and Japan at War: The Politics of Collaboration* (Stanford: Stanford University Press, 1972), 141.

44. Rōyama, "Kokumin kyōdōtai no keisei," 24, quoting from Rudolf Brinkmann, *Wirtschaftspolitik als nationalsozialistischen Kraftquell* (1939). Brinkmann's ideas are discussed more fully in Franz Neumann, *Behemoth* (1944) (New York: Harper & Row, 1966), 269.

45. On Kanai, see K. Pyle, "The Advantages of Followership: German Economics and Japanese Bureaucrats, 1890–1925," *Journal of Japanese Studies* 1, no. 1 (Autumn 1974).

46. On the "invention" of the imperial political tradition and cult, see Takashi Fujitani, "Japan's Modern National Ceremonies: A Historical Ethnography, 1868–1912," Ph.D. diss., University of California, Berkeley, 1986; Gluck, *Japan's Modern Myths*, esp. chap. 4; Robert Smith, *Japanese Society* (Cambridge: Cambridge University Press, 1985), 9–36.

47. Tanabe Hajime, "Shakai sonzai no ronri" and "Kokka sonzai no ronri," *Tetsugaku kenkyū* 20, no. 1, and 24, no. 11. On Tanabe's *Zangedō*, see the new translation and introduction by Takeuchi Yoshinori, *Philosophy as Metanoetics* (Berkeley and Los Angeles: University of California Press, 1986), with the foreword by James Heisig.

48. H. Laski, "The Apotheosis of the State," *New Republic*, 22 July 1916, quoted in *Holmes-Laski Letters* (New York: Atheneum, 1963), 1:8.

49. See, for example, R. Paxton, *Vichy France: Old Guard and New Order* (New York: Norton, 1975), for the Vichy regime's efforts to train a new elite in the early days of the National Revolution; efforts frustrated, of course, by the fragmentation of the elite that accompanied the German occupation of the entire country after the Allied landing in Italy. See also J. Hellman, *Emmanuel Mounier and the New Catholic Left, 1930–1950* (Toronto: University of Toronto Press, 1980), for the philosopher Jacques Maritain's warnings to Mounier to steer clear of too close an association with Vichy. Mounier worked briefly for Vichy at its elite training academy at Uriage.

50. On worker sabotage, see Sumiya Mikio, "Les Ouvriers japonais pendant la deuxième guerre mondiale," *Revue d'histoire de la deuxième guerre mondiale*, no. 89 (January 1973), and A. Gordon, *The Evolution of Labor Relations in Japan: Heavy Industry, 1853–1955* (Cambridge, Mass.: Harvard University Press, 1985), 318–20.

51. The career of the legal scholar and jurist Tanaka Kōtarō (1892–1974) makes for a fascinating illustration. It intersects with Nanbara's at a number of crucial points (see chap. 2 below). A convert, first to Uchimura Kanzō's nonchurch Christianity, and thence to Catholicism, Tanaka was also deeply anticommunist and fearful of anarchism. His valorization of order must be accounted extreme. Nevertheless, he did not retreat into owlish solitude, but conducted polemics with Marxists such as Tosaka Jun, traveled widely abroad, and used his political acumen to protect the procedural autonomy of Todai against Ministry of Education attack. He was in this sense far more worldly than Nanbara.

See Tanaka's essays in *Kyōyō to bunka no kiso* (Tokyo: Iwanami Shoten, 1937), for a representative statement of his ideas; for a study of Tanaka's intellectual formation, by a scholar who has followed the same path to Catholicism, see Hanzawa Takamaro, "Shisō keiseiki no Tanaka Kōtarō—chijō ni okeru kami no kuni no tankyū," in *Nihon ni okeru sei'ō seiji shisō*, ed. Nihon Seiji Gakkai (*Nenpō seijigaku*, 1975), 208–41. Tanaka's activities during the war included lecturing at the Naval College, and authoring articles in support of the *shisōsen* from a very conservative Catholic and anticommunist point of view. See for example his "Present-Day Mission of Catholics in Greater East Asia," in *Catholicism in Nippon* (Tokyo: Mainichi Shinbunsha, 1944), 40–48, where Tanaka argues for the congruence of Catholic teaching with that of the family-oriented, organicist ideologies of China and Japan, as against Anglo-American individualism and communist collectivism. At the same time, Tanaka's belief in natural law was, he knew, anathema to the right. He complained of being unable to publish his studies of "Chinese natural law" for fear of attack. (Comments of Heinrich Dumoulin, S. J., interview, Tokyo, 19 May 1984.) And, as related below (see chap. 2) Tanaka felt it prudent in mid 1945 to involve himself in Nanbara Shigeru's efforts to bring the war to as quick an end as possible through a campaign of lobbying "senior statesmen" (*jūshin*) who seemed sympathetic. The point is this: Where do we place Tanaka? Public man as opportunist? Astute reader of the signs of the times? Player of the double game in service of order? He was all of these.

52. Yoshimitsu made this remark to Heinrich Dumoulin, S.J., who worked with Yoshimitsu at Sophia University, Tokyo. They were intimate friends for a decade before Yoshimitsu's death from tuberculosis in October 1945. Dumoulin interview, 9 May 1984.

53. Quoted in Maruyama, *Thought and Behaviour*, 309.

54. Dunn, *Western Political Theory*, 55:

Nationalism is the starkest political shame of the twentieth century, the deepest, most intractable and yet most unanticipated blot on the political history of the world since the year 1900. But it is also the very tissue of modern political sentiment, the most widespread, the most unthinking and the most immediate political disposition of all at least among the literate populations of the modern world. The degree to which its prevalence is still felt as a scandal is itself a mark of the sharpness of the check which it has administered to Europe's admiring Enlightenment vision of the Cunning of Reason. In nationalism at last, or so it at present seems, the Cunning of Reason has more than met its match.

NANBARA SHIGERU

1. Minoda Muneki, *Kokka to daigaku* (Tokyo: Genri Nihonsha, 1942), 219.

2. Nanbara Shigeru, *Keisō* (Tokyo: Iwanami, 1984), 56. The poem dates from 1937. *Keisō* is a *waka* journal covering the years 1936–45, and was published originally in 1946. For biographical data, see Fukuda Kan'ichi, "Nanbara Shigeru sensei no gakuteki shōgai," in *Seiji shisō ni okeru Seiyō to Nihon: Nanbara Shigeru sensei koki kinen,* ed. Fukuda (Tokyo: Tokyo Daigaku Shup-

pankai, 1961), 2:293–328, and Iwamoto Mitsuo, *Waga nozomi: Shōnen Nanbara Shigeru* (Kyoto: Yamaguchi Shoten, 1985).

3. In putting together this discussion I have consulted the following works: Frank O. Miller, *Minobe Tatsukichi, Interpreter of Constitutionalism in Japan* (Berkeley and Los Angeles: University of California Press, 1965), 158–59, 202–7; Maruyama, *Thought and Behaviour*, esp. 25–83; R. Storry, *The Double Patriots* (London: Chatto & Windus, 1957).

4. Miller, *Minobe*, 202. See also Tsurumi Shunsuke, "Yokusan undō no gakumonron," in *Tenkō*, ed. Shisō no Kagaku Kenkyūkai, 2:81, on the anti-Tōdai attitude.

5. Miller, *Minobe*, 202.

6. Fujisawa Toshirō, *Saikin ni okeru uyoku gakusei undō ni tsuite* (Tokyo: Shihōshō Keijikyoku, 1940), 87.

7. Miller, *Minobe*, 203. Minoda's diatribe appears as *Jinken jūrin, kokka hakai, Nihon ban'aku no kakon: Minobe hakase no daiken jūrin* (Tokyo: Genri Nihonsha, 1935).

8. The term is used by Akamatsu Katsumaro in the panel discussion on "fallen liberalism." See n. 35 to Introduction above.

9. Quoted in Miller, *Minobe*, 15. Cf. also Ralf Dahrendorf, *Society and Democracy in Germany*, 143, for a more general formulation of this problem.

10. Quoted in Richard Mitchell, *Thought Control in Prewar Japan* (Ithaca, N.Y.: Cornell University Press, 1976), 41.

11. According to Harada Kumao, *Saionji kō to jikyoku*, entry for 3 May 1935, quoted in Storry, *Double Patriots*, 165.

12. Minobe, *Nihon kenpō* (1924), quoted in Miller, *Minobe*, 70.

13. Miller, *Minobe*, 83.

14. Minobe, *Kenpō kōwa* (1914), quoted in Miller, *Minobe*, 83.

15. Miller, *Minobe*, 61–113; quote, with emphasis added, from 66.

16. Miller, *Minobe*, 65.

17. Byron Marshall, "The Tradition of Conflict in the Governance of Japan's Imperial Universities," *History of Education Quarterly* 17, no. 4 (Winter 1977): 398.

18. Ibid., 399.

19. "Rōnōha kōhan ni okeru Sakisaka Itsurō, Nanbara Shigeru shōnin jinmon chōsho" (1944), in *Zoku gendaishi shiryō*, VII, *Tokkō to shisō kenji* (Tokyo: Misuzu Shobō, 1982), 731–33.

20. Paraphrase of Miller, *Minobe*, 203, "academic vigilantism."

21. Maruyama, "Nanbara sensei o shi toshite," *KGZ*, 88, nos. 7–8 (July 1975): 19–21.

22. Marshall, "Tradition," 399. On this episode, see also Tanaka Kōtarō et al., *Daigaku no jichi* (Tokyo: Asahi Shinbunsha, 1963), 116–41; Yabe Teiji, *Yabe Teiji nikki* (*YTN*) (Tokyo: Yomiuri Shinbunsha, 1974), 1:129ff. On Araki's ideology, see Maruyama, *Thought and Behaviour in Modern Japanese Politics*, 1–134, passim. The "Tomizu incidents" were the campaign to influence government policy carried out by a group of Hōgakubu professors in 1903. These were the "Seven Doctors" (*Shichi hakase*), hawks led by Tomizu Hiroto (and

including Onozuka Kiheiji) who broke precedent with a public call for a "hard" policy against czarist Russia. The government's attempt to punish the group and enforce conformity among its civil servants led to the first concerted defense of academic autonomy at the university. See Marshall, "Tradition," 391–95; Tanaka et al., *Daigaku no jichi*, 10–22; and Ishida, *Meiji seiji shisōshi kenkyū*, 250–72.

23. On the "Hiraga Purge," see Marshall, "Academic Factionalism in Japan: The Case of the Tōdai Economics Department," *Modern Asian Studies* 12, no. 4 (1978): 529–51, esp. 546–48; Tanaka et al., *Daigaku no jichi*, pp. 144–83; Yabe, *YTN* 1:176–203; Nanbara, *Onozuka Kiheiji (Nanbara Shigeru chosakushū (NSCS)* (Tokyo: Iwanami Shoten, 1974), 8:463ff; Ōkōchi Kazuo, *Kurai tanima no jiden: Tsuioku to iken* (Tokyo: Chūō Kōronsha, 1979), 63–170, passim; and the new work by Atsuko Hirai, *Individualism and Socialism: Kawai Eijirō's Life and Thought* (Cambridge, Mass.: Harvard University Press, 1986), 177–99.

24. Marshall, "Academic Factionalism," 548.

25. See Yabe's comments in *YTN* 1:199 (2 March 1939).

26. *Teikoku Daigaku shinbun,* 22 May 1939, 1. Also reprinted in Nanbara, *NSCS* 3:71–81.

27. Minoda, *Kokka to daigaku,* 5, 8, 219.

28. Ibid., 227–30.

29. Maruyama, "Nanbara sensei," 22.

30. Minoda, *Kokka to daigaku,* 237; Joseph Bendersky, *Carl Schmitt: Theorist for the Reich* (Princeton: Princeton University Press, 1983), 222ff; Maruyama, review of Schmitt's *Staat, Bewegung, Volk* (1933) in *Senchū to sengo no aida,* 36–42.

31. Nanbara, *Keisō,* 86.

32. *YTN,* 1:136 (29 August 1938), 141 (10 September 1938), 144 (19 September 1938), 342 (23 August 1940).

33. Maruyama, "Nanbara sensei," 23–27. On "national narcissism," see Robert Bellah, "Japan's Cultural Identity: Some Reflections on the Work of Watsuji Tetsurō," *Journal of Asian Studies* 24, no. 3 (August 1965), 573, and Maruyama, *Thought and Behaviour,* xiii, referring to Karl Löwith on Japanese "self-love." Löwith's article appeared in *Shisō,* nos. 220–22 (September–November 1940).

34. Maruyama, "Nanbara sensei," 24.

35. Maruyama, *Studies,* xxii; on Tsuda, see Ienaga Saburō, *Tsuda Sōkichi no shisōshiteki kenkyū* (Tokyo: Iwanami Shoten, 1972).

36. Trial records available in *Gendaishi shiryō,* vol. 42; *Shisō tōsei,* ed. Kakegawa Tomiko (Tokyo: Misuzu Shobō, 1977), 353–1089.

37. Maruyama, "Nanbara sensei," 25–27; Minoda, 239–42.

38. *YTN,* 1:134 (20 August 1938).

39. Maruyama, "Nanbara sensei," 18.

40. Biographical data from Iwamoto, *Waga nozomi: shōnen Nanbara Shigeru,* Fukuda, "Nanbara Shigeru sensei no gakuteki shōgai," and Nanbara, "Shūkyō wa fuhitsuyō ka?" (1960), *NSCS* 9:246–68.

41. Nanbara, "Shūkyō," 247–48.

42. Nanbara, "Shūkyō," 249; Maruyama, commentary to NSCS 5:505.
43. Fukuda, "Nanbara Shigeru sensei," 297.
44. Nanbara, "Waga nozomi," MS.
45. See Maruyama, "Meiji kokka no shisō" (1946) and "Kuga Katsunan: hito to shisō" (1947), in Senchū to sengo no aida, esp. 214, 238–39, 243, 281–95.
46. Oka Yoshitake, "Generational Conflict after the Russo-Japanese War," in Conflict in Modern Japanese History, ed. Tetsuo Najita and Victor Koschmann (Princeton: Princeton University Press, 1982), 197–225; Fukuda, 296; H. D. Harootunian, "The Sense of an Ending and the Problem of Taishō," in Japan in Crisis, ed. Harootunian and Bernard Silberman (Princeton: Princeton University Press, 1974), 3–28.
47. Nanbara, "Minami ryō hachiban no omoide" (1971), NSCS 10:395–405. For background, see Donald Roden, Schooldays in Imperial Japan (Berkeley and Los Angeles: University of California Press, 1982).
48. Text in Tokutomi Roka shū, ed. Kanzaki Kiyoshi (Tokyo: Chikuma Shobō, 1966), 369–74.
49. Nanbara, "Shūkyō," 251–52.
50. Nanbara, "Shūkyō," 250–51; Roden, Schooldays, 200–210.
51. Fukuda, "Nanbara Shigeru sensei," 297; Yamazaki Masakazu describes Ebina's attempt to set up an identity between the persons of the Trinity and the creator deities of Shinto. See Yamazaki, Kindai Nihon shisō tsūshi (Tokyo: Aoki Shoten, 1971), 110–17, esp. 112–13, re Ebina's "Nihonteki kirisutokyō." See also the new study by Yoshinare Akiko, Ebina Danjō no seiji shisō (Tokyo: Tokyo Daigaku Shuppankai, 1983). This reference courtesy of Matsumoto Sannosuke.
52. See Suzuki Toshirō, "'Kashiwagi' to 'Hakuukai' no kotodomo," in Kaisō no Nanbara Shigeru (Tokyo: Iwanami, 1974), 71–82. The minutes of the Hakuukai meeting on 29 March 1915 note: "Although Brother Nanbara's sermon lasted only twenty minutes, all present were greatly edified by it" (80). On the Sairin undō, in Japanese, see Yamamoto Taijirō, Uchimura Kanzō: Shinkō, shōgai, yūjō (Tokyo: Tōkai Daigaku Shuppankai, 1966), 210–19; in English, Culture and Religion in Japanese-American Relations: Essays on Uchimura Kanzō, 1861–1930, ed. R. Moore, Michigan Papers in Japanese Studies, no. 5 (Ann Arbor: Center for Japanese Studies, 1982); a good philosophical discussion of Uchimura is Mori Arimasa, Uchimura Kanzō (1946) (Tokyo: Kōdansha, 1976), esp. 48–61.
53. Suzuki, "'Kashiwagi' to 'Hakuukai' no kotodomo," 81.
54. A problem for future research would be to explore how conscience spoke, and when, to others among Uchimura's disciples. The colonial economist Yanaihara Tadao, Nanbara's friend and Tōdai colleague, took a public stand against the government's war policy in China, which resulted in his expulsion from the university in 1938. He differed from Nanbara on a number of fundamental issues, notably in his pacifism and evangelism. A contrast to both Yanaihara and Nanbara is Yoshimitsu Yoshihiko (1904–45), a philosopher who eventually left the Mukyōkai for the Catholic church and an extraordinarily ecumenical intellectual life. This three-way contrast illustrates the inherent

"centrifugal" dynamic in Mukyōkai ideology in the context of state pressure applied within an imperial university. (See also Introduction, n. 50.)

55. See Albert O. Hirschman, *Exit, Voice and Loyalty* (Cambridge, Mass.: Harvard University Press, 1969).

56. Nanbara, *Kokka to shūkyō* [*KTS*] (Tokyo: Iwanami Shoten, 1942), 380–81: "Uchimura stood *as a Japanese* before God" (emphasis added). In this respect, Nanbara considered Uchimura the superior figure. But he recognized as common to both thinkers the intuition of the "infinite qualitative distinction" that is the sign of true wisdom and the key to faith. For Uchimura's concept of *bushidō*, see Ōuchi Saburō, "Kirisutokyō to bushidō," in *Nihon shisōshi koza*, ed. Furukawa Tesshi and Ishida Ichirō, vol. 8 (*Kindai no shisō*, vol. 3) (Tokyo: Yūsankaku, 1977), 99–128, esp. 101–6. Note in this connection Nanbara's effort in *Kokka to shūkyō* to distinguish Uchimura from Karl Barth, whom he regarded as having positively rejected human culture. This is a judgment possible on the basis of Barth's major work on Paul's letters to the Romans (1912), but becomes questionable when his contemporary political activity (socialist) and later writings are taken into account. See Herbert Hartwell, *An Introduction to the Theology of Karl Barth* (London: Duckworth, 1964), 11–12, and Ulrich Simon, *Theology of Crisis* (London: S.P.C.K., 1948), 183–91. At the same time, Nanbara vigorously defended Barth's work against association with the "roots of Nazism" (*KTS*, 262–71, 364–65).

57. Nanbara, *Gakumon, kyōyō, shinkō* (*GKS*) (Tokyo: Kondō Shoten, 1946), 125, 127.

58. Nanbara, *GKS*, 135–36; Uchimura's original essay (1914) is reprinted in *Uchimura Kanzō zenshū* (Tokyo: Iwanami Shoten, 1984), 20:239–40.

59. Quoted by Nanbara in "Uchimura Kanzō sensei seitan hyakunen ni omou," in *NSCS* 9:349–50.

60. See his famous "Justification of the Corean War" (1894) in *The Complete Works of Kanzo Uchimura* (Tokyo: Kyobunkwan, 1972), 5:66–75.

61. Nanbara, *GKS*, 158.

62. Nanbara, *GKS*, 149.

63. Nanbara, *Fichte no seiji tetsugaku* (Tokyo: Iwanami Shoten, 1970), 114–15; *KTS*, 79. The quote comes from notes taken by Maruyama Masao, April 1936. See his commentary to NSCS, 4:583–85. This reference to conflict as a premise of politics is extremely rare in Nanbara's writings, both of the pre- and postwar periods.

64. Sheldon Wolin, *Politics and Vision* (Boston: Little, Brown, 1960) was very helpful to me in reading Nanbara historically. Nanbara's *Kokka to shūkyō* was reviewed with respectful criticism by Tanaka Kōtarō, Nanbara's colleague and a "renegade" convert from the Mukyōkai to Catholicism. See *KGZ* 57, no. 5 (May 1942): 102–13, and Nanbara's long response in *KTS*, 311–86.

65. Nanbara, "Kojinshugi to chōkojinshugi" (1929), *NSCS* 3:59.

66. Hata Ikuhiko, *Kanryō no kenkyū* (Tokyo: Kōdansha, 1984), 172–91, esp. 186.

67. Ishida Takeshi et al., "Zadankai," in *Naimushō shi*, ed. Taikakai (Tokyo: Chihō Zaimu Kyōkai, 1971), 4:231–86, esp. 271.

68. For background on this question, see Miller, *Minobe*; Pittau, *Political*

Thought; Maruyama, "Politics as a Science in Japan" (*Thought and Behaviour,* 225–44); Pyle, "Advantages of Followership"; Hata, *Kanryō;* and finally the classic work of Rōyama Masamichi, *Nihon ni okeru kindai seijigaku no hattatsu* (1949) (Tokyo: Shinsensha, 1971).

69. Ishida, "Zadankai," 248–70, esp. 262ff.

70. Ibid., 273–74; Pyle, "Advantages of Followership," 153.

71. Ishida, "Nanbara Sensei to Naimushō jidai," in *Kaisō no Nanbara Shigeru,* 336, 339–40. See also Pyle, "Advantages of Followership," for the hopes placed by adherents of social policy thought in the capacity of the still healthy "village community" to hold back the rootlessness and discontent that led to radicalization (154ff, 161).

72. "Left-wing" in the sense that they called in effect for a dialogue with socialism. While still rejecting its premises, they were not opposed to incorporating socialist insights into their reform programs. See Ishida, *Nihon no shakai kagaku,* 51–71; Pyle, "Advantages of Followership," 152–53, esp. re the Kyōchōkai; and Itoh, *Value and Crisis,* 12–15, 167.

73. I owe this phrase to Sheldon Garon, Princeton University, with thanks for some stimulating talk about Nanbara, whose early work he knows well. See also Fukuda, "Nanbara Sensei," 297–98, and Ishida, "Nanbara Sensei to Naimushō jidai." Nanbara's draft appears in *Rōdō gyōsei shi* (Tokyo: Rōdō Hōrei Kyōkai, 1961), 1:135–40.

74. See Thomas C. Smith, "The Right to Benevolence: Dignity and Japanese Workers, 1890–1920," *Comparative Studies in Society and History* 26, no. 4 (October 1984): 587–613.

75. On Yoshino, see Tetsuo Najita, "Some Reflections on Idealism in the Thought of Yoshino Sakuzō," in *Japan in Crisis,* ed. Harootunian and Silberman, 29–66; main texts by Yoshino collected in *Yoshino Sakuzō hyōronshū,* ed. Oka Yoshitake (Tokyo: Iwanami Shoten, 1975); on personalism, cf. Yoshino, "Kirisutokyō to demokurashii" (1919), in *Gendai Nihon shisō taikei, VI, Kirisutokyō,* ed. Takeda Kiyoko (Tokyo: Chikuma Shobō, 1965), 236–41.

76. I draw here upon language used by Maruyama, "Politics and Man in the Contemporary World," in *Thought and Behaviour,* esp. 333–48.

77. Nanbara discusses the progress and fate of the draft in "Naimushō rōdō kumiai hōan no koto nado," in *Rōdō gyōsei shi,* 1: appendix, 27–30.

78. Hata, *Kanryō,* 187.

79. Uchimura Kanzō in 1898 lamented this influence in these words: "One of the many foolish and deplorable mistakes which the Satsuma-Choshu Government have committed is their having selected Germany as the example to be followed in their administrative policy. Because its military organization is well-nigh perfect, and its imperialism a gift of its army, therefore they thought that it ought to be taken as the pattern of our own Empire. . . . Germany is certainly a great nation, but it is not the greatest, neither is it the most advanced. It is often said that Art, Science, and Philosophy have their homes in Germany, that Thought has its primal spring there. But it is not in Germany that Thought is realized to its fullest extent. Thought may originate in Germany, but it is actualized somewhere else. The Lutheran Reformation bore its greatest fruit in England and America." Quoted in Bellah, *Beyond Belief,* 58.

80. Yamazaki Masakazu, *Kindai Nihon shisō tsūshi*, 202−3.

81. Maruyama, *Thought and Behaviour*, 20.

82. Ibid., 227−32; Ishida, *Nihon no shakai kagaku*, 15−34. See also Louis Wirth's preface to Mannheim, *Ideology and Utopia* (New York: International Library, 1936), xiii−xv.

83. Pyle, "Advantages of Followership," 148−60.

84. Nanbara, *GKS*, 107−8, 115. See also Ishida, *Nihon no shakai kagaku*, 42−43. Maruyama Masao also remarks on this self-censorship, not only in Onozuka, but in Odaka Tomoo, whose *Kokka kōzō ron* (1936) attempted to place *kokkagaku* at the shared core of sociology, political science, and law; and who yet declared in his preface that his inquiries had "no direct relation to any effort to display the special State structure of the Japanese Empire in its practical significance" (Maruyama, *Thought and Behaviour*, 231n.).

85. Tetsuo Najita, *Japan: The Intellectual Foundations of Modern Japanese Politics* (Chicago: University of Chicago Press, 1974), 87, 114−27; Harootunian, "Sense of an Ending."

86. Najita, *Japan*, 109. See also Miller, *Minobe*, 8−14, and Ishida, *Nihon no shakai kagaku*, 88ff.

87. Najita, *Japan*, 110−12.

88. Gordon Berger, *Parties out of Power in Japan, 1931−1941* (Princeton: Princeton University Press, 1977), tries in excessively "positivist" fashion to disengage the vicissitudes of party influence from the failure or otherwise of the "democratic movement": "Prewar party power at its height was not contingent upon the democratic movement; nor was the decline of party power necessarily occasioned by the weaknesses of Japanese liberalism. The continuing interest in organizing parties during the war likewise had little to do with liberalism or democratic thought. The large majority of politicians who associated themselves with party organizations did so not out of ideological commitment but rather as a means of pursuing power and implementing policy objectives. It is clear, then, that the history of the political parties in imperial Japan must be examined apart from the study of democracy's failures, and in the dual context of how policies were made and how men competed for political power" (viii−ix).

89. *Mandarin* is Fritz Ringer's term. See his *Decline of the German Mandarins* (Cambridge, Mass.: Harvard University Press, 1969), 5−6.

90. For a good introduction to Stammler's thinking, see his *The Theory of Justice* (New York: Macmillan, 1925) and the critical essay by François Geny, "The Critical System of Stammler," which appears as an appendix to the volume (493−552). Also of interest is the second appendix, "Stammler and his Critics" by John C. H. Wu (553−86), in which Wu locates Stammler in relation to contemporary trends in German epistemology, social philosophy, legal history, and jurisprudence.

91. For a topical discussion of Stammler criticism, see Geny, "Critical System of Stammler," 542−52; "infinitely rich" is Geny's phrase (494); contemporary critics of Stammler ranged from Max Weber and Karl Barth to Benedetto Croce, Oliver Wendell Holmes, and Georg Lukács; for Nanbara's differences with Stammler (on the interpretation of the *Critique of Practical Reason*), see Fukuda, commentary to NSCS, 1:392.

92. Stammler, "Wirtschaft und Recht" (1906), quoted in Geny, "Critical System of Stammler," 514.

93. Stammler, "Wirtschaft und Recht," quoted and discussed by Geny, "Critical System of Stammler," 515–16.

94. Ogata Norio, commentary to *NSCS* 3:382–87.

95. See P. Gay, *Weimar Culture*, 147–55; Bendersky, *Carl Schmitt*, 21–22.

96. Richard Rees, *Simone Weil: A Sketch for a Portrait* (London: Oxford University Press, 1966), 4–5 ("Entre deux guerres").

97. Nanbara, *KTS*, 200; on Konoe see Oka, *Konoe Fumimaro*, 10–18.

98. Fukuda, interview, 19 May 1984. Quote from *KTS*, 165. See also Mitani Taichirō, *Taishō demokurashii ron* (Tokyo: Chūō Kōronsha, 1974), 122–54, on the Japanese image of America after World War I, and Uchimura's disillusionment (127, 146); and Hirakawa Sukehiro, "Uchimura Kanzō and America: Some Reflections on the Psychological Structure of Anti-Americanism," in Moore, *Culture and Religion*, 35–53.

99. Ogata Norio, commentary to *NSCS* 3:383–84; see also Kobayashi Naoki and Miyazawa Toshiyoshi, "Meiji kenpō kara shin kenpō e," in *Shōwa shisōshi e no shōgen* (Tokyo: Mainichi Shinbunsha, 1968), 150ff., for the influence of Kelsen's relativistic "pure theory" as a (less than effective) defense of liberalism.

100. Ringer, *Decline*, passim.

101. See Thomas Willey, *Back to Kant: The Revival of Kantianism in German Social and Historical Thought, 1860–1914* (Detroit: Wayne State University Press, 1978), passim, and David Lipton, *Ernst Cassirer: The Dilemma of a Liberal Intellectual in Germany, 1914–1933* (Toronto: University of Toronto Press, 1978), passim.

102. Willey, *Back to Kant*, 142.

103. See Jürgen Habermas, "Life-forms, Morality and the Task of the Philosopher," transcript of interview in *Autonomy and Solidarity*, ed. P. Dews (London: Verso, 1986), 195–97.

104. Lipton, *Cassirer*, 108.

105. Willey, *Back to Kant*, 23.

106. Ibid., 181.

107. Dahrendorf, *Society and Democracy in Germany*, 6.

108. Willey, *Back to Kant*, 135, 142.

109. Nanbara's essay on liberalism, "Jiyūshugi no hihanteki kōsatsu" (1928), first appeared in *KGZ* 42, no. 10, and is reprinted in *NSCS* 3:14–47. See also Steven Lukes, *Individualism* (Oxford: Basil Blackwell, 1973), 16–22. The essay on Kant's idea of international order first appeared in *Onozuka Kiheiji zaishoku nijū-gonen kinen ronbunshū* (1928), and later under the title "Kant ni okeru sekai chitsujō no rinen" as chap. 3 of *Kokka to shūkyō* (1942).

110. *KTS*, 142.

111. In addition to the work of Willey, I have also relied heavily on Leonard Krieger, *The German Idea of Freedom* (Chicago: University of Chicago Press, 1957) and Herbert Schnädelbach, *Philosophy in Germany, 1831–1933* (Cambridge: Cambridge University Press, 1984).

112. *KTS*, 147, 162–64, 191–206, 209–12, 366. See also Michel Despland,

Kant on History and Religion (Montreal: Montreal and Queens University Press, 1973), for a discussion of this issue.

113. *KTS,* 148–49.

114. *KTS,* 171–72.

115. *KTS,* 165. See also W. B. Gallie, *Philosophers of Peace and War: Kant, Clausewitz, Marx, Engels and Tolstoy* (Cambridge: Cambridge University Press, 1978), 16–17; Fukuda, "Nanbara Shigeru sensei," 302.

116. *KTS,* 167.

117. Gallie, *Philosophers,* 13.

118. *Kant's Political Writings,* ed. H. Reiss (Cambridge: Cambridge University Press, 1970), 183; *KTS,* 154. "War is the scourge of mankind."

119. *KTS,* 170 n. 2.

120. On the grounds that any state has the right to defend itself, Nanbara opposed the inclusion of Article 9 in the 1946 Constitution, opposition in which he was joined by the communist (then returned hero) Nozaka Sanzō. Fukuda interview, July 1984.

121. Gallie, *Philosophers,* 21; *KTS,* 178–80, 325–27.

122. *KTS,* 207.

123. Nanbara, *Fichte no seiji tetsugaku,* 92, 123.

124. Originally published in *KGZ* 54, no. 9 (September 1931). Appears as pt. 1, chap. 4 of *Fichte no seiji tetsugaku,* 101–22.

125. *KTS,* 285–86.

126. Nanbara, *Fichte,* 100; See also I. M. Bocheński, *Contemporary European Philosophy* (Berkeley and Los Angeles: University of California Press, 1969), 88–99; Schnädelbach, *Philosophy,* 161–91; Willey, *Back to Kant,* 147. The whole point about values, Nanbara would say, is that they do not exist in the sense of being susceptible to corruption. They are not contingent. As Rickert put it, "In regard to values considered in themselves, one cannot ask whether they are *real,* but only whether they are *valid*" (quoted in Willey, *Back to Kant,* 147). See also Nanbara's late work *Seiji tetsugaku josetsu* (1973), *NSCS* 5 : 117, 134, and Fukuda commentary, 5 : 444–45.

127. See esp. *NSCS* 3 : 162–224.

128. Nanbara, *Fichte,* iii.

129. Ibid., 108.

130. Ibid., 105–6. One of the few references to power in Nanbara's writings. See also his "Gendai seiji risō to Nihon seishin" (June 1938), the text of a public lecture, *NSCS,* vol. 3, esp. 82–84, where Nanbara describes politics as reflecting the inherent dualism in human nature, in which power (the tradition of the *ba dao,* Xunzi, Machiavelli, and Hobbes) is "tamed" by ideal (the tradition of the *wang dao,* Mencius, Plato, Aristotle, and Locke) through the realization of the ideal state.

131. Nanbara, *Fichte,* 110 n.

132. Ibid., 116.

133. Ibid., 115.

134. The first part of *Fichte no seiji tetsugaku* consists of a lengthy, intricate, and, I am told, superb exploration of the *Wissenschaftslehre* in all its aspects. It was originally written in 1930 and published in *KGZ* 44, nos. 11–12, and 45,

nos. 5 and 9. For an evaluation, see Murakami Takao, "Fichte kenkyūsha toshite no Nanbara Shigeru," in *Tetsugaku to Nihon shakai,* ed. Ienaga Saburō and Komaki Osamu (Tokyo: Kōbundō, 1978), 123–47. The discussion here concerns the essays on Fichte's nationalism and socialism. They appear as pt. 2, chaps. 2–4 of *Fichte,* and were published originally as follows:

   a. "Fichte ni okeru shakaishugi no riron" (*KGZ* 53–54, no. 12 [1939–40]).
   b. "Fichte ni okeru minzokushugi no riron" (*Kakehi Katsuhiko sensei kanreki shukuga ronbunshū,* 1934).
   c. "Kokka to keizai—Fichte o kiten toshite" (Tōkyō Teikoku Daigaku, *Gakujutsu taikan,* 1942).

135. Nanbara, *Seiji riron shi* (Tokyo: Tōkyō Daigaku Shuppankai, 1968), 292.

136. Nanbara, *Fichte,* 101.

137. Nanbara, *Seiji riron shi,* 281–82; Leszek Kolakowski, *Main Currents of Marxism* (Oxford: Oxford University Press, 1978), 1 : 50–56, esp. 52.

138. G. A. Kelly, introduction to Fichte, *Addresses to the German Nation* (1807–8) (New York: Harper & Row, 1968), xxix.

139. Nanbara, *Fichte,* 271, 290–94.

140. It is interesting that, just where Nanbara begins to find the greatest relevance in Fichte's life and work, his student Maruyama turns away. Maruyama, in a sensitive, but critical, review of the postwar work, writes of his disappointment at Fichte's abandonment of the cosmopolitan ideal of the Enlightenment. Aside from his difficulties with Nanbara's idealism, Maruyama obviously remained uncomfortable with his mentor's ardent nationalism. The fact that he felt uncomfortable with it, it remains to add, did not prevent him from absorbing it unconsciously and making it the critical standpoint of his entire intellectual life. See Maruyama, "Nanbara Shigeru cho, *Fichte no seiji tetsugaku* o yonde," *Tosho,* no. 117 (June 1959): 21–23; and his commentary to *NSCS* 4 : 583–85; Ikeda Hajime, *Nihon shimin shisō to kokkaron* (Tokyo: Ronsōsha, 1983), 110–11, discusses the nationalism Maruyama shares with Nanbara.

141. A reference to the "third stage" in Fichte's world-historical conception, which he set forth in his *Characteristics of the Present Age.* See Nanbara, *Fichte,* 280–88. Kelly, introduction to Fichte, *Addresses,* xx–xxi.

142. Nanbara, *Fichte,* 305ff; Kelly, introduction to Fichte, *Addresses,* xxxii, notes that while Fichte did not envision a national imperialism, nothing prevented him from embracing the "spiritual imperialism . . . of a professor determined to act on the world and seeking to tie his vision of truth to the raw materials of life in a volcanic age."

143. Kelly, introduction to Fichte, *Addresses,* xxvii.

144. Windelband, *Fichtes Idee des deutschen Staates* (1921), quoted in G. A. Kelly, *Idealism, Politics and History: Sources of Hegelian Thought* (Cambridge: Cambridge University Press, 1969), 252.

145. Nanbara, *Fichte,* 322, 334–35.

146. Frederick Copleston, *A History of Philosophy,* vol. 7, *Fichte to Nietzsche* (London: Search Press, 1971), 73.

147. Nanbara, *Fichte,* 174.

148. Ibid., 230, 334–35.
149. Ibid., 195.
150. Ibid., 335.
151. Ibid., 243–45.
152. Ibid., 237–38.
153. Ibid., 111, 245–46.
154. These were written in 1941, and appeared in *KGZ 55* no. 12, under the title "Nachisu sekaikan to shūkyō no mondai," and again as chap. 4 of *KTS*. Nanbara read the paper at a regular meeting of the Seijigaku Kenkyūkai, which Onozuka Kiheiji had founded in 1928. Commenting on Nanbara's work, Onozuka remarked in his booming voice that it seemed to him a waste of time to write about the Nazi worldview since "there was no such thing." Fearing that this impolitic view would be heard outside the room, junior members of the group rushed to close the doors (Maruyama, interview, 16 June 1984). Prior to the signing of the Tripartite Pact (May 1940) and launching of the New Order, there were Japanese who disparaged Nazism as a base approximation of the sublime *Nihon seishin*. (Minoda Muneki was one of these. An attack on Nazism, therefore, did not make one a liberal.) After this time it was "extremely dangerous" to take a view such as Onozuka's (Fukuda interview, 21 July 1984). Nanbara's paper, it will be recalled, was delivered while Axis power was at its height.
155. See inter alia Nanbara, *Fichte*, 176ff, 236ff, 324ff; *KTS*, 219ff; "Gendai no seiji risō to Nihon seishin," *NSCS* 3:101.
156. Nanbara, *Fichte*, 136.
157. *KTS*, 236–37, 288.
158. *KTS*, 243–44; Nanbara, *Fichte*, 265–66. On the "all-politicism" of totalitarian systems and Japan's "tendencies" in that direction, see "Gendai no seiji risō to Nihon seishin," *NSCS* 3:99–108, 109, 114; *KTS*, 283.
159. Nanbara, *Fichte*, 338.
160. Kelly, introduction to Fichte, *Addresses*, xii, quotes the liberal legal philosopher Erhard: "God forbid that Fichte should be persecuted, or else there might very well emerge a Fichtianity a hundred times worse than Christianity."
161. Nanbara, *Fichte*, 280–81.
162. Maruyama, review of Nanbara, *Fichte* (see n. 140 above).
163. Nanbara, *KTS*, 115.
164. Nanbara, *KTS*, 23–24, 42–43. See also *NSCS* 3:61–70, 119–22.
165. Nanbara, *KTS*, 271.
166. Nor did the end of the war in 1945 end the crisis. Japan had reached the point where reconstruction could begin, but remained susceptible to all those currents that had brought the catastrophe of 1931–45. See Nanbara's preface to the third edition of *KTS* (September 1945): "Is the 'crisis' of European culture—of all humankind—now past? No. As long as we recognize one of its aspects in a deeply rooted positivism and Marxism, we must face the fact that it is not" (5). And in the preface to *Jiyū to kokka no rinen* (1959) (*NSCS* 3:6), Nanbara asserts that the "spirit and ideas" of fascism remain despite the defeat in 1945. The possible reemergence of fascism in Japan was a common topic in the years leading to the revision of the U.S.–Japan Security Treaty in

1960. The Japanese left considered that the government had undermined the Diet (and thus the 1946 Constitution) in its efforts to ensure ratification. For an argument against the thesis of renascent fascism, see Hayashi Kentarō, "Waimāru Kyōwakoku to gendai Nihon," in id., *Rekishi to taiken* (Tokyo: Bungei Shunjū, 1972), 122–35; the article appeared originally in *Jiyū* (January 1961).

167. Nanbara, *KTS*, 25.

168. Ibid., 25–26.

169. Ibid., 27.

170. Ibid., 29–30. See also Ernst Cassirer, *The Myth of the State* (New Haven: Yale University Press, 1946), 61–77, for a similar treatment of Plato. Cassirer died in April 1945.

171. Nanbara, *KTS*, 105–6. According to Maruyama Masao, Nanbara had originally intended to use the phrase *saisei itchi*, but decided that the reference to the current regime was too obvious, and settled for the more Western-sounding *shinsei seiji* (Maruyama, interview, 16 June 1984).

172. Nanbara, *KTS*, 37.

173. See, inter alia, "Theory and Psychology of Ultranationalism" (Maruyama, *Thought and Behaviour*, 1–24, passim). Maruyama calls himself Nanbara's "unworthy" disciple in his review of *Fichte*. See n. 140 above.

174. Nanbara, *NSCS* 3:81.

175. Nanbara, "Gendai no seiji risō to Nihon seishin" (1938) in *NSCS* 3:115.

176. Nanbara, *NSCS* 3:111–13.

177. Rees, *Simone Weil*, 58.

178. Nanbara, *Fichte*, 279. That is, it was not something to be "overcome," no mere "way station," but the very condition under which "universality" on the temporal plane, and salvation on the eternal, were to be sought.

179. Nanbara, *NSCS* 3:115–16. On "communitarian democracy" compare, however, the following passage from the diary of Nanbara's colleague, Yabe Teiji (*YTN*, 1:124–25 [26 July 1938]):

> Beginning at four, meeting of Seijigaku Kenkyūkai . . . I gave a presentation, 'On the Principles of Communitarian Democracy' (Kyōdōtaiteki shūminsei no genri ni tsuite). Bit off a bit more than I could chew, and had to rush through it. After dinner there was discussion. Dr. Onozuka kindly encouraged me to put it out in book form, then left. Dr. Nanbara called attention to the point that communitarian democracy would become in effect a principle of dictatorship, and made the criticism that while the community and purposive society [*mokuteki shakai*] were logical forms [ideal types?], my intermediate form [*chūkangata*] represented a compromise rather than any logic of its own. Not a very telling criticism, I think. Dr. Kawai remarked on its differences from the English way of thinking. Quite beside the point, if you ask me. Dr. Rōyama offered the criticism that it is impossible to theorize a 'crisis' phenomenon such as the present, and that it is futile to link consideration of stereotypes to actual trends. Dr. Tozawa was alarmed at what he thought was its closeness to dictatorship. . . . None of these criticisms seems damaging in any basic way.

180. That the civil and military bureaucracy, along with "evil officials around the throne" (*kunsoku no kan*) had privatized power was, of course, the accusation made by the Young Officers at the time of the 26 February incident in 1936. Nanbara, in fact, had stunned an audience of students when he referred to the

incident in his inaugural lecture on the history of political thought in 1936: "The Young Officers who rose because they deplored the 'privatization' [*shi-heika*] of the imperial forces themselves took action that privatized the imperial forces. Wherein does such a contradiction arise? In the end it speaks for the fact that no thoroughgoing consideration was made of the intellectual significance of their action." It should be recalled that Nanbara's statement came at a time when Tokyo was still partly under martial law. The statement comes from notes made by Maruyama Masao. See his commentary to *NSCS* (*Seiji riron shi*), 4 : 582–83.

181. Miller, *Minobe*, 44.

182. Nanbara, *NSCS* 3 : 113–14.

183. Nanbara, *KTS*, 295–301.

184. Tōyama Shigeki et al., *Shōwa shi* (Tokyo: Iwanami Shoten, 1980), 227ff.

185. Nanbara, *Keisō*, 195, 205.

186. Ibid., 8.

187. Ibid., 34, 43, 47, 77, 104.

188. Ibid., 113.

189. Ibid., 122, 123, 138.

190. Ibid., 138, 139.

191. Ibid., 139, 140.

192. Ibid., 138. Nanbara very seldom gave in to this sort of feeling.

193. Ibid., 220.

194. Ibid., 157.

195. Ibid., 156.

196. Ibid., 56, 57, 65, 81, 83, 100, 156, 168, 205, 212, 219. "Yanaihara" refers to the colonial economist Yanaihara Tadao. See n. 54 above.

197. Maruyama, interview 16 June 1984, informed me that the planning had begun at this early date. Printed sources include Mukōyama Hiroo, "Min-kan ni okeru shūsen kōsaku," in *Taiheiyō sensō shūketsuron,* ed. Nihon Gaikō Gakkai (Tokyo: Tokyo Daigaku Shuppankai, 1958), 95–181, esp. 133–36; and Itō Takashi, *Shōwa jūnendaishi danshō* (Tokyo: Tōkyō Daigaku Shuppan-kai, 1981), which is based on the Yabe diary, supplemented by other sources. Among these is the Memorandum (*Oboegaki*) composed by Takagi Sōkichi.

198. Mukōyama, "Minkan," 134. Nanbara also had in mind the "Seven Doctors" affair of 1903 (see n. 22 above). The parallel, given the aims of the two groups, makes for a nice irony, which it is hard to believe was lost on any of the principals.

199. I owe this suggestion to Thomas C. Smith, University of California, Berkeley. It jibes well with the fact that Nanbara had, in February 1939, been elected chairman of the Law Faculty but declined to serve, feeling that the politi-cal atmosphere was too reactionary for him to accept; it would only have ex-posed the institution to attack for having appointed a "liberal" to a sensitive and prestigious position at a time of national crisis. Yabe Teiji, nevertheless, was among those who found Nanbara's refusal unfortunate and annoying. *YTN* 1 : 197–99.

200. Itō, *Shōwa*, 82–84. Tanaka had in fact preceded Yabe as a consultant.

But unlike Yabe he engaged in no research or planning; his duties were limited to lecturing at the Naval College.

201. Konaka Yōtarō, ed. *Tōdai Hōgakubu: Sono kyozō to jitsuzō* (Tokyo: Gendai Hyōronsha, 1976), 27.

202. Mukōyama, "Minkan," 134.

203. See *KTS,* 181, for Nanbara's statement. For examples of Yabe's political ideas, see Miles Fletcher, *The Search for a New Order: Intellectuals and Fascism in Prewar Japan* (Chapel Hill: University of North Carolina Press, 1982), 139–42, summarizing Yabe's "Seiji kikō kaishin taikō," which Yabe claimed to have written for the Shōwa Kenkyūkai; Yabe, "Kyōdōtai no seiji," in Tōkyō Teikoku Daigaku, *Gakujutsu taikan,* 396–408.

204. See Fletcher, *Search;* Berger, *Parties out of Power.* Maruyama, interview, 16 June 1984, also discussed Yabe's personality.

205. *YTN* 1:796.

206. *YTN* 1:799.

207. *YTN* 1:798–99; Itō, *Shōwa,* 283–84. Yabe expanded on this feeling in his diary for 3 June: "Vis-à-vis the Navy Ministry, matters remain as they have since my resignation. Since I am no longer required to serve at the ministry, I feel incomparably more at ease. I am no longer forced to think about the problems of the nation that crop up one after the other. I no longer have to win favor for the navy with everyone I meet, or spend money to do it. Most of all I no longer have to keep saying things I don't even believe out of consideration for the navy people—the stupid ones I mean. And I have *time*" (*YTN* 1:807).

208. *YTN* 1:807.

209. Itō, *Shōwa,* 81, 83–84.

210. Takagi Sōkichi, *Shikan Taiheiyō sensō* (Tokyo: Bungei Shunjū, 1969), 232. Takagi had some rather disparaging—and self-serving—remarks on the "sporadic, unorganized and badly timed" unofficial efforts to bring hostilities to an end (as if the navy would have done so without civilian "interference"!): "Besides [Nanbara], there were others, such as former Foreign Minister Arita Hachirō and Admiral Yamamoto Eisuke, who undertook, chiefly through written memorials [*ikensho*], to bring the war to a close. I do not believe that they had any particular effect. There seem to have been quite a few individuals who were unaware that to appeal to His Majesty—who was most scrupulous in following established channels [*kichōmen ni sujimichi o omonzerareta*]—by direct petition or backdoor connections was, indeed, counterproductive" (231–32).

211. Itō, *Shōwa,* 284–85.

212. Ibid., 285–86. Such a usage appears nowhere in Nanbara's prewar or wartime writings. The epilogue to a study of prewar Japanese textbooks on ethics, however, contains the following passage, one quite germane to the present discussion: "The Japanese themselves recognized this historical parallel [between the Meiji Restoration and the Allied Occupation of Japan]. On *Kigensetsu,* Empire Founding Day, in 1946 the President of Tokyo Imperial University, Dr. Nanbara Shigeru, used the clever paraphrase 'Showa Restoration,' coined by militarists in their propaganda of the 1930's, to indicate that this era might become a national renaissance to the lasting honor of the present em-

peror" (R. K. Hall, *Shushin: The Ethics of a Defeated Nation* [New York: Bureau of Publications, Teachers College, Columbia University, 1949], 238).

213. Yabe, *YTN* 1:811; Itō, *Shōwa*, 286, notes that despite the closeness of Nanbara's views to those of Konoe, Yabe does not mention Konoe's meetings with him at all in *Konoe Fumimaro* (1952), the definitive biography Yabe wrote after he resigned—in preference to being purged—from Tōdai.

214. Mukōyama, "Minkan," 135–36; Yabe, *YTN*, 1:817.

215. Yabe, *YTN*, 1:816–17. The same night Yabe paid a visit to an acquaintance in Takanawa. "He had just returned from the Foreign Ministry and was having dinner. Afterward, we had a few whiskies and talked until nine. Main topics were the end of the war and my reasons for resigning from the Navy Ministry. *He too says there's nothing to be done through diplomatic channels, not any more*" (27 June 1945; emphasis added).

216. Actually, the editors of Nanbara's collected works saw fit to remove a passage from *Kokka to shūkyō* on Kant's concept of war. The passage underlined was removed: "Nation in this sense is to be understood not merely as a biological or racial entity, but, inasmuch as it is a cultural-spiritual essence, rather in terms of the concept of "national individuality" [*minzoku kosei*]. And the state [*kokka*] is to be understood in its historical actuality as the political expression of this individual value [*kosei kachi*]. Nations, as values of unique and particular historical individuality must maintain and assert their existence. *Here, at the root of national existence, lies the reason that 'war,' itself an extralegal and nonrational means [to that end] may be regarded as admissible, and not only admissible, but indispensable*" (*KTS*, 3d ed., 180–81; *NSCS* 1:167).

217. Maruyama, "Nanbara sensei," 29. See also Nanbara's address "Senbotsu gakusei ni sasagu" (10 March 1946) in *Haruka naru sanga ni: Tōdai senbotsu gakusei no shuki* (Tokyo: Tōkyō Daigaku Shuppankai, 1951), 5–10, esp. 6–7.

218. Maruyama, "Nanbara sensei," 29–30.

219. See Ger van Roon, *German Resistance to Hitler: Count von Moltke and the Kreisau Circle* (London: Van Nostrand Reinhold, 1971); Alfred Delp, *The Prison Meditations of Father Delp* (New York: Macmillan, 1963).

220. Van Roon, *Resistance*, 75–81; Karl Neufeld, S. J., *Geschichte und Mensch: A. Delps Idee der Geschichte, Ihr Werden und Grundzüge* (Rome: Università Gregoriana Editrice, 1983), 80–117 passim on Delp and Heidegger. Two of Delp's articles are of particular interest: "Das Volk als Ordnungswirklichkeit," *Stimmen der Zeit* 138, no. 1 (October 1940), and "Weltgeschichte und Heilsgeschichte," *Stimmen der Zeit* 138, no. 8 (March 1941). The journal was shut down shortly after this point.

HASEGAWA NYOZEKAN

1. The German title was *Die Tochter des Samurai*. The film was made at the invitation of the Ministry of Culture as part of a film exchange program. Fanck himself was noted for his nature films, chiefly of the man versus mountain variety. Evidently Fanck had refused to join the NSDAP and had been forced to chase after work, although later he made short documentaries on Nazi art and

architecture. See *Cinegraph: Lexikon zum deutschsprachigen Film,* ed. Hans-Michael Bock (Munich: edition text + kritik, 1984), 1 : D3. Yabe Teiji, incidentally, saw the same film at the end of 1937, and found the story "imbecilic" but the photography "masterful." *YTN* 1 : 50.

2. "Musasabi wa kataru: Jibun o hakken shita hanashi," *Kaizō* 19, no. 3 (March 1937): 228–31.

3. See Hasegawa Nyozekan, "Meiji, Taishō, Shōwa sandai no seikaku" (1959), in *HNSS* 5 : 365–82, esp. 379–80. Here Nyozekan refers to an article he published in *Kaizō* ("Nihonteki seikaku no saikentō," June 1935) where, he suggests, he first used the phrase. In point of fact, Nyozekan had used it in his daily column ("Ichinichi ichidai") in the *Yomiuri:* "Nihonteki seikaku no shiren," 31 January 1935, evening ed.

4. See the special issue of *Chūō kōron* (May 1935) devoted to "a consideration of fallen liberalism" especially Hasegawa Nyozekan, "Rekishiteki jiyūshugi to dōtokuteki hanchū toshite no 'jiyū'" (96–101); and the famous article by Tanaka Kōtarō, "Gendai no shisōteki anakii to sono gen'in no kentō" (1932) reprinted in his *Kyōyō to bunka no kiso* (Tokyo: Iwanami Shoten, 1937), 1–52. Finally, see Ishida Takeshi, "Waga kuni ni okeru jiyūshugi no issokumen." On liberalism in general, see Dunn, *Western Political Theory,* 28–54; Isaiah Berlin, *Four Essays on Liberty* (Oxford: Oxford University Press, 1969); L. T. Hobhouse, *Liberalism* (1911) (New York: Oxford University Press, 1974).

5. Maruyama Masao, *Nihon no shisō* (Tokyo: Iwanami Shoten, 1961), 55ff; *Studies in the Intellectual History of Tokugawa Japan,* xxv–xxvi; Tosaka Jun, *Nihon ideorogii ron* (1937) (Tokyo: Iwanami Shoten, 1978), 211ff.

6. For a suggestive contrast of the mainstream democratic thinking represented by *Kaizō* to that of the soon to be coopted communitarian "undercurrent" represented, for example, by Kita Ikki's *Nihon kaizō hōan taikō,* see Kano Masanao, *Taishō demokurashii no teiryū,* 9–35.

7. Sōseki had reviewed Nyozekan's novel *Hitai no otoko* (the title might translate as "Cerebral man") (1909) for the Tokyo *Asahi,* and addressed a number of pointed remarks to its author. Sōseki admired the novel. He admitted that the absence of plot ("movement"), in place of which one character after another held forth on a range of subjects from the weightiest moral problems to the sheerest trivia, did not make the work a dreadful bore. This was because the opinions of the characters, all so-called "high-class loafers" (*kōtō yūmin*) and quite out of touch with the public world, were so thoroughly bizarre. (Nyozekan in turn greatly admired *I Am a Cat.*) But, Sōseki felt, *Hitai no otoko* was flawed by the very virtuosity with which its characters were drawn. If Nyozekan was seeking to portray the reality of his characters' lives, he did not succeed. Their self-presentation was too consistent in its ostentation. One even felt that wit had been placed before honesty. Natsume Sōseki, "*Hitai no otoko* o yomu," *Asahi shinbun* (Tokyo), 5 September 1909, in *Sōseki zenshū* (Tokyo: Iwanami Shoten, 1966), 11 : 214–19.

8. On the origins of the phrase, see "Kō i fukō nan [okonau wa yasuku okonawazaru wa katashi]" (1963) in *HNSS* 7 : 321–34, where Nyozekan refers to the phrase *danjite okonawazu* as "the homemade motto of my youth" (321).

A memoir of Nyozekan's published in the *Mainichi shinbun* (29 January 1967) places the date closer to 1896—a period of convalescence. I am indebted to Matsumoto Sannosuke for this reference.

9. See Yamaryō Kenji, "Aru jiyūshugi jānarisuto: Hasegawa Nyozekan," in *Tenkō,* ed. Shisō no Kagaku Kenkyūkai (Tokyo: Heibonsha, 1978), 1:324–53, esp. 325–30.

10. Hasegawa Nyozekan, *Aru kokoro no jijoden* (1950) (Tokyo: Kōdansha, 1984), 10ff; *"Warera* kara *Hihan* e" (1930), in *Hasegawa Nyozekan senshū* (*HNSS*) (Tokyo: Kurita Shuppankai, 1969), 1:377–78; "Musasabi wa kataru: Rittoru kuritikkusu," *Kaizō* 19, no. 2 (February 1937): 177–79. See also the appraisal of Nyozekan by Iida Taizō, "Hihan no kōseki: Hasegawa Nyozekan," in *Kindai Nihon no kokkazō,* ed. Nihon Seiji Gakkai (*Nenpō seijigaku,* 1982) (Tokyo: Iwanami Shoten, 1983), 157–75. Shortly after the manuscript of this book was completed, Chikuma Shobō reprinted its 1968 edition of *Aru kokoro.* This edition brings together much valuable material, otherwise available only from scattered sources, relating to Nyozekan's career after leaving *Nihon.* It should supersede the Kōdansha edition used here.

11. *Xunzi,* I ("Encouraging Learning"): "The wingless dragon has no limbs and yet it can soar; the flying squirrel has many talents but finds itself hard-pressed." In *Hsün-tzu: Basic Writings,* trans. Burton Watson (New York: Columbia University Press, 1963), 18. See also Iida, "Hihan," 173–74.

12. The question of Nyozekan's *tenkō* will be dealt with later in the chapter. See Fujita Shōzō, *Tenkō no shisōshiteki kenkyū: Sono issokumen* (Tokyo: Iwanami Shoten, 1975), passim, and H. D. Harootunian's remarks in "Between Politics and Culture: Authority and the Ambiguities of Intellectual Choice in Imperial Japan," in *Japan in Crisis,* ed. Silberman and Harootunian, 140 n. 78.

13. See Iida Taizō, "Hasegawa Nyozekan ni okeru 'bunmei hihyōka' no seiritsu," *Hōgaku shirin* 72, no. 2 (March 1975): 3–8.

14. Maruyama Masao, "Meiji kokka no shisō" (1946), in *Senchū to sengo no aida,* 221.

15. For Aizan's statement, made in 1910, see Maruyama, "Kindai Nihon no chishikijin," 101.

16. *Aru kokoro,* 180–81.

17. Iida, "Bunmei hihyōka," 17; Nyozekan, "Musasabi wa kataru: 'Hanmon jidai'," *Kaizō* 19, no. 5 (May 1937): 297–301.

18. Nyozekan was also born Yamamoto. At the age of nine, he was adopted by his great-grandmother, Hasegawa Tami.

19. The park became a gathering place for all classes of society. In addition to the crowds who came in via the ticket booth, frequent visitors included the physician to the imperial family, the future Taishō emperor, and various cabinet ministers. It is also mentioned in Sōseki's *I Am a Cat.*

20. Nyozekan, *Aru kokoro,* 71.

21. Ibid., 56.

22. Ibid., 11–14.

23. Ibid., 115.

24. Ibid., 115–22, 215.

25. Ibid., 149ff.

26. Ibid., 135.

27. Ibid., 136–37.

28. See Kenneth Pyle, *The New Generation in Meiji Japan* (Stanford: Stanford University Press, 1969), 98–117, esp. 114ff; Nyozekan, *Aru kokoro,* 167ff.

29. Nyozekan, *Aru kokoro,* 167.

30. Maruyama Masao, Nishida Taketoshi, and Uete Michiari, "Kindai Nihon to Kuga Katsunan" (round-table discussion) in *Gyakusetsu toshite no gendai,* ed. *Misuzu* (Tokyo: Misuzu Shobō, 1983), 149–87, esp. 172–75.

31. Iida, "Bunmei hihyōka," *Hōgaku shirin* 73, no. 2 (March 1976): 62–63, 88–89; Pyle, *New Generation,* 94; Barbara J. Teters, "Kuga's Commentaries on the Constitution of the Empire of Japan," *Journal of Asian Studies* 28, no. 2 (February 1969): 321–37.

32. Maruyama, "Kuga Katsunan: Hito to shisō," in *Senchū to sengo no aida,* 281.

33. Nyozekan, *Aru kokoro,* 183.

34. According to chronology attached to the Kaizōsha anthology of Nyozekan's literary work (1930) cited in Iida, "Bunmei," 11.

35. Maruyama, Nishida, and Uete, "Kindai Nihon to Kuga Katsunan," 154.

36. Maruyama, "Kuga Katsunan," 289–90. *Hasegawa Nyozekan,* comp. Yamaryō Kenji (*Jinbutsu shoshi taikei,* 6) (Tokyo: Nichigai Asoshiētsu, 1984), 7. Yamaryō's work consists of a complete bibliography and detailed chronology of Hasegawa Nyozekan's writings and public activity. Hereafter cited as "Yamaryō Chronology." It has been incorporated into *Hasegawa Nyozekan: Hito; jidai; shisō to chosaku mokuroku,* ed. Sera Masatoshi et al. (Tokyo: Chūō Daigaku, 1985), which appeared just as the manuscript of this book was being completed. It will be the chief source for researchers looking for background on Nyozekan's life and work.

37. Nyozekan had in fact promised his father, whose contacts had made possible his son's studies, that he would pursue a legal career. But, he remarks, this was only out of *giri;* only journalism fired his imagination.

38. Nyozekan, *Aru kokoro,* 232–36.

39. "Futasujimichi" was also Nyozekan's first composition in colloquial Japanese (*Aru kokoro,* 215).

40. Salary figures from Yamaryō, *Hasegawa Nyozekan,* 38.

41. I owe this suggestion to Thomas C. Smith, University of California, Berkeley (personal communication).

42. T. C. Smith, "The Right to Benevolence: Dignity and Japanese Workers."

43. Iida, "Bunmei hihyōka," 65–70.

44. Nyozekan, *Aru kokoro,* 236–38.

45. How ironic, then, to read in Smith's "Right to Benevolence" of the novelist Matsumoto Seichō's bitter experience as a lithographer at the same Osaka *Asahi:* not just of being "a cog in a wheel, but a cog of no value" (610–12).

46. Hasegawa Nyozekan, Maruyama Kanji, and Sugimura Takeshi, "Jidai to shinbun: Osaka *Asahi* hikka jiken kaiko" (round-table discussion), *Sekai,* no. 103 (July 1954): 170–82, esp. 171, 173; Nyozekan, "Osaka *Asahi* kara *Warera* e" [February 1919] *HNSS* 1 : 347–75, esp. 348, 351–52, 358–60, 369.

47. "Jidai to shinbun," 158; "Kindai Nihon to Kuga Katsunan," 176.

48. The following does not pretend to be an account of the Rice Riots, only a suggestion of their magnitude and effects. In addition to the heavily censored reports in the Osaka *Asahi* itself, I have consulted the following: Akamatsu Katsumaro, *Nihon shakai undō shi* (Tokyo: Iwanami Shoten, 1965); Matsuo Takayoshi, *Taishō demokurashii* (Tokyo: Iwanami Shoten, 1980); Yoshikawa Mitsusada, *Iwayuru kome sōdō no kenkyū* (Tokyo: Shihōshō Keijikyoku, 1939); Jon Halliday, *A Political History of Japanese Capitalism* (New York: Monthly Review Press, 1975); Arthur Young, *The Social and Labour Movement in Japan* (Kobe: Japan Chronicle, 1921) (relevant passage reprinted in *Imperial Japan, 1800–1945*, comp. J. Livingston et al. [New York: Pantheon, 1973], 322–26); and Michael Lewis, "The Japanese Rural Rice Riots: Taxation Populaire and the Tenant-Landlord Riots," available from the Asian/Pacific Studies Institute, Duke University.

49. See Osaka *Asahi* (henceforth *OA*), 8, 10, 11, 12, 13 August 1918; Young, *Social and Labour Movement*, 322–24; Matsuo, *Taishō demokurashii*, 174.

50. See *OA*, 8, 9, 13 August 1918; Nakamura Takafusa, *Economic Growth in Prewar Japan* (New Haven: Yale University Press, 1983), 141–47, esp. 145.

51. Young, *Social and Labour Movement*, 323; Yoshikawa presents a comprehensive (but for present purposes too detailed) account of the rise in rice prices in *Iwayuru kome sōdō*, 31–89, esp. 37ff. There were other costs for stubborn merchants: *OA*, 11 August 1918, reported that the father of a large Nagoya rice dealer, unable to bear the resentment of neighbors over his son's hoarding and obscene profits, hung himself in shame and chagrin.

52. Yoshikawa, *Kome sōdō*, 385–435, esp. tables on 403–12, 428–35; Akamatsu, *Nihon shakai*, 153.

53. Wakukawa Seiyei, "The Japanese Farm-Tenancy System," in *Japan's Prospect*, ed. D. Haring (Cambridge, Mass.: Harvard University Press, 1946), 151, 171–72.

54. Nakamura, *Economic Growth in Prewar Japan*, 213ff; William Lockwood, *The Economic Development of Japan* (Princeton: Princeton University Press, 1968), 56–57; Halliday, *Political History of Japanese Capitalism*, 71.

55. Young, *Social and Labour Movement*, 324–25. This suggests an interesting parallel to the use of peasant troops to crush the warrior forces led by Saigō Takamori in 1877.

56. Quote from ibid., 325; articles on relief efforts in *OA*, 14, 15, 16 August 1918; 5 September 1918. Yoshikawa, *Kome sōdō*, 495, quotes a speech by the industrialist Shibusawa Eiichi warning against corruption in relief efforts.

57. Matsuo, *Taishō demokurashii*, 175; Akamatsu, *Nihon shakai*, 154.

58. Wakukawa, "Japanese Farm-Tenancy System," 151.

59. Suzuki Bunji, *Rōdō undō nijūnen* (1930), quoted in Matsuo, *Taishō demokurashii*, 176. The English-language column in *OA*, 26 August 1918, carried a letter from "A Patriot," calling for "all tribes" under "the sway of his gracious majesty" to be "embraced with equal care and tenderness"; this to include "Formosans, Koreans, *not to say [i.e., mention] the Shinheimin and Eta.*" Although these groups were regarded as "inferior," and although they had "made the most of the disturbances originally started by the poverty stricken

multitude, no distinction should be made among them" since Japan, after all, was "soon to be the Protector of the East." Emphasis added.

60. Tsurumi Yūsuke, *Gotō Shinpei*, vol. 3 (1937), cited in Matsuo, *Taishō demokurashii*, 176.

61. Inoue Narazō, speech in Nagoya, 16 August 1918, quoted in Yoshikawa, *Kome sōdō*, 302.

62. See the table in Yoshikawa, *Kome sōdō*, 312–15, which summarizes, in quite hostile terms, thirty newspaper reports on rice prices and on the riots themselves that appeared between 24 July and 11 August. Nine of these reports came from the Osaka *Asahi*. Yoshikawa in general blamed the press (the "outside agitators" of the time) for much of the upheaval (306, 308).

63. Young, *Social and Labour Movement*, 324; Hasegawa, Maruyama, and Sugimura, "Jidai to shinbun" (*Sekai*), 172–73. See announcement in *OA*, 15 August 1918 (morning ed.) with an editorial attacking the ban.

64. Hasegawa et al., "Jidai to shinbun," 173; original in *OA*, 26 August 1918, 2.

65. Ibid., 174.

66. Ibid., 175.

67. Ibid., 173. There is some discrepancy as to who actually went to trial along with Ōnishi. In the *Sekai* article the other party is named as Tai Shin'ichi. But Yamaryō's chronology (13) lists the *Asahi*'s legal publisher, Yamaguchi Nobuo. Yamaguchi's name also appears alongside Ōnishi's in the resolution passed at the 17 August rally to protest the muzzling of the press by the Terauchi government (*OA*, 18 August 1918, 2; Yoshikawa, *Kome sōdō*, 450–51). See *OA*, 1 December 1918, for article discussing the progress of the entire case as it neared conclusion.

68. Hasegawa et al., "Jidai to shinbun," 175.

69. Kobayashi Hajime, "Nihon riberarizumu no dentō to marukusushugi," *Shakaigaku hyōron* 23, no. 4 (April 1973): 23.

70. Hasegawa et al., "Jidai to shinbun," 173–74; Yamamoto Taketoshi, *Kindai Nihon shinbun no dokushaso* (Tokyo: Hōsei Daigaku Shuppankyoku, 1982).

71. *OA*, 4 December 1918 (evening ed.); Hasegawa et al., "Jidai to shinbun," 176–79.

72. Nyozekan, "Osaka *Asahi* kara *Warera* e" (February 1919), in *HNSS* 1:347–75.

73. Marshall, "Academic Factionalism in Japan," 531–36.

74. Morito Tatsuo, *Shisō no henreki* (Tokyo: Shunjūsha, 1972), vol. 1 passim; Tanaka Hiroshi, "Hasegawa Nyozekan to 'genron shisō no jiyū': Morito jiken kara Takigawa jiken made," in *Shakai hendō to hō: Hōgaku to rekishigaku no setten*, ed. Tanaka Hiroshi and Matsumoto Sannosuke (Tokyo: Keisō Shobō, 1981), 373–79.

75. Nyozekan, "Osaka *Asahi* kara," 347.

76. Ibid., 347–48.

77. Berlin, *Four Essays*, 3–6.

78. See 202–22. "Return to the Womb."

79. Nyozekan, *Gendai shakai hihan (GSH)* (1922), *HNSS* 3:86.

80. Nyozekan, "Osaka *Asahi* kara," 365.

81. Ibid., 364.

82. Ibid., 357, 361–65.

83. Ibid., 361–63.

84. Ibid., 349. Emphasis added.

85. See "Shōrai o mukauru kokoro," *Warera* 2, no. 1 (January 1920) (*HNSS* 1 : 43–44).

86. Nyozekan, "Osaka *Asahi* kara," 368.

87. I am reminded of comments made by the head of France's Ecole Pratique des Hautes Etudes on Japanese television (May 1984). For a public servant, he said, the really important thing is not to teach the people, but to learn how to listen to them. He had heard little in Japan to suggest that Japanese civil servants felt this way.

88. See Peter Duus, "Liberal Intellectuals and Social Conflict in Taishō Japan," in *Conflict in Modern Japanese History,* ed. Najita and Koschmann (Princeton: Princeton University Press, 1982), 412–40, on the shift among Taishō liberals from a "consensus" to "conflict" model of social thought.

89. Hasegawa Nyozekan, "Yoshino Hakase to watakushi," in *Yoshino Hakase o kataru,* ed. Akamatsu Katsumaro (1934); originally in *Hihan* 4 (April 1933), 83–85. See also Ishida, *Nihon no shakai kagaku,* 80–88; Matsuo, *Taishō demokurashii,* 166–71.

90. Yamaryō Chronology (see n. 36 above) does not identify Yeroshenko (14). For detail see *Tokubetsu yōshisatsujin jōsei ippan* (1919) in *Nihon shakai undō shiryō,* ed. Kindai Nihon Shiryō Kenkyūkai, 2nd ser., no. 3 (Tokyo: Meiji Bunken Shiryō Kankōkai, 1959), 296–97, item 86D.

91. For a detailed examination of these readings, see Tanaka Hiroshi, "Hasegawa Nyozekan no 'kokkakan': Sei'ō kokka genri no juyō to dōjidaishiteki kōsatsu," in *Nihon ni okeru sei'ō seiji shisō,* ed. Nihon Seiji Gakkai (*Nenpō seijigaku,* 1975) (Tokyo: Iwanami Shoten, 1976).

92. Gianfranco Poggi, *The Development of the Modern State: A Sociological Introduction* (Stanford: Stanford University Press, 1978), 13–14. Poggi goes on to make three cogent criticisms of this theory. First, its claim to "scientific" status has not been borne out: "No one has yet specified mechanisms of social evolution with anywhere near the explanatory power of those for natural evolution worked out by Darwin or Mendel." Second, because the theory "postulates a cumulative, irreversible process of differentiation, it can shed no light, explanatory or otherwise, on those recent phenomena that are tending to displace the distinction between state and society, thus suggesting a process not of differentiation but of de-differentiation." Poggi's third criticism is of particular interest. "Any attempt," he writes, "to render the institutional story of the modern state purely in terms of a general theory of social change can at best trace the diffusion of the state as an existing entity from its European heartland to outlying areas." It cannot deal adequately with the "distinctive forces and interests" at work within a given society "from whose interaction that new system of rule emerged" (14–15). Nyozekan's *Critiques* may, I think, be accounted an attempt to do precisely the latter. The former point was taken as matter of course.

93. Nyozekan, *Gendai kokka hihan* (*GKH*), *HNSS* 2:36.

94. Herbert Spencer, *Education: Intellectual, Moral and Physical* (1854–59) (Paterson, N.J.: Littlefield, 1963), 67.

95. Iida, "Hihan no kōseki," 171–72; Kobayashi, "Nihon riberarizumu," 7–10, 21–22; Rōyama Masamichi, "Hasegawa Nyozekan no shisōteki tokuchō—sono gendai kokka to seiji no hihan o chūshin toshite," commentary to *HNSS* 2:409–20, esp. 410; Tanaka Hiroshi, "Hasegawa Nyozekan no 'kokkakan'," 157–207, esp. 176–87.

96. L. T. Hobhouse, *Liberalism*, 44–55, 66–109 passim.

97. *GKH, HNSS* 2:222–23.

98. *GKH, HNSS* 2:53, 142, 275.

99. Spencer, *Principles of Sociology* (1876–96) (New York: Appleton, 1925–29), 3:321.

100. Like Spencer, Nyozekan refused to conceive of evolution as a unilinear or rectilinear process. As Spencer wrote: "Like other kinds of progress, social progress is not linear but divergent and re-divergent. Each differentiated product gives origin to a new set of differentiated products" (*Principles of Sociology* 3:331).

101. *GKH, HNSS* 2:66.

102. *GKH, HNSS* 2:97–111 passim, 142; see also Tanaka, "Hasegawa Nyozekan no 'kokkakan'," 170–88.

103. *GKH, HNSS* 2:128.

104. *GKH, HNSS* 2:39.

105. Of "scientific truth" Nyozekan made the following pragmatic definition: "When an advance in organization demands that preexisting forms be changed, it is philosophy, science, that makes plain the reasons [*jijō*]; that work is scholarship, and the resulting clarification is truth" (*GKH, HNSS* 2:161).

106. *GKH, HNSS* 2:42, 104–7.

107. *GKH, HNSS* 2:74.

108. *GKH, HNSS* 2:182, 193, 223.

109. *GKH, HNSS* 2:222–33.

110. *GKH, HNSS* 2:62, 128.

111. *GKH, HNSS* 2:77.

112. *GKH, HNSS* 2:206–7.

113. *GKH, HNSS* 2:204.

114. *GKH, HNSS* 2:79, 196–209, 264.

115. Rōyama Masamichi, *Nihon ni okeru kindai seijigaku no hattatsu*, 118.

116. Iida, "Hihan no kōseki," 161: "However immense the reality of the state standing implacably before our eyes, from the point of view of what human life and society are meant to be, that same state is nothing other than an alienated presence; it can never be anything but a negative phenomenon. Nyozekan, in other words, invariably seeks to treat the state as a dark and depressive presence." Iida is certainly correct, but I think he overstates the case somewhat. The paradox of the state is that it is both the defender and violator of society (*GKH, HNSS* 2:57). Also, Nyozekan was very concerned about the ways in which other forces—industrial organization—served to regiment and exhaust the lives of people in conjunction with, but independently of, the state. That is

why, in the *Critiques*, Nyozekan is so insistent on the need for "positive" social organization rather than direct antistate action. He may at this point have been an anarchist, but never a nihilist. His point is that at that stage, social initiative constituted the constructive force needed to give shape to the future: the destructive movement was already under way.

117. Rōyama, *Kindai seijigaku*, 112.

118. Hasegawa Nyozekan, *Gendai shakai hihan* [*GSH*] (1922); *HNSS* 3 : 32.

119. *GSH, HNSS* 3 : 199.

120. *GSH, HNSS* 3 : 126, 175; George Lichtheim, *A Short History of Socialism* (Glasgow: Fontana/Collins, 1975), 200.

121. *GSH, HNSS* 3 : 145, 177–78.

122. *GSH, HNSS* 3 : 53.

123. *GSH, HNSS* 3 : 35–36.

124. *GSH*, pt. 2 (*HNSS* 3 : 111–52); Iida, "Hihan no kōseki," 164–65.

125. *GSH, HNSS* 3 : 132–33.

126. *GKH, HNSS* 2 : 225.

127. *GSH, HNSS* 3 : 140ff.

128. *Warera* 2, no. 6 (June 1920): 3–7. While favoring the Home Ministry Bill, the editorialist also pointed out a glaring contradiction: the same ministry was using Art. 17 of the Public Peace Police Law (*Chian keisatsuhō*) to suppress unions; and the fate of the bill was to be left not to labor and capital, but to capital exclusively. See also Marshall, *Capitalism and Nationalism in Prewar Japan*, 76–93, esp. 84–85.

129. *GSH, HNSS* 3 : 49ff.

130. *GSH, HNSS* 3 : 139.

131. *GSH, HNSS* 3 : 121.

132. *GSH, HNSS* 3 : 117.

133. *GSH, HNSS* 3 : 107.

134. *GKH, HNSS* 2 : 275.

135. *GSH, HNSS* 3 : 238, 242–43, 245.

136. *GSH, HNSS* 3 : 219–29; Ivan Illich, *Gender* (New York: Pantheon, 1982).

137. *GSH, HNSS* 3 : 231–35.

138. *GSH, HNSS* 3 : 203–4.

139. *GSH, HNSS* 3 : 249–50.

140. Takamure Itsue, "Waga kuni dansei shokun ni kenzan," *Fujin sensen* (May 1930), reprinted in *Anakizumu josei kaihō ronbunshū: Fujin sensen ni tatsu* (Tokyo: Kuroiro Joseisha, 1982), 132–40; Nyozekan's article appeared in the Tokyo *Asahi* in eleven installments between 7 and 17 January 1929.

141. Takamure, "Waga kuni," 138.

142. Ibid., 139–40.

143. See Henry D. Smith, *Japan's First Student Radicals* (Cambridge, Mass.: Harvard University Press, 1972), 25.

144. Quoted by Maruyama Masao, "Omoidasu mama ni," in *Ōyama Ikuo: Hyōden, kaisō* (Tokyo: Shin Hyōron, 1980), 215–22.

145. T. Arima, *The Failure of Freedom* (Cambridge, Mass.: Harvard University Press, 1969), 173–213.

146. "*Warera* kara *Hihan* e" (May 1930), in *HNSS* 1:377–78.
147. Iida, "Hihan no kōseki," 171, 174 n. 4. This was also true of articles Nyozekan wrote for *Chūō kōron* and *Kaizō*.
148. Tanaka, "Hasegawa Nyozekan no 'kokkakan,'" 187.
149. Rōyama, commentary to *GKH, HNSS* 2:410.
150. Tanaka, "Hasegawa Nyozekan no 'kokkakan,'" 189–90.
151. Yamaryō Chronology, 35–36.
152. This was the thesis of the 5th Comintern Congress, at which Zinoviev guided the definition of the Comintern's position. Quoted in Gavan McCormack, "Nineteen-Thirties Japan: Fascism?" *Bulletin of Concerned Asian Scholars* 14, no. 2 (April–June 1982): 21.
153. Perry Anderson, *Considerations on Western Marxism* (London: Verso, 1979), 20. It should be added that Japanese Marxists retained their interest in Soviet philosophy, and that their knowledge of the field remains unsurpassed outside the USSR. See Gino Piovesana, S.J., *Contemporary Japanese Philosophical Thought* (New York: St. John's University Press, 1969), 187–88. Piovesana is himself a specialist in Soviet philosophy; Iwasaki Chikatsugu, *Nihon marukusushugi tetsugakushi josetsu* (Tokyo: Miraisha, 1971).
154. Fernando Claudin, *The Communist Movement: From Comintern to Cominform* (New York: Monthly Review Press, 1975), 166.
155. McCormack, 22.
156. Hasegawa Nyozekan, *Nihon fuashizumu hihan* (*NFH*) (1932), *HNSS* 2:278.
157. *NFH, HNSS* 2:279–92 passim, 348.
158. *NFH, HNSS* 2:347–48.
159. Quoted in McCormack, "Nineteen-Thirties Japan," 22.
160. *NFH, HNSS* 2:280.
161. *NFH, HNSS* 2:286, 294–96, 360ff.
162. *NFH, HNSS* 2:312, 365, 372, 375.
163. *NFH, HNSS* 2:291, 325–29, 334.
164. *NFH, HNSS* 2:338, 346.
165. *NFH, HNSS* 2:280, 325–31.
166. Hasegawa Nyozekan, in *Tōyō keizai shinpō*, no. 1492, quoted in Shinomura Satoshi, "Waga kuni ni okeru fuashizumu ron no hihan," in *Fuashizumu kenkyū*, Sassa et al. (Tokyo: Kaizōsha, 1932), 323.
167. Nyozekan defined dictatorship (as distinguished from patriarchal despotism or absolutism) as "absolute control through a power configuration that results from the political supremacy of a social group with distinct political demands" (*NFH, HNSS* 2:347).
168. *NFH, HNSS* 2:293.
169. *NFH, HNSS* 2:340, 358–59.
170. But historically, he does admit, bureaucracy did constitute an autonomous force (355), and still the Japanese political system was marked by its remaining "feudal" and "factional" tendencies, which had even influenced the parties themselves. This was natural because the parties began as regionally based attempts to take "back" power, which the Meiji state, in their view, had arrogated to itself.

171. *NFH, HNSS* 2:317–20, 340–47.

172. Shinomura Satoshi, "Waga kuni ni okeru fuashizumu ron no hihan," 275–336, esp. 287–91, 323, 328. Quote from 328.

173. *NFH, HNSS* 2:298–303.

174. Misawa Shigeo and Ninomiya Saburō, "The Role of the Diet and Political Parties" in *Pearl Harbor as History*, ed. D. Borg and S. Okamoto (New York: Columbia University Press, 1973), 325; Kawahara Hiroshi et al., *Nihon no fuashizumu* (Tokyo: Yūhikaku, 1976), 148; on Adachi's early career see E. H. Norman, "The Genyosha: A Study in the Origins of Japanese Imperialism," *Pacific Affairs* 17 (September 1944).

175. Inukai (8 May 1932) and Wakatsuki (10 May 1932) are quoted by Shiraki Masayuki, *Nihon seitōshi: Shōwa hen* (Tokyo, 1949), 92–94, in Misawa and Ninomiya, "Role of the Diet," 326.

176. *NFH, HNSS* 2:336, 338–39. Nyozekan's assertion here is unsupported by any statistics. But it is borne out (at least for the period from 1932–34) by the economist Chō Yukio's examination of sources of investment capital in Manchuria. See "An Inquiry into the Problem of Importing American Capital into Manchuria: A Note on Japanese-American Relations, 1931–1941," in *Pearl Harbor*, ed. Borg and Okamoto, esp. 385.

177. *NFH, HNSS* 2:336, 407; see also Berger, *Parties out of Power*, 40–45, for Adachi's own designs on the premiership.

178. *NFH, HNSS* 2:296.

179. *NFH, HNSS* 2:294–95.

180. *NFH, HNSS* 2:387–89, 396–408.

181. *NFH, HNSS* 2:376–84.

182. *NFH, HNSS* 2:294.

183. Maruyama, "Kindai Nihon no chishikijin."

184. *NFH, HNSS* 2:376–78.

185. This had the same title as the one eventually published.

186. A. Walicki, *A History of Russian Thought, From the Enlightenment to Marxism* (Stanford: Stanford University Press, 1979), 328.

187. Nyozekan's books published from 1935 to 1945 include, for example, collected essays on Laozi (*Rōshi*, 1935), Spencer (*Supensā*, 1939), on film (*Nihon eiga ron*, 1943), and on the importance of the ceremonial (*Rei no bi*, 1944).

188. See Ienaga Saburō, "Senjika no kojin zasshi" in *Shisō*, no. 475 (January 1964): 88–99.

189. The Friends of the Soviet Union was one of the "front organizations" created by the Comintern's Willi Münzenberg in 1928. By 1931 the Friends worldwide (except in Britain) had lost whatever organizational spontaneity they had enjoyed. See E. H. Carr, *Twilight of the Comintern, 1930–1935* (New York: Pantheon, 1982), 385 and n.

190. Remarks made to the critic Sugiyama Heisuke. "Nyozekan shi no shinkyō shindan," *Yomiuri shinbun*, 27 April 1934 (but note date), quoted in Yamaryō, "Aru jiyūshugi jānarisuto," *Tenkō* 1:334.

191. Kozai Yoshishige and Maruyama Masao, "Ichi tetsugakuto no kunan no michi," in *Shōwa shisōshi e no shōgen*, 51–52, 61; for a personal account of

the organization, activities, and disbanding of the society, see Oka Kunio, "Society for the Study of Materialism: Yuiken," in *Science and Society in Modern Japan: Selected Historical Sources,* ed. Nakayama, Swain, and Yagi (Cambridge, Mass.: MIT Press, 1974), 151–57. Oka notes that "even chief secretary Hasegawa himself shamefully contemplated breaking connections with Yuiken" once police suppression began in April 1933 (153); in fact, Nyozekan did break with the organization toward the end of the same year. For other assessments see Iwasaki Chikatsugu, *Nihon marukusushugi tetsugakushi josetsu,* 173–242; Piovesana, *Contemporary Japanese Philosophical Thought,* 186–90.

192. Maruyama in *Showa shisōshi,* 61.

193. Carr, *Twilight,* 382.

194. George Beckmann and Okubo Genji, *The Japanese Communist Party, 1922–1945* (Stanford: Stanford University Press, 1969), 236–37; Carr, *Twilight,* 383–84.

195. On MOPR see Carr, *Twilight,* 395ff; on MOPR's activity in Japanese universities, see Matsumura Tadahiko, *Saikin ni okeru sayoku gakusei undō* (1941), reprinted in *Shakai mondai shiryō sōsho,* 1st ser., *Shisō kenkyū shiryō* (special collection no. 85) (Kyoto: Tōyō Bunkasha, 1972), 80–85.

196. Yamaryō, *Tenkō* 1:330–32.

197. Quoted in Yamaryō, *Tenkō* 1:331.

198. Kobayashi Hajime, "Nihon riberarizumu," 20.

199. "'Tenkō'" (July 1933), in *HNSS* 1:322–23.

200. "Ware wa Ten ni kumi sen," *Hihan* 5, no. 2 (February 1934), opposite table of contents; also in *HNSS* 1:339–40. The passage comes from Analects 11:25 ("Xian xin," 11). I have used the translation of Wing-Tsit Chan (*A Source Book in Chinese Philosophy* [Princeton: Princeton University Press, 1963], 37–38), modified where Nyozekan's rendering is different: "as if flattered" is Nyozekan's translation; Chan gives a parenthetical "[in disapproval]."

201. Miki Kiyoshi, "Chishiki kaikyū to dentō no mondai," *Chūō kōron* (April 1937), in *Miki Kiyoshi zenshū* (Tokyo: Iwanami Shoten, 1967), 13:332.

202. Hasegawa Nyozekan, afterword to *Zoku Nihonteki seikaku* (Tokyo: Iwanami Shoten, 1942), in *HNSS* 5:282.

203. Hasegawa Nyozekan, *Nihonteki seikaku* (Tokyo, 1938), also in *HNSS* 5:5–165. It has been translated by John Bester as *The Japanese Character: A Cultural Profile* (Tokyo: Japanese National Commission for Unesco, 1966; reissued by Kodansha International, 1982).

204. Iida, "Hihan no kōseki," 167, 170 n. 3, 172–74. See "Ryūgen to bōkō no shakaiteki seishitsu," *Warera* 5, no. 10 (April 1923); "Handō to bōryoku to 'kenkyū' no ichinen," *Warera* 6, no. 11 (December 1924).

205. Ralf Dahrendorf, *The New Liberty* (Stanford: Stanford University Press, 1976), 6.

206. See n. 39 to Introduction for sources on the Shōwa Kenkyūkai.

207. James Crowley, "Intellectuals as Visionaries of the New Asian Order," in *Dilemmas of Growth in Prewar Japan,* ed. Morley, 320–21.

208. Heinrich Dumoulin, S.J., the German scholar of Buddhism, who arrived in Japan in 1935, knew Miki. Dumoulin said that the deaths of Miki and

of the Catholic philosopher Yoshimitsu Yoshihiko (a close friend of both Dumoulin and Miki) deprived Japan of desperately needed philosophical direction in the postwar years (interview, May 1984, Tokyo).

209. The text of the *Principles of Thought for a New Japan* is summarized in Fletcher, *Search*, 111–14, who demonstrates the connection between the philosophy of an East Asian Cooperative Body (*kyōdōtai*) and actual government policy vis-à-vis China. On the cultural problems committee, see also Itō, *Shōwa jūnendai shi danshō*, 21–29. The text of the *Principles* (and its successor, *Continued Principles*) appears in *Miki Kiyoshi zenshū* 17:507–88.

210. Hasegawa Nyozekan, "Shinateki kokka keitai no tokuisei," *Kaizō* 19, no. 10 (October 1937), and "Nihon no bunmei to seiji," *Jiyū*, January 1938, 1–9. Funayama Shin'ichi, "Bunseki kara kōsō e," *Nihon hyōron* 16, no. 4 (April 1941): 216–21, is a discussion of Nyozekan's views.

211. On the Shōwajuku see Itō, *Shōwa*, 31–34. Nyozekan is named as a member in *YTN* 1:154 (28 October 1938). Fletcher, *New Order*, 185 n. 7, notes: "In all, 213 students attended the academy, and many of them became prominent in postwar Japan. The most famous alumnus is probably Ōkita Saburō, an economist who helped direct Japan's postwar economic development and has served as foreign minister of Japan."

212. This account follows Yamaryō, *Tenkō* 1:335–40.

213. Ogura Kinnosuke, *Sūgakusha no kaisō*, quoted in Yamaryō, *Tenkō* 1:338.

214. Kiyosawa, *Ankoku nikki*, quoted in Yamaryō, *Tenkō* 1:340.

215. Hasegawa Nyozekan, "Nihon minzoku no yūshūsei," *Nihon hyōron* 17, no. 4 (April 1942): 14–30.

216. Ibid., 24.

217. Ibid., 19–23. In Greece, Nyozekan remarks, tradition dictated that remaining property (*isan*) be passed on to survivors; in Japan, it is the headship of a living house that is transmitted (23).

218. Ibid., 28. The "spatialization of history" is a concept found in the *Shin Nihon no shisō genri*. That is, Japan's world-historical mission was to be historical both in the temporal sense that New Order cooperativism would supersede capitalism in time and in the spatial sense that the Western powers who had brought colonial capitalism to Asia would be driven out and replaced by the forces of the Japan-centered New Order. See *Shin Nihon no shisō genri*, in *Miki Kiyoshi zenshū* 17:508–9.

219. Nyozekan, "Nihon minzoku," 28–29; "Bunka ni okeru kagaku to chokkan, narabi ni kagaku bunka no kokuminsei ni tsuite," *Nihon hyōron* 16, no. 11 (November 1941): 28–38.

220. Hasegawa Nyozekan, *Nihon kyōiku no dentō* (Tokyo: Tamagawa Gakuen Shuppanbu, 1943).

221. *Nihon kyōiku*, 264–93, esp. 273–79.

222. Dunn, *Western Political Theory*, 55.

223. Compare Nyozekan, "Nihon minzoku," 28–30, with "Gendai chishiki kaikyū ron" (1946) *HNSS* 3:285–303, esp. 297–303.

CONCLUSION

1. See Nezu Masashi, *Tennō to Shōwa shi* (Tokyo: San'ichi Shobō, 1974), 322.

2. Maruyama, "Nyozekan san to chichi to watakushi," in *Hasegawa Nyozekan*, 306–8; Yamaryō Chronology, 26.

3. Ōe Kenzaburō, "From the Ranks of Postwar Literature" (paper delivered at the University of California, Berkeley, May 1983), 1.

4. Oka Yoshitake, *Konoe Fumimaro: A Political Biography*, 111.

5. See Halliday, *Political History of Japanese Capitalism*, 140–59; quotes from 149, 159 respectively.

6. See, for example, Kuno, Tsurumi, and Fujita, *Sengo Nihon no shisō* (Tokyo: Keisō Shobō, 1966); Hidaka Rokurō, "Sengo no 'kindaishugi,'" introductory essay to *Kindaishugi*, ed. Hidaka, vol. 34 of *Gendai Nihon shisō taikei* (Tokyo: Chikuma Shobō, 1964); Nakamura, *Nihon no shisōkai* (Tokyo: Keisō Shobō, 1967). Examples of recent discussions of postwar thought include Yoshida Masatoshi, *Sengo shisō ron* (Tokyo: Aoki Shoten, 1984); Sugiyama Mitsunobu, *Shisō to sono sōchi (1): Sengo keimō to shakai kagaku no shisō* (Tokyo: Shinyōsha, 1983); Ishida Takeshi, *Nihon no shakai kagaku*, 161–233; Yamada Kō, *Sengo no shisōkatachi* (Tokyo: Kadensha, 1985). Much of the important material, of course, is to be found in journals such as *Sekai*, *Shisō*, *Shisō no kagaku*, *Kokoro*, and in many others now defunct.

7. I borrow this phrase from my Wesleyan colleague, the historian of China Vera Schwarcz.

8. Hashimoto Mitsuru, "'Fuhensei' o chōkoku suru mono—minzoku," in *Senjika Nihon ni okeru minzoku mondai no kenkyū*, ed. Naka Hisao (Kyoto: Minzoku Mondai Kenkyūkai, 1986), 17–30; Ishida, *Nihon no shakai kagaku*, 147.

9. Even in Japan, the study of the theme of "overcoming the modern" and the work associated with it has barely begun. But a number of works have now appeared that will make substantive research possible. First of all, the papers presented at the actual *Kindai no chōkoku* conference in 1942, along with the transcript of the discussions, have been reprinted by Fuzanbō (*Kindai no chōkoku*, 1979). The volume also includes Takeuchi Yoshimi's famous essay of the same title (also available in the collection of Takeuchi's work, itself with the same title, published by Chikuma Shobō, 1983). In addition, the philosopher Hiromatsu Wataru has published *'Kindai no chōkoku' ron* (Tokyo: Asahi Shuppansha, 1980), which includes studies of the conference, of the Kyoto school, of Miki Kiyoshi, and a number of other essays immediately relevant to the subject. Finally, we have Kitsukawa Toshitada, *Kindai hihan no shisō* (Tokyo: Ronsōsha, 1980), which includes studies of the critique of modernity in its relation to Marxism, to the theory of *kyōdōtai*, and as it is articulated in the work of Yanagida Kunio and Miki Kiyoshi. In this connection, one starting point, in addition to the "Overcoming the Modern" conference, would be the record of the round-table discussions sponsored by the journal *Bungakkai* in 1934. These attracted philosophers, writers, and critics, many of whom also participated in the

later conference. Among the participants (in both) was the Catholic ethical philosopher Yoshimitsu Yoshihiko, discussed briefly in the present book, of whose work I hope soon to begin a more thorough study.

10. Shōji Kōkichi, *Gendai Nihon shakai kagakushi josetsu* (Tokyo: Hōsei Daigaku Shuppankyoku, 1975), passim; J. Victor Koschmann, "The Debate on Subjectivity in Postwar Japan: Foundations of Modernism as a Political Critique," *Pacific Affairs* 54, no. 4 (Winter 1981), and "The Fragile Fiction: Maruyama Masao and the 'Incomplete Project' of Modernity" (paper presented at the Conference of the Association for Asian Studies, Boston, April 1987). The "foundation texts" of modernism, including the seminal 1948 debate over "subjectivity," have been collected under the title *Kindaishugi*, edited by Hidaka Rokurō. See n. 6 above.

11. Shōji, *Gendai Nihon*, chap. 1.

12. Maruyama, "Kindai Nihon no chishikijin," 118.

13. Nakamura, *Nihon no shisōkai*, 239–40.

14. Quoted in *Authority and the Individual in Japan*, ed. J. V. Koschmann (Tokyo: Tokyo University Press, 1974), 150.

15. Koschmann, *Authority*, 150; Shōji, *Gendai Nihon*, 20–21, 66ff; Matsumoto Sannosuke et al., "Maruyama riron to genzai no shisō jōkyō" (roundtable discussion, May 1972), in *Gendai no riron: shuyō ronbunshū*, ed. Andō Jinbei et al. (Tokyo: Gendai no Rironsha, 1978), 93ff.

16. Maruyama, "Kindai Nihon no chishikijin," 113–30.

17. Ivan Morris, *Nationalism and the Right Wing in Japan* (Oxford: Oxford University Press, 1960), 105.

18. The preceding discussion is based on Andrew Gordon, *The Evolution of Labor Relations in Japan: Heavy Industry, 1853–1955* (Cambridge, Mass.: Harvard University Press, 1985), 329–48.

19. Maruyama, "Kindai Nihon no chishikijin," 116.

20. Ishida Takeshi, *Nihon no shakai kagaku*, 174–93.

21. Tanabe, *Philosophy as Metanoetics*, xvi–xviii, xxxv.

22. Maruyama, "Sensō sekinin ron no mōten," in id., *Senchū to sengo no aida*, 596–602. Quote from 597.

23. Ralf Dahrendorf, *Society and Democracy in Germany*, 16.

24. Takeuchi Yoshimi, "Kindai to wa nani ka? (Nihon to Chūgoku no bawai)" (1948), in id., *Kindai no chōkoku* (Tokyo: Chikuma Shobō, 1983), 22.

25. See Maruyama Masao, "Genkei; kosō; shitsuyō tei'on—Nihon shisōshi hōhōron ni tsuite no watakushi no ayumi," in *Nihon bunka no kakureta kata*, ed. Takeda Kiyoko, 87–152; Fujita Shōzō, "Shakai kagakusha no shisō," in Kuno, Tsurumi, and Fujita, *Sengo Nihon no shisō*, 150–81.

26. Ishida Takeshi, *Japanese Society* (New York: Random House, 1971), 31.

27. Ibid., 32–33.

28. Robert Bellah, introduction to the paperback edition, *Tokugawa Religion* (New York: Free Press, 1985), xv.

29. Dahrendorf, *Life Chances*, 141–63; on Ui's work, see for example his "A Basic Theory of *kōgai*" (1972), reprinted in *Science and Society in Modern Japan*, ed. Nakayama et al., 290–311.

30. Matsumoto Sannosuke, "The Roots of Political Disillusionment: 'Public' and 'Private' in Japan," in *Authority and the Individual in Japan,* ed. Koschmann, 31–51.

31. Germaine Hoston, "Between Theory and Practice: Marxist Thought and the Politics of the Japanese Socialist Party," *Studies in Comparative Communism* 20, no. 2 (Summer 1987).

32. Shimizu Ikutarō, "The Nuclear Option: Japan, Be a State!" *Japan Echo* 7 (Fall 1980), 33–45. I am indebted to Adam Bird for bringing this article to my attention.

33. I make this distinction in response to a challenging informal remark by Hashimoto Mitsuru, now of Osaka University.

34. J. Victor Koschmann, "Is Postwar Really Over?," conference paper sponsored by the Center for Japanese Studies, University of California, Berkeley, May 1983, 6–7.

35. Maruyama, "Sensō sekinin ron no mōten."

36. Sebastien Castilian, *De arte dubitandi* (1562), epigram in Ōe Kenzaburō, *Hiroshima Notes* (Tokyo: YMCA Press, 1981).

37. Peter Nettl, "Power and the Intellectuals," in *Power and Consciousness,* ed. Conor Cruise O'Brien and William Dean Vanech (New York: New York University Press, 1969), 25.

Bibliography

INTERVIEWS CONDUCTED IN TOKYO,
MAY–JULY 1984 AND JULY 1986

Heinrich Dumoulin, S.J., Professor of Philosophy, Emeritus, Sophia University
Fukuda Kan'ichi, formerly Professor of Political Thought, Tokyo University
Maruyama Masao, Professor of East Asian Political Thought, Emeritus, Tokyo
   University

WORKS CONSULTED

WORKS BY NANBARA SHIGERU

Fichte no seiji tetsugaku. Tokyo: Iwanami Shoten, 1970.
Gakumon, kyōyō, shinkō. Tokyo: Kondō Shoten, 1946.
Jiyū to kokka no rinen (1959). *NSCS,* vol. 3. Tokyo: Iwanami Shoten, 1974.
Keisō (1946). Tokyo: Iwanami Shoten, 1984.
Kokka to shūkyō. Tokyo: Iwanami Shoten, 1942.
Nanbara Shigeru chosakushū. 10 vols. Tokyo: Iwanami Shoten, 1974.
Onozuka Kiheiji. In *NSCS,* vol. 8.
Seiji riron shi. Tokyo: Tōkyō Daigaku Shuppankai, 1968.
Seiji tetsugaku josetsu (1973). *NSCS,* vol. 5.
"Gendai no seiji risō to Nihon seishin" (1938). Reprinted in *Jiyū to kokka no
   rinen, NSCS,* vol. 3.
"Genshōgakuteki kokkakan no mondai" (1936). Review of Odaka Tomoo,
   Kokka kōzō ron. Reprinted in *NSCS,* vol. 3.
"Hyūmanizumu no gendaiteki igi" (1938). Review of Rōyama Masamichi,
   Hyūmanizumu no seiji shisō (1938). Reprinted in *NSCS,* vol. 3.

"'Jidai no kiki' no imi" (1934). Reprinted in *Jiyū to kokka no rinen, NSCS,* vol. 3.

"Jitsuzon tetsugaku to Nachisu" (1938). Review of F. A. Beck, *Politische Gemeinschaft und geistige Persönlichkeit* (1938). Reprinted in *NSCS,* vol. 3.

"Jiyūshugi no hihanteki kōsatsu" (1928). Reprinted in *Jiyū to kokka no rinen, NSCS,* vol. 3.

"Kojinshugi to chōkojinshugi" (1929). Reprinted in *Jiyū to kokka no rinen, NSCS,* vol. 3.

"Minami ryō hachiban no omoide" (1971). Reprinted in *NSCS,* vol. 10.

"Nachisu kokka to Hegel tetsugaku" (1934). Review of Julius Binder, *Der deutsche Volksstaat* (1934). Reprinted in *NSCS,* vol. 3.

"Naimushō rōdō kumiai hōan no koto nado." In *Rōdō gyōsei shi,* vol. 1. Tokyo: Rōdō Hōrei Kyōkai, 1961, appendix.

"Ningen to seiji" (1939). Reprinted in *Jiyū to kokka no rinen, NSCS,* vol. 3.

"Seiji rironshi no kadai" (1941). Reprinted in *Jiyū to kokka no rinen, NSCS,* vol. 3.

"Senbotsu gakusei ni sasagu" (10 March 1946). Preface to *Haruka naru sanga ni: Tōdai senbotsu gakusei no shuki.* Tokyo: Tōkyō Daigaku Shuppankai, 1951.

"Shin Hegel shugi no shakai tetsugaku" (1929). Review of Othmar Spann, *Gesellschaftsphilosophie* (1929). Reprinted in *NSCS,* vol. 3.

"Shūkyō wa fuhitsuyō ka" (1960). Reprinted in *NSCS,* vol. 9.

"Uchimura Kanzō sensei seitan hyakunen ni omou" (1964). Reprinted in *NSCS,* vol. 9.

"Waga nozomi." MS. n.d.

WORKS BY HASEGAWA NYOZEKAN

Aru kokoro no jijoden (1950). Tokyo: Chikuma Shobō, 1968; repr. 1985.

Aru kokoro no jijoden (1950). Tokyo: Kōdansha, 1984.

Gendai kokka hihan. Kyoto: Kōbundō, 1921.

Gendai kokka hihan (1921). In *HNSS,* vol. 2.

Gendai shakai hihan. Kyoto: Kōbundō, 1922.

Gendai shakai hihan (1922). In *HNSS,* vol. 3.

Hasegawa Nyozekan senshū. 7 vols. Tokyo: Kurita Shuppankai, 1970.

The Japanese Character: A Cultural Profile. Translated by John Bester. Tokyo: Kodansha International, 1982.

Kokka kōdō ron. Tokyo: Kurita Shuppankai, 1969.

Nihon fuashizumu hihan. Tokyo: Ōhata Shoten, 1932.

Nihon fuashizumu hihan (1932). In *HNSS,* vol. 2.

Nihon kyōiku no dentō. Tokyo: Tamagawa Gakuen Shuppanbu, 1943.

Nihonteki seikaku (1938). In *HNSS,* vol. 5.

Rōshi. Tokyo: Daitō Shuppansha, 1936.

Shinjitsu wa kaku itsuwaru. Tokyo: Sōbunkaku, 1924.

Zoku Nihonteki seikaku (1942). In *HNSS,* vol. 5.

"Bunka ni okeru kagaku to chokkan, narabi ni kagaku bunka no kokuminsei ni tsuite." *Nihon hyōron* 16, no. 11 (November 1941).

"Gendai chishikijin ron" (1946). Reprinted in *HNSS*, vol. 3.

"Handō to bōryoku to 'kenkyū' no ichinen." *Warera* 6, no. 11 (December 1924).

"Kō i fukō nan [okonau wa yasuku, okonawazaru wa katashi]" (1963). Reprinted in *HNSS*, vol. 7.

"Make ni jōjiru." *Bungei shunjū*, December 1945 (repr. January 1972).

"Meiji, Taishō, Shōwa sandai no seikaku" (1959). Reprinted in *HNSS*, vol. 5.

"Musasabi wa kataru." Series in *Kaizō* 19 (1937).

"Nihon minzoku no yūshūsei." *Nihon hyōron* 17, no. 4 (April 1942).

"Nihon no bunmei to seiji." *Jiyū* (January 1938).

"Osaka *Asahi* kara *Warera* e" (1919). Reprinted in *HNSS*, vol. 1.

"Rekishiteki jiyūshugi to dōtokuteki hanchū toshite no 'jiyū'." *Chūō kōron* 50, no. 5 (May 1935).

"Ryūgen to bōkō no shakaiteki seishitsu." *Warera* 5, no. 10 (November 1923).

"Shinateki kokka keitai no tokuisei." *Kaizō* 19, no. 10 (October 1937).

"Shōrai o mukauru kokoro." *Warera* 2, no. 1 (January 1920).

" 'Tenkō' " (1934). Reprinted in *HNSS*, vol. 1.

"*Warera* kara *Hihan* e" (1930). Reprinted in *HNSS*, vol. 1.

"Ware wa Ten ni kumi sen." *Hihan* 5, no. 2 (February 1934). Reprinted in *HNSS*, vol. 1.

"Yoshino hakase to watakushi." *Hihan* 4, no. 4 (April 1933).

Hasegawa Nyozekan, Maruyama Kanji, and Sugimura Takeshi. "Jidai to shinbun: Osaka *Asahi* hikka jiken kaiko." Round-table discussion in *Sekai*, no. 103 (July 1954).

Warera, 28 vols.; *Hihan*, 10 vols. In reprint series, *Nihon shakai undō shiryō*. Ed. Hōsei Daigaku Ōhara Shakai Mondai Kenkyūjo. Tokyo: Hōsei Daigaku Shuppankyoku, 1983–84.

SECONDARY WORKS

Abe Hirozumi. *Nihon fuashizumu kenkyū josetsu*. Tokyo: Miraisha, 1975.

Akamatsu Katsumaro. *Nihon shakai undō shi*. Tokyo: Iwanami Shoten, 1965.

Anderson, Perry. *Considerations on Western Marxism*. London: Verso, 1979.

Arakawa Ikuo. "1930-nendai to chishikijin no mondai: Chishiki kanryō ruikei ni tsuite." *Shisō*, no. 624 (June 1976).

Arima, Tatsuo. *The Failure of Freedom*. Cambridge, Mass.: Harvard University Press, 1969.

Beckmann, George, and Okubo Genji. *The Japanese Communist Party, 1922–1945*. Stanford: Stanford University Press, 1969.

Bellah, Robert N. *Beyond Belief*. New York: Harper & Row, 1970.

———. *Tokugawa Religion*. New York: Free Press, 1985.

———. "Japan's Cultural Identity: Some Reflections on the Work of Watsuji Tetsurō." *Journal of Asian Studies* 24, no. 3 (August 1965).

Bendersky, Joseph. *Carl Schmitt: Theorist for the Reich*. Princeton: Princeton University Press, 1983.

Berger, Gordon. *Parties out of Power in Japan, 1931–1941*. Princeton: Princeton University Press, 1977.

Berlin, Isaiah. *Four Essays on Liberty*. Oxford: Oxford University Press, 1969.

Bocheński, I. M. *Contemporary European Philosophy*. Berkeley and Los Angeles: University of California Press, 1969.

Bock, Hans-Michael, ed. *Cinegraph: Lexikon zum deutschsprachigen Film*. Munich: edition text + kritik, 1984.

Borg, Dorothy, and Shumpei Okamoto, eds. *Pearl Harbor as History*. New York: Columbia University Press, 1973.

Boyle, John Hunter. *China and Japan at War: The Politics of Collaboration*. Stanford: Stanford University Press, 1972.

Braisted, Donald, trans. *Meiroku Zasshi: Journal of the Japanese Enlightenment*. Cambridge, Mass.: Harvard University Press, 1976.

Carr, E. H. *Twilight of the Comintern, 1930–1935*. New York: Pantheon, 1982.

Cassirer, Ernst. *The Myth of the State*. New Haven: Yale University Press, 1946.

Chan, Wing-Tsit. *A Source Book in Chinese Philosophy*. Princeton: Princeton University Press, 1963.

Chang, Hao. *Liang Ch'i-ch'ao and Intellectual Transition in China, 1890–1907*. Cambridge, Mass.: Harvard University Press, 1971.

Chō Yukio. "An Inquiry into the Problem of Importing American Capital into Manchuria: A Note on Japanese-American Relations, 1931–1941." In *Pearl Harbor as History*, ed. D. Borg and S. Okamoto. New York: Columbia University Press, 1973.

Chūō kōron. "Tenraku jiyūshugi no kentō." Special issue. Vol. 50, no. 5 (May 1935).

Claudin, Fernando. *The Communist Movement: From Comintern to Cominform*. New York: Monthly Review Press, 1975.

Crowley, James. "Intellectuals as Visionaries of the New Asian Order." In *Dilemmas of Growth in Prewar Japan*, ed. J. Morley. Princeton: Princeton University Press, 1971.

Dahrendorf, Ralf. *Life Chances*. Chicago: University of Chicago Press, 1979.

———. *The New Liberty*. Stanford: Stanford University Press, 1976.

———. *Society and Democracy in Germany*. New York: Norton, 1979.

Delp, Alfred, S.J. *The Prison Meditations of Father Delp*. New York: Macmillan, 1963.

———. "Das Volk als Ordnungswirklichkeit." *Stimmen der Zeit* 138, no. 1 (October 1940).

———. "Weltgeschichte und Heilsgeschichte." *Stimmen der Zeit* 138, no. 8 (March 1941).

Despland, Michel. *Kant on History and Religion*. Montreal: McGill and Queens University Press, 1973.

Dunn, John. *Western Political Theory in the Face of the Future*. Cambridge: Cambridge University Press, 1979.

Duus, Peter. "Liberal Intellectuals and Social Conflict in Taishō Japan." In *Conflict in Modern Japanese History*, ed. Tetsuo Najita and Victor Koschmann. Princeton: Princeton University Press, 1982.

Fichte, J. G. *Addresses to the German Nation* (1807–8). Introduction by G. A. Kelly. New York: Harper & Row, 1968.

Fletcher, Miles. *The Search for a New Order: Intellectuals and Fascism in Prewar Japan*. Chapel Hill: University of North Carolina Press, 1982.

Fujisawa Toshirō. *Saikin ni okeru uyoku gakusei undō ni tsuite.* Tokyo: Shihō-shō Keijikyoku, 1940.

Fujita Shōzō. *Tenkō no shisōshiteki kenkyū: Sono issokumen.* Tokyo: Iwanami Shoten, 1975.

———. *Tennōsei kokka no shihai genri.* 2nd ed. Tokyo: Miraisha, 1979.

Fukuda Kan'ichi. "Doitsu risōshugi to gendai seiji tetsugaku no mondai: Nanbara Shigeru cho, *Fichte no seiji tetsugaku* o yomu." *KGZ* 73, no. 5 (January 1960).

———. "Nanbara Shigeru sensei no gakuteki shōgai." In *Seiji shisō ni okeru seiyō to Nihon: Nanbara Shigeru sensei koki kinen,* ed. Fukuda Kan'ichi, vol. 2. Tokyo: Tōkyō Daigaku Shuppankai, 1961.

Fukuzawa Yukichi. *Fukuzawa Yukichi senshū,* vol. 6. Tokyo: Iwanami Shoten, 1981.

Funayama Shin'ichi. "Bunseki kara kōsō e." *Nihon hyōron* 16, no. 4 (April 1941).

Gallie, W. B. *Philosophers of Peace and War: Kant, Clausewitz, Marx, Engels and Tolstoy.* Cambridge: Cambridge University Press, 1978.

Gay, Peter. *Weimar Culture: The Outsider as Insider.* New York: Harper & Row, 1968.

Geny, François. "The Critical System of Stammler." Appendix to Rudolf Stammler, *The Theory of Justice.* New York: Macmillan, 1925.

Gluck, Carol. *Japan's Modern Myths: Ideology in the Late Meiji Period.* Princeton: Princeton University Press, 1985.

Gordon, Andrew. *The Evolution of Labor Relations in Japan: Heavy Industry, 1853–1955.* Cambridge, Mass.: Harvard University Press, 1985.

Habermas, Jürgen. *Autonomy and Solidarity.* Edited by P. Dews. London: Verso, 1986.

———. "The Public Sphere." Translated by Peter Hohendahl. *New German Critique* 1, no. 1 (Winter 1974).

Hall, Robert King. *Shushin: The Ethics of a Defeated Nation.* New York: Bureau of Publications, Teachers College, Columbia University, 1949.

Halliday, Jon. *A Political History of Japanese Capitalism.* New York: Monthly Review Press, 1975.

Hanzawa Takamaro. "Shisō keiseiki no Tanaka Kōtarō: Chijō ni okeru kami no kuni no tankyū." In *Nihon ni okeru sei'ō seiji shisō,* ed. Nihon Seiji Gakkai (*Nenpō seijigaku,* 1975). Tokyo: Iwanami Shoten, 1976.

Harootunian, H. D. "The Sense of an Ending and the Problem of Taishō." In *Japan in Crisis: Essays on Taishō Democracy,* ed. H. D. Harootunian and Bernard Silberman. Princeton: Princeton University Press, 1974.

———. *Toward Restoration: The Growth of Political Consciousness in Tokugawa Japan.* Berkeley and Los Angeles: University of California Press, 1970.

Hartwell, Herbert. *An Introduction to the Theology of Karl Barth.* London: Duckworth, 1964.

Hashimoto Mitsuru. "Fuhensei o chōkoku suru mono—minzoku." In *Senjika Nihon ni okeru minzoku mondai no kenkyū,* ed. Naka Hisao. Kyoto: Minzoku Mondai Kenkyūkai, 1986.

Hata Ikuhiko. *Kanryō no kenkyū.* Tokyo: Kōdansha, 1984.

Hayashi Kentarō. "Waimāru kyōwakoku to gendai Nihon" (1961). In id., *Rekishi to taiken.* Tokyo: Bungei Shunjū, 1972.

Hellman, John. *Emmanuel Mounier and the New Catholic Left, 1930–1950.* Toronto: University of Toronto Press, 1980.

Hidaka Rokurō, ed. *Kindaishugi.* Vol. 34 of *Gendai Nihon shisō taikei.* Tokyo: Chikuma Shobō, 1966.

Hirai, Atsuko. *Individualism and Socialism: Kawai Eijirō's Life and Thought, 1891–1944.* Cambridge, Mass.: Harvard University Press, 1986.

Hirakawa Sukehiro. "Uchimura Kanzō and America: Some Reflections on the Psychological Structure of Anti-Americanism." In *Culture and Religion in Japanese-American Relations: Essays on Uchimura Kanzō, 1861–1930,* ed. Ray Moore. Michigan Papers in Japanese Studies, no. 5. Ann Arbor, Center for Japanese Studies, 1982.

Hiromatsu Wataru. *'Kindai no chōkoku' ron.* Tokyo: Asahi Shuppansha, 1980.

Hirschman, Albert. *Exit, Voice and Loyalty.* Cambridge, Mass.: Harvard University Press, 1969.

Hobhouse, Leonard T. *Liberalism* (1911). New York: Oxford University Press, 1974.

Hon'iden Yoshio. "Daigaku no kakushin." *Nihon hyōron* 17, no. 5 (April 1938).

Hoston, Germaine. "Between Theory and Practice: Marxist Thought and the Politics of the Japanese Socialist Party." In *Studies in Comparative Communism* 20, no. 2 (Summer 1987).

Huber, Thomas. *The Revolutionary Origins of Modern Japan.* Stanford: Stanford University Press, 1981.

Ienaga Saburō. *Tsuda Sōkichi no shisōshiteki kenkyū.* Tokyo: Iwanami Shoten, 1972.

———. "Senjika no kojin zasshi." *Shisō,* no. 475 (January 1964).

Iida Taizō. "Hasegawa Nyozekan ni okeru 'bunmei hihyōka' no seiritsu." *Hōgaku shirin* 72, no. 2 (March 1975), and 73, no. 2 (March 1976).

———. "Hihan no kōseki: Hasegawa Nyozekan." In *Kindai Nihon no kokkazō,* ed. Nihon Seiji Gakkai (*Nenpō seijigaku,* 1982). Tokyo: Iwanami Shoten, 1983.

Ikeda Hajime. *Nihon shimin shisō to kokkaron.* Tokyo: Ronsōsha, 1983.

Illich, Ivan. *Gender.* New York: Pantheon, 1982.

Imai Juichirō. *Maruyama Masao chosaku nōto.* Tokyo: Tosho Shinbunsha, 1964.

Irokawa Daikichi. *Shinpen Meiji seishinshi.* Tokyo: Chūō Kōronsha, 1976.

Ishida Takeshi. *Japanese Society.* New York: Random House, 1971.

———. *Meiji seiji shisōshi kenkyū.* Tokyo: Miraisha, 1966.

———. *Nihon kindai shisōshi ni okeru hō to seiji.* Tokyo: Iwanami Shoten, 1976.

———. *Nihon no shakai kagaku.* Tokyo: Tōkyō Daigaku Shuppankai, 1984.

———. "Nanbara sensei to Naimushō jidai." In *Kaisō no Nanbara Shigeru,* ed. Fukuda Kan'ichi and Maruyama Masao. Tokyo: Iwanami Shoten, 1974.

———. "Zadankai." In *Naimushō shi,* ed. Taikakai, vol. 4. Tokyo: Chihō Zaimu Kyōkai, 1971.

Itō Takashi. *Shōwa jūnendaishi danshō*. Tokyo: Tōkyō Daigaku Shuppankai, 1981.

Itoh, Makoto. *Value and Crisis: Essays on Marxian Economics in Japan*. New York: Monthly Review Press, 1980.

Iwamoto Mitsuo. *Waga nozomi: Shōnen Nanbara Shigeru*. Kyoto: Yamaguchi Shoten, 1985.

Iwasaki Chikatsugu. *Nihon marukusushugi tetsugakushi josetsu*. Tokyo: Miraisha, 1971.

Johnson, Chalmers. *MITI and the Japanese Miracle: The Growth of Industrial Policy, 1925–1975*. Stanford: Stanford University Press, 1982.

Kakegawa Tomiko, ed. *Gendaishi shiryō*, vol. 42; *Shisō tōsei*. Tokyo: Misuzu Shobō, 1977.

Kano Masanao. *Taishō demokurashii no teiryū*. Tokyo: NHK, 1978.

———. "The Changing Concept of Modernization: From a Historian's Viewpoint." *Japan Quarterly* 32, no. 1 (January–March 1976).

Kant, Immanuel. *Kant's Political Writings*, ed. Hans Reiss. Cambridge: Cambridge University Press, 1970.

Kawahara Hiroshi, Asanuma Kazunori, Takeyama Morio, Hamaguchi Haruhiko, Shibata Toshio, and Hoshino Akio. *Nihon no fuashizumu*. Tokyo: Yūhikaku, 1976.

Kelly, G. A. *Idealism, Politics, and History: Sources of Hegelian Thought*. Cambridge: Cambridge University Press, 1969.

"Kiiro no rōdō kumiai hōan." *Warera* 2, no. 3 (March 1920).

Kinmonth, Earl. *The Self-Made Man in Meiji Japanese Thought*. Berkeley and Los Angeles: University of California Press, 1981.

Kitsukawa Toshitada. *Kindai hihan no shisō*. Tokyo: Ronsōsha, 1980.

Kobayashi Hajime. "Nihon riberarizumu no dentō to marukusushugi." *Shakaigaku hyōron* 23, no. 4 (April 1973).

Kobayashi Naoki, and Miyazawa Toshiyoshi. "Meiji kenpō kara shin kenpō e." In *Shōwa shisōshi e no shōgen*. Tokyo: Mainichi Shinbunsha, 1968.

Kolakowski, Leszek. *Main Currents of Marxism*, vol. 1. Oxford: Oxford University Press, 1978.

Konaka Yōtarō, ed. *Tōdai Hōgakubu: Sono kyozō to jitsuzō*. Tokyo: Gendai Hyōronsha, 1976.

Koschmann, J. Victor. "The Debate on Subjectivity in Postwar Japan: Foundations of Modernism as a Political Critique." *Pacific Affairs* 54, no. 4 (Winter 1981).

———. "The Fragile Fiction: Maruyama Masao and the 'Incomplete Project' of Modernity." Paper presented at the Conference of the Association for Asian Studies, Boston, April 1987.

———. "Is Postwar Really Over?" Paper read at conference on postwar Japan, sponsored by the Center for Japanese Studies, University of California, Berkeley, May 1983.

———, ed. *Authority and the Individual in Japan*. Tokyo: University of Tokyo Press, 1974.

Krieger, Leonard. *The German Idea of Freedom*. Chicago: University of Chicago Press, 1957.

Kuno Osamu, Tsurumi Shunsuke, and Fujita Shōzō. *Sengo Nihon no shisō.* Tokyo: Keisō Shobō, 1966.

Laski, Harold, and Oliver Wendell Holmes. *Holmes-Laski Letters.* 2 vols. New York: Atheneum, 1963.

Lewis, Michael. "The Japanese Rural Rice Riots: Taxation Populaire and the Tenant-Landlord Riots." Paper distributed by Asian/Pacific Studies Institute, Duke University, 1985.

Lichtheim, George. *A Short History of Socialism.* Glasgow: Fontana/Collins, 1975.

Lipton, David. *Ernst Cassirer: The Dilemma of a Liberal Intellectual in Germany, 1914–1933.* Toronto: University of Toronto Press, 1978.

Lockwood, William. *The Economic Development of Japan.* Princeton: Princeton University Press, 1968.

Löwith, Karl. *From Hegel to Nietzsche: The Revolution in Nineteenth-Century Thought.* New York: Holt, Rinehart & Winston, 1964.

McCormack, Gavan. "Nineteen-Thirties Japan: Fascism?" *Bulletin of Concerned Asian Scholars* 14, no. 2 (April–June 1982).

Marcuse, Herbert. *Reason and Revolution.* Boston: Beacon Press, 1960.

Maritain, Jacques. *Existence and the Existent.* New York: Vintage Books, 1966.

Marshall, Byron. *Capitalism and Nationalism in Prewar Japan: The Ideology of the Business Elite, 1868–1941.* Stanford: Stanford University Press, 1967.

———. "Academic Factionalism in Japan: The Case of the Tōdai Economics Department." *Modern Asian Studies* 12, no. 4 (1978).

———. "The Tradition of Conflict in the Governance of Japan's Imperial Universities." *History of Education Quarterly* 17, no. 4 (Winter 1977).

Maruyama Kanji. *Kenteki, yoroku.* Tokyo: Dōtōsha, 1942.

Maruyama Masao. *Nihon no shisō.* Tokyo: Iwanami Shoten, 1961.

———. *Senchū to sengo no aida, 1936–1957.* Tokyo: Misuzu Shobō, 1976.

———. *Studies in the Intellectual History of Tokugawa Japan.* Princeton: Princeton University Press, 1979.

———. *Thought and Behaviour in Modern Japanese Politics.* New York: Oxford University Press, 1969.

———. Commentary to *NSCS,* vol. 4.

———. Commentary to *NSCS,* vol. 5.

———. "Genkei; kosō; shitsuyō tei'on: Nihon shisōshi hōhōron ni tsuite no watakushi no ayumi." In *Nihon bunka no kakureta kata,* ed. Takeda Kiyoko. Tokyo: Iwanami Shoten, 1984.

———. "Kindai Nihon ni okeru shisōshiteki hōhō no keisei." In *Seiji shisō ni okeru seiyō to Nihon,* ed. Fukuda Kan'ichi, vol. 2. Tokyo: Tōkyō Daigaku Shuppankai, 1961.

———. "Kindai Nihon no chishikijin." In id., *Kōei no ichi kara.* Tokyo: Miraisha, 1982.

———. "Nanbara Sensei o shi toshite." *KGZ* 88, nos. 7–8 (July 1975).

———. "Nanbara Shigeru cho, *Fichte no seiji tetsugaku* o yonde." *Tosho,* no. 117 (June 1959).

———. "Nyozekan san to chichi to watakushi." Round-table discussion in

Hasegawa Nyozekan: hito; jidai; shisō to chosaku mokuroku, ed. Sera Masatoshi et al. Tokyo: Chūō Daigaku, 1986.

——. "Omoidasu mama ni." In *Ōyama Ikuo: hyōden, kaisō.* Tokyo: Shin Hyōron, 1980.

——. "Shisōshi no hōhō o mosaku shite—hitotsu no kaisō." *Nagoya Daigaku hōsei ronshū* (September 1978).

——, and Kozai Yoshishige. "Ichi tetsugakuto no kunan no michi." In *Shōwa shisōshi e no shōgen.* Tokyo: Mainichi Shinbunsha, 1968.

Maruyama Masao, Nishida Taketoshi, and Uete Michiari. "Kindai Nihon to Kuga Katsunan." Round-table discussion in *Gyakusetsu toshite no gendai,* ed. *Misuzu.* Tokyo: Misuzu Shobō, 1983.

Matsumoto Ken'ichi. "Rinen toshite no kindai: Maruyama Masao to Ōtsuka Hisao." In id., *Rekishi to iu yami: Kindai Nihon shisōshi oboegaki.* Tokyo: Daisan Bunmeisha, 1975.

Matsumoto Sannosuke. "The Idea of Heaven: A Tokugawa Foundation for Natural Rights Theory." In *Japanese Thought in the Tokugawa Period,* ed. Tetsuo Najita and Irwin Scheiner. Chicago: University of Chicago Press, 1978.

——. "The Roots of Political Disillusionment: 'Public' and 'Private' in Japan." In *Authority and the Individual in Japan,* ed. Victor Koschmann. Tokyo: University of Tokyo Press, 1974.

—— et al. "Maruyama riron to genzai no shisō jōkyō." Round-table discussion, May 1972, in *Gendai no riron: Shuyō ronbunshū,* ed. Andō Jinbei. Tokyo: Gendai no Rironsha, 1978.

Matsumura Tadahiko. *Saikin ni okeru sayoku gakusei undō* (1941). Reprinted in *Shakai mondai shiryō sōsho,* 1st ser., *Shisō kenkyū shiryō* (Special collection, no. 85). Kyoto: Tōyō Bunkasha, 1972.

Matsuo Takayoshi. *Taishō demokurashii.* Tokyo: Iwanami Shoten, 1980.

Matsuzawa Hiroaki. *Nihon shakaishugi no shisō.* Tokyo: Chikuma Shobō, 1973.

Mayer, Milton. *They Thought They Were Free: The Germans, 1933–1945.* Chicago: University of Chicago Press, 1955.

Merton, Thomas. *Conjectures of a Guilty Bystander.* New York: Image, 1968.

Miki Kiyoshi. *Shin Nihon no shisō genri* (1939). Reprinted in *Miki Kiyoshi zenshū,* vol. 17. Tokyo: Iwanami Shoten, 1967.

——. "Chishiki kaikyū to dentō no mondai." *Chūō kōron,* April 1937. Reprinted in *Miki Kiyoshi zenshū,* vol. 13. Tokyo: Iwanami Shoten, 1967.

Miller, Frank O. *Minobe Tatsukichi, Interpreter of Constitutionalism in Japan.* Berkeley and Los Angeles: University of California Press, 1965.

Mills, C. Wright. "The Cultural Apparatus" (1959). In *Power, Politics and People.* New York: Oxford University Press, 1963.

Minoda Muneki. *Jinken jūrin, kokka hakai, Nihon ban'aku no kakon: Minobe hakase no daiken jūrin.* Tokyo: Genri Nihonsha, 1935.

——. *Kokka to daigaku.* Tokyo: Genri Nihonsha, 1942.

Misawa Shigeo and Ninomiya Saburō. "The Role of the Diet and Political Parties." In *Pearl Harbor as History,* ed. D. Borg and S. Okamoto. New York: Columbia University Press, 1973.

Mitani Taichirō. *Taishō demokurashii ron.* Tokyo: Chūō Kōronsha, 1974.
Mitchell, Richard. *Thought Control in Prewar Japan.* Ithaca, N.Y.: Cornell University Press, 1976.
Moore, Ray, ed. *Culture and Religion in Japanese-American Relations: Essays on Uchimura Kanzō, 1861–1930.* Michigan Papers in Japanese Studies, no. 5. Ann Arbor, Center for Japanese Studies, 1982.
Mori Arimasa. *Uchimura Kanzō* (1946). Tokyo: Kōdansha, 1976.
Morito Tatsuo. *Shisō no henreki,* vol. 1. Tokyo: Shunjūsha, 1972.
Morohashi Tetsuji. *Dai kanwa jiten,* vol. 2. Tokyo: Taishūkan, 1955.
Morris, Ivan. *Nationalism and the Right Wing in Japan.* Oxford: Oxford University Press, 1960.
Mukōyama Hiroo. "Minkan ni okeru shūsen kōsaku." In *Taiheiyō sensō shūketsuron,* ed. Nihon Gaikō Gakkai. Tokyo: Tōkyō Daigaku Shuppankai, 1958.
Murakami Takao. "Fichte kenkyūsha toshite no Nanbara Shigeru." In *Tetsugaku to Nihon shakai,* ed. Ienaga Saburō and Komaki Osamu. Tokyo: Kōbundō, 1978.
Muroga Sadanobu. *Shōwa Juku.* Tokyo: Nihon Keizai Shinbunsha, 1978.
"Naimushō no rōdō kumiai hōan." *Warera* 2, no. 6 (June 1920).
Najita, Tetsuo. *Hara Kei in the Politics of Compromise.* Cambridge, Mass.: Harvard University Press, 1967.
———. *Japan: The Intellectual Foundations of Modern Japanese Politics.* Chicago: University of Chicago Press, 1974.
———. "Some Reflections on Idealism in the Thought of Yoshino Sakuzō." In *Japan in Crisis: Essays on Taishō Democracy,* ed. Harootunian and Silberman. Princeton: Princeton University Press, 1974.
Najita, Tetsuo, and J. Victor Koschmann, eds. *Conflict in Modern Japanese History.* Princeton: Princeton University Press, 1982.
Naka Hisao, ed. *Senjika Nihon shakai ni okeru minzoku mondai no kenkyū.* Kyoto: Minzoku Mondai Kenkyūkai, 1986.
Nakamura, Takafusa. *Economic Growth in Prewar Japan.* New Haven: Yale University Press, 1983.
Nakamura Yūjirō. *Nihon no shisōkai.* Tokyo: Keisō Shobō, 1967.
Natsume Sōseki. "*Hitai no otoko o yomu*" (1909). Reprinted in *Sōseki zenshū,* vol. 11. Tokyo: Iwanami Shoten, 1966.
Nettl, J. P. "Power and the Intellectuals." In *Power and Consciousness,* ed. Conor Cruise O'Brien and William Dean Vanech. New York: New York University Press, 1969.
Neufeld, Karl, S.J. *Geschichte und Mensch: A. Delps Idee der Geschichte, Ihr Werden und Grundzüge.* Rome: Università Gregoriana Editrice, 1983.
Neumann, Franz. *Behemoth* (1944). New York: Harper & Row, 1966.
Nezu Masashi. *Tennō to Shōwa shi.* Tokyo: San'ichi Shobō, 1974.
Norman, E. H. "The Genyosha: A Study in the Origins of Japanese Imperialism." *Pacific Affairs* 17 (September 1944).
Ōe Kenzaburō. *Hiroshima Notes.* Tokyo: YMCA Press, 1981.
———. "From the Ranks of Postwar Literature." Unpublished paper read at

conference on postwar Japan, sponsored by the Center for Japanese Studies, University of California, Berkeley, May 1983.

Ogata Norio. Commentary to *NSCS*, vol. 3. Tokyo: Iwanami Shoten, 1974.

Oka Kunio, "Society for the Study of Materialism: Yuiken." In *Science and Society in Modern Japan: Selected Historical Sources*, ed. S. Nakayama, D. Swain, and E. Yagi. Cambridge, Mass.: MIT Press, 1974.

Oka Yoshitake. *Konoe Fumimaro: A Political Biography*. Tokyo: University of Tokyo Press, 1983.

————. "Generational Conflict after the Russo-Japanese War." In *Conflict in Modern Japanese History*, ed. Tetsuo Najita and Victor Koschmann. Princeton: Princeton University Press, 1982.

Ōkōchi Kazuo. *Kurai tanima no jiden: Tsuioku to iken*. Tokyo: Chūō Kōronsha, 1979.

Ōtsuka Hisao. "Nanbara Shigeru sensei ni okeru minzokuai." *Sekai*, no. 344 (July 1974).

Ōuchi Saburō. "Kirisutokyō to bushidō." In *Nihon shisōshi kōza*, ed. Furukawa Tesshi and Ishida Ichirō, vol. 8 (*Kindai no shisō*, vol. 3). Tokyo: Yūsankaku, 1977.

Paxton, Robert. *Vichy France: Old Guard and New Order*. New York: Norton, 1975.

Piovesana, Gino, S.J. *Contemporary Japanese Philosophical Thought*. New York: St. John's University Press, 1969.

Pittau, Joseph. *Political Thought in Early Meiji Japan, 1868–1889*. Cambridge, Mass.: Harvard University Press, 1967.

Poggi, Gianfranco. *The Development of the Modern State*. Stanford: Stanford University Press, 1978.

Pyle, Kenneth. *The New Generation in Meiji Japan*. Stanford: Stanford University Press, 1969.

————. "The Advantages of Followership: German Economics and Japanese Bureaucrats, 1890–1925." *Journal of Japanese Studies* 1, no. 1 (Autumn 1974).

Rees, Richard. *Simone Weil: A Sketch for a Portrait*. London: Oxford University Press, 1966.

Reiss, Hans, ed. *Writings of the German Romantics*. Oxford: Basil Blackwell, 1955.

Ringer, Fritz. *Decline of the German Mandarins*. Cambridge, Mass.: Harvard University Press, 1969.

Rockmore, Tom. *Fichte, Marx, and the German Philosophical Tradition*. Carbondale: University of Southern Illinois Press, 1980.

Roden, Donald. *Schooldays in Imperial Japan: A Study in the Culture of a Student Elite*. Berkeley and Los Angeles: University of California Press, 1982.

Rōdō gyōseishi, vol. 1. Tokyo: Rōdō Hōrei Kyōkai, 1961.

"Rōnōha kōhan ni okeru Sakisaka Itsurō, Nanbara Shigeru shōnin jinmon chōsho" (1944). In *Zoku gendaishi shiryō*, vol. 7, *Tokkō to shisō keiji*. Tokyo: Misuzu Shobō, 1982.

Rōyama Masamichi. *Nihon ni okeru kindai seijigaku no hattatsu* (1949). Tokyo: Shinsensha, 1971.

————. "Hasegawa Nyozekan no shisōteki tokuchō—sono gendai kokka to seiji no hihan o chūshin toshite." Commentary to *HNSS*, vol. 2.

————. "Kokumin kyōdōtai no keisei." *Kaizō* 20, no. 5 (May 1939).

Sakai Saburō. *Shōwa Kenkyūkai: Aru chishikijin shūdan no kiseki.* Tokyo: TBS/Britannica, 1979.

Sassa Hiroo et al. *Fuashizumu kenkyū.* Tokyo: Kaizōsha, 1932.

Scheiner, Irwin. *Christian Converts and Social Protest in Meiji Japan.* Berkeley and Los Angeles: University of California Press, 1970.

Schnädelbach, Herbert. *Philosophy in Germany, 1831–1933.* Cambridge: Cambridge University Press, 1984.

Schwartz, Benjamin. *In Search of Wealth and Power: Yen Fu and the West.* Cambridge, Mass.: Harvard University Press, 1964.

Sera Masatoshi et al., eds. *Hasegawa Nyozekan: Hito; jidai; shisō to chosaku mokuroku.* Tokyo: Chūō Daigaku, 1985.

Shinomura Satoshi. "Waga kuni ni okeru fuashizumu ron no hihan." In *Fuashizumu kenkyū*, Sassa Hiroo et al. Tokyo: Kaizōsha, 1932.

Shisō no Kagaku Kenkyūkai, ed. *Tenkō.* 3 vols. Tokyo: Heibonsha, 1978.

Shōji Kōkichi. *Gendai Nihon shakai kagakushi josetsu.* Tokyo: Hōsei Daigaku Shuppankyoku, 1975.

Simon, Ulrich. *Theology of Crisis.* London: S.P.C.K., 1948.

Smith, Henry D. *Japan's First Student Radicals.* Cambridge, Mass.: Harvard University Press, 1972.

Smith, Thomas C. "The Right to Benevolence: Dignity and Japanese Workers, 1890–1920." *Comparative Studies in Society and History* 26, no. 4 (October 1984).

Spencer, Herbert. *Education: Intellectual, Moral and Physical* (1854–59). Paterson, N.J.: Littlefield, 1963.

————. *Principles of Sociology* (1876–96). New York: Appleton, 1925–29.

Stammler, Rudolf. *The Theory of Justice.* Translated by Isaac Husik. New York: Macmillan, 1925.

Storry, Richard. *The Double Patriots.* London: Chatto & Windus, 1957.

Sugiyama Mitsunobu. *Shisō to sono sōchi (1): Sengo keimō to shakai kagaku no shisō.* Tokyo: Shinyōsha, 1983.

Sumiya, Mikio. "Les Ouvriers japonais pendant la deuxième guerre mondiale." *Revue d'histoire de la deuxième guerre mondiale*, no. 39 (January 1973).

Suzuki Toshirō. "'Kashiwagi' to 'Hakuu-kai' no kotodomo." In *Kaisō no Nanbara Shigeru*, ed. Fukuda Kan'ichi and Maruyama Masao. Tokyo: Iwanami Shoten, 1974.

Takagi Sōkichi. *Shikan Taiheiyō sensō.* Tokyo: Bungei Shunjū, 1969.

Takamure Itsue. "Waga kuni dansei shokun ni kenzan." *Fujin sensen* (May 1930). Reprinted in *Anakizumu josei kaihō ronbunshu: Fujin sensen ni tatsu.* Tokyo: Kuroiro Joseisha, 1982.

Takeuchi Yoshimi. "Kindai to wa nani ka? (Nihon to Chūgoku no bawai)" (1948). In id., *Kindai no chōkoku.* Tokyo: Chikuma Shobō, 1983.

Takeuchi Yoshinori. "Translator's Preface." In Tanabe Hajime, *Philosophy as Metanoetics.* Berkeley and Los Angeles: University of California Press, 1986.

Takeyama Michio. "Karera no gawa no inshō." *Kōryō* 25, no. 2 (October 1983).

Tanabe Hajime. *Philosophy as Metanoetics.* Translated by Takeuchi Yoshinori. Berkeley and Los Angeles: University of California Press, 1986.

―――. *Zangedō toshite no tetsugaku.* In *Tanabe Hajime zenshū,* vol. 9. Tokyo: Chikuma Shobō, 1963.

―――. "Kokka no dōgisei" (1941). In *Tanabe Hajime zenshū,* vol. 8. Tokyo: Chikuma Shobō, 1964.

―――. "Kokka sonzai no ronri." *Tetsugaku kenkyū* 24, no. 11 (October 1939).

―――. "Shakai sonzai no ronri." *Tetsugaku kenkyū* 20, no. 1 (January 1935).

―――. "Shisō hōkoku no michi" (1941). In *Tanabe Hajime zenshū,* vol. 8. Tokyo: Chikuma Shobō, 1964.

Tanaka Hiroshi. "Hasegawa Nyozekan no 'kokkakan': sei'ō kokka genri no juyō to dōjidaishiteki kōsatsu." In *Nihon ni okeru sei'ō seiji shisō,* ed. Nihon Seiji Gakkai (*Nenpō seijigaku,* 1975). Tokyo: Iwanami Shoten, 1976.

―――. "Hasegawa Nyozekan to 'genron shisō no jiyū': Morito jiken kara Takigawa jiken made." In *Shakai hendō to hō: hōgaku to rekishigaku no setten,* ed. Tanaka Hiroshi and Matsumoto Sannosuke. Tokyo: Keisō Shobō, 1981.

―――. "Western Political Thought in a Japanese Context: Hiroyuki Kato and Nyozekan Hasegawa." Paper delivered at the Department of Political Science, Carleton University, Toronto, 16 September 1983.

Tanaka Kōtarō. *Kyōyō to bunka no kiso.* Tokyo: Iwanami Shoten, 1937.

―――. "Present-day Mission of Catholics in Greater East Asia." In *Catholicism in Nippon.* Tokyo: Mainichi Shuppansha, 1944.

―――. Review of Nanbara, *Kokka to shūkyō. KGZ* 57, no. 5 (May 1942).

Tanaka Kōtarō, Suekawa Hiroshi, Wagatsuma Sakae, and Ōuchi Hyōe. *Daigaku no jichi.* Tokyo: Asahi Shinbunsha, 1963.

Taylor, Charles. *Hegel and Modern Society.* Cambridge: Cambridge University Press, 1979.

Tokubetsu yōshisatsujin jōsei ippan (1919). In *Nihon shakai undō shiryō,* ed. Kindai Nihon Shiryō Kenkyūkai, 2d ser., no. 3. Tokyo: Meiji Bunken Shiryō Kankōkai, 1959.

Tokutomi Roka. "Muhonron" (1911). In *Tokutomi Roka shū,* ed. Kanzaki Kiyoshi. Tokyo: Chikuma Shobō, 1966.

Tosaka Jun. *Nihon ideorogii ron* (1937). Tokyo: Iwanami Shoten, 1978.

Tōyama Shigeki, Imai Seiichi, and Fujiwara Akira. *Shōwa shi.* Tokyo: Iwanami Shoten, 1980.

Tsuji Kiyoaki. *Nihon kanryō no kenkyū.* Tokyo: Tōkyō Daigaku Shuppankai, 1974.

Tsurumi Shunsuke. *Senjiki Nihon no seishinshi, 1931–1945.* Tokyo: Iwanami Shoten, 1982.

―――. "Yokusan undō no gakumonron." In *Tenkō,* ed. Shisō no Kagaku Kenkyūkai, vol. 1. Tokyo: Heibonsha, 1978.

Uchimura Kanzō. "Kindaijin" (1914). In *Uchimura Kanzō zenshū,* vol. 20. Tokyo: Iwanami Shoten, 1984.

―――. "Justification of the Corean War" (1894). In *The Complete Works of Kanzo Uchimura,* vol. 5. Tokyo: Kyobunkwan, 1972.

Ui Jun. "A Basic Theory of *kōgai.*" In *Science and Society in Modern Japan: Selected Historical Sources,* ed. Nakayama Shigeru, D. Swain, and E. Yagi. Cambridge, Mass.: MIT Press, 1974.

Van Roon, Ger. *German Resistance to Hitler: Count von Moltke and the Kreisau Circle.* London: Van Nostrand Reinhold, 1971.

Wakukawa, Seiyei. "The Japanese Farm-Tenancy System." In *Japan's Prospect,* ed. D. Haring. Cambridge, Mass.: Harvard University Press, 1946.

Walicki, Andrzej. *A History of Russian Thought, From the Enlightenment to Marxism.* Stanford: Stanford University Press, 1979.

Weber, Max. *Economy and Society* (1922). Berkeley and Los Angeles: University of California Press, 1978.

Weil, Simone. *The Need for Roots* (1943). Boston: Beacon Press, 1952.

———. "East and West: Thoughts on the Colonial Problem" (1943). In *Selected Essays,* ed. and trans. Richard Rees. Oxford: Oxford University Press, 1963.

———. "The Power of Words" (1937). In *Selected Essays,* ed. and trans. Richard Rees. Oxford: Oxford University Press, 1963.

Willey, Thomas. *Back to Kant: The Revival of Kantianism in German Social and Historical Thought, 1860–1914.* Detroit: Wayne State University Press, 1978.

Wirth, Louis. Preface to Karl Mannheim, *Ideology and Utopia.* New York: International Library, 1936.

Wolin, Sheldon. *Politics and Vision.* Boston: Little, Brown, 1960.

Wu, John C. H. "Stammler and His Critics." Appendix to Rudolf Stammler, *The Theory of Justice.* New York: Macmillan, 1925.

Yabe Teiji. *Yabe Teiji nikki,* vol. 1: *Ichō no kan.* Tokyo: Yomiuri Shinbunsha, 1974.

———. "Kyōdōtai no seiji." In Tokyo Teikoku Daigaku, *Gakujutsu taikan.* Tokyo, 1942.

Yamada Kō. *Sengo no shisōkatachi.* Tokyo: Kadensha, 1985.

Yamamoto Taketoshi. *Kindai Nihon no dokushasō.* Tokyo: Hōsei Daigaku Shuppankai, 1982.

Yamamoto Taijirō. *Uchimura Kanzō: Shinkō, shōgai, yūjō.* Tokyo: Tōkai Daigaku Shuppankai, 1966.

Yamaryō Kenji, comp. *Hasegawa Nyozekan* (*Jinbutsu shoshi taikei,* no. 6). Tokyo: Nichigai Asoshiētsu, 1984.

———. "Aru jiyūshugi jānarisuto: Hasegawa Nyozekan." In *Tenkō,* ed. Shisō no Kagaku Kenkyūkai, vol. 1. Tokyo: Heibonsha, 1978.

Yamazaki Masakazu. *Kindai Nihon shisō tsūshi.* Tokyo: Aoki Shoten, 1971.

Yanaihara Tadao. *Kokka no risō: Senji hyōronshū.* Tokyo: Iwanami Shoten, 1982.

———. *Watakushi no ayunde kita michi.* Tokyo: Tōkyō Daigaku Shuppankai, 1975.

Yoshida Masatoshi. *Sengo shisō ron.* Tokyo: Aoki Shoten, 1984.

Yoshikawa Mitsusada. *Iwayuru kome sōdō no kenkyū.* Tokyo: Shihōshō Keijikyoku, 1939.

Yoshinare Akiko. *Ebina Danjō no seiji shisō*. Tokyo: Tōkyō Daigaku Shuppankai, 1983.

Yoshino, M. Y. *Japan's Managerial System: Tradition and Innovation*. Cambridge, Mass.: MIT Press, 1968.

Yoshino Sakuzō. *Yoshino Sakuzō hyōronshū*. Edited by Oka Yoshitake. Tokyo: Iwanami Shoten, 1975.

————. "Kirisutokyō to demokurashii" (1919). In *Kirisutokyō*, ed. Takeda Kiyoko. Tokyo: Chikuma Shobō, 1965.

Young, Arthur. *The Social and Labour Movement in Japan*. Kobe: Japan Chronicle, 1924.

Index

Compositor: G & S Typesetters, Inc.
Text: 10/13 pt. Sabon
Display: Sabon
Printer: Maple-Vail Book Mfg. Group
Binder: Maple-Vail Book Mfg. Group